THE ETIQUETTE
ADVANTAGE
in BUSINESS

SECOND EDITION

OTHER BOOKS FROM THE EMILY POST INSTITUTE

THE ETIQUETTE
ADVANTAGE
in BUSINESS

SECOND EDITION

Personal Skills for Professional Success

PEGGY POST *and* PETER POST

HarperResource

An Imprint of HarperCollinsPublishers

HarperCollins books may be purchased for educational, business, or sales
promotional use. For information, please write: Special Markets Department,
HarperCollins Publishers Inc., 10 East 53rd Street, New York, NY 10022.

First Collins edition published 2005.

Designed by Joel Avirom and Jason Snyder

Library of Congress Cataloging-in-Publication Data has been applied for.

ISBN-10: 0-06-076002-8
ISBN-13: 978-0-06-076002-1

07 08 09 ❖/RRD 10 9 8 7 6

ACKNOWLEDGMENTS

We want to specially recognize the efforts of Fred DuBose and Royce Flippin for the invaluable insights they have offered and the dogged diligence with which they worked to make this book possible. It is hard to imagine bringing this book to fruition without them.

Special thanks also go to Greg Chaput at HarperCollins, who has worked hard to keep us on track and focused on reviewing, revising, and updating the business etiquette advice for today's workplace.

We also thank the following for their research and great ideas: Courtney Denby, Inge Dobelis, Martha Leslie Hailey, Tad Harvey, Beth Landis, Alexis Lipsitz, Dierdre Van Dyk, and Bryce Walker.

Our appreciation goes to those who shared their expertise in their respective professional or business fields: Regis Canning, Lois Ebin, John Fowler, Greg Gregory, Dr. Judy Harkins, Mimi Irwin, Nancy Maniscalco, Knox Massey, James B. Miller Jr., Bob Moore, Susan Onaitis, Morgan Rich, and Evan P. Spingarn.

Thanks to these for their critical eye: Linda Ambrose, Keith Anderson, Kate DuBose, Stacy Kravetz, Kenneth Santor, and Burke Stinson.

Not least, we want to thank the following for their helpful suggestions: Katherine Cowles, Elizabeth Howell, Alfred Kennedy, Janet Kenny, Nelson Kenny, Alan Klavans, Anne McCarver, Larry McCarver, Allen Post, Anna Post, Tricia Post, Toni Sciarra, Carl Raymond, Monica Sapirstein, Cindy Post Senning, and Sally Dee Wade.

CONTENTS

PART THREE | RISING TO THE OCCASION

PART FOUR | COMMUNICATION

INTRODUCTION

In 1922, Emily Post wrote that "to make a pleasant and friendly impression is not only good manners but equally good business." Today, even as business attire, work schedules, and office arrangements become ever more flexible, Emily's words continue to ring true. Just because you might wear jeans to work without causing a stir doesn't mean people have stopped caring about manners: No matter how formal or informal your own workplace might be, good social skills are still absolutely essential to your professional success. Knowing how to behave in a wide variety of professional settings not only makes you a more pleasant, confident, and enjoyable person to work with; it also provides you with all-important tools for building solid, productive relationships with your business associates—relationships that will help propel you and your company toward your mutual goals. In fact, given today's greater job mobility, the growing popularity of the "team" concept in business, and the increased need to take different cultural sensitivities into account in a global marketplace, a knowledge of business etiquette is now more in demand than ever.

So . . . what exactly *is* good business etiquette? For starters, it is *not* a set of ironclad "rules." In fact, most of what people call business etiquette is really little more than common sense driven by being considerate, respectful, and honest with others in your business life. As you'll see in the pages that follow, this combination, used correctly, can guide you safely through even the most difficult situations. Among other things, *The Etiquette Advantage in Business* will show you how to

- Negotiate the tricky ground of a job search

- Dress appropriately for any situation, no matter what your professional field

- Interact more confidently and effectively with coworkers and business associates

- Steer away from situations that might be ethically awkward

- Handle business conflicts with ease and grace

- Get along better with your boss

- Gain the respect of your boss, subordinates, coworkers, and customers

- Run a disciplined, productive business meeting

- Communicate effectively in both speech and writing (including e-mail)

- Conduct yourself with aplomb when dining out or hosting or attending a business party

- Respect and enjoy cultural differences when traveling overseas

- Increase your chance of success if you're striking out on your own

Our aim in *The Etiquette Advantage in Business* is to instill the self-confidence that comes with knowing not just *what* to do, but also *why* a certain behavior is appropriate. In the business seminars we conduct around the United States, we've found time and again that many of today's office workers have never learned the underlying principles of etiquette and are often uncertain about how to behave as a result. Throughout this book, our focus is always on etiquette's bedrock principles of consideration, respect, and honesty, and how these inform and guide what people think of as good manners. With this knowledge, you will be able to judge for yourself what constitutes "correct behavior" in any given situation.

The underlying lesson of the book is this: By engaging in the right behavior, you will virtually always elicit a positive response from those you're dealing with. Our own professional backgrounds (more than sixty years of combined experience in finance, service industries, and public relations) have given us a deep appreciation of Emily Post's belief that everyday manners and workplace manners are inseparable. Just as people everywhere strive for pleasant personal encounters, people in business want and need standards of behavior that make their professional relationships smooth, enjoyable, and productive. Today, more than ever, knowing the proper way to behave can make all the difference between getting ahead . . . and getting left behind.

WHAT YOU'LL FIND

Reflecting the ever-accelerating pace of business today, this revised edition of *The Etiquette Advantage in Business* has been condensed and reorganized to spotlight the aspects of business etiquette that are most essential to your personal and professional success. Significantly more compact than our previous edition, it nonetheless contains a good deal of new material. Like our previous edition, this book is written for businesspeople of all types and backgrounds—including office workers, those who work at home, and those who regularly do business overseas.

While devoting considerable space to the needs of employees in the junior to mid-level range, *The Etiquette Advantage in Business* also offers counsel to top management on matters such as how to maintain good relations with employees and how to deal with knotty ethical problems. Much of the book's advice is universal: Whether you're a pin-striped corporate executive or a sneaker-wearing dot-commer, knowing the ins and outs of cell-phone etiquette, picking an appropriate business gift, or hosting a business dinner will always be valuable.

Section by section, here's what you'll encounter:

The Keys to Success. These three chapters concentrate on the most important part of the etiquette equation: you. They address the basic principles of etiquette, including why and how it enhances your interactions with others; feature a brand-new chapter on the importance of behaving ethically at all times, including guidelines for setting and maintaining high ethical standards; and finally, give soup-to-nuts advice on all aspects of business attire and grooming for men and women.

At the Workplace. Nowhere is etiquette more important than in your work environment, where harmonious relationships are essential for business success. These seven chapters cover every aspect of office life, including how to get along with your coworkers and super-visors; your attitude toward your workspace (be it cubicle or corner office); relations between the sexes; how to be a considerate and effective manager; the art of running a pro-ductive, on-time meeting; and the issues that can arise when you're telecommuting or working out of a home office.

Rising to the Occasion. The practical advice offered in these five chapters will help you feel confident and at ease when dealing with business associates both inside and outside your workplace. They include tips on pleasing the customer, choosing an appropriate business gift for a customer or associate, and decoding even the most formal table setting at a busi-ness dinner or lunch. You'll also find comprehensive etiquette advice for when you are entertaining or being entertained.

Communication. This section is devoted to the etiquette of self-expression. Its four chapters cover the spoken word—including the importance of introductions, the art of conversing well, and considerate phone behavior—and how to express yourself skillfully in writing, both in the traditional way (on paper) and in electronic form.

On the Road—Here and Abroad. These four chapters focus on the etiquette of business travel, including advice on domestic travel; behavior at conventions and trade shows; and the special challenges of international travel, where understanding and respecting your hosts' culture is the indispensable first step in any successful business negotiation.

The Job Applicant. These final three chapters explore how to use etiquette to your advantage when conducting a job search, applying for a job, updating your résumé and cover letter, and going through the job interview process.

The goals of *The Etiquette Advantage in Business* are many: to bring a level of comfort to the businessperson who never had the chance to learn the basics of etiquette; to provide a refresher course for those who did; to equate good manners with good business sense; and to instill the self-confidence that sets you on the road to success. We hope our book will make a difference for employees and executives everywhere and serve as a helpmate that grounds people in the timeless fundamentals as they work their way through a fast-changing world.

PEGGY POST
PETER POST
April 1, 2005

PART ONE

THE KEYS
TO SUCCESS

1 | *Why Etiquette Matters*

***Etiquette* is one** of the most misunderstood words in the English language. Most people, when asked what etiquette means to them, reply, "Manners," "Politeness," "Thank-you notes," "Rules." Over the years, in thousands of interviews, Emily Post was repeatedly asked what *etiquette* meant to her. Here's how she defined the term:

> *Whenever two people come together and their behavior affects one another,*
> *you have etiquette. Etiquette is not some rigid code of manners, it's simply how*
> *persons' lives touch one another.*

Emily Post understood that etiquette is not about rules; etiquette is about building relationships, plain and simple. Etiquette gives us clues as to how we should act and what we should do in any given situation, so that we can be as successful as possible in our interactions with the people around us. Far from stifling your personality in a straitjacket of do's and don'ts, etiquette—by giving you the confidence to handle a wide variety of situations with ease and aplomb—actually lets you focus on being your own, relaxed self: the real you.

"I WANT YOU TO DO A BETTER JOB BUILDING RELATIONSHIPS"

That's what your boss could tell you in a job performance review. If she did, how would you go about fulfilling such a request? Chances are, you wouldn't have a clue where to begin. If, however, you shift your focus from improving your "relationships" in general to evaluating how well you handle *the specific factors* that influence all relationships, this goal will start to look much more attainable. This is easier than you might think, because there are really only three things that affect a relationship: your actions, your appearance, and your words.

- ACTIONS. The things we do can have various impacts. Imagine: You sit down at a restaurant table with a client. After a few minutes, your cell phone starts ringing. You answer it and start talking. Clearly, we are all aware that this action would create a negative atmosphere at your business lunch. What is a better action, one that will improve your relationship with your client? Simple: Either turn off your phone before meeting your client or let your client know that you're expecting a call, and then excuse yourself to the lobby or restroom area when your phone vibrates.

- **APPEARANCE.** The importance of clothes and grooming is obvious. Dress like a slob, and the people you are with will think of you as a slob. Body odor and bad breath—those are no-brainers. But what about body language? That falls under appearance as well: Twitching your foot during a meeting says you are either nervous or apprehensive, or you can't wait for the meeting to end. Improve your appearance by keeping your foot still—and staying calm, alert, and twitch-free in general—and you will build better relationships with the people you do business with.

- **WORDS.** Coarse language is clearly out of bounds. But say you're in a meeting and you blurt out, "Oh my God, Sally, what a great idea!" Later, you discover that some of the people present were offended that you took the Lord's name in vain. Suddenly, instead of thinking about Sally's great idea, those participants are focused on you and their negative perception of you.

One of the hallmarks of good etiquette is that it never calls attention to itself. When everything is going well as far as your actions, appearance, and words are concerned, your focus—and the focus of the people you are with—will be on the content of your discussion. Slip up with any one of these factors, however, and the focus will suddenly shift to the failure ("I can't believe he just did that"). By being aware of your actions, appearance, and words, and working to improve your performance in all three areas, you can directly enhance the quality of your relationships.

JOB SKILLS VERSUS PEOPLE SKILLS

Being successful in your job or your job search hinges on two critical factors: your job skills and your people skills. Your job skills are the capabilities you bring to your work. If you're searching for a job, it's unlikely you'll be invited for an interview if you don't have the requisite job skills. The same goes if you're up for a promotion, or if your company is up for a job or contract with another firm: The reason you are being considered for the promotion or your company is being considered for the work is the set of job skills and capabilities you or your company possesses.

THE DANGERS OF STEREOTYPING

Never has it been more important for people of different generations, be they older or younger, or of different cultures, to avoid making knee-jerk assumptions about one another. Everyone has something to offer, both in skills and attitude. The voice of experience and a view to the future don't have to be mutually exclusive but can merge to create rich company cultures that benefit everyone.

The job hunter or coworker who is quick to stereotype can easily offend or get off on the wrong foot. Human beings are infinitely complex and don't always reveal themselves by how they wear their hair or clothes. Although the assumptions people have about one another may sometimes be right on the money, often they're nowhere close; assuming that a workplace "isn't your type" because of what you see on the surface is a snap judgment that could keep you from a rewarding job and cut you off from people who could help you grow. Such shallowness has no place in business. The person who knows to delve beneath the surface is the one who is most likely to succeed.

Once you enter the room for an interview, however—whether as a job applicant, or a candidate for a promotion, or a salesperson—your personal skills are what will most likely get you the job. Your ability to connect with that person across the table more readily than any of the other candidates is critical to your potential success. In short, your job skills will get you in the door, but your *people skills* are what will land you the assignment.

Fair? Perhaps not. Reality? You'd better believe it.

It makes sense, too: Imagine you're a CEO who's considering three employees for a promotion, so you invite each of them in turn for a talk over lunch. Jane knows her job cold but can't quite make or hold eye contact with you. Kevin is friendly and outgoing, but he eats holding his fork like he's going to stab someone and chews his food with his mouth open. Jonathan, on the other hand, walks into the interview dressed for the job he wants, rather than for the job he now has. His table manners don't draw attention to his eating; instead, you find yourself focused on the conversation you are having with him. He smiles, and he holds eye contact—but not for too long.

Considering the three applicants, you realize that while they all have the necessary job skills, clearly Jonathan is the person you want representing your company. And that decision is made based completely on his personal skills.

The skills that Jonathan employed are exactly what Emily Post was talking about when she defined etiquette. The actions and behavior of these three people affected you in some way, and influenced your choice.

ETIQUETTE = MANNERS + PRINCIPLES

Etiquette is the power that fuels our relationships, by helping us know how to act and how to expect others to act in any kind of situation. Etiquette accomplishes this through a powerful combination of manners and principles.

MANNERS

First of all, manners aren't rules—they are guidelines. In many situations, manners can help us determine the right thing to do, but there are always exceptions, and so we use judgment to decide when a manner applies and when we should do something differently rather than by the book.

Manners tell us two types of things:

- What to do in all kinds of situations

  - What fork to use

  - Whether to hold a door for someone else

  - How to introduce yourself to another person

- What we can expect other people to do

  - If you extend your hand to shake hands, you fully expect the other person to reciprocate. When he does, everything is fine. If he doesn't extend his hand, however, you immediately start to wonder if you have body odor or bad breath, or if you did something to insult him.

In essence, manners are guidelines to help us as we interact with the people around us, by sketching out the appropriate actions, appearance, and words that will help us build successful relationships.

THE THREE PRINCIPLES THAT GOVERN ALL ETIQUETTE

Principles are the guiding concepts on which all manners are based. Among other things, they tell us

- Why a certain manner is called for

- What to do when there is no prescribed manner or a manner doesn't work

- How to resolve relationship situations

For example, while attending a business dinner, an elderly client begins to excuse herself from the table. Because business etiquette is meant to be non–gender specific, the appropriate "manner" states that you, as a male, shouldn't stand as she gets ready to leave the table. But you also know the client is old-school—and so you decide that, despite the latest guideline or "rule," you will stand. As you do, she smiles and says, "Thank you." By understanding the unique circumstances of the situation, and showing respect for your dinner companion by standing in spite of what the "rule" says, you have made her appreciate you just that much more. In turn, you've helped yourself and your company build a better relationship with her.

Virtually all the manners that you'll find in etiquette books—and, indeed, all the choices that you'll ever make about your actions, appearance, and words—are governed by three principles: *consideration, respect,* and *honesty.*

In order to understand these principles and how they are used in etiquette, it is necessary to define each of them:

- CONSIDERATION means looking at the current situation and assessing how it affects everyone who is involved.

- RESPECT means looking at how your possible actions will affect others in the future.

- HONESTY means acting sincerely and being truthful, not deceitful.

Being in command of proper etiquette really means knowing how to use your own common sense in applying one or more of the above principles to determine the best course of action in any situation. The man standing up at the dinner table knew that in this case, being respectful of his companion was more important than following the "rule"—so he rose.

THE IMPORTANCE OF SINCERITY

Contrary to what some people may think, a concerted effort to make a good impression through the use of etiquette doesn't mean putting on airs, playing games, betraying yourself, or compromising your integrity. Phoniness and pretentiousness are one thing; observing guidelines of behavior that have evolved over time to serve the common good is quite another. Therefore, it's not enough to be considerate, respectful, and honest; you must also be sincere in the use of these principles. If you aren't, people will see through your veneer. "Jim seems like a nice guy, but there's something about him that strikes me as phony." That's *not* the impression you want to make.

The more considerate, respectful, and honest businesspeople *sincerely* are to one another, the better their relationships will be with coworkers, employees, customers, and suppliers. Etiquette greases the wheels of social interaction.

THE IMPORTANCE OF FLEXIBILITY

Conforming to certain customs and principles doesn't mean forsaking who you are. You may not like doing some of the things expected of you—whether it means putting on a suit or being expected to show up for work at nine o'clock sharp—but pragmatism dictates that you must. Only the most rigid of individualists won't make some accommodation to the demands of the workplace; and in most companies, refusing to do so means, as they say, cutting off your nose to spite your face. Being willing to adapt makes the difference between getting a job or doing without one—and between keeping a job or being fired. The goal is to strike a delicate balance between being yourself and conforming to the standards and expectations of your company, your colleagues, your clients, and your prospects. This is where etiquette—defined simply as being sincerely considerate, respectful, and honest—is invaluable. Etiquette allows the real you to thrive, by giving you the skills and confidence to build the best relationships possible, which in turn will give you the opportunity to be as successful as you want to be. With the help of etiquette, the sky is the limit.

2 | *The Ethical You*

In Emily Post's 1927 edition of her groundbreaking book *Etiquette*, she wrote, "Etiquette must, if it is to be of more than trifling use, include ethics as well as manners. Certainly what one *is*, is of far greater importance than what one appears to be." For Emily, treating others honestly and taking only what you have fairly earned was at the very essence of who you are—not your station in life, or your monetary wealth, or where you live. She understood that the way we behave *ethically* matters in our day-to-day lives, and that the way we treat each other reflects on who we really are, rather than who we appear to be.

Ethical behavior influences every aspect of our lives and our relationships, but it's especially important in the business world, for a number of reasons:

- *An ethical company is a more positive and more effective company.* Employees of businesses that actively promote ethical behavior report higher levels of job satisfaction and thus employee retention, make decisions more readily, and are less afraid of making mistakes. Their focus is on doing the work to make the business successful.

- *Good ethics is good for business.* Ethical behavior has become an absolute necessity for corporate success. In this day and age of unethical behavior at the highest levels on the corporate ladder, an ethical lapse by any employee not only undermines a company's reputation, but also carries the risk of potentially damaging lawsuits, scandals, and even criminal charges accompanied by jail time for the guilty.

- *Business is inherently competitive.* Without a clear sense of ethics, pressure to hold down costs and meet sales targets can all too easily cross the line into a willingness to cut corners or overstate earnings. On the other hand, by exhibiting consistently ethical behavior under even the most pressured circumstances, you'll stamp yourself as a trustworthy, confident, and reliable person—the type of individual others will want to do repeated business with.

- *In a business setting, unethical behavior can affect the lives—and livelihoods—of many other people.* When Enron went under because top executives engaged in fraudulent bookkeeping, thousands of employees lost their retirement savings as a result. Because a junior staffer on the *New York Times* lied about his work, two senior managers resigned. The examples go on and on, but the conclusion is basic: You not only owe it to yourself to hew to a strict ethical approach—you owe it to your coworkers as well.

- *Your own behavior on the job influences the way others act in the workplace.* An active commitment on your part to ethical behavior in all aspects of business life— from honest accounting practices to seemingly minor issues like taking credit for a colleague's idea—will help set a positive tone for your entire firm. High personal standards send the message that you expect only the finest business ethics from yourself, your coworkers and/or employees, and your company.

- *Ethical behavior is simply the right thing to do.* This fact in itself is truly the key reason to behave ethically—at all times, both professionally and personally.

A QUESTION OF VALUES

Good ethics is based on a set of *values*—not just on compliance with legalities (although legal requirements matter, too [see box, "It's a Legal Matter," page 20]). When you have a firm grasp of the underlying values of good business ethics, you hold the keys to solving even the toughest ethical problems.

SIX ETHICAL VALUES TO LIVE BY

The Better Business Bureau lists the following six core values in its code of ethics:

Equality—recognizing equal rights for all and displaying a sense of justice

Truth—being both accurate and open in all business transactions

Honesty—being fair in our own dealings and intolerant of deceptive behavior in others

Integrity—following the spirit as well as the letter of the law and avoiding schemes that take advantage of "ignorance or gullibility" in others

Cooperativeness—supporting an open, ethical marketplace for all participants

Self-regulation—including honoring all commitments and guarantees, selling safe products and services, and resolving any disputes in a "fair and expeditious manner"

Most important of all: True ethics mean holding yourself to the highest level of behavior because you *want* to—not because you're afraid of getting caught and punished for flouting a specific rule. Commit these six values to memory. They'll help guide you through even the thorniest ethical dilemmas.

BLACK AND WHITE, OR SHADES OF GRAY?

Even with your ethical values firmly in place, some ethical decisions will invariably be harder than others. We all know we shouldn't steal from petty cash, for example. But what about such "gray areas" as where to draw the line when submitting your travel expenses; how to respond to the boss who asks you to tell a white lie; and whether you can ethically accept a job that you plan to hold for only a few months, until something better comes along? As we'll discuss below, situations like these will often require making a judgment call and deciding for yourself whether a given action fits your own ethical standards.

Tougher still are those ethical decisions that involve conflicting values—whether to be a "team player" and go along with a questionable company policy, for example, or to air your misgivings, especially when to do so could actually hurt your company's performance and/or cause you to lose your job.

In these cases, it's important to weigh carefully the positive and negative consequences of your various potential responses. Ask yourself, "Who will be helped by a given potential action, and how—and who will be hurt by it, and how?" Consider both the short-term and long-term consequences. After you've made this evaluation, ask yourself, "Which response produces the best mix of positive benefits compared to harmful outcomes?" With careful thought, your answer should come through loud and clear.

Keeping these steps in mind, let's take a closer look at some common ethical issues you're likely to encounter in the workplace.

THE ETHICAL EMPLOYEE

Whether you're just starting out in an entry-level position or you've risen to become chairman of the board, being an ethical employee requires balancing a variety of ethical obligations. These include your obligations to your coworkers; your obligations to the company that's employing you; your obligations to clients, vendors, and other business partners; your obligations to the public at large; and your obligations to yourself and your family.

YOU AND YOUR COWORKERS

As the "Common Ethical Pitfalls" box on page 13 shows, behaving ethically toward your coworkers involves more than simply being honest with them. Good ethics also means treating your colleagues fairly and without discrimination, and giving them whatever support and information they need to do their jobs effectively. Key areas to be aware of include the following:

ABUSIVE BEHAVIOR

You may disagree with the way a colleague is doing his job, or even dislike him for some reason, but that is *never* an excuse to berate or intimidate a coworker. Abusive behavior on the job is more than bad manners—it's an infringement of basic workplace rights. If you're so upset that you can't conduct a job-related discussion calmly and professionally, put off the discussion for another day or sit down with the other person and your manager to hash out a constructive solution.

Similarly, if someone behaves abusively toward you, calmly tell them that their behavior is not only inappropriate, but unethical—and offer to continue the discussion at another time, when emotions have cooled. If the other person's abusive behavior continues, bring it to your immediate supervisor's attention.

DISCRIMINATION

Just like abusive behavior, treating a coworker differently because of his or her race, religion, gender, or age is an affront to workplace ethics, as well as being illegal. If you are aware of discrimination taking place in your office, muster up the confidence and conviction to have a private conversation with the person who is at fault, and point out that what he or she is doing not only is ethically wrong and personally unfair but is also undermining office morale and cohesion. If the behavior persists, contact your company's human resources department or ethics officer and register an official complaint.

COMMON ETHICAL PITFALLS

Can bluster in the workplace actually constitute a breach of ethics? You bet it can, if it crosses the line into abuse or intimidation. In fact, a recent survey of American workers by the Ethics Resource Center found this type of misconduct to be the most common of all, while stealing from one's own company ranked sixth in prevalence. The types of unethical behavior most often cited were

- Abusive or intimidating behavior toward other employees (reported by 21 percent of all respondents)
- Misreporting of hours worked (20 percent)
- Lying to other employees, customers, vendors, or the public (19 percent)
- Withholding needed information from other employees (18 percent)
- Discriminating on the basis of race, color, gender, age, or similar categories (13 percent)
- Stealing, theft, or related fraud (12 percent)
- Sexual harassment (11 percent)
- Falsifying financial records or reports (5 percent)
- Giving or accepting bribes, kickbacks, or inappropriate gifts (4 percent)

SEXUAL HARASSMENT

Any sexually oriented talk or behavior in the workplace that makes a fellow employee uncomfortable is unethical and illegal and should not be tolerated. If you observe such harassment in any form, you have an ethical obligation to confront the offender about his or her behavior—and to take it up with your human resources department or ethics officer if the behavior persists. (If you believe you are the victim of sexual harassment or have witnessed it, see "What Is Sexual Harassment?" pages 93–95.)

WITHHOLDING INFORMATION

As the box above indicates, this is the fourth most common form of ethical misconduct in the workplace. Holding back information that a fellow employee normally should have access to, either to hurt that employee's performance or to enhance your own, is wrong—period. If you believe someone is withholding information from you that should rightfully be yours, ask them about it directly. If they aren't responsive, follow up with your immediate supervisor or—if your supervisor is the problem—seek out someone else in a position of authority.

RESPECTING PRIVACY

Just as you're obligated to share appropriate job-related information, you also have a responsibility to avoid being privy to your coworkers' personal correspondence, e-mails, faxes, and phone calls. In other words, don't snoop! As you sift through faxes, look only at the cover sheets. Similarly, if someone has left an original sheet in the copying machine, glance at the sheet just long enough to ascertain whom it belongs to. Then return the sheet to the person, letting him know you didn't read it.

KEEPING CONFIDENCES

If a coworker tells you something in confidence, whether it's work-related or personal, you are ethically obligated to keep the conversation private—*unless* that information involves something clearly harmful to your company, a fellow employee, or the public. At that point, it becomes incumbent on you to tell the person that this cannot remain confidential—and that if he or she doesn't take the issue to the appropriate person, you will have to do so.

GIVING CREDIT

In the business world, coming up with innovative new ideas and strategies is essential to job performance and advancement. Taking credit for someone else's ideas—either passively or actively—is a form of stealing. If you bring up a new idea that originated with someone else, quickly credit the person who first came up with the idea, whether or not he or she is present. Similarly, if you find out after the fact that someone has mistakenly credited you with an idea, go to the appropriate people *immediately* and tell them who actually generated the idea.

It's just as important to act quickly and decisively when it's *your* idea that's been lifted. If someone takes credit for an idea of yours during a meeting that you're attending, be sure to respond with a comment of your own that starts, "You know, Tom, when I brought this idea up to you the other day . . ." Later, take Tom aside and tell him that either he corrects the false impression he created or you'll do it for him.

Should you hear about such an incident after the fact, approach the person who wrongly took credit and ask him or her to go to your supervisor at once to clear up the matter—adding that if he or she doesn't, you'll do so yourself. (Note: One way to prevent this sort of thing from happening is to write up your idea in memo form at its very inception and e-mail it or circulate a hard copy prior to any meetings or discussions.)

ACCEPTING BLAME

A serious mistake has been made, and now someone must be held accountable. If the error was yours, it's incumbent on you to stand up at once and openly accept responsibility. Allowing another person to take the blame for something that wasn't their fault—or even running that risk — is flatly unethical. Similarly, if someone blames you unfairly, you have every right to demand that your colleague set the record straight — and to do it yourself if he or she refuses.

BACK-STABBING AND UNDERMINING

A negative comment in the right ears can be a death knell to someone's prospects in a company. That is why the ethical employee will avoid back-stabbing or undermining his or her colleagues. On the other hand, what if your boss or a fellow employee openly invites your critique of another coworker? When discussing a colleague with management, it is your responsibility to objectively outline the positive and negative aspects of your colleague's performance, focusing only on work-related matters, while avoiding any overtly personal criticism. If, in your opinion, your coworker clearly isn't pulling his or her weight, this is a legitimate time to say so.

As for bull sessions among your peers about a colleague's work performance, the ethical thing is to demur politely — explaining simply, "I don't care to get into that sort of thing."

YOU AND YOUR COMPANY

When you joined your firm, you entered into an agreement to abide by all company policies and to fulfill the contractual obligations of your job. In return, your company took on the obligations of living up to its financial agreement with you and treating you fairly. Here are some of the key ethical issues that commonly arise on both sides of this arrangement:

YOUR THINGS OR THEIRS?

Office supplies have a way of becoming interchangeable between the office and the home. While the occasional pen or box of paper clips may seem like nothing to worry about, even the smallest pilfering could easily be the first step down a slippery slope. The best ethical approach is simply to avoid taking any office supplies out of the workplace. The only exception would be if you are explicitly working on work-related projects at home and you have your company's permission to bring home any needed supplies.

AN HONEST DAY'S WORK

Overstating the hours you work, or leaving the office early if you're on a fixed salary, is the equivalent of taking money from your company's till. Again, the ethical approach is to avoid shaving even a few minutes off the hours you're contracted to work. If you are forced to miss work time — to keep a doctor's or dentist's appointment, for example — schedule the appointment for the beginning or end of the day to minimize the impact on your work schedule, and offer to work late or through lunch to make up for the lost time.

A trickier issue involves time spent in the office on personal phone calls and e-mails, or in non-work-related conversation with colleagues. Clearly, some personal communication is unavoidable during office hours, while some degree of office chat is important for morale and camaraderie in the workplace. Still, the ethical employee will minimize the time spent on such distractions. If you do have to spend a significant amount of time on a personal call for some reason, keep track of your time on the phone, and make it up by working overtime.

Taking a strong ethical position on your work hours is even more important when you're telecommuting. Since no one is watching to see if you're actually at your desk, it's up to you—and your inner ethical compass—to make sure that you're providing your employer with an honest day's effort.

SICK DAYS

Unlike vacation days and personal days, which are yours to do with as you wish, sick days are set aside by your company strictly for illnesses that are debilitating or contagious enough to require you to stay out of the office. Again, it will often be up to you to make the ethical call. If you're not truly sick but simply feeling a little run-down, and you honestly think a day's rest at home could improve your productivity, then you may be justified in calling in sick, provided you don't overstate your physical condition in the process. On the other hand, using a sick day to catch up on your shopping or go to the ball game is flat out unethical—and could also put your job in jeopardy if someone spots you in the act.

If you have an unavoidable personal obligation and have already run out of vacation and personal days, go to your manager and explain the situation, adding, "I'd like to try and work something out with you." You might offer to give up a day's pay, for example, or use a vacation day from the next calendar year.

RESPECTING PROPRIETARY INFORMATION

While some information is meant to be shared within a company, other information—such as key financial data, employee records, or future business plans—may be disseminated only on a need-to-know basis. If you stumble across data that is not meant for your eyes, it is your ethical obligation not only to avoid scrutinizing this information, but to call attention to the lapse in confidentiality.

Many companies also ask their employees to sign confidentiality pacts, in which the employee agrees not to reveal certain information about the company. Typically these agreements continue to have effect even after you leave a company's employ. You have an ethical responsibility to be clear on the details of any such agreement before signing on with the firm—and then living up to it.

EXPENSE REPORTS

Asking your firm to reimburse you for expenses that aren't actually business-related is both unethical and a form of stealing. Most companies have explicit policies about how expense reports are to be filed and what type of expenses are acceptable. Make sure you know exactly what your company's policy is, then follow it to the letter. (Should you have doubts about a given expense, listen to your inner ethicist and err on the conservative side.) If your company doesn't have a policy about allowable expenses, suggest that they adopt one.

COMPANY PERKS

Unless your company's policy explicitly says otherwise, you must assume that company perks are intended strictly for you and your coworkers and are to be used only for business-related purposes. This includes riding in the company car or plane, using company facilities, and taking any company-related discounts. If your company does make exceptions for certain perks—by allowing employees' families to fly with them on the corporate jet, for example—you should still double-check with management before going ahead. If there is any uncertainty, offer to pay the full value of any perks in question.

CONFLICT OF INTEREST

Most companies have strict conflict-of-interest rules, and it is your responsibility to know the details of your firm's policy. Beyond this, the ethical businessperson is careful to avoid even the *appearance* of a conflict. For example, if you have a particularly close personal relationship with someone at a potential vendor that could possibly leave you open to a charge of favoritism, you should pass this information on to your company's management, along with a request that you not be involved in any procurement decisions involving that firm.

REPORTING ETHICAL MISBEHAVIOR

The fellow in the next cubicle has been gone all afternoon—for the third day in a row. What do you do? While you may feel a tug of loyalty toward the guy (he's really not such a bad egg), your duty is clear. Besides behaving ethically yourself, it is also your responsibility to be intolerant of any unethical behavior on the part of your coworkers.

In practice, how you actually respond to such behavior will vary depending on the severity and nature of the transgression. If it's a matter of a few ballpoint pens slipped into a briefcase or someone ducking out of the office an hour early now and then, you may weigh the pros and cons of saying something and then decide to remain silent for the time being. If the transgression is more serious—such as repeatedly going missing from the office for hours at a time, acting abusively toward a fellow employee, or lying about a work-related issue—you should approach your colleague and give him the opportunity to redress the situation before you do: "Jack, lying about that sales call was unethical and reflects badly on the company and the rest of us. You need to approach [the manager] and explain what really happened—and if you don't, I will."

If the other person ignores you and continues the unethical behavior, or tells you to take a hike—or if the transgression violates the law or is so serious that you don't feel you should approach your colleague about it—then your next step is to talk to someone in your firm's management. Your choices include your immediate supervisor, your company's human resources department, and your firm's ethics officer.

One thing to bear in mind is that supervisors and human resources staff are obligated to investigate any complaints brought to them. The advantage of going to your firm's ethics officer first—especially if you are uncertain about whether the behavior is ethical or not or want to learn more about your company's guidelines before acting—is that the ethics officer is not required to take any action and doesn't have to divulge your name to management, the courts, or any regulatory agency.

If you are worried about repercussions, or simply want to keep your name out of the affair, many companies—including all publicly held corporations—now offer a simpler option: The Sarbanes-Oxley Act of 2002 requires public companies to have anonymous "hotlines" or similar whistle-blower systems, so that employees can report ethical violations without revealing their identities.

WHEN THE CULPRIT IS YOU

What if—through ignorance, carelessness, or a lapse in judgment—you do something yourself that is clearly unethical?

There will always be a strong temptation in such cases to keep quiet about your misstep and hope that no one notices, but ethics experts agree that the best move is to admit what you've done and offer to make restitution as appropriate. Tell your supervisor that you're sorry for your actions, and that you'd like to start over with a clean slate. While you may still lose your job, this is better than living with the knowledge of what you've done and the anxiety that your actions may eventually be uncovered.

LYING FOR YOUR BOSS—
AND OTHER ETHICAL DILEMMAS

What if your manager or some other company leader asks you to do something that you believe to be unethical, or even illegal? The request could be as "harmless" as asking you to lie about your boss's whereabouts, or as potentially damaging as ordering you to falsify your firm's financial records. Either way, you're on the spot.

You should *never* lie for your boss or be put in a situation where you're forced even to consider it. If your boss doesn't want to deal with a visitor or a telephone call, suggest that you say your boss is "unavailable," rather than telling a fib like "He's in a meeting" or "She's out of the office." (The same holds true, by the way, when it comes to keeping confidences your boss has shared with you. If a nosy colleague tries to pry some confidential information out of you, instead of lying and saying, "I don't know," simply tell your coworker, "You know that's an area I can't talk about.")

In a more troubling situation—if, for example, your boss asks you to alter the minutes of a meeting—your best response is to say, "I'm sorry, but I'm uncomfortable with that." Most managers will respect your ethical stance and back down.

Perhaps the toughest of all ethical dilemmas is when a manager or colleague asks you to do something that you feel is unethical, "for the good of the company." Ethics researchers have found that in this situation, all too many employees are willing simply to follow orders. In one 1996 survey of 400 executives, 47 percent said they would be willing to commit financial fraud by using an accounting trick to inflate corporate profits.

The ethical employee, on the other hand, will always look carefully before leaping into an ethically dicey assignment. Rule number one when confronting an ethical business dilemma, say ethicists, is to "ask before you act." If you're feeling pressure to do something questionable—or observe someone else being so pressured—your first step should be to discuss the pros and cons of the situation with a supervisor who isn't directly involved in the assignment. If that doesn't clear up the matter, contact your firm's human resources department or ethics officer (if you have one). As a last resort, you can go to your company's legal counsel or compliance officer.

If you attempt to turn down the questionable assignment but the pressure to act unethically continues, you'll need to consider resigning. At the very least, you'll want to take an unflinching look at your entire company. Is the pressure you're feeling an aberration, or is it reflective of the general corporate culture?

The final step, in cases where you believe your firm's activities are dangerous or illegal, is to become a whistle-blower and report the company's ethics lapses to the appropriate oversight agency.

IT'S A LEGAL MATTER

From the ban on insider trading by investment bankers to the Hippocratic oath taken by doctors, every profession has its own unique set of legal and ethical requirements. It's your responsibility to keep abreast of all the legalities regarding your particular trade. Review these rules carefully when you first join a firm, and periodically update your knowledge. One of the best ways to do this is to confer regularly with someone from your company's legal department. Insist, too, that your company have a policy of quickly disseminating any changes or modifications in your field's legal requirements. In a courtroom, ignorance of the law is no excuse—which means that if you're not up to speed, it's your head that will be on the chopping block.

THE ETHICAL MANAGER

As a company manager, you have three additional sets of ethical responsibilities, beyond your obligations as an employee:

- You have a responsibility not to abuse your position when interacting with your subordinates.

- You have a responsibility to serve as an ethical role model for others in the company.

- You have a responsibility to actively promote an ethical environment within your firm, including putting systems into place to help accomplish this goal and encouraging employees to come to you with their concerns.

Let's consider these points one at a time:

NOT ABUSING YOUR POSITION

Being a manager means you have direct power over the careers of others. As with any type of leverage, this power must be handled with care and consideration. The ethical manager will never ask an employee to lie or misrepresent the facts, or to perform an action that is ethically dubious. The ethical manager is also scrupulously fair in his or her treatment of all subordinates, including when hiring and promoting employees. Finally, the ethical manager never exploits his or her position to demand a favor or other consideration from an employee; to harass or vent displeasure toward an employee in an abusive, belittling, or intimidating way; or to ask an employee to put in more work than he or she is being paid for.

Conversely, the ethical manager makes every effort to support his or her staff within the company and also in regard to their long-term career paths, and works with each employee in good faith to resolve any problems or difficulties that might arise. The ethical manager is also careful to be clear and accurate in all interoffice communications, and to pass along important information about the company in an appropriate and timely fashion.

SERVING AS AN ETHICAL ROLE MODEL

Experts agree that corporate ethics are defined from the top down. When a company's leaders are perceived as having high personal ethics, that company's employees are more likely to have high ethical standards as well. The higher your leadership position, the more effect your words and actions will have. The ethical executive is scrupulous when handling company funds and assets and makes every necessary effort to avoid even the appearance of nepotism, favoritism, or other personal conflicts of interest. In addition, the ethical leader is prepared to take ultimate responsibility for all ethical lapses on the part of subordinates that occur on his or her watch.

PROMOTING AN ETHICAL WORKPLACE

As a leader, you are in a position to influence the future course of your organization's business activities. The ethical leader insists that his or her firm adopt ethical goals and means, and encourages an open decision-making process that includes a full discussion of the ethical implications of various business opportunities.

Your role as an ethical leader also involves making sure your company has systems in place that support ethical behavior. These include a corporate code of ethics that applies to all employees at all times; in-house communication strategies that emphasize the importance of ethical behavior and encourage the discussion of ethical issues within the company; training programs to help educate employees on how to make good ethical decisions; resources for employees who wish to seek guidance on ethical issues; a mechanism for reporting unethical behavior; and an established process for dealing with ethics lapses if and when they occur, including an ethics officer who reports directly to the CEO.

The Sarbanes-Oxley Act—passed by the U.S. Congress in 2002, in the wake of the Enron collapse and other corporate scandals—now requires such systems in all publicly held companies. If a firm is not big enough to justify an ethics officer, this function will typically be taken on by the human resources department or by an ethics committee made up of members of the management team.

If you work in a privately owned company or organization that doesn't yet have an ethics program in place, you should consider raising the issue with your fellow managers. Such programs help ensure an ethical, high-functioning workforce, while also serving as a symbol of your commitment to integrity. Ethics programs have become so popular, in fact, that a large number of ethics-consulting firms have been formed in recent years to help companies set them up. It could be the best investment your company ever makes.

THE ETHICAL VENDOR

Clients and customers are the lifeblood of any business. Treating your customers ethically is not just the right thing to do—it will also help ensure that they remain your customers over the long haul. The ethical vendor

- Works diligently to finish every assignment professionally within the agreed-upon time frame, while charging a fair price for it

- Gives honest reasons for any problems and/or delays, and offers legitimate, honorable solutions

- Provides an accurate estimate of the costs for any services or goods ahead of time, when appropriate, and makes good on that estimate

- Never promises anything that can't be delivered

- Will never offer cash or other unethical inducements in an attempt to secure business

- Will never collude with a customer to get around regulations, manipulate fees or prices, or secure business in an unethical fashion

- Avoids even the appearance of any unethical behavior in its business relationships

An ethical company will typically have a policy against working for two clients who are competitors, for example, and will place a limit on the value of gifts that be given to or received from clients. (What should you do if you do get a present that's too expensive? Simply return the item in question with a note saying, "I appreciate your gift, but I'm afraid the rules here won't allow me to keep it.") (See also "Declining Gifts," page 151.)

"TALK TO MY AGENT"

If you're in an inventive or creative line of work, any new ideas are actually intellectual property and have to be guarded especially carefully. It's your responsibility to be discreet when discussing your ideas, and, where appropriate, to patent, copyright, or trademark them as soon as possible. You should also be cautious about playing audience to other people's ideas—especially if the idea being pitched is similar to something you're already working on. If another party *does* present you with a concept that's close to one of your own, you run the risk of later being accused of stealing their idea—a risk that could force you to drop the idea altogether.

If someone tries to share something you'd rather not hear, you can avoid this ethical trap by telling the person politely but firmly, "I'm sorry, but I can't discuss this with you." If the other party persists, ask them to contact your agent, manager, or other representative. Your agent can then field the idea without getting you involved, shielding you from a potentially compromising encounter.

THE ETHICAL CUSTOMER

Being an ethical customer or client doesn't mean you can't push hard for the best possible service or product at the best possible price. It does mean, however, that you always conduct your negotiations in an open, honest fashion and are careful not to use your position to exploit or manipulate the vendor—for instance, by asking a firm to spend time preparing a proposal "on spec" when you know that you have no intention of hiring them. In addition, the ethical customer

- Pays vendors within the agreed-upon time period

- Lives up to all contractual obligations

- Doesn't pressure the vendor to provide goods or services beyond the scope of their agreement

- Never allows a choice of vendor to be influenced by favors, gifts, or kickbacks

- Avoids even the appearance of any conflict of interest or discrimination when selecting vendors

- Will work in good faith with creditors to resolve outstanding debts if financial difficulties make it impossible to meet contractual obligations

THE ETHICAL JOB-SEEKER

Whether you're between jobs, looking to change positions, or just starting out on your career path, searching for new employment has its own set of ethical hurdles. It's always a good idea to head off disruptive speculation by being as discreet as possible when looking for a new job—for example, by conducting all interviews and job-related phone calls at a safe distance from your office. But these activities should be done only on your own time, either outside normal work hours or in the context of a personal or vacation day. You also owe it to your employer to give at least two weeks' notice before leaving your current job.

In addition, the ethical job-seeker

- Never lies or exaggerates in a résumé or cover letter

- Focuses only on legitimate accomplishments during interviews

- Avoids bad-mouthing his or her former employer when leaving a job

Ethics experts also suggest taking advantage of the job-interview process to inquire about your prospective employer's ethical policies and enforcement systems. If a firm has shaky or nonexistent ethical standards and practices, the time to learn this is *before* you jump on board—not after.

3 | *Dress and Grooming*

Business dress has undergone such radical shifts in the past ten years that people simply no longer know what is "appropriate" anymore. Standards that used to speak for the entire work world now barely suffice for an individual profession. For instance, some law offices still require men to wear suits, while others opt for a jacket-and-tie look and some go so far as to permit full-blown business casual anytime. A few firms still subscribe to a casual-Friday mode, although that particular term is fast dying out.

Does all this tremendous change mean that anything goes? Of course not. Figuring out which clothes are appropriate for your particular business simply means assessing the particulars. It boils down to (1) dressing to fit in at your company and (2) dressing to meet the expectations of those with whom you do business. In a word, it's situational. But that doesn't mean you should get complacent. Some things about clothing never change: First, people judge you by your clothes; how you attire yourself is a vital ingredient in making a good first impression and is a signifier forever after. Second, dressing as your peers do but with a bit more style gives you an advantage no matter where you work.

ATTITUDE AND ADAPTATION

Remember the days when the preferred business look for women was the man-tailored dark skirt-suit with the floppy bow tie? Such lockstep uniformity has disappeared, to the relief of many. Today, the emphasis is on situational dress, with a businessperson's choice of what to wear to work determined by his or her profession and the attitudes of the company. Fields such as finance, law, banking, insurance, and health care typically call for traditional business clothing in almost every case, whereas industries that provide design or content — advertising, publishing, entertainment, fashion, and information technology — allow for more personal expression.

As a result of these variable standards, the big picture of business dress has become more complex — or simpler, depending on how you look at it — than the old dichotomy of traditional versus nontraditional. In short, the modern business dresser is chameleon-like. What to wear to work depends on what the businessperson plans for that day. If he's doing nothing special, a man might wear his usual open-collar shirt; if meeting with clients who are sure to be wearing ties, he wears one, too. Or, if he's going to be meeting with clients who wear nothing but jeans and T-shirts, he knows that wearing a suit could build a wall between him and his clients.

A CAVEAT. Dressing for "what I'm doing today" can be risky. You never know when an invitation to see a valued customer, client, or contractor may come out of the blue. Avoid getting caught by either (1) keeping a change of clothes in your office, including an extra jacket and tie, or (2) dressing daily in a way that's appropriate regardless of the situation—the wiser of the two choices.

EIGHT KEY POINTS

Whether your workplace is stodgily conservative or more casual, there are some timeless axioms that always apply to dress:

1 KEEP IT UNDERSTATED. Understatement—allowing your clothes to speak without shouting—has always been the hallmark of the well-dressed. Yet this, too, is relative. What is considered too flashy by a conservative law firm is no doubt a far cry from what's too "out there" at a recording studio. Still, the philosophies of these very different environments have at least one thing in common: In both settings, bosses and coworkers alike may view veering wildly from the resident norm as an act of flippancy or even contempt—behavior that's unwelcome anywhere.

2 DRESS FOR THE JOB YOU WANT, NOT THE JOB YOU HAVE. Take a look at how your manager dresses, or the people in the sales division where you really want to work. Show your employers that you're focused on growing with the company, rather than pushing the envelope on corporate dress policy.

3 REPRESENT YOUR COMPANY. Whenever you deal with people from outside, your clothes reflect on your company. No matter what the dress code is at the office, be prepared to look your best by keeping a change of conservative clothes in your office. An even better solution is to dress every day so that you're prepared for any situation that comes your way.

4 **KEEP IT NEAT.** The blouse with the ripped seam and the trousers with the grease spot should stay in the closet until they can be mended and cleaned. The same goes for footwear, even on casual days: Dirty canvas shoes should be saved for gardening or puttering around the house, not for wearing to work.

5 **KEEP IT CLEAN.** Obviously, clean clothes are just as essential in fields where standards of dress are the most relaxed (information technology and music, for two) as they are in more formal companies. Soiled jeans and an unironed T-shirt speak more of slovenliness and poor personal habits than of rebellion and cool.

6 **DON'T REVEAL TOO MUCH.** Clothes that are too revealing are unsuitable in any workplace. Whether intentional or not, low-cut blouses, too-tight pants, and see-through fabrics send a sexual message. The smart business dresser knows that the key is to look authoritative and highly competent.

7 **DRESS FOR THE TIME OF DAY.** Arriving at work in clothes more suitable for evening is a bad idea. If you choose something dressier than usual because you have an important lunch or a special evening event, forget the black cocktail dress. You can change your daytime wear after the official workday. Knowing which kinds of clothes are appropriate for day wear is one of the first lessons anyone in business should learn.

8 **DON'T BE A FASHION VICTIM.** Because your work clothes are the kind of investment that should last for several years, don't let "what's hot" be your guide. Besides, following a trend can be a giant mistake if it doesn't fit who you are.

BUSINESS CLOTHES FOR MEN

The following notes on clothes and accessories are to help you make choices when you shop, no matter what your field. Choosing suitable fabrics and materials has to do with seasonality and practicality, but what is "in style" is more than ever in the eye of the beholder. Nevertheless, erring on the side of subtlety is generally the best course, a philosophy reflected below:

THE SUIT

Your business suit may spend more time hanging in the closet than it used to, but it remains an essential, if only for weddings and funerals. While you want to select a suit with care, think less of making a fashion statement than of finding something that fits well and feels comfortable, and that will stand the test of time.

There's only one ironclad rule in choosing a fabric for a suit: No matter what the color, the surface should be matte—not shiny or iridescent. The choice in fabrics boils down to wool or cotton.

- **WOOL**. With its many textures, wool is the suit fabric of choice because of its ability to stretch yet still keep its shape; its matte finish; its ability to breathe (keeping you warmer in winter and cooler in summer); and its long shelf life.

- **COTTON**. In summer, cotton and linen are popular suit fabrics because they're so comfortable. But be careful, especially with linen. Unless you aspire to the fashionable nonchalance associated with wrinkles, remember that linen will look as if you slept in it after only a few hours.

- **A HINT**. Not only will wool wrinkle less, but a lightweight variety is actually cooler than linen and some cottons for summer.

Dark colors have always been associated with authority, but tradition has also embraced suits in lighter shades of brown (tan and beige) and gray. Pastel-colored suits in blue, mint green, or rosy beige just won't do in a traditional work environment. Solids are always a safe choice, while pinstripes are a handsome alternative, with a very thin, light gray stripe preferred.

SPORT JACKETS AND BLAZERS

The most versatile style is the single-breasted jacket with a classic shape, with the three-button version as the more modern. Small checks, muted patterns, and tweeds are the usual designs, while solids come in almost every color imaginable. If the sport coat is the most casual item of business wear and the three-piece suit the dressiest, the navy blue blazer occupies the middle ground. A blazer paired with gray flannel slacks creates a casual look that's unsurpassed.

SLACKS

Slacks should be worn with the waist high enough to rest the waistband over your hip bones. Non-pleated pants tend to make you look slimmer. Cuffs are classic, while no cuffs present a more modern look.

DRESS SHIRTS

At work, more muted colors work better than loud colors. The only caveat is to make sure the jacket, shirt, and tie complement one another. White remains the dressiest choice.

OVERCOATS AND RAINCOATS

One of the most popular coats is the trench coat. The traditional and most versatile length for an overcoat is just below the knee. Shorter, knee-length coats such as peacoats, parkas, and duffle coats are also perfectly fine to wear with casual clothes or even a suit, especially in colder climates where practicality has to prevail over style.

SHOES

From the dressiest on down, the traditional business shoe is the oxford (plain toe or cap toe), the wing tip, and the plain or tasseled loafer. Your shoes shouldn't so much contrast with your outfit as harmonize with it: black with gray, brown with tan.

SOCKS

Beyond these three basics, few rules apply to socks: (1) Use dark socks for business wear, (2) match them to your pants, and (3) make sure they're high enough not to show your bare shins when you sit down. Natural fibers such as cotton and wool are preferable to synthetics because they are better insulators and more breathable, keeping feet warmer and deterring foot odor.

ACCESSORIES

As basic as a tie, as small as a pen, as infrequently used as an umbrella—the smaller items of the businessman's wardrobe can dress up your look, giving it an expensive sheen—or dress it down. And, like garments, these accessories should change character according to the situation.

THE TIE

For the great majority of men who dress for business, the tie remains the most important of all accessories. There are two schools of thought about ties: The first says that your tie is a way for you to express your individuality. The second says that defining your personality with your tie may make you feel good, but nobody else really cares; plus, some people find idiosyncratic ties unprofessional. (Though your coworkers get a kick out of your tie with the mermaid motif, some of your customers may not be amused.) One solution to this problem is to keep a "safe" tie in your office. Regardless of the design, make sure your tie color coordinates with your shirt and jacket.

HATS

Hats carry more connotations than other accessories, so choose them with care: a fedora that suits you can look smart, while one that doesn't can make you look a little disreputable. Avoid hats that are too large or unusual.

THE UBIQUITOUS BASEBALL CAP

The most important consideration for the cap-wearing businessperson is to know when to take his—or her—cap off. Wearing a baseball cap to work is perfectly fine, but keeping it on once you've stepped in the door is not. The cap is so much a part of some men that they forget they have it on, and more than one worker has come to an early morning meeting and had to be reminded to remove it. Also, if a conservative client comes in and you take him to lunch, leave the baseball cap at the office.

BELTS AND SUSPENDERS

The fact that belts should be coordinated with your shoe color means you need more than one—a black, a brown (both dark and light), and possibly a cordovan. The standard belt width is 1¼ inches; anything wider should be saved for clothing other than your suit. Materials of choice are fine-grade leather and real crocodile, alligator, or lizard; and for casual wear, braided leather, suede, or canvas. Avoid showy buckles, obvious stitching, and other trimmings.

The alternative (not companion) to a belt is suspenders, which have about as much to do with holding up your pants as ties do with keeping the middle of your chest warm: They are not about function, but style. Suspenders are coordinated to the tie, with the quietness or wildness of the pattern determined by the company culture in which the wearer operates.

JEWELRY

Two words sum up the well-dressed businessman's use of jewelry: *minimalism* and *subtlety*. A wedding band, a class ring, and a good watch aren't quite the limit, but they're close. Anything else on the hands or wrists should be limited to a very simple ring and cuff links.

Chains around the neck are never suitable in a conventional work environment and are often out of place even in casual settings. Bracelets are not a good idea at most conservative companies, although thin and expensive ID bracelets usually won't cross the line.

BRIEFCASES

Laptop computer cases are now challenging the traditional briefcase in popularity, especially since many now build in additional room for documents and other materials. Whichever you use, it should be in excellent condition. For a simple sheaf of papers, another option is a leather envelope carried under the arm.

WATCHES

Think simple. Keep that dive watch with several timers and multiple buttons for nonbusiness situations. Even more important than the style you choose is making sure you turn off any electronic sounds your watch makes. A sudden beep announcing the hour can interrupt a meeting or presentation.

SUNGLASSES

Don't wear sunglasses with people you're meeting for business unless you're walking outside in bright sun. Obviously, you should make eye contact, and sunglasses render that impossible while at the same time making you look inscrutable (or worse, suspicious). Wearing sunglasses indoors is an affectation that's going to make most people think you're trying to shout "Hollywood!"—unless, that is, you're really lunching with a movie mogul.

STAYING WELL-GROOMED

Most men learn not to be a mess when they start to date as teenagers: The better groomed they are, the better their chances of having a girl on their arm. As adults, the better groomed men are, the more points they score in business.

Staying well-groomed means staying clean, odor-free, and untousled. It's a practical thing: A man with greasy hair and dandruff is going to be less appealing to be around, his sloppy personal habits erecting a wall of sorts between him and his coworkers and—perhaps even more important—his business associates from outside. The idea is to attract, not repel. Here's an everyday grooming checklist, including some items to keep on hand:

- **HAIR.** Wash your hair often enough to keep it from looking greasy. Avoid both the super-blow-dried look and the gelled-to-the-skull look. If you tend to have dandruff, use a dandruff shampoo and keep a small brush in the office for whisking flakes off your shoulders.

- **FINGERNAILS.** Keep a nail clipper with a cleaning tool in your desk drawer. Dirt can mysteriously appear under your fingernails when you least expect it. Nails should be trimmed straight across with about one-sixteenth of an inch of white showing; push back the cuticles occasionally, too.

- **FIVE O'CLOCK SHADOW.** This can be a problem if you have very dark hair. An electric shaver will smarten you up if you have a late afternoon meeting, so keep one in your desk drawer if necessary.

- **NOSE AND EAR HAIR.** One morning a week, check to see if your nose hairs need to be clipped (special blunt-end scissors are made for the purpose) or your ears tweezed. Your barber can take care of the ear hair; otherwise, do it yourself at home, not in the office restroom.

- **BODY ODOR**. A daily shower is the best defense against body odor, and a deodorant or antiperspirant is the second best. Deodorants only mask odor (and can actually make body odor worse when used as a bath substitute), while antiperspirants block sweat. Combination deodorant/antiperspirants are available, but don't apply them too thickly, or the scent could become obvious later in the day.

- **BREATH**. To keep your breath fresh, bring your toothbrush to work and brush after lunch. Brushing the back of the tongue helps control odor, and a breath mint or two during the day should keep you from offending.

- **WELL-HEELED, SHINY SHOES**. Shoes with the heels worn down should be worn only at home. As for shoe polish, your shoes needn't be mirrorlike, but they shouldn't be noticeably scuffed or dirty either.

- **IRONED CLOTHES**. The wrinkled look at the office makes you look like you're not tending to business. A touch-up with an iron before work will take a coat-hanger crease out of slacks and make any less-than-smooth shirts more presentable.

- **CLEAN CLOTHES**. Don't be tempted to wear that shirt, tie, or pair of pants with the grease spot, thinking that no one will notice. If it turns out you have to meet a client, you'll regret the decision. Wearing clean clothes is as essential as combing your hair.

YOUR COLOGNE

If some scents for men are meant to conjure up a woody glade or a citrus grove, they should merely hint at those bucolic places—not plop you down in the middle of them. No element of the businessman's wardrobe requires more subtlety than cologne. Filling a meeting room with the smell of citrus, balsam, or musk is the job of an air freshener, not you. Wearing too much cologne is even worse at an interview, where the "moderation in all things" approach is key. The toilet waters that refresh the skin after a shower are probably the best choice for the workday, with full-fledged cologne saved for night.

PROFESSIONAL AND CASUAL BUSINESS CLOTHES FOR MEN AND WOMEN

MEN—PROFESSIONAL

ACCEPTABLE

- Suits—three piece, two piece, two button or three button, wool or cotton
- Blazers or sport jackets with ties
- Slacks
- Dress shirts or oxford button-downs with ties
- Vests
- Overcoats or raincoats
- Oxfords, wing tips, or loafers
- Dark socks

NOT ACCEPTABLE

- Loud colors or bold patterns
- Spread collars without ties
- Athletic shoes
- White socks
- Fur coats
- Showy belt buckles

MEN—CASUAL

ACCEPTABLE

- Blazers or sport jackets
- Oxford-style shirts with button-down collars
- Turtleneck shirts
- Short-sleeved knit shirts
- Khaki slacks
- V-neck or crew-neck sweaters
- Informal ties

NOT ACCEPTABLE

- T-shirts with slogans, sayings, or cartoon characters
- Torn or worn-out jeans
- Anything shiny or too tight
- Sandals
- Tank tops
- Shorts

WOMEN—PROFESSIONAL

ACCEPTABLE

Three-piece suits: jackets, trousers, and interchangeable skirts

White or cream-colored blouses

Matching-colored blouses

Sweater sets

Status silk scarves—standard size, 34 inches

Quality microfiber all-weather coats—wool or twill

Good-quality handbags

1½-inch black leather pumps

Good-quality loafer-style shoes or flats

Tights and/or stockings

Umbrellas (arriving for a meeting soaking wet is not impressive)

NOT ACCEPTABLE

Jewelry that dangles, jangles, sparkles, or is gaudy

Athletic shoes

Fur coats (depends on locale)

Metallic, glittery, or sheer fabrics

WOMEN—CASUAL

ACCEPTABLE

Casual blazers over nice-quality plain knit blouses

Tailored pants or Bermuda-length shorts (depends on locale)

Jumper-style dresses (long or short)

Khaki pants

Washable linen pants

Twin sweater sets

Tunic-style sweaters

Loafers or flats

Open-toed pumps

NOT ACCEPTABLE

T-shirts with slogans, sayings, or cartoon characters

Tattered jeans

Spandex miniskirts

Strapless, stretchy bandeau tops

Exercise clothing, sweatpants, or sweat suits

Tank tops

Bare midriffs

The issue of jeans: Wearing jeans or not is determined by the workplace. At some places jeans are fine and at others they are not. However, it is never acceptable to wear jeans that are torn, have holes, are stained, are too tight, and/or are worn out. This applies to men and women. The same guidelines apply to T-shirts where in some companies the company shirt with a logo is perfectly acceptable.

TATTOOS AND PIERCINGS

A tattoo on a part of your body that no one will see is not an issue, but one on a hand, an ankle, or any other potentially visible place is different. Will the exotic salamander tattooed on your arm or upper neck affect your chances of getting a job or being promoted? No one knows for sure—but as soon as the tattoo becomes part of the image you project, it cannot help but affect what people think of you.

By comparison, most body piercings are benign. Unlike tattoos, piercing ornaments can be removed at will, which means that people who like them can have their cake and eat it, too. Most American businesses, however, still think piercings are strictly for earlobes. The smart man or woman in business takes cues from his or her peers and bosses before wearing any piercings to work.

BUSINESS CLOTHES FOR WOMEN

While today's businesswoman has more choices available to her than her predecessors of a generation ago, the principles underlying the traditional dress code are still in place in most professional fields—to wit, that good taste is never showy, whether in color, fabric, style, accessories, hairstyle, or makeup. Yes, customs change rapidly, but the smart woman in business will ground herself in the traditional styles and then branch out from there.

Here's a basic wardrobe for almost any working woman to start with:

- A three-piece suit (jacket, slacks, and interchangeable skirt) or two suits (one with jacket and skirt, one with jacket and slacks)

- A white, cream-colored, or solid conservative-colored, non-sleeveless blouse

- A sweater set suitable for the workplace

- A fine silk scarf, conservative and in good enough condition for the workplace

- A microfiber all-weather coat

- A good-quality handbag

- A pair of black-leather pumps, with a stylish, not-overly-high heel

- A pair of good-quality flat shoes, loafer-style or similar

- Stockings and knee-highs

- An umbrella

To these you can add garments and accessories that will individualize your look without taking it outside of your workplace norm.

COLOR CONSIDERATIONS

When it comes to color, what is considered appropriate varies by region as much as by professional field. As always, the smart dresser starts by observing the conventions in her area and her workplace, taking her cues from those around her. But she also knows something about the general perception of various colors.

- Navy blue, burgundy, black, charcoal gray, and taupe are the traditional colors of the businesswoman's wardrobe, with the darker hues worn through the winter. Neutral colors, or tonals, are preferable to pure colors—sea green over kelly green, for example, or peach over orange.

- As for other colors, red is strong and assertive—the reason it's known as a power color. Bright orange, magenta, and other loud and flashy colors can cross the line into tackiness in conservative businesses if not worn with care; these bright colors may be worn, but when in doubt, tone them down with a dark color, such as a navy suit.

COORDINATE AND ACCENT

Coordinating color in an outfit is equally important. For the more traditional look, start with basic business colors for the major garments and then accent them with brighter colors in small amounts—an eye-catching ensemble that ensures you won't fade into the background. A classic example is the paisley scarf used with a gray or camel suit. A brighter-colored blouse with complementary earrings, necklaces, and bracelets serves the same purpose and balances the overall look.

FABRICS

The enduring preference for natural fabrics is rooted in the fact that cotton, wool, silk, and linen breathe while keeping the wearer cool or warm. The new microfibers are synthetics reborn, providing breathability, comfort, and ease of care.

The acceptance of synthetics and knits is particularly good news for working women: These fabrics that were once thought of as suitable only for casual wear can now go into the workplace depending on how they're styled. It's even better news for businesswomen who travel: A garment that blends a natural fiber with a synthetic is more flexible, easier to care for, and less seasonal, making it perfect for wearing on a trip that goes from chilly Boston to steamy Houston.

NOTES ON ACCESSORIES

The wide range of accessories that you're able to select from gives you more leeway to achieve a look of authority and style. Choose them to reflect both your own attitude and that of your organization. Remember that accessories, conventional or not, project an image, and you want that image to be positive.

HANDBAGS
A quality handbag is a valuable accessory that need not break the bank. Focus first on neatness and functionality, making sure the bag is large enough to hold all the items you carry with you other than makeup—a day planner, for example.

BRIEFCASES
The traditional briefcase is giving way to the protective laptop computer case, the purchase of which demands the same attention to good design and quality as you would devote to a briefcase.

BELTS
When a woman's outfit requires a belt, the classic style is ½- to ¾-inch-wide leather. Buckles can be metal or leather in any simple, quiet shape; if metal, coordinate it to other metal—earrings, necklaces, watchbands, buttons. The belt's color should harmonize with shoe and garment colors. Wear belts loose enough to ride with the waistband of your skirt, not above it.

GIVING OLD TABOOS THE BOOT

At what time of year, exactly, are you not supposed to wear white shoes? Did your mother say before Easter, or was it Memorial Day? A few taboos and customs hold fast, while most others have either relaxed or fallen by the wayside on the road to sartorial correctness.

SEASONAL COLOR

The answer to the white shoes question? Apply common sense. If the shoes are strictly summer wear—white straw sandals, for example—you might want to follow the old Memorial Day to Labor Day rule. These days, this seasonal injunction against the *color* white no longer applies. The determinant applies only to white fabrics and materials—and loosely, at that. White suede pumps in November? Sure, if they go with your outfit. The white gabardine skirt is fine for winter, too. Thin white cotton slacks in Minnesota in January? No, for obvious reasons.

Lighter colors are more acceptable at all times of year and are not limited to spring and summer, especially in seasonless fabrics. And vice versa: Forest green, for example, was considered a fall and winter color but is now perfectly fine for a linen springtime garment.

FABRICS

Objections to certain fabrics for business clothing have largely disappeared, with style a more important issue than "natural versus synthetic" or "woven versus knit."

- As recently as the early 1980s, knitwear was perceived as too casual for the traditional business look. But after top designers put knit suits on the map, this attitude changed. Knits have also gained favor because they don't wrinkle, making them ideal for business travel.

- Linen is still mostly worn in spring and summer, but as a linen blouse paired with a winter jacket it is perfectly acceptable in winter.

SUEDE AND PATENT LEATHER

Suede is no longer worn just in fall and winter, yet it remains seasonal for handbags. For shoes and handbags, patent leather is no longer a spring-and-summer-only choice. Black and dark browns and other earth colors (but not bright ones) have traditionally been preferred. But even white patent leather has its place in the business wardrobe.

SCARVES

A scarf can heighten focus on the face or provide visual relief in a monochromatic outfit. Scarves can also dress up a casual outfit or soften a tailored look. Coordinate a multicolored scarf to your ensemble by making sure it picks up a color in the outfit.

JEWELRY

If you have a passion for jewelry, curb it during the workday—at traditional offices, at least. Keep in mind that jewelry should accent, not take center stage, meaning you should let nothing dangle, jangle, sparkle, or be gaudy. (See also the "Tattoos and Piercings" box, page 35.)

- **EARRINGS.** Simple button earrings in silver, gold, or pearl are classic because they harmonize well with jacket outfits. Diamond, pearl, or gold studs or small drops are also always correct. Hoops that are hollow are lighter and more comfortable to wear, while heavy earrings will stretch your earlobes over time. Another consideration: Large clip-ons can make talking on the telephone difficult. Make earrings compatible in size and shape with a necklace. If you wear glasses, small earrings that won't compete with your frames are the best choice.

- **NECKLACES.** Two necklace styles are traditional for business wear—small-scale silver or gold chains or classic (i.e., small) pearls in white or off-white. Let the neckline of the garment decide the shape: V-shaped neckline, V-shaped necklace; rounded neckline, rounded necklace. To coordinate a colored necklace with your outfit, make sure its color is repeated somewhere—in a print, the belt, or the skirt or blouse color.

- **RINGS.** With simplicity as the guiding principle, the maximum number of rings for traditional business wear is one per hand (wedding and engagement count as one ring).

- **WATCHES.** Two kinds of bands are preferred in conservative offices: leather in black or brown; and metal in matte stainless steel, silver, or gold. (Match the metal of your watch to that of your other jewelry.) Sport watches have become more acceptable so long as they're not the heavy, deep-sea-diver type. A watch worn with a bracelet is fine, but a watch with multiple bracelets is not. Remember to turn off any electronic noises the watch makes.

FOOTWEAR

Shoes no longer have to look orthopedic to keep arch and back problems at bay. Beyond this development, the traditional taboos against open-toed shoes, backless shoes, sling backs, and other informal styles still exist in conservative workplaces but have gone by the board in most others. Figuring out what's undesirable in most offices is simple: clogs, hiking boots, boat shoes, or chunky, thick-soled shoes. Knowing what's appropriate anywhere is equally easy: the pump.

PUMPS

The classic business pump has a 1- to 1½-inch-high heel (and the wider, the more comfortable), but any becoming height can be appropriate depending on the workplace. Extreme spikes (3 inches or higher) and flat heels look the least professional. Shoe color is less of an issue than it once was, but the traditional business colors remain black, navy, chocolate brown, and taupe. (Note: Very inconspicuous trim details can be appropriate but might limit the number of outfits that go with the shoes.) Whatever the color, under no circumstances should you wear shoes that are dirty or scuffed, or have worn-down heels.

Save heels over 1½ inches to wear with skirts; they look too dressy for the office when worn with slacks. Other choices for pants are an oxford-style shoe and a sleek leather loafer that covers the instep.

BOOTS

New boot styles designed with commuters in mind are cross-functional: The upper portion is less casual, while the rubber soles grip the pavement securely. These new styles make it possible to wear boots to the office without having to change to heels.

ATHLETIC SHOES

Athletic shoes at work are a definite *never* except at the most nonconformist companies and on some casual days. To wear them to or from the office is fine, however, especially in cities where heels become a problem when negotiating sidewalks and public transportation. Many women keep a pair of shoes at the office or carry them in a tote bag to change into at the office.

STAYING WELL-GROOMED

Grooming is every bit as important as what you wear, from tip to toe. Hair, in fact, has proved its potential to make a statement as well as or more strongly than clothes do. The amount of makeup sends an unavoidable message, too—and in most workplaces, understatement in both is key.

THE "DON'T LEAVE HOME WITHOUT IT" EMERGENCY KIT

The smart businessperson keeps a stash of emergency items in the office. It's wise to have a change of professional clothes on hand for use as needed: a jacket, as well as an extra ironed shirt and tie or blouse, and a skirt or pair of slacks. Here's a checklist of other emergency items:

- Wash-and-dry towelettes
- Marker for touching up shoe scuffs
- Lint roller
- Tape to hold up hems
- Safety pins
- Small sewing kit
- Brushes for hair, clothes, shoes
- Spot remover
- Eyeglasses
- Dental floss, toothbrush, and toothpaste
- Extra pair of hose
- Static guard
- Nail polish—clear for panty-hose runs, your current nail color to repair chips
- Lipstick and compact

HAIR

A woman will attract attention with her hair when she has a flattering cut or healthy, shiny hair that simply begs to be admired. What about length? There's no longer a true rule, but on the job, hair should be kept out of the eyes: Tuck it behind your ears, pull it back in a ponytail, or pull it out of your eyes with a barrette. Unusual ornaments are risky unless you're a senior vice president who has earned the right to be a little au courant. The clamps that create an instant upswept twist are also popular and make for a nice professional look.

MAKEUP

As a rule, use a light touch—makeup should enhance, not dominate. Extreme eye makeup, very unusual lip color, a lot of lip liner that is in obvious contrast to the lipstick—these are poor choices in most workplaces.

NAILS

The best length for nails in most business environments is just over the tip of the finger. The appropriateness of talons, extreme colors (black, blue, purple, neon), and fake nails decorated with designs or pictures is in direct proportion to the conservatism of your workplace. Clear nail polish is the best choice if you're uncertain. In conservative offices, it's not so much the painting of nails that matters but the colors that are chosen: A clear red, an understated pink, or clear polish are all fine. Still, remember that red on a simply manicured hand is one thing, while bright red on talons is another.

PERFUME

Like it or not, the perfume you wear to the office may be offending someone's nose. At the same time, there has been an appreciable jump in the number of people who claim they are "allergic" to most smells in general, especially manufactured ones. But you don't have to go to work scent-free. Just make sure the scent is light and clean, not one of the more exotic or muskier "romantic" blends more appropriate for evening. And use it sparingly: If your scent still lingers in the room when you leave someone's office, you're wearing too much.

AFTER DARK

Evening business functions allow women more opportunity to step out from the pack. First, determine whether the event you're attending is a short-dress cocktail affair or a formal occasion, and then proceed accordingly. Find out from someone who has a long history with the company about the best course to take.

When choosing what to wear, take special care with how you'll be perceived, erring on the side of less-than-flashy. Remember that at evening functions you might be sized up by managers or clients, plus their spouses or dates—in fact, it's often said you're truly dressing for your boss's significant other.

PART TWO

AT THE WORKPLACE

4 | *You and Your Coworkers*

Whether you're starting a new job or have been settled into one for years, you probably find yourself occasionally asking the question: "So just who *are* these people, anyway?" Here you are for forty-odd hours a week, sharing your time and space with a group of individuals whom you had no part in choosing. The fact that you work in the same field should give you at least one interest in common, but that's not necessarily so—not in an age when more and more people regard their jobs as a means to a wholly unrelated end. The office secretary may be taking dictation only until her screenplay is sold. The accountant in the next cubicle may be crunching numbers but thinking about his plan to win the Boston Marathon. How do you get to know these people? What are the secrets to getting along with them?

Those questions aside, an ill wind blows in some quarters of the workaday world, spawning a fashionably cynical attitude about the people we work with: "My job is terrific it's the people I can't stand." Besides being self-centered, this sort of attitude is also self-defeating. Even the evolution toward less formal work styles—flex-time, temporary employment, and electronic commuting—doesn't free employees from the obligation to make the best of things with their fellow workers and work toward a harmonious atmosphere. Nowhere is the Golden Rule more important than in the workplace. By treating your coworkers with consideration, whatever their title or level of responsibility, you'll gain their trust and respect—and establish yourself as a valuable and cohesive part of the team.

THE SAME POOL

You and your coworkers are in the same pool, and whether you sink or swim has a great deal to do with your ability to treat your workmates—even the difficult ones—with courtesy and respect. From a strictly self-serving perspective, it pays to have allies rather than enemies and to assume that everyone you work with can give you a boost up the corporate ladder. (For all you know, that fumbling mail boy might turn out to be the boss's grandson and heir apparent, while that caustic secretary could have a direct pipeline to the CEO.) Even if you don't regard yourself as a "people person," you can win friends and gain influence by observing the common courtesies and being tolerant when others don't. Rather than focusing on your coworkers' shortcomings, work to appreciate the contributions they make, recognizing that you are all part of a larger company culture with its own rules and standards—and eccentricities.

GRASPING COMPANY CULTURE

A culture is broadly defined as a group that shares beliefs, interests, values, goals, and living styles. Applied to businesses, culture refers to the common characteristics that set one workplace apart from another, including everything from the way major decisions are made and communicated to how the lowliest cubicle is decorated. All new employees not only have to learn a new job but also have to adapt to a new workplace culture.

Every company's culture, no matter how formal or informal, is governed by two realities: First, in business, culture is hierarchical—the rules of the game come from the top down. Even those companies that tout their participatory management and flattened pyramidal structures are not exactly democracies. Second, good intentions notwithstanding, business cultures develop over time, become ingrained, and are slow to change. In fact, CEOs who attempt to radically alter a well-established corporate culture will find themselves frustrated and sometimes tossed out of the executive suite.

In the days when workers typically had one or two employers during an entire working lifetime, accepting the prevailing company culture was relatively easy. In today's business world, however, workers are likely to have many employers and possibly even several career changes during their employment years. Every change requires adaptation, often to widely varying business styles and manners.

Your success in any new job depends on how quickly and thoroughly you master the company culture. Fortunately, you've got plenty of teachers. Along with taking your cues from your bosses, interacting with coworkers will give you all the practice you need. Your coworkers are all individuals—people from diverse backgrounds and with diverse ambitions and objectives. Some you will like; others you won't. But you can learn something from each one of them about how to get along inside the company and, in turn, in the business world in general—lessons that only work to your advantage.

FACE-TO-FACE

Positive interactions with your coworkers are founded on considerations as basic as respecting their personal space, understanding rank, and giving thought to the way you handle everything from small talk to humor to disagreements.

When you engage in conversation—whether it's chitchat or strictly business—one of the quickest ways to alienate others is to violate their physical space.

- Instead of crowding the people you talk to, step back (about 18 inches is a reasonable distance).

- If someone is very soft-spoken, you may have to lean in to catch their words, but back away when it's your turn to speak.

- Make solid eye contact. An open and interested expression, which begins with the eyes, is far more engaging than an in-your-face stance or posture.

- Be conscious of height differences: Stand sufficiently far away so that the person doesn't get uncomfortable having to look up or down at you.

- Be considerate of persons with disabilities—such as a person in a wheelchair or with a hearing impairment.

- If you're dealing with international coworkers, be sure that you know and observe their conversational customs and taboos.

RESPECTING RANK

In business, rank is power, so be conscious of the position of the person with whom you're talking. On the one hand, you don't want to be overly familiar with peers and superiors. Maintain a respectful conversational distance: no back-slapping, nudging, hugging, elbowing, or other touching that implies nonexistent intimacy. And just because you're chatting with your supervisor about the Super Bowl, don't assume that the casual nature of the conversation allows you to dispense with the common courtesies: Don't prop your feet on the desk, drop down on the couch without an invitation, or fidget with the bric-a-brac on the coffee table.

On the other hand, when talking with workers in subordinate positions, you don't want to abuse your rank. Use of courtesy titles is often dictated by company culture, but it is always polite to address people who are considerably older as "Mr." or "Mrs." or "Ms.," whatever their jobs may be (unless they insist you do otherwise). A twenty-five-year-old junior executive may get a power rush from addressing his sixty-year-old secretary by her first name, but in a very conservative organization the rush could be short-lived if his boss doesn't approve.

REQUESTING AND OFFERING HELP

No one likes the office shirkers who never seem to get their own projects finished on time and habitually impose on peers for assistance. Everyone avoids the employee who can never learn the filing system and is constantly seeking on-the-job training. As a result of these bad eggs, good workers sometimes hesitate to ask for help because they fear being lumped in with the shirkers, the indolent, and the incompetent. But in most workplaces, coworkers will willingly volunteer to lend a hand to someone who has helped them.

The best way to get help is to give it. For instance, if you see an office mate working through lunch to collate a large client packet and you pitch in to help, your generosity will likely be returned in kind. Be mindful that a voluntary act is not overtime; your reward is a coworker's gratitude, not extra pay. Don't store your own good deeds away in your mental favor bank, awaiting repayment, or remind everyone of what a good person you are.

When you receive a helping hand, a thank-you is always necessary, no matter how small the favor. If a coworker gave up his lunch hour to help you, then a funny card, a little gift, or an invitation to lunch may be in order. When possible, you might also compliment helpful coworkers to their superiors.

HELP FOR THE NEWCOMER

Be particularly conscious of newcomers. New employees may have crackerjack skills, but they will have a lot to learn about how your business works—names to remember, places to locate, policies to master, reporting relationships to understand. Be helpful and forgiving within reason. Try to recollect how you felt when you were first employed and what information you needed. Volunteer answers, even if the questions haven't been asked yet: "Ms. Hernandez wants those weekly reports in a folder, but Mr. Wilson prefers a memo." Or "If you have a doctor's or dentist's appointment, tell Mrs. Shipman, and she'll clear your schedule." Just remember that help doesn't include office gossip; leave it to the newcomer to make his or her own judgments about coworkers and bosses.

GIVING AND ACCEPTING COMPLIMENTS

You and everyone you work with need occasional pats on the back. Corporate executives hire consultants and take courses to learn how to give compliments, but the real key is to be an empathetic person, capable of feeling with and for others. This is no touchy-feely exercise. Paying compliments when and where compliments are due is a kind of day-to-day justice. Saying "Well done" or "Good job" to coworkers raises their spirits a notch or two; it also communicates that you are a thoughtful and observant person, capable of giving and sharing credit where it is deserved. Just don't overdo it; handing out compliments too freely and too frequently devalues both your words and your sincerity.

"AW, SHUCKS!"

Receiving compliments graciously is hard for many people. Taught from childhood not to be show-offs, they have the impulse to negate good comments by going into great detail about why the compliment is undeserved. But this kind of modesty rings hollow. In fact, a momentary burst of genuine immodesty ("I did handle that well, didn't I?") is usually preferable to the calculated obsequiousness of rejecting a reasonable compliment.

Two simple words can solve all compliment dilemmas: "Thank you."

CAREFUL WITH THE JOKES

A mature sense of humor enables people to tease and laugh with others in a kind and gentle way, and to laugh at themselves without any trace of self-consciousness. The ability to make others smile is a gift; the ability to elicit laughter is also a business tool. But you should always use humor with care.

Whenever you feel like injecting a joke into a conversation, make sure it is at no one's expense; ethnic, racial, religious, or gender-based humor is not worth the risk of hurting someone else's feelings or soiling your reputation. Also, be careful about naming names, insulting your own and other companies, or attacking causes.

WHAT TO SAY WHEN . . .

Hearing news of one kind or another about your coworkers' personal lives is inevitable. In some cases, you will want to congratulate; in others, commiserate. If the person is a close friend, you'll probably have no trouble coming up with something to say; for those you know less well, a simple acknowledgment will usually do. (See also "Marking Milestones," pages 148–149.) Before venturing any comments, consider the following whenever . . .

- **SOMEONE BECOMES ENGAGED OR MARRIES.** "Congratulations," "Best wishes," "All happiness." Genuinely wish your coworker well. Don't be too inquisitive about his or her choice of spouse (that's what in-laws are for), and don't be too free with marriage advice or horror stories.

- **SOMEONE IS PREGNANT.** Be happy for your coworker, but don't pry. Avoid giving advice that may conflict with current medical opinion; future parents need confidence in their physician, and it is unfair to undermine that relationship even from the best of intentions. Also refrain from sharing terrible labor and childbirth stories.

- **SOMEONE MISCARRIES.** A miscarriage is a death that requires grieving. Be sympathetic by recognizing the depth of the loss. Never offer up phrases such as "It was for the best" or "It was just God's will." And never, under any circumstances, imply that the miscarriage may have resulted from something your coworker did or did not do.

- **SOMEONE DIVORCES.** Divorce is another kind of death. It's better to listen than to talk, although you might offer practical advice (such as how to find child care or file income tax as a head of household) when needed. (See also "Your Divorce," page 97.)

- **SOMEONE IS ILL.** If a coworker or a coworker's relative is seriously or terminally ill, your actions will speaker louder than words. Show sympathy by helping the person on the job. Don't complain about absences from the office. Be alert should anyone else try to undermine your coworker's position during an illness or loot his or her office or files. (It happens.) Keep the person informed about business happenings.

- **SOMEONE DIES.** When a coworker loses a loved one, write and speak your condolences. If you are close, attending pre-funeral and funeral services will be comforting. But merely working with someone is not a reason to take a funeral day off. Never make comments such as "It was really a blessing" or "Be thankful his suffering is over." Offer practical assistance where you can, and be understanding. The death of a loved one will change your coworker, so don't expect him or her to bounce back in the space of a few weeks to become the person you used to know.

- **SOMEONE IS FIRED OR DOWNSIZED.** Be sympathetic, but don't prolong the agony by talking it into the ground. Accept your coworker's official explanation for a firing, and don't engage in speculation. If you can give practical assistance, do so—a recommendation, help with a résumé update, information on other job openings. But don't let sympathy lure you into encouraging or participating in destructive behaviors such as binge drinking or firing off threatening letters. Finally, don't be surprised if a former coworker drifts out of your life; he or she needs to move on, and because you are still part of the old workplace and old hurts, you may be left behind.

TAKING RESPONSIBILITY

Everyone makes mistakes. What matters is how you handle the situation once the mistake has been made.

Consider the case of Brad, who was editing the alumni newsletter at a small college in upstate New York. He discovered he had misspelled a word in a prominent headline he had written. The word was not just wrong it had an embarrassing connotation. After collecting his wits, Brad immediately called the printer, found out how fast the newsletter could be reprinted, and got a price for the job. He then went to the college's president, explained the error, took responsibility for it, told the president how he proposed to fix it, and gave the costs. Quickly weighing the facts, the president approved the reprint, and nothing more was ever said about Brad's slipup.

Brad did two things right and saved himself a lot of grief. First, he took responsibility for his mistake, and he apologized for it. Second, he worked out a solution to resolve the problem *before* he went to his boss. Instead of putting a problem on the boss's back, Brad presented him with a solution.

In today's high-stakes business games, not all errors are forgiven and forgotten, of course. Some may even cost a person his or her job. But in many cases, by taking responsibility and by solving the problem, you may navigate the troubled waters with little if any negative effect on your career. To deny that responsibility—to reflexively say, "That's not my fault!"—is almost guaranteed to infuriate everybody.

HANDLING PROFESSIONAL DIFFERENCES OF OPINION

You and your coworker have different ideas about how to proceed on that new joint assignment. How do you resolve the situation without ruffling anyone's feathers?

When differences of opinion arise on the job, the first rule is not to avoid disagreeing if you feel strongly about an issue. If you have honestly and critically reached a position that is contrary to your coworker's, you have an ethical obligation to state your case as strongly as you can. But it's also wise to pick your battles with care. If it doesn't really matter all that much to you whether the office soda machine stocks Coke or Pepsi, leave that debate to others.

Ideally, disagreements between coworkers should be handled in private, but there are times when conflict is integral to the work process—during a brainstorming session, for example, or a policy meeting. In these situations, be considerate of bystanders. State your case clearly and engage in debate if necessary, but don't be mulish. Pay attention to the reaction of others: As soon as you pick up signals of resentment or annoyance, bring the conversation to a close for the time being; otherwise, it could degenerate into personal attacks. "Actually, I think it would be better if we talked about this later" is one way of defusing the situation. Or you could try "Let's take this up when we can get [the supervisor] to help us figure out the direction the company wants to go in."

Don't get drawn into other people's disagreements, but at the same time don't feign ignorance if you can really help find a resolution. If, for example, you have factual information that can settle an argument, speak up. Remember, telling what you know or offering reasonable compromises is not the same as taking sides. Expect to be attacked, but maintain your objective role even if the parties to the disagreement unite against you.

DON'T MAKE IT PERSONAL

Never allow a professional disagreement to become personal. Apart from being rude, name-calling and personalizing weaken your case in any argument. The instant you call Joe an "idiot" for preferring to file alphabetically rather than by invoice number, or make a snide reference to Marcia's lack of higher education during a lunchtime political discussion, guess what happens? Joe or Marcia just won the war, even if you won the battle. If someone calls you a name or challenges your competence, chalk it up to frustration in the heat of conflict and try your best not to hold grudges.

Three more bits of advice:

- **STICK TO THE SUBJECT.** Don't allow a disagreement to wander into nongermane issues. Be especially careful to avoid referring back to old conflicts. Remember that even if you were proved right in the last argument, you may be wrong in this one. And beware when others try to sidetrack an issue: Diversion, deflection, and tossing red herrings onto the trail are classic tactics of those with the weak side of an argument. If you fall for this trick, learn from your mistake and listen more closely next time.

- **BE OPEN TO COMPROMISE**. Although you may not get everything you want, resolution is usually better than continual hard feelings. Be sure to document the outcome of the disagreement; if it is business-related, you should also confirm the final resolution with a memo to your "opponent." Documentation and confirmation are important if it becomes necessary to take the matter to a higher level of authority.

- **DON'T GLOAT**. Avoid the temptation to gloat or say "I told you so." If everyone recognizes that you were right, you will only undermine yourself by engaging in petty smirking and arrogance. (You want your colleagues to say, "Josh really knows his stuff," not "Josh knows his stuff, but he's still a jerk.")

WHEN CONFLICT GETS PERSONAL

It is going to happen. Sooner or later, you'll find yourself at loggerheads with a coworker, or you'll be dragged into somebody else's quarrel. You'll hear gossip or, worse yet, become the target of gossip. Or you may find yourself subjected to language, a dirty joke, or offensive comments that disturb you. No matter what form it takes, a situation like this is a real test of your mettle as a mature adult.

How should you respond when a coworker makes blatantly sexist or racist remarks, calls you (or someone you know who is trustworthy) a "liar" or a "cheat," or treats coworkers and subordinates with snobbish and arrogant disrespect? A couple of centuries ago, you might have challenged the offending person to a duel. Today, however, you must rely on your wits.

For starters, you have an obligation to yourself and your company to confront or report verbal offenders, just as you would a thief or an arsonist. If you merely sit back and listen, you become a collaborator — passive, but nonetheless guilty. Also, your company can be held liable for the hateful remarks of employees, and while you are in their employ, you owe loyalty to the greater good.

If you find yourself in a situation that you feel demands to be addressed, here are some basic strategies to help resolve the conflict and build relationships rather than brick walls:

GET CONTROL OF YOURSELF

Trying to engage a person in a debate, especially about a behavior or action of theirs that you think is egregious, is hard enough. Trying to do it while your blood pressure is elevated and you're seeing purple is a sure way *not* to correct the situation. The perpetrator is far more likely to react to your anger than to your criticism of the behavior. So disengage for a time and then later ask to speak to the person in private

While you're collecting yourself, spend a few minutes asking yourself what you want to see as an outcome of any conversation you have with the other person. In most cases, the best outcome would be a combination of changing the behavior of the perpetrator *and* maintaining or building a constructive working relationship with him or her.

DISCUSS THE SITUATION ONE-ON-ONE IN PRIVATE

If you can talk with the other person in private, do so. Frame your statements as criticism of the behavior, not the person, and be specific: "You probably didn't realize it, but that comment you made about Leslie's short skirts really was sexist, and I could see that she was offended and hurt." People who repeatedly offend or degrade others are rarely subtle and usually don't take hints. But they may respond if you address them directly and indicate that your concern is for their own welfare and reputation.

IN THE OPEN

Some remarks require immediate and public response. Be direct, but remember to confront the *remark* rather than the speaker. However great the temptation, control your anger and avoid patronizing the person. For example, if a coworker's subject is racial politics run rampant, try something on the order of "People are treated fairly here, Ralph, and I know that your boss got his job because of his ability, not because of his race." If you can (it isn't always easy), give the person a graceful way to retreat from his or her offensive remarks: "I think we talk too much about people's races, don't you, Ralph?"

Whatever you do, don't become involved in a shouting match. You simply cannot outshout a dedicated bigot or snob. If the offending remarks are habitual, it's time to take the matter to a superior or human resources manager, or ethics officer. If you fear retaliation, make your complaint in confidence.

HANDLING HARMFUL GOSSIP AND RUMORS

What can you do to avoid becoming the subject of office gossip? Simple: Keep personal information to yourself on the job – and don't invite inquiries. Even seemingly innocuous questions about your age, income, personal relationships, sexuality, and politics can set you up for gossip and innuendo.

If you become the subject of malicious gossip or a false rumor, you'll want to uncover the source. Begin your detective work by talking to the person who clued you in; explain to him or her that the story is untrue and you want to stop it. If you promise confidentiality, there's a good chance you will learn the name of the initial source of the falsehood.

You should then confront the gossip – but stage your confrontation in private. Adopt an attitude of concern rather than anger: "Sally, I hear you told a couple of people that I'm looking for a new job and I've been meeting with a headhunter. The truth is that I had lunch last week with my old college roommate, and he happens to work for an employment firm. But I am not looking for a job, and that story could really cause me a lot of trouble here." Even if the gossip denies spreading the tale, she'll be stung because she has been caught, and she'll think twice before gossiping about you again.

Remember also that it takes two to tango; a person who is eager to hear the latest gossip is an active participant and hardly blameless, even if he or she doesn't spread the story. Gossiping, whether you are on the giving or receiving end, can be hazardous to your professional reputation. You never know who's chummy with whom, and you could wind up covered in mud if you dish dirt about the wrong person. If you're faced with gossip from your colleagues, be tactful but firm: "I honestly don't want to hear the details of anybody's private life." If the gossiper pushes ahead anyway, you should politely refuse to listen – "Oh, that sounds interesting, but I'd just rather not know" – and quickly excuse yourself.

OFFER A RESOLUTION

Stating your feelings is just the first part of the healing process. Remember, your goal is to both change a behavior and hopefully avoid creating an enemy. Before you meet with the other person, develop what you think is a reasonable strategy for resolving the situation and moving forward. Then, once you've made your statement and the other person has responded, check to make sure that your strategy still sounds reasonable. If it does, suggest your solution and ask the other person for his or her buy-in. It's not enough simply to state your demand and walk away. In order to reach a resolution, you need to be prepared to work with the other person to refine your solution until it works for both of you.

SMALL-TALK TIPS

Small talk is one very big deal—an important part of building business relationships. It is when you and your coworkers let down your guard while sitting at a cafeteria lunch table, waiting for a meeting to begin, or hanging out in the copier room that your personality and real interests come to the fore. Almost any topic is up for grabs, so long as it's not malicious, derogatory, inflammatory, or indiscreet.

By being open to opportunities for small talk, you'll discover who the resident expert on grand opera or NASCAR is, as well as who's the movie buff, the gourmet cook, the night-school scholar. If you're attentive, in a matter of minutes you'll be able to identify the office gossip, the snob, and the back-stabber. Through small talk, your coworkers also get a chance to become better acquainted with you and find out if you're sociable and easy to talk to—something that's to your advantage in the workplace. (See also Chapter 16, "The Good Conversationalist," page 209.)

- When initiating small talk, be attuned to the other person's receptiveness. If he or she seems distracted or unresponsive, take the hint and back off.

- Even when the person is willing to chat, don't overstay your welcome.

- Ask for the other person's opinions and show genuine interest in his or her ideas. Don't try to dominate the conversation.

- If other people come along, make an effort to include them in the conversation. You may need to switch topics to something that everyone can discuss.

- Avoid subjects that are too personal.

- It's fine to disagree with someone, but phrase your comments politely. "You're wrong!" is hostile and combative, while "Actually, I just don't agree with you about that, but I'd like to hear more of your opinion" is tactful.

- Keep abreast of the world outside. Read the daily newspaper and a weekly news magazine. Watch the entertainment shows on television once in a while. Listen to your kids' music station on the radio. Watch the latest, hottest show so you know what people are talking about.

- After making an effort to be informed, think up some questions to ask others when you join a conversation.

- To end small talk, excuse yourself after you, not the other person, has made a concluding statement. Finish with a remark such as "Well, I think it's time I got back to work" or "This was really interesting. We'll have to talk again."

- If a coworker who just wants to chat interrupts you while you're working, suggest another time. "You've caught me at a bad moment. Can we touch base after I've finished these letters?" If you do the interrupting, be sensitive to the other person's reaction. If your coworker says he or she can't stop, take no for an answer and don't take offense or feel rejected.

FOUL LANGUAGE

In company cultures where obscenity and profanity are permitted in the workplace, their use tends to be widespread, and you can't correct everyone. If foul language makes you uncomfortable, signal your distaste by never using these words yourself, and by excusing yourself politely from office gatherings whenever the language becomes too raw. Some people will label you a prude, but you may be pleasantly surprised by others who welcome your attitude and even imitate your behavior.

If you sometimes use offensive language yourself, make sure you do so only with people who won't be made uncomfortable by it. Anytime you're not sure how your colorful language will affect others, throttle back a bit and save the saltier expressions for another time.

DEALING WITH PETTY ANNOYANCES

What should you do when a coworker has an annoying little idiosyncrasy that is threatening to drive you up a wall? The first thing you'll have to decide is whether to deal with the situation or to ignore it. Because you work with people you might not choose to associate with on a purely social basis, you may find yourself putting up with behaviors you might not accept in your friends. Still, while you're obligated to grin and bear most of your coworkers' follies and foibles, you *can* try, with courtesy, to correct problems that literally affect your work. Before tackling the failings of others, however, it's a good idea to take a look in the mirror: Is it possible that you annoy your coworkers every bit as much as they annoy you?

SMOKING
Smokers are the literal outcasts of most businesses these days—banished to the out-of-doors in rain, sleet, snow, and hail for periodic puffing. Yet despite (or perhaps because of) this arrangement, tension still persists among smokers and non-smokers, which means that consideration on the part of both groups is more necessary than ever before.

If you're a smoker, understand that some people's "smoker's breath" is more powerful than others'—and yours may be on the high side. Breath mints may help, but a good tooth-brushing and a dose of mouthwash is better. There's also the problem of smoke-permeated clothing. Try to smoke in ventilated places, and consider taking a stroll in the fresh air before you reenter a smoke-free space.

If you are a non-smoker, on the other hand, show a little tolerance. If you want some-one to put out a cigarette, ask *politely*. Most smokers have no desire to offend or cause dis-comfort or health problems for others.

THOSE EMBARRASSING MOMENTS

Spinach stuck in the front teeth, an open fly, an unbuttoned blouse—while these are the sta-ples of situation comedy, they are also very real embarrassing moments. When they happen to you, all you can do is laugh and blame bad luck. When you realize they are happening to others, step in and help. Discreetly tell the person (in private if possible), and, if need be, help to repair the damage. If you are a woman and are too shy to tell a male colleague that his zipper is undone, quietly ask another male to do it. When a coworker alerts you to the fact that there's a blob of mustard on your tie or a poppy seed in your teeth, don't take offense or get huffy. Be grateful; a friend has just saved you from an embarrassing moment.

Some problems, on the other hand, should just be left alone. Someone's dandruff, a hairpiece that looks like a shag rug, or raccoon-eyes makeup does not affect the workplace in any serious way and is really nobody else's business. It's up to the person with the problem to realize that it may be jeopardizing his chances for advancement. Only if you're close to the person should you gently suggest that something he is doing might be hurting his career.

BAD ODORS

A coworker's body odor, smelly feet, or bad breath is an extremely sensitive issue. We are all loath to tell a person about body odor, yet every time we ask our business seminar partici-pants which they would prefer—*not* to be told about an offensive odor or to be told about it by a friend or a manager—invariably, 100 percent say they'd want to be clued in by a friend. So the next time you have a friend who has body odor, consider what *you* would want *him* to do if the roles were reversed. Be a friend: Enlighten him.

Here's how. Do it privately, and start out with something like this: "Bill, because I'm your friend, I'm going to say something that is really difficult. But I know if the roles were reversed, I would want you to say something to me. So here it goes. I don't think you are aware of it, but you have a problem, and it has to do with body odor. Some of us have noticed it and we're worried that it may have an effect on your advancement in the company. I'm telling you this only to help. Can we talk?"

Be warned: Your colleague's response may surprise you. You may discover that your colleague's body odor is the result of poor hygiene, for example, but it's also possible that personal odors can be caused by medical conditions, medications, or dietary deficiencies.

If you simply cannot do the deed yourself and the problem becomes unbearable, you can discuss the situation with a sympathetic supervisor or human resources manager, either alone or with other coworkers. (This is an instance when a group of concerned employees is more impressive to a boss than an individual complainer.)

TOO MUCH SCENT

Perfumes, aftershaves, colognes, and other cosmetics are meant to be pleasant but can quickly become oppressive in a crowded office. Many companies are adopting policies regulating the use of scents on health grounds. Meanwhile, you can help by not overdoing your own toilette. Don't spritz in the office, and test any new scent before wearing it to work; body chemistry affects the power of fragrances and can intensify it. Finally, save the musky, heavy scents for nights on the town. (See also "Your Cologne," page 32; "Perfume," page 42.)

CHEWING GUM

There's nothing inherently wrong with chewing gum; the problem with doing it at work is that you run a constant risk of annoying people who think your gum-chewing is socially graceless or simply a disgusting habit. Chewing gum when you're alone is fine, of course, so long as your smacking or bubble-popping can't be heard in the next cubicle. But chewing gum in business meetings or with clients and associates is a little like eating with your mouth open: It feels better to you than it looks to everyone else.

"WANT TO CHIP IN?"

Office collections by workmates for birthdays, weddings, the birth of a baby, or school charities are perfectly acceptable, but they can also nickel-and-dime people to the point of distraction. If the frequency of collections seems to be getting out of hand, you might want to adopt a personal policy of giving only for certain events, like showers. (Don't refuse across the board, or your workmates may make negative assumptions about your generosity.) Chances are, other employees feel office collections are an undue burden, too. If a bit of discreet investigating confirms that they do indeed feel this way, go as a group to talk to a supervisor about setting up or enforcing some collection guidelines. One idea: a general office kitty to which everyone contributes.

TEMPS AND PART-TIMERS

One of the most dramatic changes in the contemporary workplace is the growing use of nontraditional employees. Once, not that long ago, the typical office was filled with nine-to-fivers who worked for the same company for years, receiving the traditional compensation of a salary or hourly wage plus a package of benefits that might include vacation and sick days, health and life insurance, and pension plans. Today, the person working next to you is just as likely to be a temporary worker or a part-time employee. As a result of this shift, permanent and full-time employees are having to adapt by modifying their thinking about and behavior toward these new-fashioned coworkers.

WORKING WITH TEMPS

It's a fact that many traditional employees resent the arrival of a temp, because of the not-unreasonable fear that their own jobs may be the next to be converted. But it's important to separate your behavior toward the individual from your views about your company's hiring policy. If you want to protest the use of temps, take it to senior management or the corporate board. Do not take it out on the temporary employee.

Welcome temporary employees graciously, and be ready to offer your assistance as they settle into the job. Assume that the temp worker is both skilled and ready to learn, and treat him or her with the same professional courtesies you would extend to a permanent employee. Be aware that temp workers may well expect a chilly reception, and that it is largely the responsibility of the staff to bring them into the team, show them the ropes, and introduce them in a positive way to the company culture.

If it is your workplace custom to take a new employee to lunch in the first week, do the same for the temp worker who is there on an extended assignment. Get to know the temp worker and include him or her in normal office socializing. You may be pleasantly surprised to discover that temps are not so different from you and your full-time colleagues.

Finally, just as coworkers should avoid blaming temps for company hiring policies, you should be careful not to draw temps into office debates about company policies. Don't subject them to your complaints and insecurities, or try to elicit their sympathy and support.

IF YOU'RE A TEMP

Temporary employees should do their best to adapt to the customs and culture of a new office as quickly as possible. If you are a temp, your agency should provide you with basic information about your new assignment. Sometimes, though, your assignment may come too quickly for a thorough orientation and your agency may be unfamiliar with the personality of the workplace they are sending you to. Until you get the lay of the land, dress conservatively and behave with maximum decorum. You'll quickly learn whether the office style is casual or formal.

Try not to judge your new coworkers too harshly if they are cold or stiff with you. You may have dropped unwittingly into a major downsizing or a shift in company employment policies. Unfortunately, temps are easy targets for the resentments of long-time employees who sense that the rug is being pulled out from under them. A thick skin can help, but you don't want to be so aloof that coworkers avoid you or, worse, undermine your job. Keep your antennae up, and respond when someone makes a friendly overture. It can't hurt to accept offers of assistance, even when you don't really need the help; doing so shows collegiality and respect for the knowledge and experience of long-timers.

As for socializing with coworkers, be guided by the policies of your agency and explain your situation to the people you're working with. Never discuss salary or benefits, because comparisons will inevitably be drawn. Because you have two bosses—the service employing you and the company contracting with your agency—keeping confidentiality is doubly important.

WORKING PART-TIME

Part-timers are employed by the company but work nontraditional schedules—coming in for a few hours a day or for a few days a week, or telecommuting from home at least part of the time. Some part-timers share a single job.

This type of arrangement comes with its own unique set of issues. One of the biggest challenges facing a part-timer is proving to coworkers that he is just as serious about his work as any full-time employee. Whether he is there forty hours a week or twenty hours, the part-time worker should put in the same professional effort whenever he is on the job.

BE ON YOUR TOES

Good work habits are the best offense for the part-time worker. Be where you are supposed to be, when you are supposed to be there. Your supervisor will doubtless announce the part-time arrangement to the entire office, but be sure that everyone also has a copy of your schedule, including the company receptionist who will have to field your business calls when you aren't there. (You should also make it a habit to check your messages and voice mail regularly in your off-hours.)

You may want to give your home e-mail address to colleagues as well, so you can receive memos and announcements. Check in occasionally with your supervisor so that you don't miss out on news and information that affects your job. Do not drop out entirely from the social side of the office, although you'll probably have to reduce the number of on-the-job breaks in order to get your work done.

Whatever you do, *don't* complain to your office mates about being overloaded with work; your full-time coworkers will have a hard time sympathizing with your plight. If you are overburdened, talk with your supervisor as soon as possible and be specific about your problems.

Finally, when you discuss your off-hour activities with coworkers, be very careful that you don't appear to gloat; keep in mind that a perfectly normal remark about having lunch at your son's school or volunteering mornings at the food bank may strike full-time coworkers as insensitive. Also, avoid scheduling any non-work-related activities such as doctor's appointments or haircuts during your scheduled work hours.

COURTESIES FOR THE DISABLED

People with disabilities comprise the largest minority group in the United States—some 17 percent of the population. Behind this statistic are more than 45 million individuals who are human beings first, and who have special needs second. So when you work with someone who's disabled, put aside any anxiety you might feel ("Am I saying the wrong thing?"), and be yourself. Act just as you would with anyone else; if the disability is brought up, it should be the disabled person who does it, not you.

SENSITIVITY IN LANGUAGE

While it's important to be considerate about sensitive topics, you don't have to be excessively careful about your language: The words *deaf* and *blind* have not been banished from the vocabulary (but *handicapped* is on its way out). It's perfectly fine to ask a blind person "See what I mean?" or to invite someone in a wheelchair to "go for a walk." Trying to eliminate common words and phrases like these from your conversation is awkward and implies that the person with disabilities should be treated differently from everyone else.

Never leave a person with disabilities out of a conversation because you feel uncomfortable or because you assume she will. Include her as you would anyone else, and leave it up to her to decide whether to participate or not.

TO OFFER HELP?

It is always courteous to ask if a coworker with a disability would like assistance, but don't automatically provide help that may be unwanted. Follow the person's cues, and don't be offended if your offer of aid is refused: It is everyone's choice to be as independent as he or she wants to be.

WITH THE DEAF OR HARD-OF-HEARING

Face the person, maintaining eye contact throughout your conversation, since many people with hearing loss can get a lot of information from both listening and reading lips. If the person is hard-of-hearing, it's helpful to speak up and speak slowly and clearly, but never shout or exaggerate your lip movements. If speech alone isn't working, it is perfectly acceptable to gesture or write notes.

If you have dealings with a deaf person who has an interpreter, always direct your attention to the deaf person rather than the interpreter. (This can feel uncomfortable because the courteous worker doesn't want to exclude anyone from the conversation. Don't worry, however; trained interpreters, including those for non–English speakers, understand their role and won't expect to participate.) Speak at your normal rate, being sure the interpreter can hear you clearly.

WITH WHEELCHAIR USERS

When you meet, offer a handshake if you would normally, unless it is clear that the person does not have the use of his or her arms. Under the Americans with Disabilities Act, most businesses are legally required to accommodate the physical needs of people who use wheelchairs. Even so, don't hesitate to offer your help if you spot someone in a tight situation. Don't push someone's wheelchair unless you are asked. But do offer to push if the two of you are approaching a steep ramp or an obstacle.

WITH THE BLIND OR VISUALLY IMPAIRED

When you greet a blind coworker in the early days of his or her employment, identify yourself by name; your voice will be recognized before long. Whenever necessary, offer to read written information, such as the latest office memo or the cafeteria menu. It's appropriate to offer your assistance in selecting food from a buffet or in getting coffee when everyone is gathered around the conference table. But be an observant friend, and follow your blind or sight-impaired coworker's lead as to how far to go. Don't pet guide dogs or try out equipment that the person with a disability may be using. But do feel comfortable asking a blind person if he or she would like to take your arm when navigating an unfamiliar area.

WITH THE SPEECH IMPAIRED

Listen patiently and carefully to someone with a speech impediment. Your understanding of his or her speech (or of any device used by the person) will improve as you continue to listen. Remain attentive to the conversation even if there are delays. Don't complete the person's sentences unless he or she looks to you for help. If you don't understand something, ask a question to help the person clarify the part you missed.

BUILDING PERSONNEL

Naturally, the people who maintain your building—doormen, front-desk personnel, cleaners, security guards—deserve the same cordiality as anyone else you see on a daily basis: a morning hello (or at least a smile and a nod) and a thank-you when they've helped you in any way. You may never actually have been introduced to them, but that's no reason to treat them as if they were part of the lobby furniture.

If you're in the habit of working late, be courteous to the regular cleaning person by saying hello or asking his or her name and introducing yourself. You're not obliged to get involved in a conversation, but being respectful will make the cleaner feel less anxious about intruding on your space and interrupting your work.

POST-9/11 BUILDING SECURITY

One of the most visible changes that occurred after 9/11 is the increase in security at office buildings, especially in major metropolitan areas. Where previously you might have looked at a directory and taken an elevator to your destination, now you may often be required to sign in, show ID, and wait for an escort to take you to your destination. Treat the security personnel with the same respect you show to others in the building and in your office. Don't ask them to break the rules for you—they're the ones who will get in trouble. If they ask to inspect or scan your briefcase, give it to them politely.

If you go in and out several times during the day, expect to have your briefcase or laptop case inspected each time. Don't be frustrated. It's part of their job to check no matter how often you go in and out.

Also, if you're expecting visitors, make sure to contact security ahead of time so that passes for your guests will be ready when they arrive.

SIDEWALK SMOKING

Now that smoking has been banned in most offices, front sidewalks have become salons of sorts for smokers, who puff and schmooze on intermittent breaks. If you're a sidewalk smoker, be mindful of those who aren't. If, for example, your building entrance is recessed from the street and has an overhang, stand out near the curb so that a curtain of smoke won't collect in the space. In fact, you should stand away from any doorways, no matter what the layout of your building. If there's no out-of-the-way spot to indulge, consider taking a walk around the block or into the parking lot. Always be sure to put the cigarette butt into a proper receptacle.

A Note of Caution. Don't think people don't notice when you're outside having a cigarette several times a day. Someone who's seen standing outside virtually every time anyone walks in or out of the building is going to gain a reputation not only as a smoker but a slacker. This is one time when a smoker's behavior can reflect on him and his company: "If this guy's allowed to spend most of the day on the sidewalk," people might be thinking, "what does that say about the way things are run inside?"

THE GREAT COFFEE DEBATE

Should an employer expect a member of the support staff to make and serve coffee daily? The great debate continues: A recent survey revealed that only 7 percent of administrative assistants now consider making and serving coffee to the boss to be a part of their job description. This one-time "duty" is now considered a courtesy, similar to offering to get coffee for a coworker. The bottom line? Serving coffee to the boss is not expected and generally not considered part of an assistant's job description. Nevertheless, it is always polite, if anyone—and that includes the boss—is going for coffee, tea, or snacks, to offer to bring something back for other people in the vicinity.

5 | *You and Your Workspace*

It doesn't matter whether you have a cubicle or a corner office—your workspace says a lot about you. This chapter tackles the practical issues of you and your office, including: What messages does your office decor send? How proprietary should you feel about your space? What does your attitude toward your cubicle say about you? What rules of behavior apply when a workmate or visitor enters your space?

A DOSE OF HUMILITY

The fact is, the window office/cubicle divide doesn't always equate with senior/junior status. In some companies, cubicle dwellers at a certain job level graduate to window offices whenever one becomes available; whoever is next in line wins the prize. If this explains your good fortune, then humility, not gloating, is the demeanor to strive for. When someone drops by, get up and lean or perch yourself on the edge of the desk, or take a chair next to him or her; this de-emphasizes the inequities, if only subliminally.

No matter who the visitor or what the situation, anytime you come around from behind your desk and sit near someone, you set up a friendly climate for a more relaxed discussion (see also "Your Meeting," page 73). The behind-the-desk position is formal and signifies that this is your turf. Bosses, too, will do well by occasionally removing themselves from behind the desk and democratizing the scene.

CLOSING YOUR DOOR

Keep in mind that a closed door is a stark reminder to cubicle dwellers that you have a door and they don't; for this reason, close yours only when there's a legitimate reason to do so. As a rule, privacy is warranted when you need quiet to concentrate, when you're meeting with a visitor, or when you're discussing a confidential matter with your employer or a coworker.

RESPECTING THE PRIVACY OF OTHERS

Don't snoop! As you sift through a fax in-box or remove someone else's just-transmitted documents from the machine, look only at the cover sheets. Similarly, if you open the lid of a copier and find someone has left an original sheet, don't get curious if it looks like something private. While the page would usually go in a communal receptacle for forgotten sheets, this is one time when you should deliver it in person. Save the person any worry by volunteering, "I didn't read this when I opened the copier lid, but I could tell it was private. Thought I'd drop it by."

Furthermore, don't abuse the privilege. A closed door doesn't give you the license to make personal calls all day long or to complete personal tasks. As much as it feels like your home away from home, your office is still the property of your employer—and you're there to do the business you were hired to do.

ANOTHER REMINDER. No slamming! If you're bothered by a conversation going on outside your door, either wait it out or take the opportunity to run an errand elsewhere on the floor. If it drags on, get up and shut the door as softly as possible; the talkers will no doubt catch on.

YOUR CUBICLE—A MATTER OF ATTITUDE

The ease with which you handle having to work from a cubicle says much about your resiliency. It also slots you somewhere along the personality scale that runs from crybaby to stoic—and don't think your attitude won't be noticed: When the time comes for raises and promotions, the person who accepts his or her fate with good graces has the edge over the perennial whiner. Regardless of how you really feel, rolling with the punches doesn't mean you're a weakling; it demonstrates a firm grasp of the realities of life in business.

Resentment toward your immediate superiors is usually misplaced, since decisions on office design are probably beyond their control. Don't hesitate to make your wish for a window office known to your supervisor, but at the same time make it clear that you understand the possibility is contingent on other factors. Stay upbeat, as if you know she'll do what she can when and if the opportunity arises. Looking bitter and defeated may leave a sour taste and work to your disadvantage.

TERRITORIAL IMPERATIVES AND PRIVACY

Because the worker in a cubicle is so visible (and all the more so in the half-wall design), there is a subconscious assumption on the part of passersby that he or she is automatically available.

This notion couldn't be farther off the mark. In fact, some companies have gone so far as to distribute red baseball caps for workers to don whenever they don't want to be disturbed.

However compact or noisy your cubicle domain might be, you still have the right to expect visitors to respect your time and space. The cubicle is your office territory and should be treated as such. Just as visitors refrain from barging into an office or opening a closed door, they shouldn't sashay into your cubicle without knocking lightly or saying "May I come in?"

The same applies to your next-door neighbors. The phenomenon that has come to be known as "prairie-dogging"—standing up or hanging over cubicle walls to communicate—can be annoying and invasive. Here, plain common sense is called for: Employees intensely involved with coworkers in team projects may find prairie-dogging the best and most efficient way to communicate quickly, while employees working on individual projects usually prefer that others respect their need for privacy.

If prairie-dogging seems out of line and bothers you, choose your words to a coworker with care: "Bruce, I know it's easiest for you to talk over the wall, but would you do me a favor and come around? The fewer reminders that we're in cubicles, the better, don't you think?"

"QUIET, PLEASE!"

Noise is the enemy of the cubicle dweller, a constant threat to concentration in a space that can't be soundproofed with the closing of a door.

- If you have an exceptionally loud voice, get in the habit of speaking more softly, especially in open-plan offices.

- Many people tend to unconsciously talk louder when they're on the phone. As silly as it sounds, leaving a Post-it marked "Sotto Voce" or some such message in plain sight will remind you to lower your voice while talking on the phone.

- Never shout a request or response to someone in a nearby cubicle. If it's too much trouble to walk over, pick up the phone instead.

- If you must listen to music at your desk, keep it low or use headphones if your company allows them.

- When you ask the people in the next cubicle to quiet down, do it as politely as possible. Remember that minor resentments are magnified by someone who is dissatisfied at being consigned to a cubicle, and ruffled feathers can quickly lead to frayed tempers.

CHATS, PHONE CALLS, AND EAVESDROPPING

An unfortunate by-product of cubiclization is the ability of those around you to hear every-thing you say—and vice versa. It takes a very strong-willed individual to tune out the voices around him or her; in fact, many cubicle workers find this possible only with the help of earplugs or earphones. But remember, too, that this issue cuts both ways:

- When entertaining visitors, go to a common area so as not to disturb your neigh-bors. Also try to dissuade people from loitering or socializing around your cubi-cle. (A polite "Larry, I'm working on something right now that demands my full concentration" should do the trick.) And be discreet—a cubicle is not the place to talk about sensitive matters; discuss anything confidential in a private place.

- Whenever you don't want a phone call to be overheard, find an empty office or a pay phone in the lobby, or make the call after hours. If that's impossible and a next-door neighbor seems to be listening in on even your most mundane calls (as evi-denced by under-the-breath chuckles or mutterings of surprise), try drowning out your voice with an air filter or a white noise device. If that doesn't work, take the matter up with your colleague: "Don, I know we're in close quarters, but would you mind giving me privacy when I'm on the phone?" Don may not stop eaves-dropping, but at least you've made your point.

- If you walk up to someone in a cubicle and find he's on the phone, don't hover there waiting for him to hang up. Leave and try again later.

MORE UNWELCOME SOUNDS

One of the stickier wickets in the culture of cubicles is the office mate who makes inappro-priate or offensive sounds. Burping, the slurping of soup or coffee, loud yawning, and worse are all amplified in close quarters.

Be thoughtful of neighbors by maintaining some decorum at your desk. The rest-room, of course, is the place to relieve yourself of any physical discomforts. A quick nose blow is one thing, but any major honking should be done where it won't disturb others.

CREATIVE ADJUSTMENTS

Many cubicle residents have found smart ways to both achieve some level of privacy and mute some of the noises around them. Removable entryways can be arranged into a kind of semi-maze entrance, for example. Plants or corkboards placed strategically can help to muffle outside sounds and create a sense of privacy at the same time. Before moving panels or putting up makeshift sound buffers, however, be sure to get permission from your employer or office manager.

If business is moving toward the paperless office, it isn't there quite yet: A messy workspace is still the enemy of the efficient worker. Here are four tips to beat the clutter:

- *Keep a pad by the phone for jotting.* Even if you have to nail it down, keep a notepad for just this purpose next to the phone on your desk.

- *Clear the decks daily.* Straightening up the office at the end of the day serves two purposes: You're likely to find something you thought was missing, and you'll find it satisfying the next morning to walk into an uncluttered space.

- *Use folders.* Set aside part of a file drawer purely for miscellany: circulated journals and magazines, schedules from the production department, postcards mailed from traveling friends. Label folders and then put in them the flotsam and jetsam as it accumulates rather than leaving it on your desktop.

- *Ask yourself whether you really need it.* If you can't come up with a specific reason for keeping a piece of paper, throw it away.

PIN-UPS

Cubicle walls often become billboards and are a great way to share a cartoon, a joke, or an article that's particularly apropos. But be careful with your choices: While something a little risqué may be permissible in your office, never put up materials that cross the line to gross or obscene. Anything with racist or sexist undertones is equally out of the question.

A FURTHER NOTE OF CAUTION. Never pin anti-corporate articles from magazines or newspapers to your cubicle wall, whether they are written about your own company or the corporate world in general. Those in view of anyone passing constitute a direct affront to management.

WORKSPACE DÉCOR

The decoration of your workspace depends on a number of things, with the type of work and the amount of customer interaction conducted there being among the most important. If you deal face-to-face with clients and customers on a daily basis, the décor will generally be customer driven. In a service industry such as banking, for example, the environment is often homogeneous, with personal effects kept to a minimum. In an office where creative work is done, such as a graphic design studio, décor is often more personalized. Know the expectations of your company before you start to personalize your workspace. It's not your task to risk a promotion or even your job itself by pushing the limits.

MORE WORKSPACE MANNERS

There are some things that apply to workspace etiquette in general, without regard to walls and doors. This grab bag of concerns includes whether you should stand when someone enters, how to play the good host to visitors, and the more mundane (though no less potentially annoying) matters of using a speakerphone and lunching at your desk.

WHEN TO STAND?

Male or female, a well-mannered person rises when either a superior or someone elderly enters the workspace. You also rise for clients and prospects, of course. It's even nice to stand to greet any workmate who hasn't dropped by your office or cubicle for a while. Rising is not an empty gesture done for the sake of "etiquette," but a way of showing respect.

EATING AT YOUR DESK

Eating at your desk is often unavoidable, particularly in busy offices or those without cafeterias. Besides eating quietly (especially in a cubicle), think "smell." (See also "Storing Food" and "Cooking and Microwaving," pages 76–77.)

USING A SPEAKERPHONE

For some people, the effort of picking up the phone receiver is too great; they rely instead on talking or listening to messages by speakerphone. This forces everyone around to suffer the noise, especially those who work in an open-plan office or have thin walls. A speakerphone should be used only in closed offices.

If possible, make conference calls using speakerphones from a conference room. Even closed doors can't always muffle voices, since people talk more loudly to be heard. (See also "Using a Speakerphone," page 224.)

OFFICE APPOINTMENTS

Meetings around your desk can be highly productive if you observe a few courtesies. First, is your space really conducive to discussion with a colleague or with a prospect? Evaluate your private space. Is it comfortable physically and psychologically? Does it provide a sense of privacy the visitor will be comfortable with? If not, reserve a meeting room for appointments.

When the receptionist calls and says your visitor has arrived, go out to greet him. If you have an assistant, you can ask her to escort the visitor in, but it's even more impressive if you greet him yourself.

Early arrivals. If a visitor arrives more than ten minutes early and you are not ready, try to keep her from feeling awkward. If there is a receptionist, ask him to make the visitor comfortable, telling her you'll be out as soon as possible. If you work in a small office without a receptionist, come out of your workspace and greet the visitor. Accept her apologies for arriving early, offer her an available chair, ask her if there is anything you can get her, and tell her you'll be with her in just a few minutes.

Late arrivals. If a visitor arrives so late you won't be able to squeeze him into your schedule, accept his apologies and arrange another meeting. Or, should he arrive after you are already indisposed, ask the receptionist or an assistant to tell him you waited as long as you could and that you would like to schedule another date and time to meet.

Keeping someone waiting. Never keep a visitor waiting more than five or six minutes past the appointed time. If you have no choice but to do so, walk out and apologize in person. (People today are smart enough to know a power play when they see one, and remaining out of sight contributes to the assumption that you're making one.) An offer of a cup of coffee and a magazine is also a nice gesture. If something has come up that is going to delay your meeting for more than fifteen minutes, apologize for taking up your visitor's time and ask if she prefers to reschedule on another day.

YOUR MEETING

In addition to extending a greeting, there are two things you should always do when a business associate from outside enters your workspace: (1) Offer to hang up his coat if he has one, and (2) ask him to be seated. Remember that sitting behind a desk is less personable than taking a chair next to your visitor (see "A Dose of Humility," page 67). If you want the meeting to remain private, close your door; if you're in a cubicle, go to a common area or meeting room, which you should have reserved in advance.

Be sure to have all the necessary materials at hand, so that your visitor won't have to navigate through piles of files. If coworkers are participating in the meeting, arrange for them to be present in your office when the guest arrives, and then make introductions.

If the phone rings, it is generally bad form to answer it when a visitor is present. If you have a "Do Not Disturb" button on your phone, use it. If you have an assistant and she considers a call important enough to interrupt your meeting, use your intuition to decide whether this particular visitor will mind or not. (See also "Phone-Call Faux Pas," pages 225–226.)

If you expect the meeting to be a long one, you might offer your visitor a beverage. Keeping a coffeemaker, tea bags, and a couple of china cups and saucers in your office simplifies things by saving you from having to rely on orders from outside, which are difficult to time.

If a visitor overstays his or her welcome, you can politely end the meeting by stating that you have another appointment or duty.

SEEING VISITORS OUT

Walk your visitor back to the reception area. Do this even if it's a straight shot and he won't have to make his way through a maze of corridors. Exchange a few pleasantries when saying good-bye; if he shows signs of chatting at length, you can simply explain that you have to get back to work.

SAYING "GOOD MORNING"

Creating a workplace where courtesy reigns doesn't mean feeling obligated to say hello every time you pass someone in the hall; being preoccupied with what you're doing is only natural when you're busy, and shouldn't be taken as an affront. Of course, you'll want to greet coworkers the first time you see them with "Good morning" or "How's it going?" but after that a quick smile or nod will do. More important is what *not* to do when passing people in the hall—staring straight down at the floor with a sour look on your face. Even though it's unlikely to be taken personally, ignoring people does little toward creating the kind of atmosphere that makes the day go better.

HALLWAY SCHMOOZING

When chatting in the halls, stand to the side so as not to block traffic—an obvious courtesy, but one that a surprising number of people ignore. If that includes you, remember that making busy coworkers detour around you a couple of times is little to worry about, but after three or four repetitions it can start to get annoying. Less obvious is what people might be thinking when your conversation goes on for more than ten minutes or so; besides disturbing people in nearby offices, you could be seen as a slacker if you make a regular habit of gabbing away in the corridors.

COMMUNAL EQUIPMENT

Communal office equipment, which has a way of needing maintenance more regularly than it should, is a lightning rod for the "it's not my job" attitude among workers. Keeping the office technology in good working order is assumed to be the responsibility of someone else, and frequently it is. (Besides, in many offices you probably don't have access to toner cartridges and such.) Still, even if it's technically not your responsibility, you should take care of things if you know how. If the signal lights show that a fax machine, printer, or copier needs toner or has a paper jam, either do the job yourself or call the person in charge of machine maintenance right away. This applies doubly in a small business, where, in the spirit of team play, everyone—including the boss—should pitch in.

COPIERS

Copying machines run at different speeds, with some processing thirty pages in half the time that an older machine might take. Those that are on the slow side are ticking bombs, just waiting to create frustrations if not conflicts. But even the use of state-of-the-art copiers requires remembering the needs of others.

The most obvious courtesy is for someone who has a large copying job—say, twenty pages or more—to let anyone who has a small job go first. It's another matter if you've set the machine for finishing (sorting, stapling, enlarging, or the like) and you need four copies of a twenty-page manuscript. In this case, give anyone who comes to use the machine an estimate of how long your job will take. After any large job, check the paper drawer and top it off as necessary.

Also check company policy for personal copying jobs. Whenever copying personal papers, be especially careful not to leave documents in the machine. If you work for a small business with a "no personal copies" policy, always abide by it or ask special permission from your boss. If you are making copies secretly and a coworker reports it, be angry with yourself, not the tattler.

FAX ETIQUETTE

Proper fax etiquette is relatively simple, with six main points:

- **USE A COVER SHEET.** Don't be tempted not to use one, or a fax could get lost in the shuffle.

- **DON'T COUNT ON PRIVACY.** You can mark a fax "Confidential" or "Personal," but remember that your fax may pass through many hands before reaching the intended recipient.

- **NUMBER THE PAGES IN YOUR DOCUMENT.** This allows the recipient to ascertain that all pages have arrived.

- **BE CONSIDERATE OF THE RECIPIENT.** If you must send a lengthy fax during business hours, call the recipient first. There may be a number for an alternate fax machine that is not in heavy use, or the recipient may want to alert others that a long document is expected.

- **DELIVER IT.** If it's no trouble to drop off a business fax to someone (or at least mention that they have one) as you pass by their office or cubicle, by all means do so.

- **PERSONAL FAXES.** Don't send personal faxes on company equipment unless the company specifically allows it or unless you receive permission.

PRINTERS

If a printing job hasn't been picked up by a coworker, don't just throw it aside. Place it faceup where it can be clearly seen, or put it in a space designated for finished jobs. As with faxes, it's a nice gesture to drop off a job if it's obvious whose it is.

When the printers are down, don't take out your frustration on the technical support staff, who are undoubtedly doing all they can. Alert them at the first sign of trouble (or call the help desk if you have one), and then turn your attention to something else until the problem is solved.

FURNITURE

Treat any tables in the reception room, conference rooms, or the kitchen as you would treat your furniture at home. That means putting a sweating glass or soda can on a napkin or coaster to avoid leaving a ring on a table made of wood. The same goes for your office furniture, which may be expensive and will more than likely be inherited one day by someone else. Don't wipe greasy fingers on a fabric-covered chair, and don't let the crumbs of your morning muffin fall on the floor where it can be ground into the carpet. Both acts can leave unsightly oil stains.

IN THE KITCHEN

The kitchen has the potential for being the messiest room on the floor, so it's only fair that everyone does his or her part to keep it clean. If you spill something—on the counter, in the fridge, on the floor—*wipe it up.* Don't leave your dirty dishes in the sink. If necessary, wipe down appliances after you use them.

Besides cleanliness, there's courtesy. If your fridge doesn't have an ice maker, refill the ice cube trays when you empty them. If there's a communal coffeemaker, refill it and start a new pot when you take the last cup. Report any problems with the vending machine; if management hasn't made it clear who to tell when it goes on the fritz, find out from whoever is responsible for maintenance, then report the problem and post the information for the future benefit of others.

STORING FOOD

When it comes to the refrigerator, one rule is paramount: Don't leave milk or leftovers inside until they start to smell. It's your responsibility to dispose of food you never got around to eating.

THE FOOD THIEF

You could wring somebody's neck, couldn't you? Nothing is more frustrating than finding that the smoked turkey sandwich your mouth was watering for has mysteriously disappeared from the fridge. "How could they?" you think. Personalizing a food package by clearly labeling it with your name may disabuse the potential thief of the notion it's communal, but don't count on it. The annoying little crime of food theft is all too easy for some people to commit.

It is almost impossible to catch a food thief unless your kitchen has surveillance cameras. (The evidence, after all, has probably already been digested.) Your only way of getting back is to announce the deed to the world. Compose a note for the refrigerator door and leave it posted there for a few days.

COOKING AND MICROWAVING

Just as you're responsible for washing your own dishes, you're responsible for cleaning up any appliances you use. If anything you've placed in the microwave or conventional oven boils over or splatters, wipe down the inside of the oven with a wet paper towel.

WASHING DISHES

Don't leave dirty coffee mugs in the sink or food scraps in the garbage disposal. It's each person's responsibility to wash his own dishes as soon as he has finished his meal. Remember, nobody wants to clean up your mess. To avoid the awkwardness of confronting messmakers in person, post a gentle reminder above the sink. Be aware, too, that a messy kitchen may lead management to simply close the kitchen.

COMMUNAL LUNCHES

Having lunch together in the cafeteria is a great time to get to know your coworkers. More important, it's a great time for them to get to know *you*. Both the quality of your small talk and decent table manners will help contribute to your reputation as someone who's a pleasure to be around.

Having a regular group to lunch with is only natural, but you should occasionally mix your lunch partners so that you don't become too isolated from your workmates as a whole. Either invite workers from another department or try going at different hours so that you'll encounter a wider range of people.

If you bring your lunch and always eat at your desk, be aware that becoming too much of a creature of habit can start to make you look unsociable. If a coworker who eats in the cafeteria (especially if he or she is your boss) sometimes drops by and asks if you want to go get a bite, think seriously about leaving your sandwich in the fridge and having it tomorrow.

TABLE CONVERSATION

Avoid discussing sensitive work topics over lunch, since people at other tables may overhear. Things that are too personal—the hot date you had last night, the trouble you're having with a child—are also not a good idea. For the benefit of your lunch partners, don't talk about your or anyone else's skin conditions, stomach problems, or operations; these subjects are not exactly appetizing at the best of times. Lunch is a time for relaxing and taking a break—not the place for conversation that would be better conducted in a bar after work, if at all.

IN THE RESTROOMS

Depending on the frequency of maintenance, the office restrooms can be more disorderly than the kitchen. Do your part by always using the trash can, wiping up water that splashed out of the sink, and replacing toilet paper rolls as necessary.

YOUR TOILETTE

A woman putting on her makeup, a man shaving, or anyone brushing their teeth in a workplace restroom should remember that they are not at home. The important thing is to go about things discreetly, clean up after yourself, and not take over the space.

THE TOILET

Some people are uncomfortable about talking while they are in a toilet stall, so be cautious about initiating a conversation between stalls.

The position of the toilet seat can also be a major issue in offices with unisex bathrooms. The best practice is for everyone to agree to put the lid and seat in a down position before flushing. If there is no lid, men should make the effort to put the seat back down after they're done. This is simply not an issue that is worth fighting over. If you prefer to use one of the disposable sanitary covers or arrange sheets of toilet paper on the seat before sitting down, make sure to flush the paper when you leave, instead of letting it litter the floor.

Finally, there's the inescapable but rarely acknowledged problem of a more delicate nature: odor. Use any air freshener that is kept there.

DOORS, DOORS, DOORS

Doors are the most common spot for close encounters. At busy times of day, people rushing through doors tend to think of the meeting that's starting, the lunch date they're late for—anything but the person coming the other way or right behind them. Yet preoccupation could lead to injury if your unknown partner in transit happens to be disabled, elderly, or just inattentive. Another consideration is never to squeeze into a revolving-door compartment that is already occupied.

The best policy for two people approaching a door together—whether they are a man and a woman or two people of the same gender—is communication. "Here, let me get that for you" or "Please, go ahead," said by either person, avoids confusion.

ANOTHER BIT OF DOOR ETIQUETTE. Stand away from entryways and elevator doors whenever you're biding time in the lobby. If you're waiting for someone, stand against a wall so as not to impede traffic.

AROUND THE BUILDING

The same issues of consideration and respect hold when you're not in your immediate workspace. In particular, doors, elevators, and other points where people are likely to come into close physical contact are places where a little thought can go a long way to easing things for everybody.

ELEVATOR ETIQUETTE

The old-style elevator operator, nattily attired in a jacket with gold braid, has gone the way of the Edsel in most office buildings. But however casually he or she is clothed, any operator is due a "please" and "thank you" whenever you request a floor or disembark. That's not all you need to remember as you ride, however.

GETTING ON

The rules for entering an elevator are much the same as those for going through a door—gender is not the issue, communication is. Remember, the elderly or incapacitated go first. After pushing your floor button, move as far to the back as possible, leaving room for others. If you're unable to reach the button to push it, don't be embarrassed to ask someone else to do it for you.

If the elevator is already jammed with people before you get on, don't squeeze your way inside, even if you work in a building where the elevators seem to take forever to arrive.

Likewise, patience is a virtue when you find the door closing as you approach. Although it's a nice gesture for a passenger to hold the door for you or push the "Door Open" button, it's equally thoughtful of you to allow the passengers already aboard to go ahead and get to their floors.

Also, mind your manners. Don't stare at other people, smack your gum (which you should hesitate to chew in public anyway), or sing along with your iPod. If there's a mirror or reflective wall in the elevator, women and men alike would do well to leave their primping for later.

CHATS IN TRANSIT

If you're on the elevator and you see someone you know, say "Hello," say "How are you?" or say "How 'bout those Broncos?"—but be careful about going further, unless you're the only two people aboard. A quiet chat is fine, but talking and laughing loudly may annoy fellow passengers, trapped as they are for the length of the ride.

As important as the volume is the subject: Discussing a client's business or anything else confidential while riding a crowded elevator is on the same level as not having the sense to come in out of the rain. If you need to talk about personal matters or exchange trade secrets with someone you see on the ride up or down, wait until you can have your discussion in private.

GETTING OFF

When the elevator door opens, common sense prevails: Those nearest the front exit first. If several people need to exit on a floor, the first person out should pause just outside the elevator and hold his or her arm across the open door to prevent it from starting to close while others exit. Alternatively, the other passengers still in the elevator should press the "Door Open" button so everyone can exit as easily as possible.

RIDING ESCALATORS

Escalator manners are more obvious: Keep to one side so that other people are able to continue walking up or down. If you're the one in a hurry to get off, don't be surprised to find that most people are standing square in the middle of the steps. Unless the escalator is so clogged that it's useless to make the attempt, politely say "Excuse me, please" to every person you want to move past. Squeezing by with a sour look does little but add one more minor annoyance to the workday.

6 | *You and Your Supervisors*

Despite endless jokes and situation comedies to the contrary, bosses are people, too. As Shakespeare might have said, prick them and they bleed the same as everyone else. In fact, whatever name he or she goes by (boss, supervisor, employer, manager, middle manager, executive), there's not a boss in the world who doesn't have a boss. The CEO must report to the board of directors, the board of directors to the shareholders. Even the highest-flying entrepreneur must answer to his or her lenders and the market. What separates you from your boss is power and responsibility. He or she has the power to direct and demand your performance; your boss is then also responsible for your performance to everyone above him or her in the chain of command.

THREE STEPS TO COMPATIBILITY

Over a lifetime of work, most of us will experience good bosses, mediocre bosses, and a few truly atrocious bosses. In every case, three straightforward steps will set the stage for getting the relationship off on the right foot:

- Understand that your boss is a human being.

- Accept the reality that your supervisor is in charge.

- Do your job, and do it on time.

WHEN YOU'RE NEW TO THE JOB

When you take a new job or a new position within your company, your primary challenge is to master your own duties. But to be fully effective, you must also uncover your new supervisor's modus operandi. Different bosses may have widely differing ways of operating: Your old boss required written project reports delivered punctually at the end of each week; your new boss prefers verbal updates and only occasionally asks for written reports.

Your old boss got a kick out of the rubber crocodile collection on your desk; your new boss frowns on cluttered cubicles. When you step into a new job, be open to your new boss's ideas. Stay flexible and remember that there's no absolute right way to run an office.

You can quickly pick up on the most obvious characteristics of your new boss's style by observing your coworkers and their interactions with him. Don't be hesitant about asking questions, because your job description will tell you only what is expected of you—not how to do it. If the boss isn't available, it's fine to talk with your fellow workers about office procedures. Just be sure that your questions don't carry any implied criticisms. In particular, avoid the "At my last job, the boss would never tolerate . . ." approach.

GETTING ALONG WITH YOUR BOSS

Frankly, how you get along with supervisors is more your responsibility than theirs. Their job is to get the company's work done in the most productive and profitable manner. Your ambitions and goals are your own concern. The challenge facing all workers is how to get the most out of their relationships with their bosses.

- **SPEAK UP AND OFFER IDEAS.** Bosses generally welcome fresh thinking from the people they supervise.

- **BE PREPARED.** Bosses appreciate the difference between those who shoot from the hip and those who do their homework before speaking.

- **DON'T WASTE YOUR BOSS'S TIME.** Be concise and clear. Have your materials and support documents ready, as well as copies of any pertinent papers. You'll not only save your boss's time, but also show yourself to be organized.

- **LOOK FOR PROBLEMS YOU CAN SOLVE.** Bosses look favorably on employees who show initiative.

- **ASK FOR HELP WHEN YOU NEED IT.** Most bosses enjoy teaching and guiding their employees. Asking your superior for help is not a sign of weakness; it is an appropriate recognition of the boss's broader knowledge and experience.

- **BE A TEAM PLAYER.** It may be a cliché, but bosses prefer directing a cohesive group rather than a hodgepodge of self-centered individualists. Prima donnas may be high achievers, but many bosses believe that a group of steady workers is ultimately more productive than the loftiest star.

- **SHOW ACCEPTANCE.** Accept your boss's final decisions graciously even when they are contrary to your thinking.

FOUR KEYS TO SUPPORTING YOUR BOSS

1 *Be observant.* If, for example, you see that your boss is snowed under with reports to read before a big meeting, you might offer to help by summarizing one or two.

2 *Offer a compliment.* Once in a while, when she does something that impresses you, tell her. "The way you handled that client was perfect. You defused the situation and ended up getting us more work. That was great!" Just be careful to do it sparingly, or you may look like you're trying to curry favor.

3 *Support your boss's decisions in public.* It's generally wise to stay loyal to the person above you. Whatever the outcome (and even if your supervisor gets the ax), your loyalty will be noted by others.

4 *Cover, but don't lie.* Don't make up false explanations, but you also don't have to completely answer a question about your boss. If the CEO calls you and angrily demands why your boss missed an important meeting, you can politely claim ignorance even if you suspect he was at the gym. At the same time, you should warn your boss that the CEO was wondering where he was for the meeting.

DO NOT UNDERMINE

Never try to undermine your supervisor's position. There are a few legitimate situations when you must go above or around your boss (see "Going over Your Boss's Head," page 88), but it is extremely dangerous when ambition drives an employee to connive. Keep in mind that a company has a large investment in its supervisors and department heads. In a conflict between boss and worker, the boss will almost always win — and the loser will gain only a reputation for ruthlessness and deceit.

THE ART OF COMPLAINING

There are times when you may have to go to your supervisor and complain, whether it's as minor an issue as grumbling about a messy restroom or as major as being sexually harassed. You may have a private gripe or your dissatisfaction may be shared by others. In any case, the boss is almost always the person to talk with. To complain effectively is something of an art form; by asking yourself the following questions ahead of time, you can avoid some common pitfalls:

- Is your complaint worthwhile? Is the problem persistent and serious enough to warrant intervention by a supervisor? Does it affect the quality of your work or overall productivity? Is it worth the boss's time, or will you be perceived as crying wolf?

- Have you documented the problem? What is your evidence that a problem even exists? It is extremely important that you be able to support your complaint, both to show your seriousness and to validate your claims.

- Are you the right person to make the complaint? Be honest with yourself. If you lack the credibility to make the complaint, see if there's someone else who can do it.

- What results do you want? Be clear about how you would like to see the situation resolved. Your boss may ask you for your opinion. You will want to have a well-thought-out solution ready.

- What's the best approach? Decide if your boss prefers to read or to listen. Then, either prepare a memo detailing the situation or ask for a private meeting.

- What's the right time? Don't wait until the whole office is tied up in a crash project to express your dissatisfaction. By respecting your boss's other obligations, you greatly improve your chances of being listened to.

- How long should you wait for a response? Never expect immediate action on a complaint. You may not see results for a long time, especially when your complaint involves changing a company policy. A good boss will eventually tell you what came of your complaint, but understand that there may well have been consequences that he or she cannot discuss, such as the disciplining of a colleague.

If a problem persists after you've registered your dissatisfaction, carefully weigh the pros and cons of further complaints. What seems like reasonable follow-up to you may quickly become pestering to a boss. There are times when it is better to back off, face reality, and let the issue drop.

COMPLAINING ABOUT CONDITIONS

Complaints about workplace conditions can involve anything from poor janitorial service to excessive overtime. If you belong to a union, many working conditions are covered by your union agreement, and you will report problems to your steward or union representative. Otherwise, go to your boss, his or her assistant, or the office manager. Minor problems with the physical environment (you need a new chair or the photocopier consistently malfunctions) can usually be covered in a brief memo or e-mail. More serious or physically threatening problems (loss of a security card, locked fire doors, the presence of unauthorized persons) should be reported as quickly as possible by the fastest means available. Don't hesitate to call the boss directly if the situation is potentially dangerous.

OVERTIME AND WORKLOADS

Problems such as excess overtime and short-staffing are a bit trickier. Don't jump to the conclusion that your boss is at fault. She may already be working to get relief. If your boss is unaware of the problem, it's wise to inform her in a polite, conciliatory manner. The employees may decide it is best to choose a representative to bring the complaint to the boss. Make sure he or she has adequate documentation of the problem. (No angry mobs at the castle gate!) You stand the best chance of getting the results you want if you frame the complaint in terms of productivity: For example, show your boss how the lack of staff is causing missed deadlines and increased work errors.

THE GROUP COMPLAINT

If conditions don't improve, it may be time to gather your troops and meet with your supervisor as a group. The advantage of a group (made up of department representatives or the whole department) is that numbers can impress even the most insensitive supervisor; most bosses want to avoid serious and widespread morale problems.

THE BIG NEXT STEP

If group complaining doesn't work, you and your colleagues will have to consider very carefully what your next step will be. Openly taking your complaints to your boss's boss could create an untenable situation. You may find out that the company values your boss's efforts and style, and that suddenly you are in a very difficult situation. Instead, you may want to approach your boss's boss or someone in human resources on a confidential basis without naming names to get a sense of how valid your complaint is and to discuss how you can best approach the problem to resolve it. If you choose to openly go over your boss's head, it's preferable to let your boss know what you are doing. Copy him or her on all letters and memos to higher-ups. Document the problem, and keep the tone of all communications professional. Remember, once the dust settles, your boss will still be the boss.

SERIOUS COMPLAINTS ABOUT COWORKERS

Sometimes you'll need your boss to step in directly on a problem, especially if it is serious or has legal implications. Sexual harassment, racist remarks, religious proselytizing, theft, lying, fighting, threatening behavior —these are all examples of serious problems that can affect the entire company, and your direct supervisor needs to know about them immediately. If you become aware of a serious problem, go straight to your supervisor. Be precise; don't elaborate beyond what you actually know; don't feel obliged to cover for coworkers or explain their behavior. Then leave it to the supervisor to manage the situation.

IS IT WORTH IT?

As for run-of-the-mill irritating, obnoxious, or difficult coworkers, you'll have to decide whether complaining about them is worth the effort. Scott is late to work nearly every day and expects you to cover for him. Rachel is driving everyone crazy with her bad moods. Ben's divorce is really affecting the quality of his work. And somebody is stealing food from the office fridge.

Ask yourself if your complaint is valid or merely a personal issue. Does the behavior affect the way the person or other workers do their jobs? Is the problem persistent or short term? Is there an underlying condition such as alcoholism or drug use that may be the cause? Finally, can you talk to the person and work things out, or is the boss's intervention necessary?

Like it or not, sometimes you must simply grin and bear it, tolerating difficult people whose value to the business outweighs their quirks. The egomaniacal salesman who is always the top producer, the temperamental art director who wins all the prestigious awards, the sharp-tongued secretary who is a genius with complex computer programs—they may irritate your boss even more than they bother you. But bosses have the responsibility to balance the general good against the feelings of individual employees.

TAKING ACTION

If you decide to complain about a colleague, arrange a private meeting with your boss instead of writing a memo. (*Never* complain via e-mail, unless you're prepared for your words to become public property.) In your meeting, be calm and focus on the troubling behavior, not the person: "Roger leaves a half hour early at least three days a week, and we're having a problem getting his time sheets" is far better than "Roger is totally irresponsible and deceitful." Be as objective as you can, and don't be tempted to express moral judgments.

OWNING UP TO THE GOOD AND THE BAD

Occasionally, you may find yourself on the receiving end of a heartfelt compliment from your manager. When this happens, the most important thing you can do is to accept it graciously, with, for example, a simple, "Thank you. I really appreciate that you realize how hard I worked on that proposal." If others were involved, make sure you point out that the proposal was really a team effort. Don't take all the glory for yourself.

On the other side of the coin, there will inevitably come a time when you screw up. Don't deny your culpability. When you find yourself in the hot seat, rule number one is to take responsibility for your actions. First and foremost, don't wait for your supervisor to come to you. Instead, go to her, explain the situation, apologize, and then offer a solution. As frustrating as your mistake may be for your supervisor, having a problem you caused suddenly land on her desk is even worse. By providing a solution, you not only exhibit responsibility but you also show consideration for the impact your mistake could have on your supervisor and others.

DEALING WITH CRITICISM

In order to learn and profit from criticism, it may be necessary to grow a little armor over that thin skin. Learn to listen to what the boss is really saying, without inferring hidden meanings. Learn not to react until you have fully digested the criticism. Control the instinct to become defensive; defensiveness in the face of legitimate criticism is about as productive as the infantile instinct to suck your thumb. Count to ten or mentally recite the preamble to the Constitution before launching a counter-offensive. It also helps to hone your sense of humor; don't take the boss's favorite joke about "the bumbling junior executive" as suggesting something negative about *you*.

It's not easy to learn to value criticism, but doing so is a triumph of intellect over raw emotion. In fact, receiving criticism well—understanding that criticism is an opportunity to learn and improve—is a classic characteristic of good or excellent bosses, and it no doubt helped them to rise through the ranks.

RESPONDING TO CRITICISM

If the boss is sensitive or if you need to discuss her criticism in some depth, arrange a private meeting, preferably at a time when the boss is at ease. Try not to be confrontational. Even if the criticism was totally unjustified, phrase your response in terms of what you can do to remedy the situation: "When you were criticizing the Alpha project yesterday, I know you forgot that I didn't work on it. But you've said often enough that these short deadlines hurt everybody. It could be my group next time, and I want to get your ideas for avoiding the problem." You have corrected the boss, but you've also given her an out and moved the discussion forward to a more productive area.

You can learn from all valid criticism, even criticism directed at others. But sooner or later, there's a good chance you'll have a boss who is just plain mean and abusive. In this case, your options are limited; you can stay and take it or you can get out. If you stay in the job, you'll have to work hard not to become a victim of the boss's evil ways. Be your own critic, and don't take his or her complaints to heart: The criticisms of a truly abusive boss are neither valid nor well-intentioned.

DEALING WITH DIFFICULT BOSSES

Tough bosses are different from difficult bosses. There are tough, demanding bosses who drive you to perform above and beyond anything you thought yourself capable of. A difficult boss, on the other hand, is one whose demands hurt your performance more than they help.

Difficult bosses may be control freaks, credit hoggers, or pass-the-buck types, and their personalities can range from merely hard to get along with to near abusive. But difficult bosses are not, as a rule, out to get you, and they are generally unaware of how their behavior affects their employees.

DISCUSSING THE PROBLEM

It can help to talk with a difficult boss in a nonconfrontational meeting. You may want to include several office representatives in the meeting to demonstrate that the problem is widespread. Be specific about your complaints and show the boss how the problem is affecting overall productivity and morale. Try not to blame; instead, offer to help and have possible solutions in hand. Be aware that defensiveness may be the first reaction, and that change may come more slowly than you'd like. But if your boss shows a willingness to make adjustments in his behavior, be ready to meet him with cooperation.

GOING OVER YOUR BOSS'S HEAD

If you have to go over or around a difficult boss, keep the boss informed of your actions if possible. If your business has an experienced human resources staff, they may be able to help you decide on the strategy that is most likely to achieve the results you want within the unique structure and culture of your business. Keep in mind that your objective is positive change for everyone, including your difficult boss—not a bloody palace revolution.

ABUSIVE BOSSES

Abusive bosses are neither tough nor merely difficult; they are mean and unpredictable. They pick their victims for no apparent or logical reason. They afflict their workers with physical and emotional tortures from ulcers and migraines to failures of self-confidence. Abusive bosses are deliberately harmful to the people around them.

Before you personally tackle an abusive boss, it's always wise to gauge his or her role in the company. Remember, not only are people who are rude and uncivil in the workplace three times as likely to be superiors but they're also likely to be valued employees in the eyes of senior management.

For employees with abusive bosses, there may be no totally happy solution other than escape. But it is not always possible or desirable to transfer or find a new job. Normal complaint and reconciliation mechanisms don't often work with abusive bosses; heart-to-heart talks are rarely helpful either, and may even be counter-productive if the boss labels you as the enemy.

Employees may be able to combat abusers through group action. (If you have a union, try taking your issues there.) Documentation and unity are powerful weapons, but you'll need to face up to the fact that even they may not solve the problem. The best defense when you can't leave your job is to identify your boss as an abuser and to understand in your heart and mind that you are not the cause of the problem.

YOUR CAREER PATH

Your supervisor will have a major impact on your career. He or she has the power to satisfy your immediate objectives and influence your long-range goals. But when you deal with the boss on issues that affect your career, remember that his or her primary concern is not your future or your personal situation, but rather things that are happening here and now. And that's where you should focus any career discussions with your supervisor, as well.

ASKING FOR A RAISE OR PROMOTION

If ever a meeting needs to be conducted professionally, it is the salary or promotion discussion. Here are some tips on how to be as successful as possible in the meeting:

- **MORE MONEY MEANS MORE RESPONSIBILITY.** When you are seeking a promotion, be ready to tell the boss what you can bring to the job. Know what the new position entails and how you plan to manage it.

- **NEVER, EVER, BRING UP PERSONAL ISSUES.** The boss doesn't care about your second mortgage, your kid's orthodontia, or your grandmother's nursing-home bills.

- **KNOW WHAT THE MARKET IS FOR YOUR SKILLS.** You may want to provide information about the general market standards for a person with your responsibilities. Be careful not to bring up other offers as a threatening or coercive tactic; threats can blow up in your face. If you choose to mention an offer from another company or a headhunter, carefully present it as a means of helping the boss to evaluate your position relative to comparable companies. If you're genuine in your representation, the boss will not be riled—and if he or she senses that you may be in demand elsewhere, so much the better.

REFUSING OFFERS

What do you do when the boss makes you an offer you have to refuse?

Think about it very hard. Weigh all the pros and cons. Talk with the people who mean the most to you. If you really cannot take on the added hours or excessive travel, turn down the offer. No matter how reasonable your reasons and how sympathetic the boss, your refusal of an offer may well stall your career ambitions for a time. You may face a period of repair work as you rebuild your image with the boss.

LEAVING YOUR JOB

If you're leaving your job by choice, don't signal your intention too early or to the wrong people. If you are looking for a new position, be discreet. Don't, for instance, leave your updated résumé in the office photocopier or get your secretary to type your application letters. Ask headhunters to phone you at home. Don't schedule a luncheon interview with a potential new employer at your current boss's favorite bistro. People love to gossip about who is planning to head for the door, and your boss will soon get wind of your plans.

YOU'VE BEEN LET GO

If you've been fired or asked to resign, not only should you not leave mad, but you also shouldn't leave the *impression* that you're mad. You don't want to burn any bridges in your professional career. Five years from now, you may be pitching a contract to a prospect and discover that your old boss has moved as well—and that *he's* the prospect. Remember, too, that you'll want recommendations and references.

WHEN YOU RESIGN

If you're resigning, be courteous and appreciative in your meeting with (or letter to) the boss. You may want to sound off about every rotten moment you've endured and every idiot you've had to work with (the "take this job and shove it" syndrome). Don't do it. You never know when you might need your boss's help down the line, and old employers have a way of becoming new customers if you haven't alienated them. You might even want to return to the company in the future. So make sure you leave on a graceful note, no matter how you truly feel.

THE EXIT STATEMENT

Whether you are resigning or have been fired, you should work with your boss on an appropriate exit statement. It is important for you to participate in the composing of it, whether the statement is for in-office circulation only or is intended for wider distribution, including news releases. By working with your supervisor on the exit statement, you'll make certain that you and your former employer are telling the same story. Naturally, it's a good idea for the statement to include something about your achievements. If you've been fired, it is unnecessary to explain why. A generic statement is adequate: "Jerry will be leaving Acme this Friday to pursue new career opportunities." An exit statement for a person moving to a new job can be more specific: "All of us at Acme will miss Rebecca, but we know she will be a great success in her new position as human resources director of Manderley Enterprises."

7 | *Women and Men Together— and Other Personal Matters*

The concept of "the weaker sex" has been rightly consigned to the dustbin in a business world where women have proved themselves every bit as capable as men. Driving home the point, more women than ever are emerging as business leaders: Not only have they reached the top rungs in major corporations, but they also own almost 50 percent of America's small businesses. But with their rise in the workplace has come a new set of concerns: How do women react to men who have yet to adjust fully to the change? And is chivalry dead, a casualty of equality? (See also "Gender-Free Chivalry," page 98.) More important, how do both sexes deal with sexual attraction—which has nothing to do with one's work but merely with being human?

ROMANCE IN THE WORKPLACE

It is naive to think that romance, whether your own or someone else's, won't be a factor in the workplace, not to mention the field. When people are thrown together in the same building for most of the day (and often well into the night), flirting and relationships will be inevitable. Statistics tell the story: Roughly half of all married couples first met at work.

While it is true that romances are an eternal part of office life, it is also true that relations between the sexes have become a potential minefield. Hand in hand with the growing number of women in the workplace has come a heightened awareness of discrimination and harassment, making office affairs touchier and more risky than ever. Questions regarding conflicts of interest, distraction from work, and the unpleasant ramifications of a fling's sour ending are very much on the minds of workers and human resources departments alike.

Given this tricky state of affairs, how do you – as a woman or a man – proceed when you find yourself attracted to an office mate, or vice versa? Is even flirting off-limits? No.

Does the way in which you flirt matter? Yes. Is the fact that your love interest and you are at different levels on the corporate ladder an issue? Yes.

It goes without saying that not all relationships are fraught with danger or even trouble, but entering into a romantic involvement at the office requires no small measure of thought and care. (See also "Your Love Life," page 96.)

MAKING THE FIRST MOVE

Someone new to your workforce is physically attractive, dresses well, seems pleasant, and is single—and so are you. In most cases, it is perfectly acceptable after you've become acquainted to extend an invitation for a cup of coffee or drinks after work. But if the invitation is declined, stop and leave it there—unless, of course, the person seems flattered and genuinely disappointed not to be able to accept. Otherwise, repeated bids not only paint you as a pest but also could end up putting you at significant risk. You can never be sure when your attentions might be perceived as sexual harassment.

HOW TO SAY NO

If there's no mistaking that an office mate is interested in you and you are not interested, try a polite rebuff: "Really, Dan/Donna, there's no chance of our going out"—followed by either "I have a boyfriend/girlfriend" (if true) or "I'm just not interested in changing our friendship into something else." If he's persistent, be frank: "Dan/Donna, we're friends. Period. Will you *please* stop asking me out?" If this doesn't shame him/her into backing off, state that you will inform a supervisor or Human Resources.

THE FLIRTEE

Responding to interest is perfectly acceptable as long as it doesn't interfere with work or break company rules. Conversation at the watercooler or on the way to a meeting can be a fine start. But what happens if you're *not* interested? When this is the case, try to be as honest as possible without causing offense.

A SECRET TO KEEP?

If your company has no policy on dating office mates, respect the company's trust in you by proving that your work remains paramount during the day; you have no more license to canoodle at the vending machine than you did before. It's in poor taste—not to mention unprofessional—to subject coworkers to displays of affection.

If your office bans romances between workers at different levels, consider the options: You could continue the affair in secret, at the risk someone will discover the truth and spread the news; you could ask to be transferred to another department; you could end the relationship; or you could find a new job.

Even if office romance is permissible, there are the couples who prefer to be discreet. If you feel uncomfortable revealing your relationship to coworkers, remember that you have no obligation to do so. A simple "I'm sorry, but I try to keep my personal life private" is a good enough answer to someone who pries, although some couples find it easier to deny everything.

ROMANCES BETWEEN MANAGER AND EMPLOYEE

No matter how professional a front you maintain during the workday, a relationship between two people of unequal standing in the office will raise suspicions of unfair treatment or questionable motives, especially if one person supervises or reviews the other's performance. Inherent here are issues of power, preferential treatment, and manipulation, which don't necessarily play a part in a romance between equals.

If the relationship is serious, one of you (almost certainly the partner of lower rank) should consider requesting a transfer. If this seems rash, look at the alternatives: If the relationship were to continue for any length of time, the more junior partner could never be promoted without the risk of people crying unfair advantage. On the other hand, if the relationship were to end badly, there could be issues of harassment or misuse of power that would be traumatizing to both parties.

ROMANCES WITH ASSOCIATES FROM OUTSIDE

If you work closely with someone from another company, you face a difficult situation if a romantic relationship results. If the relationship becomes serious, consider removing yourself as the company contact; otherwise, there could be charges of preferential treatment. Also bear in mind that if the relationship *doesn't* last, it may cause tension or even the loss of an account.

WHAT IS SEXUAL HARASSMENT?

Because sexual harassment is often in the eye of the beholder, the government and the courts go to some lengths to define it. According to Title VII of the Civil Rights Act of 1964, sexual harassment occurs in two forms:

- **QUID PRO QUO.** This translates as "this for that" harassment, in which a supervisor (1) offers a job, promotion, or raise in return for a date or sexual favors, or (2) a supervisor threatens negative consequences if his or her advances are not accepted.

- **HOSTILE ENVIRONMENT CLAIMS.** More of a catch-all, this section of the law refers to cases that include but are not limited to unwanted flirting, touching, unwanted e-mail, offensive pinups, inappropriate comments, lewd gestures, foul language, sexual innuendos, repeated requests for sexual favors, demeaning sexual inquiries, and inappropriate comments on a person's dress or appearance.

It is particularly important for workers to remember that what they consider funny may be insulting to someone else. For instance, telling dirty jokes or describing the previous night's sexual activity around the water fountain or at the lunch table may seem innocent and natural to the person doing the talking—but appalling and offensive to others. A smart office worker carefully considers the wide range of sensibilities that's inevitable in any group of individuals.

RESPONDING TO HARASSMENT

Given the open-ended nature of the law as stated, it is important to understand more about the nature of the behavior in question before deciding to make a claim. According to the Equal Employment Opportunity Commission, sexual harassment is defined as "Unwelcome sexual advances, requests for sexual favors, and other verbal or physical conduct of a sexual nature . . . when submission to or rejection of this conduct explicitly or implicitly affects an individual's employment, unreasonably interferes with an individual's work performance or creates an intimidating, hostile or offensive work environment."

The EEOC also notes that:

- both victim and harasser may be either a woman or man.

- the victim may be the opposite or the same sex as the harasser.

- the victim of harassment doesn't necessarily have to be the person being directly harassed, but could be anyone affected by the harasser's offensive behavior.

If these criteria are met, you need to decide what action to take next.

1 Depending on the seriousness of the situation and your comfort, you may choose to discuss the problem directly with the person doing the harassing. It's possible there has been a simple miscommunication, which can be cleared up with a frank and open discussion. Tell the person to cease, and state in no uncertain terms that you don't condone his or her advances or comments. Depending on the response, you may choose to give an additional warning or two, but make it clear that if the behavior continues, you will report him or her.

2 Check your employee handbook and follow the instructions for combating sexual harassment outlined there. You should speak to a supervisor or a member of the human resources staff to put your employer on notice about your situation. Representatives of the company should find it in their best interest to support you, especially when you show them that you are serious about your complaint.

3 If the company doesn't take your complaint seriously, consider contacting an outside agency and/or an attorney who concentrates in the area of employment law as a step toward ending the harassment. One organization offering help is the Equal Employment Opportunity Commission (EEOC). In most states, your first recourse is through a state agency or division that handles sexual harassment claims often related to the attorney general's office. In most cases, depending on the nature of the claim, the state agency will conduct an independent investigation of the claim.

4 Whatever action you choose to take, keep a record of the encounters you've had with the person who is harassing you and with any contacts in the company from whom you have sought help. It may seem paranoid to jot down the nature of every communication you have with the offending person and to keep copies of any written communications, which may include examples of the harassment, such as e-mails, and of your discussions with human resources or your supervisor, but if the harassment continues you will need to have accurate and detailed examples: what was said and done, who might have been a witness, and what your employer said and did in response to your complaints. It's also wise to keep copies of your performance reviews at home for safekeeping; if your harasser tries to discredit your work, your documentation of good performance will speak for itself.

YOUR PERSONAL LIFE

When it comes to talking about personal matters, employees can be their own worst enemies. Without intending to, they often divulge private information about themselves that ends up becoming watercooler gossip. How (and how much) you talk about personal issues—dating, marriage, children, divorce, sexual preference, death, personal finances—is up to you. Proceed at your own risk.

YOUR FAMILY
Who you are is intimately related to your family. Some people will be genuinely interested in your background—that your grandmother was a suffragette, that your father fought in

Vietnam, that your uncle once worked for Elvis—but beware of imposing any family problems on your workmates. People you work with will be concerned that someone close to you is suffering a serious illness, for instance, and you may want to tell colleagues as a way of explaining periodic absences from the office. But they neither expect nor want daily updates on Grandpa's arthritis or Aunt Tillie's gynecological problems. Be especially careful about discussing medical matters that may come back to haunt you. If, for example, news of your family history of a serious disease reaches your employer, you can't be fired, but you may become known as a "health risk"—affecting future employment or promotion opportunities.

YOUR LOVE LIFE

Discussing the details of your love life, especially with coworkers you don't know well, can be obnoxious. Moreover, employees who are too free with intimate details can be putting themselves in danger of sexual harassment charges. Also, don't expect your workmates or supervisors to be your romance counselors or to keep your deep, dark secrets confidential.

YOUR MARRIAGE AND CHILDREN

Marital and parental status are usually the first two pieces of personal information that circulate about a new employee. A wedding ring, family photos on your desk, the "Baby on Board" sticker on your car—all are invitations to questions. It's up to you how much or how little you decide to share about your spouse or your children.

Family relationships can forge bonds with other workers. They can also explain and ameliorate some behaviors. (For example, knowing that you have children whom you must pick up from day care or after school will help colleagues understand why you can't schedule late-afternoon meetings.) But if you bring family problems to work, be prepared to become the subject of office talk, attract unwanted advice, and possibly risk more serious consequences.

TERMS OF ENDEARMENT

"Sweetie," "Honey," "Hey, beautiful"—these are at best terms of endearment that should not be part of a person's vocabulary at work. The simplest test is, if he or she wouldn't say it to a man, he/she shouldn't say it to a woman. It's not likely you would give Tom a squeeze on the shoulder and say, "Nice job, sweetie." So don't squeeze Mary's arm or say it to her either. Her name is Mary. Use it—and keep your hands to yourself.

Avoid imposing your family on others. Don't expect your colleagues to buy your daughter's Girl Scout cookies by the dozens or sponsor your son's soccer team. A few photos are fine, but don't turn your office or cubicle into a family portrait gallery. Don't bring your children to work unless it's allowed; even then, be sure that your youngsters are quiet and respectful of your coworkers' need to get their work done.

YOUR DIVORCE

When you walk through your office's entrance, you should try as much as possible to leave your personal problems at the door. A divorce is one of the most difficult emotional issues anyone can face, but if you're in the process of one, don't use your coworkers as therapists. Turn to friends, family, and professionals outside the office for support and guidance.

You should talk with your supervisor if the divorce process is likely to affect you on the job—requiring time off for meetings with lawyers, court appearances, the sale of house and property, the care of children. If you experience any emotional or behavioral difficulties (occasionally being short with coworkers, forgetting appointments, becoming distracted in meetings), seek counseling and, if appropriate, discuss it with your supervisor. A good boss may be able to help by shifting some of your workload for a while.

There's no need to go into details about the cause of the divorce—and never berate or demean your ex- or soon-to-be-ex-spouse to colleagues or bosses. Simply state the facts and any problems you have or anticipate having.

DIVORCE IN THE SAME COMPANY

When a divorce happens between two employees of the same firm, the stress can affect everyone. The worst circumstance is when a divorcing couple expect their coworkers to take sides, thus turning a private matter into a company-wide tangle. Hard as it may be, divorcing couples have an obligation to keep their personal lives private, except for appropriate notification of supervisors. If the acrimony can't be contained and threatens to infect an entire office, it may be necessary to consider a change of job or transfer for one or both parties. If the ex-couple won't consider making a change themselves, they may find that the company will do it for them.

At the same time, don't expect to keep the divorce under wraps. On the other hand, it's not necessary to stop every Tom, Dick, and Harry in the hall and regale them with your story. Nor is it wise to send out divorce announcements or, as one divorcing couple did, to write personal notes to every coworker.

YOUR SEXUAL ORIENTATION

Revealing sexual orientation or preference to an employer is tricky. Although many states and localities have enacted laws that protect gay and lesbian workers against employment discrimination, the majority of jurisdictions do not recognize them as a protected class. The issue is a political and social minefield, and court decisions as yet offer little consistent guidance.

Legal status and fairness aside, homosexual employees must take a hard look at their individual workplaces and corporate cultures when deciding whether to disclose their orientation. It is not easy to leave a life partner at home when the company hosts its annual family day, or to be denied insurance coverage for a person who is your true dependent. Fortunately, many enlightened employers realize that sexual orientation, whether heterosexual or homosexual, is irrelevant to job performance.

GENDER-FREE CHIVALRY

Thankfully, chivalry itself has not gone out of style. Instead of men taking care of women, today's ideal is people taking care of people. Holding the door for someone, helping to put on a coat, standing to greet a newcomer—a polite person extends such gestures to everyone, regardless of sex. Nevertheless, many men still insist on playing the perfect gentleman, and a woman who is treated to the old courtesies should never consider such behavior an affront. Kindness is kindness, whatever the motive behind it. Among the chivalries that today are gender-free:

- *Holding a door.* Whoever arrives at the door first holds it for others.

- *Getting off an elevator.* The person closest to the door exits first.

- *Helping put on a coat.* Anyone having difficulty putting on a coat or sweater should be helped, regardless of gender.

- *Paying for a meal.* Today, whoever does the inviting does the paying.

- *Standing.* Male or female, standing to greet someone is always polite—and is especially important when the person is of higher rank, a client, or elderly.

- *Walking on the outside.* The custom of a man taking the outer position on a sidewalk dates from the days when carriages splashed mud and ladies needed shielding. Needless to say, the practice is, if not already obsolete, waning.

- *Shaking hands.* In today's world a man doesn't need to wait for a woman to offer her hand before he extends his. Whether you are a man or woman, shake hands.

- *Helping to carry something.* A workmate who is overloaded with books or packages will appreciate an offer of help from *anyone* nearby.

8 | *The Smart Manager*

One key measure of a manager's success is how adeptly she earns and *keeps* respect in the workplace—from clients as well as from everyone top to bottom in her department and company. Why is respect so important? Because being respectful means understanding how your actions will affect other managers, employees, suppliers, clients, and prospects. Actions that tear others down will hurt productivity, profits, and retention; actions that build will do just the opposite.

Today's smart manager not only knows when to lead and when to get out of the way, but also respects her employees as people. She uses praise when she means it—and usually gets better results in the bargain. She can also be an enforcer when necessary, but she knows that managing by fear and threats is counter-productive.

Much of the secret of successful management is simply keeping your eye on the company's targets while applying common courtesy, respecting other people, communicating clearly, and keeping calm under pressure. But when the pressure starts to build—whether from your boss, your staff, or your inner voice—all that is easier said than done.

A POSITIVE CLIMATE

"Creating a positive climate in my office is so important to me," says the head of a cutting-edge Internet company, "that when I hire people, I tell them that one of the non-negotiable requirements for working at my company is being able to get along with their coworkers. If they can't, that is grounds for dismissal. Work is already pressure-packed enough. No one should have to tolerate the additional pressure of a negative atmosphere created by people who can't get along."

The way a manager manages directly affects the atmosphere of the workplace. Manage in a positive manner, and the atmosphere will be positive. Manage with fear and threats, and the atmosphere quickly becomes pressure-charged and negative. Although the relationship between employee morale and productivity is always shifting and difficult to pinpoint exactly, there is little doubt that the psychological environment of the workplace directly affects the productivity of employees. Creating a negatively charged atmosphere will lead sooner or later to reduced performance. Efficiency, quality, and productivity all go down the drain.

MANIPULATION'S MANY FACES

The smart manager will avoid manipulative behavior at all costs—no matter how tempted you might be to use such behavior as a motivational club. Not all manipulative managers use fear and threats. Some use more subtle kinds of pressure. One of the most common ones is "Everybody is saying that . . . [you don't seem to be a team player . . . you don't seem to respond well to criticism . . . you seem less interested in manufacturing than marketing . . .]" Another common ploy is preceded by the apparently gentle question "Don't you think that . . . ?" which implies that if you really *don't* happen to think what follows is true, you are in the minority. Subtle and crass manipulation both originate from the same source: a person who wants his or her own way more than anything else.

THE EUPHEMISM SCOURGE

The fact is that many employees are ready to distrust any "official" statements that come out of the company front office. Why? One reason is that companies tend to speak in a convoluted, self-protective way, employing euphemisms by the dozens. Corporations use euphemisms for basically two reasons: to sugarcoat bad news and to spare feelings. Used in moderation, euphemisms can amount to simple good manners. Most people would probably rather hear "We are eliminating your position" than "You're fired," even though both mean you're out of work. But is it really necessary or helpful for companies to talk about "rightsizing" and "reengineering" when what they mean is mass firings?

Many management experts attribute worker cynicism to the fact that most employees see right through the euphemisms and conclude that the company thinks it can pull the wool over their eyes. If a manager faces such a climate of distrust, perhaps the best he can do is tell his staff the unadorned facts as he understands them and ask them to ignore the irritation they feel about euphemistic company pronouncements.

BEING ACCOUNTABLE

Every good manager should have the courage to be accountable for his or her own actions. Owning up to your staff that you made a mistake—say, by admitting that you misread the deadline for a project, causing you and several of them to work late into the night—is the mark of strength, not weakness. Making the occasional mistake is only human: Taking blame for an error—and immediately setting about correcting it—shows you as an effective problem-solver, not a dodger. Blaming another person, another department, or "circumstances beyond my control," on the other hand, marks you as a whiner and buck-passer—and raises a serious question about your integrity. Respect is too valuable an asset for you to risk it just to save some embarrassment or pretend that you're infallible.

The smart manager is also willing to admit that she's not all-knowing, whether in regard to the business at hand or otherwise. When she doesn't have the answer to a question that has been posed in a meeting—the approximate quarterly sales figures of a competitor, perhaps—a straightforward "I don't know" is perfectly acceptable. At the same time, she acknowledges that she's accountable for finding the answer: "I'll find out and let you know by five o'clock today." Pretending to know more than you actually do makes you look not only phony but insecure—characteristics that stand no leader in good stead. If you claim always to have the answer, you'll lose credibility among your employees, and that will ultimately weaken your ability to lead.

TAKING CREDIT

Of course, owning up to your mistakes doesn't mean you shouldn't take credit for your successes—bringing a project in under budget, for instance, or delivering on a promise to step up monthly production. Don't be so modest that you undersell your achievements. Just remember to recognize other people's contributions and acknowledge them quickly, openly, and generously.

"TRY THE TRUTH"

A top executive in a Texas public relations firm has a favorite saying for clients who are at a loss about what to reveal: "When all else fails, try the truth." In business, as in life, telling the truth—no matter what the short-term consequences—is far more beneficial than getting caught in a deception. People are generally forgiving, almost to a fault. But deceive them and they will remember it for a long, long time. "Try the truth" applies to everyone in the workplace: the boss, the manager, the new employee, the client, the contractor.

COMMUNICATING DOWNWARD

In the executive suite, being available also means communicating downward, as well as sideways and upward. Many managers are most comfortable talking with their organizational peers about shared interests and common concerns. And few want to miss a chance of schmoozing with their bosses. That leaves people below them last in line. Be that as it may, every manager should make an effort—at least once a day—to hear what's on the minds of employees further down the corporate food chain.

Communicating downward is not only good for office morale; it's also very good for the business. Those frontline employees who rarely see the inside of an executive office—salespeople, customer service reps, telemarketing personnel—are usually the first to know what's going right and what's going wrong. A smart company makes them feel they have access to the planners and decision-makers—a chance to tell the unvarnished truth as they see and hear it every day, unfiltered by middle managers who might try to tone down bad news before it reaches the top.

INSPIRING AND MOTIVATING

The smart manager doesn't leave it to the human resources department to inspire employees to do their best, to remain loyal to the company, and to maintain high standards. Making yourself available to answer questions and concerns, along with giving frequent feedback about job performance, is really the best kind of motivation, and it keeps the employee headed consistently in the right direction. The old-style taskmaster, who treats employees as little more than cogs in a wheel, is asking for low morale and low productivity.

FOCUS ON NEW EMPLOYEES

Two common mistakes made by managers are (1) assuming that employees know exactly what their jobs are and (2) failing to provide adequate training. A new worker must be given a job description that includes every duty that is expected of him. No one, neither the boss nor the employee, should suppose that certain tasks "come with the territory" while others do not. Even an employee who has been doing the same job at another company is going to need direction, since expectations vary from workplace to workplace.

Investing time up front in training an employee will pay off in fewer hassles later, ultimately saving time and effort. A manager should meet, if only briefly, with the employee every day for the first month if possible (or at least three times a week) and provide him with a list of activities that are important for getting a solid start. Make sure the employee understands why each activity is important, how you want it handled, and what level of proficiency you expect of him—now, and six months from now. In follow-up meetings, review his progress to date. These meetings afford an opportunity for intensive one-on-one training and allow you to reinforce desired approaches and skills. While the employee is learning exactly what you want, you're discovering his strong points and weaknesses. Keep your advice practical, specific, and to the point.

Just be sure that you never renege on a promise to give feedback. If you do, you show the employee that follow-through is not important to you. That sets a bad example, and it could come back to haunt you.

RECOGNIZE AND COMPLIMENT

If a job is truly well done, give it all the praise it deserves. Mentioning one or two specific things that especially impressed you makes your praise all the more convincing. It shows that you understand the difficulties the job posed. And don't delay. Leaving your compliment for a few days keeps the worker in suspense, and you may risk forgetting to deliver it.

If a job is done well enough, but parts of it would benefit from a little constructive criticism, save the latter for later. Allow the recipient to bask in the praise until the next time the subject comes up; then say something such as "As great as that proposal was, I think it could've used a few more examples of outside competition. Do you think you could find a few and add them?"

THE POWER OF COMPLIMENTS

The power of a compliment is greater than you might realize. It makes people feel good—and people who feel good generally are better, more productive employees. That means, of course, that giving compliments is good business as well as the nice thing to do. For the owner of a small business on a tight budget, praise is often the only reward she can afford. In that case, it becomes just that much more important to recognize and compliment a job well done, an effort that went above and beyond, or a great idea.

Make your compliments count. Just as important as giving them is *not* giving one for every little thing any employee does, which will cheapen the value of your praise. For the giver and the receiver, compliments are best when they are not only sincere but also well deserved.

WHAT'S YOUR STYLE?

Sometimes, the medium amplifies the message. Many managers like to deliver their highest praise face-to-face. Others prefer to put it in writing. It's a matter of personal style—and usually employees know which style their manager uses when he or she is most pleased. For managers of the terse kind, this could be a brief phone call or e-mail, or even just a handshake and a "Nice job" when passing in the hall. Others go further. One executive, when extremely pleased, composes a handwritten message, seals it in an envelope, and then delivers it in person. She gives the compliment verbally and then hands over the written note as well. Employees will hold on to those notes as part of their official record.

BE AVAILABLE

Remember that your first priority as a manager is to get results, and the way to get results is through managing people, not paper. Instead of hiding behind a closed door and your desk, surrounded by a defensive barricade of paperwork, keep your door open—and especially your eyes and ears. You'll learn much about employee attitudes and morale simply by being alert.

There is no better way of finding out who's feeling overlooked or overwhelmed than watching the passing parade and tuning in to the office chatter—and you can ask unhappy workers in for a chat on the spot. That way, their discontents have less chance of spreading to the rest of the staff.

The telephone can be just as effective a barrier to people management as paperwork. So can e-mail. (Try talking to a manager's back as he or she sits hunched in front of a computer screen!) The best managers learn to take control of their telephone and e-mail time, rather than having it control them. This leaves time for face-to-face meetings and spontaneous conversations—the source of almost all the good ideas that arise in a corporation.

One energy company manager tries to allot no more than one hour per day to the telephone and e-mail. She gives her e-mail a half hour in the morning and makes her telephone calls in a half-hour slot in the afternoon. People she deals with inside and outside the company know she's a paragon of organization, and if they don't hear from her today, they'll hear from her tomorrow. Some days her calls and e-mail take a little longer, but other days she's done in minutes. It evens out, she says—and the discipline makes her a better manager.

THE POWER OF "PLEASE" AND "THANK YOU"

More often than not the small courtesies get lost in the shuffle of today's do-it-now, faster-better-cheaper business world. But saying "please" and "thank you" is not just an empty gesture. Adding the word "please," for example, before "Come to a meeting in my office at ten o'clock" or "Fax this to Bob Johnston" turns a demand into a request. People respond much more positively when something is asked of them rather than demanded.

The same goes for "thank you." When you say "Thank you," you are showing appreciation. When you don't say "Thank you," you are showing that you expected someone to do something. People much prefer to be appreciated.

Manners project a kind of easy confidence. They say, "No matter how crazy our jobs get, let's not forget the social amenities that hold our lives together. Let's not let a bad day destroy our mutual respect. If we keep our heads, things always work out." One manager on the news desk of a national newspaper makes a habit, no matter how harried or exhausted he feels, of greeting everyone he passes in the corridor with a smile and his or her name. If he knows an employee's relative has been in the hospital, he asks, "How's your mother doing?" He has a reputation as one of the most demanding managers on the paper—but he is also one of the most respected and admired. By using "please" and "thank you" yourself, you are setting an example for your staff by making it clear that these common courtesies are part of your team or company culture. Model the behavior, and your employees are likely to follow suit.

YOUR SUPPORT STAFF

Today's assistant is likely to be something of a generalist, involved in much more than just secretarial work. Increasingly, he or she is likely to have been placed on a career track by the company, with the understanding that the eventual goal is to graduate to a higher position or even a managerial one. Such changes make it all the more understandable why the term *secretary* has fallen from favor, symbolizing as it does the era of the low-level, low-paid "gal Friday" with little prospects of advancement. Today the preferred titles include *administrative assistant* and *executive assistant*.

Part of most executives' daily routine is to spend time with an assistant going over projects, dictating letters, discussing appointments to be made. It's easy to forget the basic courtesies that make your interaction more pleasant. Shouting "David, come in here!" or running through the litany of things to do without a smile seems demanding if not overbearing. "David, when you're finished with that letter, would you please come in so that we can discuss the next project?" shows recognition that he is busy and turns an order into a request.

Likewise, using "you" rather than "I" when making requests implies that David has a participatory place in the process. "I want you to work on the Welt project this afternoon" is better phrased as "David, the Welt project needs some attention—would you please fit it into your schedule this afternoon?"

A SPECIAL RELATIONSHIP

Because you, as a manager, spend more time with your assistant than with other employees, you have the opportunity to give him or her a day-by-day performance evaluation of sorts— the ideal situation for any employee but usually impossible in all but the smallest offices. The same goes for the receptionist, whom you come into contact with every morning and

BUDDY OR BOSS?

Most managers have found, some through bitter experience, that it is best not to form close friendships with subordinates. Here are the perspectives of three executives who have faced the situation and reflected on it:

- *"Professional only."* The thoughts of the president of a design firm: "As my firm has grown, I've found relationships with my employees have become more professional and less personal. When it was three of us, we knew everything about each other, and we worked closely together in one big open space with no secrets. Now, with nine people and doors and offices, the relationship between me and the employees is much more 'professional only.' I do care about each of them, but I also care about the business. And no matter how hard I might try, the business would be part of any outside-the-office friendship we might have. So I don't seek or encourage close office friendships. In some ways that's a little sad. But it keeps things simple."

- *Awkward versus rewarding.* From the president of a bank: "Any manager has to be extremely careful about becoming too friendly with an employee. For starters, if you're trying to socialize with your subordinates, they could feel obligated to socialize even if they don't want to—and you've put them in an awkward position. Any socializing should be for the purpose of learning things from employees that will help you do your own job better. That's not the same as socializing with people for the fun of it. Just as you don't want to be your child's friend instead of his parent, you want to be a boss first and a friend second."

- *Fun, but with limits.* From the president and CEO of a real estate development company: "I'm a people person, so personal contact with my employees is very important. It's how I learn about what's really happening in the company, because the information isn't filtered through other levels. In-house lunches, special outings, and an occasional office party are fine—and I saw nothing wrong with taking a bunch of my accounting people recently for drinks at my house and then out to dinner, since they were getting ready for a very tough time with long hours. But even though I get to know my people in a personal way, I usually don't socialize outside the office, with the exception of a few senior managers."

occasionally during the day. Giving a compliment for a job well done (and a little constructive criticism when a lapse is noticed) works both to their advantage and yours.

Some secretaries are of the old school and take pride in having mastered secretarial duties to a tee. Your relationship with an assistant of this sort is relatively cut and dried; there's little or no question as to what each other's duties and obligations are. Other assistants are often those who aspire to a higher level, and it is here that the definitions become less clear.

9 | *Hosting, Attending, and Speaking at the Perfect Meeting*

If any aspect of life at the office makes workers want to cup their heads in their hands and emit a piercing collective scream, it's the business meeting. It has been estimated that today's businesspeople spend at least a quarter of their working hours in meetings—and the higher you rise in the company, the more you'll attend.

You may love meetings, hate them for all you're worth, or fall somewhere in the middle. But take a moment to reflect: Business meetings give you, the participant, a chance to display your skills and talents—to show off in a positive way—and to take the measure of your colleagues. Consider this, too: More than a few advancement-minded workers have undercut their own interests by failing to demonstrate the most basic meeting etiquette.

MANAGING A MEETING

Managing a meeting successfully is an art, not a science. A science is a set of rules for doing things; an art form draws on the ability to adapt creatively and appropriately to each new situation. This explains why some people put on great meetings, while others consistently botch the job. Artfully adapting requires that you be observant, be yourself, be firm in your willingness to lead and control, and be respectful of individuals and the group as a whole.

A QUESTION OF PURPOSE

Unfortunately, far too many meetings end up being unproductive time-wasters—a discourtesy that falls directly on the shoulders of the people who call them. A genuine business meeting has a genuine business purpose. Know exactly *why* you want to have a meeting and what outcome you want to see from it. What do you want to accomplish? Do you want to inform your participants about the issue and get their feedback? Do you want to brainstorm ideas? Do you want to assign tasks? Is there more than one issue to consider? Is decision-making involved?

At the same time, be careful that your stated purpose isn't overly ambitious or unrealistic. For example, a meeting in which a wholly new problem is presented may not accomplish your goals if you also rush your attendees into making decisions based on the new information. They need time to mull the issues privately. Remember, meetings are designed for discussion—*not* thoughtful reflection.

Once you're clear on the purpose of the meeting, you can then proceed to fill in the how, who, where, and when. When it comes to planning a successful session, the devil, as the saying goes, is in the details. In addition to basic logistics, you'll want to be certain that you've prepared for every aspect of the meeting. Remember, it's your meeting and your responsibility.

ISSUING INVITATIONS

Let the nature of your meeting decide how you issue the invitations. If you're calling a small, informal meeting, a telephone invitation may be just fine, but a written notice (memo, letter, or e-mail) is even better. *Always* send written invitations for formal meetings. But only gatherings such as corporate shareholders' meetings and annual board meetings require formal, printed invitations.

Try to give your invitees as much advance notice as possible—at least one week for inhouse meetings, two to four weeks for formal meetings. Remember, too, that the longer the meeting, the more schedule-shifting it will require for participants. If your invitees will be coming from distant locations, four to six weeks' notice is appropriate.

For all but the most informal meetings, you'll want to include the agenda with your invitation. You may also want to include a list of all participants. (Advance lists of attendees are normally provided for large, professional conferences and international meetings.) Be sure to provide some kind of response mechanism—your name and phone number for an informal notice, RSVP information or a reply card for formal invitations. It's a good idea to ask for the response by a certain date so that you can reschedule the meeting if too many invitees are unable to attend. To guarantee good attendance, you or your assistant should give your invitees confirmation calls on the day before the meeting and remind participants of time, location, and any materials they need to bring.

Many companies now make use of integrated calendar-scheduling software programs that simplify the scheduling of meetings. After you type in the participants' names, the time, the date, and the duration, the software tells you if anyone has a scheduling conflict. Invitations and responses are also made through the software, establishing an electronic trail that makes it hard for anyone to claim that they didn't know the meeting was being held.

WHOM SHOULD YOU INVITE?

When developing your list of invitees (whether all in-house, all clients or customers, or a mix of both), decide who will help accomplish your purpose. Resist the temptation to include anyone else, but consider the list carefully so that you won't inadvertently leave out a key player. In short, the size of a meeting depends entirely on its purpose. When the meeting objective is clear, the participants almost choose themselves; you invite the people who can help achieve your goal.

PART-TIME ATTENDEES

You may want to plan for certain people to attend only part of the meeting. Example: An advertising executive calls a morning-long meeting to discuss creative planning for a new client; she asks representatives from the media department to attend for the first hour only, and thoughtfully plans a break at the hour mark for coffee and snacks, allowing the media buyers to make a gracious getaway. Segmenting like this allows busy people to participate only when they are needed, without feeling obliged to remain once their involvement is done.

WHAT'S THE AGENDA?

Even for informal weekly staff meetings, you'll want to have some sort of agenda. Depending on the purpose of the meeting and the company culture, this can range from a list of topics the leader has jotted down on a pad to printed copies for all attendees, laying out the agenda in detail.

Some planners recommend scheduling action items (decision making and problem solving) first, as a way to motivate prompt attendance. Others prefer scheduling discussion first and then proceeding to decisions. However you decide to organize your meeting, you want to include adequate time at the end for wrapping up—summarizing discussion points, clarifying assignments, reviewing decisions, setting deadlines, and (only if necessary, remember) scheduling a subsequent meeting.

A HINT. As the meeting leader, keep a private agenda that lists the items that absolutely must be acted on. As the meeting progresses, make sure you steer the proceedings so as to accomplish your must-do's before a key player has to excuse herself from the meeting.

As you organize your agenda, you'll be able to estimate closely the amount of time needed for each agenda item. Plan breaks if the meeting will be lengthy; no one should be expected to sit for longer than an hour and a half.

WHEN AND WHERE?

With the list of invitees and the agenda determined, you have the tools to decide on time and location. The number of participants, format, and style of the meeting (casual or formal, in-house or with clients) will tell you what size room you'll need and how it should be furnished. If it's a simple announcement meeting for employees, you can jam a lot of people into a small room for five or ten minutes and ask them to stand without any discomfort. If you're planning an all-day seminar, you'll need a room with comfortable tables and chairs and plenty of elbow room. Be sure to book and confirm your meeting space well in advance; many a meeting has had an embarrassing start because the proposed meeting site was already in use.

When you set the meeting time, think of your invitees' schedules. Friday afternoon, for example, is usually disastrous because participants' minds have already left for the weekend, even though their bodies are still in their chairs. Also be attuned to the rhythm of your workplace: Are your coworkers most harried in the morning? Then meet in the afternoon. The more people invited to your meeting, the more difficult scheduling will be. While you may not always be able to clear your starting time with everyone, you should at least check with key participants (including any guest speakers) before settling on your schedule, to avoid locking in an inconvenient time.

PRE-MEETING PREPARATION

The last step in planning your business meeting is to walk yourself through the actual process of the meeting. Consider your meeting subject, your participants, and your own past experiences. Try to visualize everyone together in your meeting room: How are they interacting? What is being done? Is your vision of the meeting accomplishing what you want? What would make it more effective? You might want to employ techniques you've learned elsewhere to activate your participants: A role-playing session, for example, may help salespeople identify hidden customer service problems.

Try to anticipate problems that are likely to bog down the meeting, as well: Is that lengthy statistical presentation really necessary, or can it be handled with printed handouts and a short summary? Review your agenda to be sure you haven't planned too much; you can always revise the agenda before the meeting if need be.

What materials do you need to provide? Always bring sufficient copies of the agenda to the meeting. Be sure, too, that you have copies of any necessary background information, reports of previous meetings, and research reports for all participants. (For the participants' convenience, you can prepare labeled file folders.)

Try to know something about each person you're inviting to the meeting—especially if you have included people who don't know one another, or with whom you have never worked. Meetings often begin with a meet-and-greet period, in which case you will have to be the spark plug to get things moving. Be sure that you are prepared to make friendly, courteous introductions.

NEEDS OF THE DISABLED

If any of the meeting's participants are disabled, pay special attention to seating. Check beforehand to see whether any accommodations are needed, such as reserving seats next to electrical outlets for people who need to use electrical equipment. Attendees who are deaf or hard-of-hearing will need a good seat for viewing the speaker and an interpreter or transcriber if there is one. If a wheelchair user will be attending, think about how the person can best get around the meeting space. Remove chairs if necessary to give him a choice of seating areas and a clear path in and out of the room. Someone with low vision or blindness will face a barrier if visual aids are used; make sure the person sitting next to her is prepared to quietly describe any visuals so that the person won't feel left out.

OFF AND RUNNING

The biggest mistake a meeting organizer can make is to assume that a well-planned meeting will run itself. That's like assuming that if you peel the vegetables and cube the beef, the stew will make itself. Managing a meeting is analogous to a chef cooking a great meal: Following a recipe, you prepare the raw ingredients, set the temperatures, mix and blend the ingredients, juggle pots and pans, time everything to perfection, and finally bring the finished elements together on a plate.

Four essential actions will ensure that your meeting runs smoothly:

1   **START ON TIME.** A late start sets an unfortunate tone, signaling to participants that you are not in control and that you're not altogether respectful of their schedules.

2   **KEEP THINGS ON TRACK.** Every meeting is rife with opportunities to run off onto interesting but irrelevant tangents. Your job is to keep the proceedings focused on your agenda points. Be polite but firm. "That's an interesting point, Sarah, and I'd like to discuss it with you after the meeting. But right now, I want to stay with the problem of . . ."

DEALING WITH PROBLEM PARTICIPANTS

Every meeting has them—the manager who is happy only when he is dominating the discussion, the department head who can't stick to the subject, the know-it-all who can't resist displays of her superior grasp of the facts, the devil's advocate who feels compelled to shoot down every new idea, the constant interrupter, the chronic latecomer. You can't change them, so you'll have to deal with them as best you can.

The Dominator, the Know-It-All, and the Devil's Advocate usually thrive in open discussions, but you can thwart them by either directing questions to others or, if necessary, politely cutting them off. You can stop the Interrupter with comments such as "Can you save that thought until the Q and A?" and "I think Mrs. Rodriguez was getting to that point. Let's let her finish." For the Shooter-Downer a simple reminder will do: "Tom, let's get the ideas on the table first and look at the pros and cons before we dismiss any possibility, no matter how out-there it is. Thanks." As for the Latecomer, she'll usually slip in and apologize later, but if she enters armed with elaborate excuses, signal her to be quiet and hope she gets your message. Some meeting leaders manage latecomers by the simple expedient of locking the door when the meeting begins.

The point is that you can't fully control everyone's bad habits. You do, however, want to make a polite but firm effort to deal directly with problem people and difficult situations in order to keep the meeting moving forward smoothly. Even if you're ultimately ineffective, your other participants will see that you recognize the problem and are willing to try to correct it within the limits of common courtesy.

3 **ENCOURAGE FULL PARTICIPATION.** Be alert to who is speaking and who isn't. Some people simply reserve their comments until they have a full grasp of the issues, and you don't want to pressure them. But others—especially junior-level employees or attendees who are new to your group—may need to be drawn into the discussion.

4 **END ON TIME.** If you can consistently accomplish this simple but elusive goal, your colleagues will be eternally grateful.

WRAPPING UP

Leave enough time near the end of the meeting for a purposeful summing up. Your wrap-up gives you the chance to delineate what has been accomplished in the meeting in an organized manner and to clarify assignments and responsibilities. It also allows you to

1   Present a basic action plan, including deadlines for assigned tasks and a future meeting date or dates

2   Address any final questions (although you don't want to open up new discussion at this point)

3   Thank special guests and participants

If the meeting has been heated or rancorous, you can also use your conclusion to smooth any ruffled feathers. Even the smallest, most casual meetings need a summing up so that the participants leave with a clear understanding of future expectations.

FOLLOWING UP

It is always smart to follow up your meeting within a day or two with a thorough recap memo or letter to all of the participants. Your memo should elaborate on the details of your summary assignments and schedules and include confirmations of any formal decisions or votes. In most cases, the memo itself is a sufficient thank-you to participants, but you will want to write formal thank-you notes to speakers, special guests, and anyone else who has contributed to the success of the event.

In addition, set aside some personal time to evaluate your meeting. Be ruthlessly honest. Did the meeting accomplish what you wanted? If not, why not? Was the agenda flawed? Did you lose control at any point? Did you invite the right people for your purpose? Was your organization too rigid or too loose? Did a problem crop up that you should have anticipated but didn't?

Too many managers become wedded to a meeting format, instead of learning from their mistakes. But by analyzing each meeting you hold—good, bad, or indifferent—and doing it while the particulars are still fresh in your memory, you open the door to constant improvement.

ATTENDING A MEETING

People attending a business meeting have their own responsibilities for helping to ensure that the meeting is a success. Your first mannerly step is to respond to all meeting invitations, whether your attendance is compulsory or not. As soon as you receive a notice for a meeting, check your schedule to make sure there's no conflict and then make your reply. Even if your invitation doesn't specifically ask for a response, do it; a quick phone call will usually suffice. If you're unable to attend an optional meeting, it's a good idea to explain why, particularly if you have a business-related conflict. This tells the person calling the meeting that your absence is justified; it may also prompt him or her to reschedule the meeting at a more convenient time.

IF YOU'RE ATTENDING

If you're able to go to the meeting, prepare in advance. Study the agenda and determine what you can do to be ready to join in the discussion. If you don't receive an agenda or your invitation doesn't include particulars of the meeting, ask the meeting organizer what you can do to prepare and whether there are any materials you should bring. To avoid implying the organizer has been remiss by not including an agenda, couch your questions in terms of seeking direction: "I just want to be sure that I'm up to speed for the meeting."

YOU CAN'T ATTEND?

If you can't attend a last-minute meeting, let the organizer know immediately. You may want to send a surrogate to the meeting, but always check with the meeting organizer first. Follow up on meetings you miss: Find out what happened and if you have any assigned tasks. If possible, make an effort to get a detailed report of the proceedings.

YOU'RE NOT INVITED?

Try not to interpret exclusion as an affront. It may simply be that the organizer believes your time is better spent at something else, or that decisions will be made that are above your level. If you have a close relationship with your supervisor, you may want to ask why you weren't invited; if the exclusion was a mistake, your supervisor is in the best position to correct it. But whatever the cause, take it in stride, and never try to force or wangle your way into a meeting. Being excluded is a temporary disappointment, but a reputation for manipulation and bad temper has longer-lasting consequences.

THE IMPORTANCE OF PUNCTUALITY

Arrive on time—not too early, and certainly not late. First, the early bird: Most meeting specialists warn strongly against arriving more than a few minutes early. The person holding the meeting may be involved in last-minute preparations or may be trying to clear away other business before the meeting's start, and he or she will feel compelled to stop and greet early arrivals.

COMING IN LATE

Arriving late is sometimes unavoidable, whether the meeting is in-house or elsewhere. If you know you're going to be tardy, tell the meeting organizer as soon as you can; he or she may want to adjust the agenda if your participation is needed at a certain point. With advance notice, the organizer can also save a chair for you in a spot least likely to cause distraction. If you're delayed on the way to a meeting, try to call ahead. If you can't call, then do everything possible to get there as quickly as you can.

When entering a meeting in progress, be as unobtrusive as possible. Walk in, apologize briefly without interrupting anyone (save your excuses until after the meeting is ended), and take your seat. It helps to have everything you need, such as pen and pad, at hand when you enter the room. Above all, don't disturb the meeting by rattling papers, snapping a briefcase open and shut, shedding a coat or jacket, getting coffee, or whispering to your neighbors. Use your printed agenda to determine what is going on.

If a formal presentation is in progress when you arrive, you may want to delay your entrance until there is a natural break and you can slip inside the meeting room. Late arrivals are the bane of speakers because they inevitably distract the audience and break the flow of the presentation.

OTHER TIMING ISSUES

Even the best-planned meetings can run overtime, so it's wise to pad your schedule a bit to accommodate late endings. Allow an extra twenty or thirty minutes to cover most situations, and don't make appointments based on the exact end time on the agenda.

If you must leave a meeting early or right on schedule, tell the leader in advance. Seating can be arranged so that you can depart without disturbing others.

THE BRAINSTORMING SESSION

Many companies have meetings to brainstorm ideas, and these lively sessions have an etiquette all their own. The meetings can range from four people wheeling extra chairs into someone's office to three-day, off-site meetings where groups keep to a tight schedule and then either record or make presentations of ideas.

Some things to remember:

- The notion that "nothing is off-limits" applies to ideas, not manners. Although brainstorming is blissfully free-form, talking over one another and interrupting will most likely neither contribute to the freshness of the concepts nor spark any new ones. If you're bursting to get an idea out, jot it down on paper and wait until there's an opening to speak.

- Don't shoot other people's ideas down with "We've tried that before." Also, never disparage an idea, no matter how bizarre it may be. Remember that brainstorming is the forum for off-the-wall concepts that will eventually be reshaped into marketable ones. If, however, someone's idea is so ill-conceived that it's ludicrous, don't say so flatly. When you point out its shortcomings, start with the positive things about it and then come up with ways it could be made stronger.

- If a group has to work individually at a communal table to get their ideas on paper or disk for a presentation, keep distractions to a minimum. Bringing in food (especially the crunchy kind) can not only affect other people's concentration, but also drive them up the wall.

- If your writing skills are strong and you know someone else's aren't, offer to look over their work, but only if they've made noises about how "I can't do this! I'm an engineer, not a writer!"

A note to brainstorm leaders. If the meeting is off-site and the word processing equipment is different from that at work, arrange for tech-support people to be on the premises.

THE POLITICS OF SEATING

If seating isn't assigned, let the key participants take their places first and then fill in around them. Don't head for the top or bottom of a conference table unless you're the leader. A good organizer will tell everyone where to sit, but if the seating order is unclear, ask the leader where he or she would like you to be. Even if you're an important guest (the client rep at a business presentation, for instance), check with the meeting leader about seating; there may be a reason, such as vision line, to seat you somewhere other than the head of the table. In a seminar or open seating arrangement, find a place where you can see and hear clearly, and leave the bad seats to the latecomers.

DO YOUR PART

Whether the organizational skills of the meeting manager are brilliant or nonexistent, you have not been invited to a meeting to sit on your hands. Your participation is needed regardless. When you've prepared well and followed the proceedings attentively, participating should be no problem. If your opinion is requested, give it. If you have an idea, state it. If you need more information or clarification, ask for it.

There are times, of course, to remain quiet. Example: Your department is making a new business pitch to a prospective client. Although the mood of the meeting is as folksy and casual as a country hoedown, every step has been carefully choreographed and rehearsed. You and the other members of your team have been assigned specific roles in the presentation. This is not the occasion to speak out of turn or propose an untested idea.

Most meetings, however, get their energy from full participation; you don't want to be the only dud match in the box.

AVOID INTERRUPTIONS

Leave behind your pager, cell phone, watch with timer, and anything else that tends to go off noisily and unexpectedly. (Another hint is to eat something before a meeting to avoid a grumbling stomach.) If you have an assistant, inform him or her (or the office receptionist if necessary) that you will be in a meeting until such-and-such time and under what circumstances, if any, you are to be disturbed.

AT MEETING'S END

Wait until the meeting is over to gather your things; then leave. Naturally, you'll want to thank the leader politely, but unless a post-meeting event has been scheduled, it's best to depart promptly. You have other business to attend to, and so does everyone else. If there has been a guest speaker and you want to have a word with him or her, be extremely conscious of the person's time constraints. If you have questions that weren't answered during a presentation, it's preferable to write any speakers, telling them where and when you met and asking for a response at their convenience.

WHAT'S NEXT?

For participants, following up a meeting generally means doing what you were assigned to do. You may need to clarify assignments with the meeting leader, although you should receive a post-meeting confirmation or summary memo. Thank-you notes are not appropriate for the majority of meetings, but it's always nice to compliment the meeting organizer at the first opportunity. Thank-you notes or letters may be written for large conferences, seminars, and formal meetings that involve social activities, as well as for some informal meetings, such as lunch at the invitation of a client.

IF YOU'RE A GUEST SPEAKER

Should you ever be called on to speak at a meeting, you won't necessarily be taking part in the meeting itself but imparting your wisdom from a podium. Unless you're an old hand at public speaking, you'll have to learn that there's more to the assignment than the content of your speech, regardless of the size of the meeting you're asked to address.

First of all, you must understand the assignment thoroughly. What is the subject? Are you the only speaker or one of several? Are there particular issues you need to address? Are there problems or situations you should be aware of? (Your surefire joke about the CEO on his deathbed will not go down well if your host business has just lost its beloved president.)

There's a story about a well-known chef who was invited (and handsomely paid) to address the spring luncheon of a prominent Jewish women's organization. He duly spoke to the group, delivering a fulsome presentation on the planning of Easter activities and preparation of the perfect Easter ham! This is an extreme example of poor preparation, but it illustrates some of the common pitfalls of public speaking.

ELECTRONIC MEETINGS

Teleconferences and videoconferences are one of the small miracles of our age. They allow real-time voice-to-voice or face-to-face communication between people in multiple locations and time zones. But to make the most of electronic conferencing requires some forethought.

First, timing and notification are critical. Be alert to time differences when planning the conference. Three in the afternoon may be perfect for you, but not for your colleague in London, where it is ten at night. Be sure that everybody who will participate in the call has been notified and their availability confirmed. If specific materials are needed, send them early and confirm that they've been received. Check your conferencing equipment in advance; if you are uncomfortable with the technology, you may want to book an off-site location where knowledgeable folks can manage the conference for you. Also, be prepared for the worst: Have a backup plan ready for when your lines go dead in the middle of the meeting or you lose one of your parties. It's a good idea to have a second phone line ready so you can fall back on old-fashioned dialing and talking if necessary.

Also, long-distance conferencing can be expensive, so have an agenda and stick to it. Try to focus on a single topic or issue; an electronic meeting is generally not the best venue for brainstorming sessions or freewheeling discussion. If you are videoconferencing with large display screens, visual aids can be very effective—but don't expect your colleague with the standard computer screen to be able to decipher complex growth charts held up to the camera. Finally, end your meeting on time and avoid extended good-byes. (See also "Using a Speakerphone," page 224.)

GETTING THINGS STRAIGHT

A speaker should always research the inviting group and the location of the event: Who will comprise the audience? How many? What are their interests? What are the unique characteristics of the business or organization and its location? An attentive speaker can win friends and influence people by customizing even a canned speech with local references.

At the same time, you should provide all necessary information to the organizers. What will you need for your presentation? Equipment such as easels and projection screens? Also relay any other special requirements such as transportation or dietary needs. Once prepared, proceed:

- **APPRECIATE THE AGENDA.** Arrive on time, stick to the program, and don't run over your allotted time. Clarify in advance whether your presentation is to include a question-and-answer session. Be alert to time cues from the organizer.

- **MEET AND GREET.** Plan to arrive early if you can. Check out the environment. Get a sense of the audience and mingle if possible. Speakers can learn a great deal from a relatively few minutes of pre-event chitchat with some of the audience members.

- **BE GRACIOUS.** When something goes awry—a glitch in the microphone or a last-minute change of room—don't take it as a personal insult.

- **SAY THANKS.** Highly paid speakers are sometimes all too aware that they are not speaking from the goodness of their hearts. But all speakers should be grateful for the opportunity and the platform to express themselves. Thank-you notes to organizers are a must.

10 | *Telecommuting and the Home Office*

Working at home: What a great concept. Whether you're self-employed or you telecommute instead of going into your office every day, toiling out of a home office has real benefits. Not having to commute is a big one. Being more independent and in charge is another.

Whether you work for yourself or someone else, however, you are responsible for getting your work done. Goof off, and it will catch up with you: Either you'll stop getting a paycheck from your employer or your own checking account will quickly dry up.

Success, in other words, depends very much on your own initiative. Fortunately, there are a number of things you can do to help motivate yourself and stay focused on the job at hand.

SETTING YOUR PARAMETERS

For many home-based workers, the chief advantage of the home office is that it lets them achieve a more equitable balance between work and family. The key word here is *balance.* One of your most difficult tasks will be to convince loved ones that you really are working. Unless you lay down specific ground rules and communicate these clearly, you will defeat the purpose of working at home. The same goes for friends and neighbors, who require a special set of considerations. You'll want to make things run as smoothly in your relations with them as you do with your business associates.

When you explain your working rules to family and friends, be neither apologetic nor mealymouthed. Even the most considerate family and friends may suffer from the common misconceptions about home-based work. Make it clear that you are earning your livelihood, not indulging in a hobby.

DON'T CUT YOURSELF OFF FROM...

...FORMER EMPLOYERS

Just because you're on your own now, don't overlook your old employers. Assuming that you left your former jobs in good graces, past employers can be a gold mine of information, referrals, and actual work. Many a home-based freelancer has discovered that an old boss, who already knows your skills and capabilities, makes an excellent new client. But be aware that the relationship has changed, and that the person who was your boss is now a business peer. Aim for professional accommodation when you work for an old boss—not servility. Remember, too, that your old boss may have trouble adjusting to the new relationship, so tread carefully.

...FORMER COWORKERS

You should make an effort to keep in touch with former coworkers as well. In addition to the personal benefits of maintaining friendships, you'll find that old colleagues usually want to see your business thrive and can be valuable allies. They may be able to send opportunities your way, serve as references, and keep you informed about what's happening in the larger business community. (Be considerate, however, of their confidentiality, and don't expect "insider" information that is proprietary.)

There is one serious mistake that home-based workers tend to make in the early phase of going it alone: Unused to the solitude, they may become excessively dependent on old office friends. It is fine to lunch with or call your colleagues occasionally; it's rude (and more than a bit desperate) to call or e-mail daily. You don't want to transform yourself from friend to pest.

"OH, THOSE KIDS!"

Just as children have different needs at different ages, they also have different levels of understanding. Whatever your children's ages, they will need constant reminders of your rules. Think of home-office education like sex education—provide the information appropriate to the child's age, repeat it often, and update it when needed. A three-year-old will understand that Daddy is working; a seven-year-old may be ready for a definition of "breadwinner" and a lesson in family economics; a teenager will probably require serious discussion about the importance of advance scheduling for school activities or trips to the mall.

Here are some guidelines for helping you and your children adapt to a home-based work situation. Ask other family members to reinforce any rules you lay down. Spouses, grandparents, older siblings—many adults serve as models of behavior for children. When the other adults in the family show support for your work and respect for your rules, your kids will probably follow suit.

- **MAKE A SCHEDULE.** Since you are no longer on a strict nine-to-five schedule, you can arrange your busy times to suit your family's needs. But being flexible doesn't mean being totally free-form; you need structure in your workday. This means, for example, that your child-care arrangements may not be too different from the days when you left for the office, especially when caring for preschool children. If two parents work at home, try to schedule work hours so that family responsibilities can be alternated. Make it absolutely clear that your work hours must be honored.

- **BE HONEST.** Don't make promises to children that may not be kept. Spurred by love and guilt, all working parents are quick to promise to do things "later" or "tomorrow" in order to get through the moment peacefully. Unless you're certain you can keep your word, however, resist the temptation. Don't, for example, promise to attend the school play when you have an important deadline on the same day. Children will be disappointed when you must say no. But they will be resentful when you say yes and then fail to meet your commitment.

KNOWING WHEN TO STOP

Long hours are not a reliable measure of productivity, so it's important to know when to stop. If you are working at home in order to see more of your family, don't stay cooped up in your home office all hours of the day and night. Even if you live alone, you still need time for yourself. The old saying that "all work and no play makes Jack a dull boy" applies to today's home-based workers as well. You need R&R if you are to be effective at your work. There's no need to give up your regular weekly round of golf or tennis, or lunching with friends; clients will come to respect your Thursday afternoon off, knowing you'll give them more in return if you come back relaxed and fresh.

Other Tips. Don't promise yourself a future vacation while you fail to take daily breaks, don't work when you are truly sick, and don't give up on housework. (Some people report that their most creative thinking comes while washing the breakfast dishes or doing a load of laundry.)

- **DRESS THE PART.** Although one of the enticements of a home office is the end of everyday dressing for success, you may find that a business-like appearance helps younger children distinguish between work time and play time. If children see you in your bathrobe when they leave for school and you're still in your bathrobe when they return, they will logically conclude that you haven't been doing much business during the day. Without sacrificing too much of your independence, you can assemble a work "uniform" as casual as jeans and a jacket that nevertheless signals to children that your workday has begun.

- **DEFINE "EMERGENCIES."** Of course, you want your children to interrupt your work when a real problem occurs. But don't expect children instinctively to know what constitutes an emergency. When they bother you with what seems trivial, use these experiences as teaching opportunities. A fall from the swing set does require your immediate attention—but a lost Barbie or a dirty soccer uniform does not. Be patient and explain repeatedly, especially during the early stages of your business when children are making their own adjustments to your new lifestyle.

- **NO TRESPASSING.** Your office is an office, not a playroom. Until children are sufficiently responsible, they should probably not be allowed to enter your office unless you're present.

"...AND THIS IS ROVER"

Pets are not a social problem for the home-based worker unless you receive clients or customers in your home. Pet owners can be a myopic lot when it comes to their beloved Fluffy or Spot. But not everyone loves pets, and some of your important guests may have genuine aversions to them. Allergies to pets are relatively common, and your meeting will not go well if your client is sneezing and tearful. Inform any visitors of your pet situation ahead of time, and vacuum away all pet hair before they arrive. If your dog is large and likely to pounce on strangers who knock at your door, keep it leashed or penned during meetings. Even better, put the family pet outside or in the garage when clients are expected. Also, don't "introduce" your pet to clients, expecting that they'll form long-term relationships. Clients who don't enjoy being licked, pawed, or even cuddled will probably be too well-mannered to say so—and all too anxious to take their business elsewhere.

- **DO NOT TOUCH**. As a rule, do not allow children to use your business computer for homework or surfing the Internet. It's always possible they could erase an important file or put in a disk that introduces a virus with disastrous results. (Note: This is only one of the reasons why an antivirus program is essential for a home-office computer.) Also put your work supplies and materials off-limits. Just about every home-based worker with children has at least one horror story of the critical meeting notes or the client's private phone number that turned up months later, glued to an art project or crumpled in a toy box.

TO TAKE THEM ALONG?

Include your children when appropriate. It is perfectly acceptable to take your child when you make your drop-off deliveries or do your routine errands. It is unprofessional to bring your children to meetings with your clients or employer. And never expect busy secretaries to mind your kids while you are meeting with the boss.

PHONE HOURS

Make it clear to the people you do business with what hours you keep—you don't want to be on call at virtually any time of day and night. By the same token, find out from individual clients what their set business hours are. If they have none, ask them to give you a time frame for calling so that you don't risk waking them up or calling when they have something regularly scheduled.

TELEPHONE TANGLES

Perhaps the most persistent and annoying conflicts between work-at-home parents and their children involve the telephone. Young children seem to have a special radar to detect when a parent is taking an important call; it tells them exactly when to cry or yell or bang on the floor. Older children will fight you for phone time. There's really only one solution that works—install a separate business telephone line. Take business calls in your office (and remember to shut the door to keep toddlers at bay). Be sure your business number is listed in the business section of your telephone directory and not included with your residential number. It's also advisable to invest in separate answering machines or voice mail services for your household and your home office—many an important call has been missed because someone in the family erased an important message by mistake—and to record distinctly different messages for each.

In addition, it's important to teach your children good telephone etiquette early. Your stodgiest client will be mightily impressed when your youngster replies with a polite "Yes, sir" or "Thank you, ma'am." Develop a simple response for your children to use when they answer your business phone: "Hello, this is Brown's Custom Draperies. May I help you?" or "Hello, this is Richard Mazurek's office. May I help you?" Be sure they are equally polite when answering your residential line, because you never know who's calling. Your biggest challenge will probably be training your children not to scream for you; kids are kids, after all, and inclined to follow the shortest route between A (the phone receiver) and B (you). For those times when you're away from the office, older children can be taught to take careful message notes, and they will usually be flattered to be trusted with this important chore.

TIMES WILL CHANGE

Conventional wisdom holds that home-based workers have their shoulders to the wheel every waking hour of the day. This is true for some, but by no means all. Many home-based workers find that they are more productive if they work fewer hours, or that their best work comes in intensive bursts followed by extended downtimes. Others adopt a traditional nine-to-five schedule and rigorously observe their self-imposed office hours. The point is to use your time as *you* see fit; so long as you are meeting your goals, there's no need to feel guilty about working shorter hours—or to feel overly compulsive about working longer hours. Remember, however, that corporate America still tends to arrive at work at nine and leave at five or six. You can be as flexible as you like with your own time, but when doing business with others, some degree of conformity is required.

FRIENDS AND NEIGHBORS

Even the most supportive adults may find it difficult to accept the proposition that you are "at home but unavailable." People who would never arrive unannounced at your office building will unthinkingly expect you to be ready for long chats whenever they drop by your home office. You will have to be polite but firm—*very* firm. Make it clear that, except for emergencies, you are not to be disturbed between such-and-such hours. Your business phone is for business calls only. Your fax machine and photocopier are not neighborhood resources. Another suggestion: Don't answer the home phone while you're "at the office." Let the home answering machine be your secretary.

"WOULD YOU MIND . . . ?"

One problem common to home-based workers is coping with requests for free services. The graphic designer who sets up at home is suddenly a prime target for everyone who wants "a little help with the church newsletter" or "a nice-looking flyer for the yard sale."

The accountant who works at home is deluged with friends and neighbors who want him to "look over" their 1040 forms at tax time. The best (and most difficult) course is to refuse everyone; a well-intended exception or two will cause resentment among those you turned down. One effective strategy is to meet such requests with a cost estimate. Put a dollar value on your time, and most people will quickly get the message.

Charities and nonprofit organizations are notorious for soliciting free work, often while promising (but rarely delivering) paying jobs in the future. Don't let your sympathetic nature get the best of you. From a humanitarian and business standpoint, charitable work is good for you and your community—but charity clients can also be the most demanding of all, with little sympathy for your time and professional obligations. If you take an assignment from a charity, be clear from the start that you expect payment; you may be willing to work for cost, but be certain the charity understands that your first priority is your paying clientele. Set reasonable goals and deadlines; if they want your work free *and* in a rush, say no immediately.

Another option is to choose a group that you really care about and limit your "donations" to that organization. (You may want to select a charity that is not the traditional beneficiary of large donor funding.) The advantage of selecting only one or two charities is that you can get to know them well, become familiar with their needs and goals, and establish long-lasting relationships.

BE A GOOD NEIGHBOR

Placating the neighbors is an ongoing process. After all, your home office is probably in the midst of homes full of people who are grateful to be *away* from their offices. Your neighbors are in constant need of good public relations. They want honest assurances that your business will not disrupt their lives, endanger their safety, or impact their property values. Chances are, you won't please everyone in your neighborhood; but if you follow the Golden Rule and do for your neighbors as you'd like them to do for you, then you will avoid most hassles and unpleasant surprises. Be a good neighbor by doing the following:

- Inform close neighbors that you plan to have an office or open a business in your home, and keep them apprised whenever you make any changes that may affect their peace and quiet. Most people are understanding once they know what's going on.

- Consider the aesthetics of the neighborhood. Even if zoning laws permit signage, exercise good taste in the look, size, and placement of all signs and advertising.

- Control noise. Running a power saw in your workshop or cranking up the volume in your home recording studio may be acceptable at midday, but not during early-morning or evening hours.

- Hold meetings or receive customers at home during standard business hours. Traffic before 9:00 A.M. and after 5:00 P.M. should be kept to a minimum.

- Do not subject your neighbors to an endless flow of cars and deliveries. Don't expect a neighbor to sign for your deliveries on a regular basis.

- Never hog the available parking. If your neighbors depend on street parking, they will not appreciate walking for blocks because your customers have taken all the convenient spaces. If you share a driveway with neighbors, be sure their access and egress is never blocked.

PART THREE

RISING TO THE OCCASION

11 | *Pleasing the Customer*

Just as Olympians fervently compete for their trophies, so today's companies vie for a singular prize—the best customers. The most successful go to great lengths to keep their customers happy and coming back for more, and that effort to please extends to contractors and vendors as well. Without satisfied customers and suppliers, no profit-seeking organization is going to survive for long. When everybody is happy, on the other hand, the sky's the limit.

Whether your buyer is a one-time client or a regular customer, your aim in all of your dealings should always be to establish a positive, long-term relationship. You never know when that one-time customer will decide to come back again, with an even bigger order—or refer other business your way. With your regular customers, nurturing an enduring, ongoing relationship will help cement your long-term business partnership and enable you to respond quickly and effectively to any issues that may crop up in the course of doing business.

BUILDING THE BEST RELATIONSHIP

The first rule for building strong business relationships is to treat everyone with your full respect. This includes starting off on the right foot. From your very first encounter with any potential customer, make that person feel that he or she is important in your eyes by listening attentively, being prompt for all scheduled meetings and phone conversations, and carefully following through on any promises or commitments you make.

BEFORE MAKING A BUSINESS CALL

When it comes to making a good impression on a new business associate, preparation makes all the difference. You shouldn't be wasting your own time—and you certainly shouldn't waste a colleague's, client's, or prospect's time—by meeting with him or her without knowing what the session is about and what outcome you are looking for.

- Before you make the call, jot down a list of the topics and questions you need to discuss.

- Identify how long you think it might take to cover each discussion item.

- Realistically assess what actions you or the person you are calling on will take as a result of the discussion.

- Identify several potential meeting times on your calendar.

- Call or write your colleague beforehand, and spell out the topics you want to discuss and the length of time you would like to meet.

AT YOUR INITIAL MEETING

Time is money. You want to be personable when establishing a new business relationship, but it's also important to know the difference between friendly introductory conversation and time-wasting, non-business-related chatter. After a few minutes of talk, shift to the business at hand. Use your discussion points and time line as an agenda for the meeting and try to stick to this agenda. As discussion for each item wraps up, focus on the next action for that item and who is to take it. At the end of the meeting, review the full list of items discussed, along with the actions that have been decided on and who will be carrying them out.

Once the meeting comes to an end, thank the participants and then take your leave— or, if you are the host, escort your visitors to the door.

Within twenty-four hours, prepare minutes of the meeting, briefly recounting the discussions and listing the action items. Distribute these minutes to the participants and, if appropriate, to your manager as well, to keep him in the loop.

MAINTAINING THE RELATIONSHIP

If your new business contact blossoms into an ongoing, productive association, then the process of doing business will automatically give you plenty of opportunities to develop that relationship further, both at formal meetings and at more casual business meals and business-social events. Still, use consideration and your common sense in gauging how often to call or schedule a get-together with a client: You want to be a receptive and available business colleague, not a pest.

In cases where there's no active business relationship, but you still want to keep up with a potential client on the chance that future business opportunities may materialize, an occasional phone call or lunch invitation is a good way to stay in touch without going overboard. Sending holiday or birthday greetings is another excellent way of maintaining ties; some savvy businesspeople file away their contacts' birth dates on computerized calendars so that they pop up a week early, allowing time to drop a card in the mail. With such intermittent relationships, you *don't* have to send a gift—a card is plenty. Indeed, a gift in this case may even backfire and be seen as excessive.

THE HAZARDS OF BAD-MOUTHING

Although it shouldn't, it happens in every office. A couple of employees start talking about the difficult situation that just developed with a contractor or, worse still, a customer. Venting is the order of the hour: "Can you believe that jerk had the nerve to deliver that sorry excuse for a report, and then blamed us for the problem? And he calls himself a professional!" Then there's the annoying behavior variation: "She talked my ear off again today. I swear, that woman never shuts up. She's driving me nuts!"

Disparaging the offender may relieve the employees of some of their own frustration, but it has the potential to do real harm. For one, it can prejudice coworkers who overhear the ranting, possibly affecting the way they behave with the object of scorn the next time they talk or meet. Worse yet, the ranters' comments may make their way back to the customer. What happens if a phone call that was meant to be on hold actually isn't, and the customer overhears the following: "Hey, Tom, it's that cantankerous old fool you were just talking about on the phone for you"? End of relationship.

DEALING WITH AN ANGRY CUSTOMER FACE-TO-FACE

When you are face-to-face with an angry customer, your biggest challenge is to immediately guard against letting yourself get angry in response. Anger feeds on anger; if you get hot under the collar as well, you are more likely to exacerbate the situation than defuse it. Instead, let the customer vent, listen carefully to separate the anger from the problem, and then focus on the problem. Possible outcomes include the following:

- It may be possible for you to solve the problem on the spot.

- You may need to ask the customer to wait while you look into it.

- If you can't solve the situation then and there, set a time when you can get back to him, and give him your contact information so he can get in touch with you if necessary. Note: Be sure to follow up when you say you will.

- Finally, it may be a problem that you can't resolve. Get a supervisor, let her know the situation, and introduce her to the customer.

THE CLIENT AS FRIEND

One of the benefits of doing business is that you get to meet all kinds of people. Sometimes you'll meet people who end up becoming good personal friends as well as customers. Having a client who is also a close friend can help cement a long-term relationship. But each person also has to maintain a careful balance between friendship and business. Don't let your friendship get in the way of the following:

- *Deadlines.* Deadlines affect more than just the two of you. Other people's jobs and livelihoods depend on the work being done on time. Using a friendship to allow a deadline to slip is a fast way to abusing the friendship and losing it altogether.

- *Bids.* It is especially important when doing business with friends to spell out clearly what you are doing for the friend and how much it will cost. Approach this part of your work just as you would with any client. If someone is doing work for you, insist on an upfront bid in order to ensure that there is no problem when the work is done.

- *Payment.* It's amazing how fast money can come between good friends. If you're the person providing the service, it's your responsibility to prepare and send an invoice in a timely manner and to spell out the particulars, just as you would for any client. If you're the client, it's your responsibility to pay your bills in your next regular cycle of payment. Don't use your friendship as an excuse for dragging out payment.

- Finally, don't make any promises motivated by feelings of friendship that you can't keep.

HANDLING DEMANDING PEOPLE

Handling an angry or difficult customer is never pleasant, but it doesn't have to be complicated. Many books try to break down difficult people into various personality types and then tell you how to tailor your response accordingly. But all you really have to do is listen very carefully to what a customer with a complaint or a client with an attitude is saying and *how* he is saying it, while at the same time keeping your own emotions in check. Once you do this, difficult people will actually tell you how to respond. Simply set aside any general or non-constructive criticism, and focus on the customer's specific complaints—then work toward resolving them. You'll find this approach works equally well over the phone or in person.

DEALING WITH ANGRY CALLERS

Everyone gets them occasionally: calls from customers who have some sort of bone to pick. Luckily, most customers with a problem are neither out of control nor insulting. They realize that mistakes and oversights occur from time to time, and that you're not the one to blame. If you sound genuinely interested in helping them, they'll usually keep their cool.

But then there are the firecrackers with short fuses—the ones who literally explode in your ear. With these folks, it's essential that you try to keep from taking any remarks personally, even though you may in fact be under personal attack. If you reach a point where you've had enough ranting, personal abuse, or profanity, you are fully justified in saying good-bye and hanging up. If this does happen, report the incident in detail to your boss, quoting the abusive caller verbatim if possible.

Fortunately, it's rare that callers behave so badly. Most, infuriated as they may be, will calm down before you're driven to desperation. Here are some tips on getting past a customer's (or anyone's) anger as quickly as possible:

- Let the angry caller rant for a minute or two. That usually relieves the rage he has built up.

- Don't interrupt—even if he pauses or says something that sounds like the beginning of an apology, such as "I don't like to get this mad, but . . ." A comment by you at this point may set off another round of explosions.

- As the caller is venting, try to detach yourself from the emotional context of what he is saying and, almost like a scientist, objectively consider and remember the words he uses.

- When you sense the caller's anger has run its course, make a brief comment that demonstrates that you've listened closely and that you understand how important the problem is to him.

- If that goes well, introduce yourself (if you haven't already), spelling out your name and giving your title, then explain that you want to help solve the problem. This may pleasantly surprise the caller, whose fury is likely due in part to his anticipation of a hostile reaction to his plight.

- If the caller explodes again, ask for his number and say you'll call back in a couple of hours or at a specified time the next day. Use this breather to collect your thoughts and to talk to your coworkers or supervisor about how you should proceed with this tough case.

- When you've decided how to resolve the situation, always emphasize to the caller the actions you *will* take (even if they don't fully meet his demands), rather than the actions you *can't* take. Never promise to do something you can't deliver on.

- If the problem turns out to be the customer's fault—a failure to follow a basic instruction, for example—never adopt a superior tone. Doing so implies that if only he'd been smarter, he could have saved you both a lot of turmoil. Instead, patiently walk the customer through the required steps.

Sometimes, despite your best efforts and extraordinary self-control, nothing you say satisfies an angry caller, and your company loses a customer. This happens to everybody. Don't let it eat away at you, because it's not your fault.

CONTENT VERSUS TONE

Listening to a complaint from an irate customer often triggers an immediate defense mechanism, leading you to reject what the person is saying because of the *way* it's being said—not because of what it means. Don't let a person's tone of voice prevent you from getting to the gist of the matter. The problem may be real, and it may need real attention regardless of how it's presented. Even if you can't win back the irate customer, by hearing her out and actually understanding her complaint, you may prevent someone else from calling with the same problem—something that's good for business in the long run.

MAKING PROMISES

When dealing with an aggressive, angry, or puzzled customer, it is absolutely essential to tell the truth (without revealing company secrets) and to follow through on any offer or promise you make. Not to do so is almost as bad as losing your temper and yelling or slamming down the phone.

When you pick up the phone and get greeted with a tirade about a defective product, the caller obviously wants action immediately. If you can promise to send her a replacement, that's what she wants to hear—not some general discussion about warranties or your company's excellent quality-control procedures. (That can come later, if need be.) If you can't promise an immediate solution, stress the urgency you feel about the customer's problem by responding "I'll look into it immediately" or "I'll ask my supervisor the minute I hang up" or "I'll ask our technical staff what could have happened."

If you promise you'll ask someone else about the customer's problem, go ahead and ask that person as soon as possible. If you have to explain why you can't do what the customer wants done, be sure your facts are accurate. If you offer to call back and report what you've found out, before ending the call ask the customer for the best time to reach her—then be sure to phone at the appointed time. A particularly effective tactic, and good manners to boot, is to tell an irate customer that if, for some unforeseen reason, you can't call her back at the specified time, she should call you collect or at an 800 number. Though this courteous act may seem as if it's letting you in for trouble you could avoid, it is the kind of graciousness you would expect from a friend in the business—and that's exactly what an irate customer is afraid she doesn't have.

DON'T TAKE IT PERSONALLY

At a busy passport office in a major Southern city, the U.S. government has decided that one employee is enough. There are times when the waiting line snakes out of the cavernous main hall and spills into the long main corridor of the vast old post office building. "Disgruntled" is a mild description of most of the waiting people. Meanwhile, behind the passport window, Polly, the one employee, is also responsible for answering telephone inquiries—and the line never stops ringing. Yet when she answers the phone, she is unfailingly courteous and helpful. Incredibly, she maintains the same calm pleasantness when passport applicants, some of whom are ready to explode, finally reach her window.

How does she do it? "I keep telling myself not to take it personally," Polly explains. "Being the only one here is not my fault. It's not under my control. I think these people have a right to be mad, but all I can do is be as quick, careful, and helpful as I can." Once in a while, after standing in line for an hour or more, a passport applicant gets to her window so hot under the collar he can't stop venting. When that happens, Polly says, "I ask them to go talk to my supervisor down the hall and tell him that I need help. That often makes people feel better, though it really doesn't get me any more help. I'm lucky because my supervisor *does* have a nice manner."

This harried but even-tempered worker's experience illustrates the two most important rules of dealing with unhappy customers or clients—in fact, almost any peeved person:

- Don't ever take a customer's anger or criticism personally. If you do, you will probably lash back in kind—and that makes everything worse.
- Always remember that you are not alone—you have coworkers and supervisors you can turn to for support when you need it.

WHEN YOUR COMPANY IS IN THE WRONG

Often, a complaining customer will have a legitimate gripe regarding a slipup on the part of your own organization. There are two steps involved in effectively accepting responsibility for a problem or error. The first is to apologize to the person. "Mr. Smith, I'm really sorry that the person you were talking to didn't follow through. I can understand your frustration fully. I'm going to . . ." The second step is to offer whatever solution or action you feel you're capable of pursuing. This solution may simply be a promise to look into the matter and then get back to the person. You don't have to admit liability or culpability—but you *do* need to show the person that you're willing to pursue the matter and to try to find a resolution that will be satisfactory to everyone.

DEALING WITH CONTRACTORS AND VENDORS

The importance of treating customers with respect goes without saying. Some firms, however, make the mistake of turning around and treating their contractors and vendors as if they were lower down in the pecking order. In view of the fact that your contractors and vendors can make or break your relationships with your customers, giving them anything less than the same consideration you would show to a customer or client is a serious blunder for the smart businessperson—as well as bad etiquette.

SIX STEPS FOR KEEPING CONTRACTORS HAPPY

Treating your contractors well can pay major dividends, especially when you need their extra effort on a project. Here are six simple steps you can take to ensure extra service from any contractors with whom you do business:

1 Treat the contractor courteously at all times.

2 Be reasonable with deadlines. Don't ask for the impossible. (When you do ask for the impossible, make sure the contractor knows how grateful you are for the extra effort he or she is giving you.)

3 Don't ask for a rush job when you don't need it.

4 Let the contractor know when the job isn't time sensitive.

5 Pay promptly.

6 If you ask for a favor, be ready to return the favor in the future.

The business card...

- Invites a new bu... ...ouch with you
- Defines your po... ...Vice-President, Sales)
- Provides a numb... ...address, telephone, fax, e-mail address, and som... ...ne number and alternate phone numbers for you...

The smart bus... ...without at least a few cards in a jacket pocket—and the new... ...You never know when you might need a card (at a dinner in... ...xt to someone in a baseball stadium's bleachers), and they s... ...when you present them. Stationery and department stores sell... ...vent smudging and creasing.

How to hand out...

- If you're reasonably... ...eone in the future, ask for a business card and gi... ...e one exception is when you encounter a top exec... ...if such a senior person wants your card, or wants y... ...so.
- When given a card, d... ...o your pocket. Take a moment to look at it, perhaps... ...slip it into your wallet or date book.
- Offer cards one to a pe... ...fistful, as if you were trying to flood the market wit... ...itle.
- Offering your card priv... ...t is perfectly fine—but suggest holding off on d... ...her day. *Don't* pop out your card in the middle of a... ...ith business; if you want to present one, wait until y...

MEETING DEADLINES

Of course, there may be times when you have to hold a contractor's or vendor's feet to the fire in order to meet your obligations to your own customers. In particular, missed deadlines and ignored delivery dates can bring a company to its knees—and lose you a customer in a New York minute. If the holdup is internal, you can apply several kinds of pressure to the tardy individual or group, from gentle nagging and prodding (don't be afraid to ruffle feathers, the stakes are too high), to a company's ultimate weapon—the threat of firing. If you are a manager, you may also be able to reallocate people and other resources to get the job done. (See Chapter 8, "The Smart Manager," page 99.)

With an outside contractor or vendor, you have less control—and all the more reason to be extremely alert to deadline slippage. As you do with an internal project, set a schedule up front with deadlines that must be met. Have everyone concerned buy into and sign off on the schedule. A paper trail is essential so that nobody down the line can claim they "weren't consulted" or "weren't informed" about a deadline. (It's also a good idea to insert stiff penalty clauses into all contracts, though these can be difficult to enforce—and may be small consolation if the project fails to meet its final deadline.)

A good manager is sufficiently on top of things to know when a contractor's work is falling behind. At the first sign of danger, you should meet with the project team and ask what it needs to get back on schedule. At this point, you betray no lack of confidence that the project will go smoothly after a few minor adjustments. In fact, let it be perfectly clear that there is simply no alternative—because, you remind the group, "everybody here knows the dire consequences of not bringing this project in on time."

At the same time, if deadline problems still seem to be cropping up, be doubly sure that you are holding up your end of the bargain. Ask yourself whether you and your subordinates are meeting all of your own deadlines and getting all necessary materials or information to your contractors in a timely and effective way.

SOFT SPEECH, BIG STICK

As long as the contractor demonstrates the ability to meet the schedule (or get back on it quickly if there is a slipup), you can be Mr. Nice Guy. But remember Teddy Roosevelt's remark about speaking softly and carrying a big stick. Your big stick is the schedule and any upcoming payments linked to it. No matter how pleased you are with the creativity of the team and the quality of its work, always keep the schedule at the forefront of discussions. Not-so-subtle remarks like this are not out of line: "I'm very pleased with progress so far, Mr. Henry. I see we have a delivery of prototypes due nine days from today, on the fifteenth, and a review session on the twenty-second. I'm assuming you have no problem with those dates. We're very tight on this one, as you know."

If, despite all your watchfulness, a critical deadline is missed, don't make the often fatal mistake of trying to keep it a secret between you and your contractor. You should tell your direct superior, and if he or she agrees, you should bring in the lawyers. Keeping quiet about a lagging project could cost your company millions, and cost you your job.

12 | *Business Gifts*

The giving of gifts is a time-honored and thoughtful way of tending to business relationships. Whether the exchange takes place with an outside client or associate or within your own firm, a thoughtful present to mark a holiday or some other occasion can be the perfect way to tell a colleague, "Our relationship is important to me." But gift-giving has its risks as well: If you choose a present that's inappropriate, or too personal, or in the wrong price range, even the best of intentions can quickly backfire. This is a time when the use of careful consideration and tact becomes especially important.

GIFTS TO OUTSIDERS

Gifts from the company or its individual senior employees run the gamut from standard holiday gifts sent to customers and clients to more individualized gifts thanking business associates for a favor or entertainment. Gifts may also be sent to congratulate a client on a promotion or an award, or to express sympathy for an illness or a death.

FROM THE COMPANY
Clients and customers are the usual recipients of gifts sent by the company as a whole. These may be annual holiday presents, or tokens of appreciation as varied as coffee mugs, appointment calendars, paperweights, pen and pencil sets, T-shirts, and umbrellas. If gifts of this kind are going to bear the company logo, they should be of a certain standard—well made and in tasteful colors, with the logo understated enough not to look like an advertisement.

Some companies prefer to show appreciation at holiday time by giving a donation in the recipient's name. Charitable gifts are a perfect example of a win-win situation: The recipient is glad to be recognized, the company giving the gift makes its appreciation known, and both companies are helping society at large—showing themselves to be good corporate citizens. Corporate giving also engenders pride in the company and sets an example for employees.

FROM INDIVIDUALS TO CUSTOMERS AND CLIENTS

Individuals in the company who give gifts to outsiders are usually at the executive to mid-manager level. If this includes you, it goes without saying that you must abide by company policy and follow company traditions. Some firms forbid *any* corporate gift-giving. If your company does allow exchanges with clients, you should still make sure your gifts don't seem too stingy or expensive compared with those given by your colleagues, and that the gift doesn't exceed the financial limits set by either your own company or the recipient's. Many businesses don't allow employees to accept anything costing more than $25. When in doubt, check with your intended recipient's human resources department; sending a gift to a client who's unable to keep it is awkward for both giver and receiver. (See also "Accepting and Declining Gifts," pages 150–151.)

Finally, never give a gift of any sort to an outside business associate who is either currently involved in a bidding process with your firm or receiving a bid from you or your company—no matter what time of year it might be. Also, avoid giving a gift in any situation in which the gift might embarrass the recipient or risk a rebuke from his or her employer.

GIFTS FROM OUTSIDE

Rather than setting a ceiling for the cost of gifts received, some companies have a policy that any gifts costing more than $25 must be disclosed to management. This is a way of keeping tabs on what's coming in from outside and seeing to it that everything stays aboveboard.

Most companies allow employees to receive token gifts from customers and clients because sending them back could insult the giver, especially during the holidays. Some businesses also require that any foodstuffs received from outside be divided up and shared; this is because the usual recipients of such gifts tend to be those employees who have the advantage of dealing face-to-face with customers—whereas the people who work behind the scenes often go unrewarded.

EXCHANGING GIFTS WITH COWORKERS

Holiday gift-giving is such a long-standing tradition in some workplaces that it can't be ignored. To ease the financial strain of providing every coworker with a gift, many companies have a holiday grab bag or Secret Santa system that ensures everyone gives and receives one gift, with expenditures limited (usually to around $10). Just be sure to abide by the spending limits. It is fine to give humorous (but not off-color) gifts to coworkers at holiday time, and homemade gifts are a thoughtful and frugal way to spread good cheer.

If you decide on your own to give gifts to colleagues you're close to, be sure to give gifts to selected individuals in private so that no one's feelings are hurt. Something to brighten up his or her workspace is usually the best choice. Tailor gifts to the individual: You probably know what types of ornaments or gadgets would make someone's office more pleasant. (See also "Accepting and Declining Gifts," pages 150–151; "'Thanks!'" page 152.)

GIFTS FOR BOSSES: YES OR NO?

Don't give a gift to your supervisor that's just from you. Other employees may resent what they see as your effort to suck up to the boss. Also, jealousy may quickly spread if your gift is twice as expensive as another employee's gift. The best solution is for the employees to get together and give a gift jointly to their supervisor. A group gift lacks the hint of favor-currying that a personal gift may have.

A GIFT FOR YOUR ASSISTANT

If you're a manager in a large office, the company may provide annual holiday gifts for employees, but you may also want to reward your secretary or assistant yourself. The gift choice depends on his or her length of service: If it is less than five years, a gift costing $25 is sufficient; with longer-term assistants, you may want to be a little more generous.

The number one rule for employer-to-assistant gifts, be they for holidays or for birthdays, is to make sure they're not too personal. Perfume, lingerie, and jewelry are all out of bounds. That *doesn't* mean picking the most impersonal item you can find, however. Always consider your assistant's likes and interests in choosing what to give him or her. Below are a few possibilities.

TIME ON JOB	GIFT SUGGESTIONS
Under 5 years	Books, CDs, personal organizers, fruit baskets
5 to 10 years	Movie or theater tickets, gift certificates (furniture, home, garden, or appliance stores)
More than 10 years	Spa getaway, leather briefcase

GIFT CHOICES

Whether you're giving to a coworker or a business associate from outside, your choice of gift depends on the occasion, your relationship to the recipient, and your position in the company. Whether you know the recipient well or not, keep the gift professional. Select a gift that can be used in the workplace—perhaps a reference book, a nice calendar, a pen and pencil set, or a picture frame.

BUSINESS GIFT IDEAS

There are two key rules in picking out a business gift: Don't make it too personal, and don't buy something that's inappropriately expensive. Also, be aware of any price limits that have been set by your firm or the recipient's company. Many organizations have a $25 cap on gifts—which is also the maximum amount you're allowed to deduct on your taxes for an individual business gift. If there are no limits, you can appropriately spend as much as $50 to $100 if you wish. Anything more expensive than that should be purchased as a group gift.

Gifts that are appropriate for business colleagues include the following:

ITEMS FOR THE OFFICE

Attractive wall calendar

Daily calendar featuring a favorite sport, travel destination, or comic strip character

Paperweight

Pen and pencil set

Desk caddy

Dictionary, thesaurus, or other reference book

Picture frame

Date book

Letter opener

Leather tablet holder

Bookends (leather or otherwise)

Plant (choose one that doesn't need much light or maintenance)

Magazine rack

Framed poster of an artwork or featuring a favorite sport or activity

TRAVEL ITEMS

Folding umbrella (a high-quality one)

Tote bag

Pocket calculator (to calculate exchange rates)

Leather passport holder

Travel clock

Watch that shows global time zones

Foreign dictionary (paperback, for easy portability)

Book listing holidays around the world

Pre-printed luggage tags

Folding cosmetic or toilet kit

Shoe bags

Elastic resistance bands or other portable fitness equipment

GENERAL ITEMS

Leather business-card case

Briefcase (for celebratory occasion—
should be a group gift)

CD player (again, should be given by
a group)

CD(s) by favorite musician or group

Job- or hobby-oriented magazine
subscription

Fruit basket

Pin, tie clasp, or cuff links (for
colleagues you're especially
close to)

Computer case

Movie or theater tickets

Gift certificate to a favorite restaurant

Tickets to a sporting event

Business-related book

Book on history or travel, or a special
interest or hobby

Coffee-table book on a favorite sport,
activity, or travel destination

Golf or tennis balls

Cooking utensils

Gourmet food or fruit basket (check
on recipient's food preferences
before selecting)

Subscription to a "food of the month"
club (again, check on preferences
first)

Flowers and vase (for a special
occasion such as an engagement
announcement)

Engraved paperweight, pen, or
pocketknife

TEMPORARY GIFTS

Flowers, foodstuffs, candy, and beverages fall into the temporary, or perishable, gift category. These are appropriate for most occasions—but especially when a more enduring gift could become a lasting reminder of an illness, a hospitalization, or the death of a family member.

■ FLOWERS. A great all-purpose gift, flowers can be sent to anyone at any time, thanks to credit cards, teleflorists, and the Internet. You can also pair cut flowers with another gift (say, a vase or a mug) or attach theater tickets or a gift certificate to the arrangement. But don't choose flowers without thinking: A classic spring arrangement is appropriate no matter what, but a delivery of long-stemmed roses will imply romantic sentiments. Similarly, when sending flowers internationally, take care to learn about local customs so that you don't choose flowers with the wrong connotation. At any time, consider the occasion and circumstances before choosing what flowers to send:

□ For an office mate, choose either an arrangement or a potted plant.

□ A get-well card is usually a sufficient gesture when someone is ill, unless you have a close relationship with the person. If you choose to send flowers or a potted plant to someone who is hospitalized, check with the hospital first to make sure they are allowed.

- □ When sending a plant, pick one that's easy to care for; the last thing the patient or worried family members need is a failing plant that needs reviving.

- □ For a funeral, check the obituary to find out whether flowers are desired and to which funeral home they are to be sent.

- **FOOD.** This is one gift that can be shared with others and, with a little research, can be personalized. Find out from the recipient's assistant or spouse if there are any particular favorites; at the same time, make sure the person has no food allergies. If time isn't a consideration, scan catalogs and the backs of magazines for mail-order firms, which offer everything from prime steaks to out-of-season fruits, specialty cakes, and smoked salmon or trout. Or you can keep things economical and impart a special touch by preparing the food yourself—your prized recipe for cheese sticks or brownies, perhaps, or a basket of exotic fruits—and packaging it attractively.

- **WINE AND LIQUOR.** Avoid giving wine or liquor as a business gift. There are plenty of other gifts to choose from without the downside of giving alcohol and potentially insulting or sending the wrong message to the recipient.

MARKING MILESTONES

Your business associates from both outside and inside the office may live in different worlds, but all share life's major milestones. Acknowledging birthdays, weddings, and other events shows you respect someone's life outside of work. You're not expected to give a gift for every significant day in every client's or colleague's life, of course, but some occasions call for at least a card. While chipping in for a group gift is perfectly fine, you might also want to send a separate card to people to whom you are especially close.

- **A BIRTHDAY.** Though you may have ignored a colleague's or client's birthday in previous years, it's a good idea to recognize a significant one—say, forty or fifty. But note that within the office there exists a double standard for birthdays: It's appropriate for a boss to give an employee a gift, but when it's the other way around, a birthday gift might be interpreted as kissing up. Use your judgment to decide whether a simple card is the better gesture.

- **A WEDDING.** If you've received a wedding invitation from a coworker or client, send a gift, even if you don't attend. (There are exceptions to this, however, including an invitation from someone you barely know.) Then again, it may be that you know of an associate's wedding but *aren't* invited. If so, don't be offended; some people prefer to keep their work and personal lives separate. If you still want to send a gift, either do so or organize a group gift from the office or your department.

- **THE BIRTH OF A BABY.** Unless you're close to the parent(s), a group gift is the best idea. Standard gifts include baby clothing, stuffed animals, toys, picture frames, and receiving blankets—but try for some originality. A gift with a truly timeless quality is a hardback edition of a classic children's book; inscribe it with a message that will be understood by the child when he or she reaches reading (or read-to) age.

- **A DEATH.** The standard gifts of condolence when a business associate is dealing with the death of a close relative are (1) flowers with a card, (2) a donation to the deceased's favorite charity or a related medical organization, and (3) food, which gives the family one less thing to think about as they grieve. Consult the obituary to see whether it includes instructions on where to send flowers or donations. Remember that when someone is mourning the death of a family member, the most important thing is to offer condolence and support. This can be done effectively through a note or a simple verbal acknowledgment; express your sympathy and your willingness to help as soon as you hear of the person's loss.

THE ART OF PRESENTATION

Even a gift that's thoughtfully chosen, timely, and wonderful in itself can have its effect dulled by a sloppy presentation. Wrap your present carefully; if you're unable to do a professional-looking job, have it wrapped at the store or ask a proficient friend for help. Two other things to remember:

- Modesty may be an attractive quality in other situations, but never belittle a gift you are giving; be as positive as possible, emphasizing that you thought especially of the recipient when choosing it. Gifts mean more when you're proud to give them.

- Whether a gift is sent or given in person, attach a card—especially if the gift is one of many the person is receiving. Cards serve not only as an expression of your sentiments, but also as a useful reminder when thank-you notes are written. A correspondence card is ideal, but a business card can also be used. With the latter, draw a line through your printed name and write a short, personal note. A mere phrase will do: "Best wishes, Beth Landau."

ACCEPTING AND DECLINING GIFTS

When receiving a gift at the office, you may open it as soon as possible; usually, the giver will want to see your reaction and be thanked on the spot. At a shower or retirement party, the opening of presents is often a party in itself. If the occasion for giving is formal, however—a wedding or an official ceremony—gifts are generally put aside, to be opened later.

Act delighted when receiving a gift, regardless of what you actually think of it. Effusing comes naturally if you're thrilled with the gift, but not so easily when you're not. Even if the present is the last thing you wanted, thank the giver for his or her thoughtfulness, letting the actor in you mask any disappointment. Be pleasant but noncommittal: "It's so nice of you to think of me this way!" or "What an imaginative choice!" Do the same in your thank-you note, the sending of which is mandatory.

APPROPRIATE OR NOT?

Besides good taste, two things determine the appropriateness of a business gift: its cost and how personal it is. Cost is mostly an issue when giving to customers and clients, with the smell of bribery or favor-currying growing in direct proportion to expensiveness. Too-personal gifts are also out of place in business, including gifts between close colleagues that are exchanged at work. Consider carefully your relationship to the person to whom you're giving and what he or she will think appropriate. If you're unsure, it's always safer to err on the less personal side.

- Gifts that "show," such as jewelry and clothing, are less appropriate than consumable or perishable items, such as food or flowers. (There are two schools of thought about jewelry: A gift of cuff links to a man or a pin to a woman may seem fine to some people, while others say even jewelry of this kind crosses the line.)
- Tickets to an event are appropriate, but airplane tickets are not.
- Gifts of perfume, roses, or lingerie have obvious romantic overtones and should never be given in a business environment.

DECLINING GIFTS

Having to pretend a little pales in comparison to the discomfort of declining a gift, which may be necessary for either of these reasons: (1) its cost is over the limit allowed by your company or (2) it is too personal or sexually suggestive.

In the too-costly case, there is really no need for embarrassment: In effect, it is the company, not you, who is declining. A hand-written note clearly stating this is all that's needed, regardless of the giver's motivation. The note that follows is an example of one that will spare hurt feelings on the part of someone who had good intentions yet, at the same time, will also dissuade anyone who was trying to curry favor from doing so again.

> *Dear Mr. Sharpley:*
>
> *I found the carved bowl you sent delightful, but I'm afraid the rules here won't let me keep it ($30 or more at Kettle & Black, and it's automatically "return to sender"). I'm sure you understand that I really have no choice. Still, I greatly appreciate your thoughtfulness and look forward to maintaining our productive business relationship.*
>
> *Sincerely,*
> *Diana Dickson*

A gift with obvious romantic overtones is more difficult. You don't have to return a dozen long-stemmed red roses, but you could let the sender know (verbally or via a note) that while you know he meant well, sending such gifts are inappropriate in light of your professional relationship.

More serious is something sexually provocative, like lingerie. If you're given such a gift in person by a member of the opposite sex, return it on the spot, making it clear that the gift is improper: "Honestly, I don't know what you were thinking. I can't accept this, and I think it's obvious why." Then put the same statement in writing and send it. Make a copy of your note and keep it as a record in case any repercussions arise down the line; in an era when legal ramifications are an ever-present possibility, you may need evidence of your reaction.

GIFT-GIVING ABROAD

In countries outside the United States, many rules pertain to the giving of gifts, and failing to follow them is a serious breach of etiquette. One rule common to virtually all countries is to have the gift beautifully wrapped.

A sampling of customs: The Japanese give and expect gifts on numerous occasions, and the wrapping is perhaps as important as the present itself. In some Asian countries, clocks and handkerchiefs symbolize mourning and are not given as gifts. In other countries, bringing wine to a dinner party indicates that you think either that the host will not have enough or that it won't be of sufficient quality. The French, it is said, appreciate music or a book, and the fatter the book, the better; American best sellers are a good choice. In any country, it would be hard to go wrong giving a fine pen or pen and pencil set or a coffee-table picture book with an American theme.

Whether here or abroad, never give liquor to someone of the Muslim community or non-kosher food to an Orthodox Jew. Nor should you give gifts of clothing, perfume, or cosmetics, which are in poor taste almost everywhere—as are corporate gifts with a logo that is less than subtle. (See also "Gifts," page 298; "Suggested Reading for Business Travelers," pages 309–310.)

"THANKS!"

When thanking someone verbally for a gift, emphasize their thoughtfulness rather than your gain. Besides the usual "I love it," praise the giver with "You were so thoughtful" or "You always think of the perfect gift."

Like the verbal thank-you, a note of thanks should be sincere and enthusiastic, and preferably sent within a day or two of receiving the gift. (Try not to let a thank-you note languish on the shelf of good intentions: A late one not only is more difficult to write, but can sound less enthusiastic.) Handwrite the note, making it short, personal, and familiar enough to sound as though you're saying it aloud. To acknowledge a gift given by an entire department, it's fine to offer a general thanks to the group, either by posting a note on the bulletin board or sending out a group e-mail message. Whatever the medium, though, make certain that your message recognizes everyone who contributed.

13 | *Business Events*

Business events can run the gamut from formal business dinners to freewheeling office parties. But no matter what form an event may take, the general purpose remains the same: To connect and spend time with your colleagues and business associates. In order to accomplish this, you need to be able to focus all your attention on the people you're with. Being familiar with the protocol of various business affairs—whether they're held in a restaurant, a club, a private home, or your own offices—leaves you free to partake and enjoy, confident in your ability to handle any etiquette issue that comes your way.

BUSINESS MEALS

Business meals (essentially meetings with food) can take many forms, from casual to more formal. What they all have in common is a measure of sociability over and above that of an office-bound appointment. But your own behavior at business meals is every bit as important as the fellowship they foster. Remember: These are the only times when your conversational abilities, your self-possession, and your table manners are all on display at once. Bear in mind, too, that your manners reflect on the company you represent. The desire to make a good impression hardly means rehearsing your across-the-table banter or becoming a wine connoisseur. It *does* mean knowing how to use the cutlery, eating your food with civility, and conveying the sense of being at ease with those around you.

LUNCH, BREAKFAST, OR DINNER?

Obviously, the decision whether to meet over lunch, breakfast, or dinner depends mainly on which of these meals best fits the time constraints of the participants. Also, take into account what you wish to accomplish. A breakfast gathering, for example, may be ideal if the aim is a quick, straight-to-the-point meeting—while evening is undoubtedly the best time for a more leisurely paced business meal.

THE BUSINESS LUNCH

Lunch is the traditional workhorse of business meals. Because the participants have to return to the office, the meeting stays relatively short and focused. There are other advantages as well: Unlike a business dinner, lunch is faster-paced, it doesn't cut into someone's personal time, and it doesn't raise the issue of the inclusion of a spouse or partner.

The typical business lunch lasts from just over an hour to two hours, but a participant who is on a tight schedule shouldn't take this for granted. Instead, she should announce her time constraints from the start: "Before we get busy, I should tell you that I have a meeting at the office at one-thirty—bad luck, I know, but it was called at the last minute." (Note: The excuse should be real, not made up.) This not only puts the person's mind at ease, but also avoids catching her lunch mates by surprise when the time comes for her to leave.

THE BUSINESS BREAKFAST

Even a garden-variety breakfast meeting has real benefits: Many people are at their sharpest early in the morning; as with lunch, the timing of a morning meeting helps it stay short and focused; *unlike* lunch, it barely interrupts the workday, if at all; plus, breakfast is less costly than either lunch or dinner.

A business breakfast can be held at any location that is handy to both host and guest: a restaurant or coffee shop, a hotel dining room, or perhaps a private club. If it's convenient for all concerned, guests can even be invited to breakfast in the host's office. Putting out a selection of Danishes or muffins and coffee or tea requires little preparation and lends the meeting the affable touch of an away-from-the-office meal.

THE BUSINESS DINNER

Whether it takes place at a table for two or involves a large group, this most special of business meals is generally oriented toward camaraderie. Because no one has to get back to work, dinner also proceeds at a more leisurely pace. At the same time, dinner's longer time span can be an advantage when doing serious business is the goal.

Dinner is the most meaningful meal with which to mark special occasions—the retirement of a long-time employee, for instance, or the welcome of a new client into the fold. It is also the more logical choice when entertaining a business associate from out of town who is traveling with his or her spouse. On occasions such as these, business will doubtless come up as a conversational topic, but the aim is usually the strengthening of relationships, with an eye on mutual rewards to be gained in the future.

THE FORMAL CORPORATE EVENT

Some business entertainments are in a class by themselves: large formal or semiformal events put on by the company, including affairs in which the dress is black tie and no expense is spared. The purpose may be to launch a new product, to garner publicity, or simply to create goodwill among customers and clients; large parties limited to the company's employees might be held to mark an anniversary or toast the retirement of a prominent executive. In days past, most events of this kind were held in the ballroom of a hotel, at a full-service party facility known for its elegance and efficiency, or at a private club. Today, there are many more choices: A museum, a park, a historic house, a botanical garden, or a zoo are all feasible locales.

DRINKS AND HORS D'OEUVRES

At a business event with a formal dinner as its centerpiece, pre-dinner drinks and hors d'oeuvres will more than likely be served—from a bar, buffet tables of various kinds, trays carried by waiters who circulate through the room, or any combination thereof.

The Bar

If there is no true bar on the premises, bartenders will serve from a table, mixing drinks or pouring wine or beer as requested. Before ordering, be certain it's your turn; if you're in doubt, ask anyone who arrived at the bar or drinks table before you whether he or she is being served.

Waiters, too, will probably be passing through the room with trays, serving drinks. Don't make a beeline to a waiter to grab a glass or place your order; either wait patiently until the waiter comes your way or go stand in line at the drinks table or bar. Keep the drink in your left hand so that your right one is ready for handshakes. When your glass is empty, look for a sideboard or tables where used glasses and plates are deposited; if you can't find one, ask a waiter or the bartender what to do with your glass, and then thank him when he more than likely takes it.

Do not tip the bartender unless there is a cash bar, in which case you will also pay for your drinks—an arrangement that's unlikely at most formal affairs, but a possibility.

Passed-Tray Food Service

This may be the only food service, or it might be combined with self-service at a buffet table. Waiters circulate with trays of hors d'oeuvres, stopping to offer them to guests. Finger foods and bite-sized hors d'oeuvres can usually be taken in your fingers and eaten directly. The server will also have small napkins that you can take to clean your fingers.

What to do with food skewers or toothpicks after you've eaten an hors d'oeuvre? There's usually a small receptacle on the waiter's tray for used ones. If not, hold any items (including drink stirrers) until you find a wastebasket. Don't place used items on the buffet table unless you see a waste receptacle there.

Another question: How on earth do you juggle your drink and your plate and shake hands at the same time? Only with great difficulty, of course—meaning that a nod and a smile might have to substitute for a handshake. Standing close to a table could solve the problem, by giving you a place to put your plate. Another option is to limit your intake of food, thus freeing up a hand. If you suspect that you'll be hungry and tempted to spend more time eating than mingling, have a snack before the event.

The Buffet Table

Hors d'oeuvres and canapés will be set out on a buffet table, with guests picking up plates and helping themselves to both finger foods and dishes that require a fork. Take small portions, and don't return for plateful after plateful; the food at this stage of the party takes a backseat to the people around you—not the other way around.

Food Stations

Food stations are smaller tables set up in strategic locations around the room. Each holds a different kind of food—ethnic specialties, perhaps, or all-vegetarian dishes. The idea behind this arrangement is to create several shorter lines instead of one long one.

GREETINGS AND COURTESIES

As a rule, punctuality is stressed more at a business affair than at a purely social one. For a business dinner, arriving on time is not only expected—it's also the considerate and smart thing to do. Even if the event is a large reception at which guests' arrival times are fluid, it's still wise to arrive close (within ten to twenty minutes) to the time stated on the invitation.

IS THERE A RECEIVING LINE?

Because a receiving line speeds introductions, arranging one is a smart company choice for functions of more than sixty people. Guests who arrive too late and find the line disbanded must accept not only that they may not meet the host, but also that the host may never know they were present.

It's fine for guests to hold a drink while waiting in a receiving line, but they should set their glasses down before it is their turn to go through. There are usually servers with trays standing by for that purpose; if you see none, then it's imperative that you find a nearby table for disposing of your glass. Once the moment arrives, a guest shakes hands and briefly exchanges a few pleasant words with each member of the line. Be careful to avoid lengthy conversations, so as not to hold up those behind you in the line.

If the party has no receiving line, the host may appoint two or three people as introducers. Introducers make sure that every person who arrives eventually meets the host at some point during the evening. Do make it a point to locate the host on your own if necessary, so that you're able to briefly thank him or her for the hospitality.

THE ART OF MINGLING

Don't be embarrassed to introduce yourself to someone. When another person is standing alone, this ritual poses no problem (see "Introducing Yourself," page 221). Introducing yourself into a group conversation is slightly more difficult. Try to find a group that has at least one person whom you know. Approach with a smile on your face. Nod a greeting as you join the group and then, at the next small break in the conversation, introduce yourself: "Hi, I'm Jim Sanders from MNO." Remember, attendees at business functions realize that strangers will be introducing themselves, so they're likely to be open to meeting you.

What do you do if you don't know anyone in a group and you wish to join? Approach the group, but be careful not to interrupt a person in mid-sentence. Instead, wait and listen for a break or for the person to finish his or her thought. Then make eye contact with one of the group, reach out your hand, and introduce yourself: "Hi, I'm Sally Smith from LMN." Remember: At a business event people are encouraged to meet people, so it's an expected thing for a stranger to join a group.

Here are some other tips for mingling:

- Put aside any shoptalk of the critical or confidential kind. It can be tempting to relax when you're outside the office, but remember to keep your professional demeanor. A slip of the tongue can cause you problems—plus you never know who might overhear.

- Avoid any political or religious issues that you feel passionate about; save these for friends, to avoid offending a stranger who may not share your views.

- Be an attentive listener. Stand up straight and show your interest by making eye contact and occasionally paraphrasing what the other person is saying to show you understand.

- Keep your voice volume to a reasonable level, so as not to add to the din.

- Keep a close rein on drinking. Nothing has as much potential to undermine a good impression as alcohol. Even if, after a few drinks, you imagine yourself a *raconteur par excellence*, remember that a relatively small amount of alcohol is enough to loosen the tongue. You may be mortified to wake up the next morning and realize that you were, in fact, simply blabbering on. Decide ahead of time what limits to place on your drink consumption—say, one cocktail or glass of wine during the pre-dinner gathering, one glass of wine at dinner, and an after-dinner liqueur if one is served. Then do not give in and go over your limit, no matter how festive the occasion and how great the temptation.

HOW TO BE AN EXPERT AT SMALL TALK

Some people seem to be natural talkers. They approach total strangers and are immediately able to be completely at ease and conversational. How do they do it? Here are six tips to help you be a great conversationalist:

1. *Become familiar with various topics.* Read newspapers and news magazines to be knowledgeable about world and national events. Read your local paper and tune in to the local news as well, and peruse general-interest magazines and watch television news-magazine programs to keep up to speed on what's happening in entertainment and the arts. Know which sports teams are succeeding and which aren't. Make it your assignment to be a generalist and to know something about a lot of different things.

2. *Ask people their opinions.* Before you go to an event, list three or four questions you can ask at the start of a conversation. Always couch these questions in terms of asking a person for his or her opinion. Remember, people love to be asked for their views on any number of subjects.

3. *Stay away from controversial topics.* Politics, sex, and religion: Don't go there. These are potential argument-starters that can backfire on you.

4. *Know about your host(s).* If possible, learn their interests ahead of time. Do they enjoy skiing, traveling, hiking, collecting stamps? You can ask colleagues or your boss, or if the event is in your host's home or office, take note of pictures and other objects for clues.

5. *Listen. Listen. Listen.* Become a great listener by learning to focus on the person who is talking and to tune out the other distractions around you.

6. *Practice. Practice. Practice.* Try talking to people who are "safe" (that is, non-business-related) conversational partners: cabdrivers, people at the supermarket checkout counter, the package delivery person. Becoming comfortable with these folks will help you to be comfortable with strangers at company functions, when the small talk may really matter.

GREETING THE HOST

At a formal dinner you may or may not be able to spend time with your host, but at some point in the evening you must seek him out (and preferably his spouse as well) to offer your thanks for a wonderful evening; not to do so is rude. If it's impossible to thank the host—this can happen, particularly at the party's end, when he may be swamped by people trying to do the same—write a note the next day (see box, "The Thank-You Note," page 196) in which, along with your thanks, you express your regrets that you weren't able to thank him in person.

AT THE TABLE

At a large sit-down dinner, you'll often be seated with strangers—but only momentarily, since making introductions all around is essential. People seated together at a table always introduce themselves to each other as a sign of courtesy and respect, even when they expect to conduct separate conversations.

PLACE CARDS AND MENU CARDS

The presence of place cards on the table—or, alternatively, a card given to you citing your table number—means that the host has decided where you are to sit. Only the most boorish guests will alter the arrangement of the cards or switch them with those from another table as a means of getting closer to the head table or obtaining a better view.

OPEN SEATING

If no place cards are on the tables, guests may sit wherever they choose. At the same time, they should never seat themselves without asking those already at the table for permission: "Do you mind if I join you?" or "Excuse me—are these chairs taken?" (A chair tilted against the table is the traditional signal that the place is reserved, but this custom is seen less often today.) If you're given the go-ahead, introduce yourself, along with your spouse or partner, as you sit down. Shaking hands with everyone at the table isn't necessary; after the meal ends, however, a handshake is a nice parting gesture for anyone with whom you've spoken.

DINNER IS SERVED

At most formal dinners, an empty service plate—also called a charger or place plate—will be set at each diner's place from the beginning; a folded napkin may also be in the plate's center. Alternatively, a cold first course may already be set on the service plate when the diners are seated, with the napkin to the left of the forks. The only time a plate will not be set before guests is just before dessert, when a waiter clears all the dishes from the table and crumbs from the tablecloth.

Throughout the meal, the waiter will serve the food from your left side and remove your empty dishes from your right side. When your soup course is finished, the waiter will remove the soup bowl and its underplate from the service plate and replace them with a warm dinner plate or a plate already holding the main course. If a first course is followed by soup, the service plate remains until the soup course is finished.

Possible additions to the usual china, flatware, and glassware of a formal dinner are finger bowls (see "What Do You Do With a Finger Bowl?" pages 186–187) and salt cellars (see "Plates, Et Cetera," pages 197–198). The former are used if any finger foods are part of the meal. The latter, small bowls with spoons, replace salt shakers.

No matter how elaborate the table setting may be, remember that the way you treat those around you—not to mention your sparkling wit and tasteful attire—will be remembered far longer than your misuse of a fish fork. Table manners are a vital concern, but they should never be fretted over so much that your anxiety overshadows your comfort and sense of ease. (See also Chapter 14, "Table Manners: Navigating the Meal," page 175.)

MAKING TOASTS

At many large parties, toasting the guest of honor or the host with wine or champagne may be expected. Anyone considering making a toast should prepare beforehand, if only to mentally rehearse what you plan to say so as not to fumble the words. Unless your toast has been designated as the principal one of the evening, keep your remarks short and to the point. The principal toast is a small speech of sorts, and it should be composed in writing and rehearsed by the speaker in advance. A glance at your notes is acceptable, but try to speak as extemporaneously as possible.

The protocol points of toasting:

- The host is the first to toast, attracting the crowd's attention by standing and raising his or her glass; banging on a glass with a knife should be considered a measure of last resort.

- At formal occasions, the toaster stands, as do the people toasting; the person being toasted remains seated.

- The guests respond by taking a sip of their drinks—but never draining the glass. A person who doesn't drink alcohol should join in as well, toasting with a soft drink or even water.

- The person being toasted does not drink to himself.

- After the toast, the person who is being toasted rises, bows his acknowledgment, and says thank you. He may also raise his own glass to propose a toast to the host, the chef, or anyone else he sees fit to so honor.

- At private or small informal dinners, it is acceptable for everyone—toaster and toastee included—to remain seated.

IS A THANK-YOU NOTE IN ORDER?

The answer to "Should I write a note?" is that it's never wrong, but you don't always have to do it (see box, "'Thanks!'" page 152, and box, "The Thank-You Note," page 196). If the invitation was made by phone, a phoned thank-you the next day is appropriate. If the invitation was made via e-mail, then an e-mailed thank-you is appropriate. If the invitation was written, then a written thank-you note is called for. In any of these cases, it is always appropriate as a guest to write a short thank-you note to your host.

If you're the host and you've invited a prospect or major client to lunch, you may also write a short note to her, thanking her for taking the time to meet with you.

Remember, a thank-you note isn't a chore—it's an opportunity. In business, being thought of as a gracious, "with it" person sets you apart from your competition on both a personal and corporate level. A thank-you note is a quick, easy, and inexpensive way to accomplish this.

ENTERTAINING AT HOME

A more personal way to entertain is to invite people to your home. Though the purpose of a business party is primarily social, as the host you'll want to stay on your toes even more than usual. For better or worse, your spouse or partner, your home, and your entertaining style all reflect who you are. How well you carry off a social gathering is part of a larger picture. Showing your proficiency in getting the party organized, keeping it running smoothly, and staying cheerful and relaxed will inevitably strike your business associates favorably and help you stand out at the office.

INVITING GUESTS

How formal should your invitations be? This varies according to the situation: If you're inviting, say, a client who's in town for a few days, a simple phone call is sufficient. The same goes for inviting local clients or customers—although in this case you should include spouses or partners, too. Depending on the circumstances, you may also want to invite a few non-business friends, whose presence will lessen the likelihood of your company or professional field ending up as the evening's one and only topic.

A written invitation is more appropriate when inviting your boss (or others of high rank), unless the two of you have developed such a close working relationship that it would seem artificial to stand on ceremony. Inviting others with whom you work presents the special challenge of not offending those coworkers or associates who aren't invited. Either keep the invitation private or invite those who weren't on the list the last time you entertained.

Some executives and managers who entertain regularly make a ritual of inviting each staff member to their homes once a year, one at a time; others choose to throw parties with small groups; still others may prefer to invite the entire staff at once. Just remember to invite the person's spouse or partner as well.

THE SPOUSE'S ROLE

It goes without saying that when businessmen or -women entertain at home, their spouses or partners need to do their part to get things organized and make guests feel comfortable. Since there will undoubtedly be a great deal of job-related chat among people they may or may not know, spouses should appear interested and make it a point to listen and to ask questions. At the same time, they should also feel free to discuss their own professional or personal interests.

MEETING AND GREETING

Your spouse isn't expected to join you as you greet arriving guests at the door. Instead, introduce him or her as soon as the opportunity arises. (If you're cohabiting with someone but aren't married, it's up to you whether you want to inform arriving guests of your living situation. All that's necessary is a standard introduction that gives your partner's full name.) You (or your spouse or partner) should then take newly arrived guests around the room, introducing them to anyone they haven't met.

SINGLE HOSTS AND HOSTESSES

A single man or woman might consider asking a friend to act as a co-host. This makes sense because some of the guests (the business associates) will already be acquainted, whereas many of the rest (mostly wives, husbands, or dates) will not be. With two hosts sharing the duties of refilling drinks, replenishing food trays, and chatting with guests, it's less likely that spouses, dates, or unattached guests will be left standing alone and feeling awkward.

HOSTING A SIT-DOWN DINNER

Whatever cuisine or serving style you choose, there are a number of things to consider beforehand—most obviously, your available space and the tastes of your guests. While it's nice to try to accommodate invitees' idiosyncrasies and special food needs, remember that the goal is to offer enough variety in the cuisine to please everyone, without tailoring the meal to any one person's needs.

BEFORE-DINNER DRINKS

If pre-dinner drinks or cocktails are being served, plan for dinner to start about an hour later than the time specified on the invitation. If drinks are not part of the plan, you should still wait twenty to thirty minutes before serving the meal; this allows time for any late arrivals to say their hellos.

Don't forget to provide soda, juices, and mineral water for those who want to forgo alcohol. If you offer snacks or hors d'oeuvres, keep them fairly light so that they don't compete with the meal. At the same time, be sure to replenish hors d'oeuvres as necessary.

THE CALL TO DINNER

Before you call your guests to dinner, the butter and condiments should already be on the table, the water glasses filled, any candles lit, the plates warming in the oven or on a hot tray, and the wine either in a cooler beside the host or within reach of the table. Tip: Uncork the red wine thirty minutes before dinner to give it a chance to breathe. If the first course is served cold or at room temperature, it should also be set out before the guests are seated. (Note: Long-stemmed glass bowls holding shrimp cocktail or other seafood appetizers are set on underplates, with both dishes removed before the main course is served.)

When the time to eat arrives, simply say, "Dinner is ready. Shall we go in?" Suggest to guests who are holding drinks that they bring them to the table, and then lead the way into the dining room.

Plan your seating arrangement ahead of time, while you're setting the table. Either use place cards or indicate where people are to sit as you approach the dining area. (See "As You Approach the Table," page 179 and "Place Cards and Seating," page 204).

When guests are seated at two tables, it's only polite that the host sit at one table and the hostess at the other. If there are more than two tables, ask a good friend to act as a surrogate host at his or her table, seeing to it that wine is served and plates are refilled.

SERVING THE FOOD

As the host, you can either serve your guests' food onto their plates and pass them, or let the guests pass the serving bowls to one another as they serve themselves. If you choose to do the former, have the warm dinner plates stacked beside your place setting, along with the food and the necessary serving implements. When guests are seated, serve food into the first plate and hand it to the guest of honor (if any), saying "This is for you"; this lets her know not to pass it down. Give the second plate to the honored guest and ask her to pass it on. It should be passed from person to person until it reaches the person sitting opposite you. Continue serving and passing plates to your right until everyone has a plate. Then repeat the process with the people on your left until everyone is served. Finally, prepare a plate for yourself.

There are other ways to serve your guests as well. You could place dishes on a sideboard, buffet-style, and let guests serve themselves before being seated. Another option is to hire someone (a few high school or college students, for example) to serve dinner and clean up; they could also pass hors d'oeuvres before the meal.

If the meal includes two or more sauces or other condiments, it's smart to serve these in a divided dish or on a small, easily managed tray; this ensures that they are passed together and that the guests see all the choices.

When it comes time for dessert, your pièce de résistance can either be brought to the table on individual dessert plates or served from a bowl or pan that has been set by your place at the table. In the latter case, the filled dishes are then passed to the guests.

WHICH WAY IS THE FOOD PASSED?

Traditionally, food is passed counterclockwise—to the right—among diners. Practicality comes into play here, however: If someone nearby to your left asks you for an item, it's perfectly okay to take the shorter route and pass the item to your left.

SERVING WINE

The simplest way to offer wine at the dinner table is for you, as host, to do the pouring. Place the opened bottle on the table in front of you, preferably on a coaster or in a wine holder to prevent any drops from staining the tablecloth. At a small table, you may remain seated and pour for each person. At a larger table, you may need to stand and walk around the table, pouring for each guest. If you are entertaining a number of guests, a second bottle is placed at the other end of the table, with your spouse or a guest doing the pouring and refilling.

CLEARING THE TABLE

When it comes time to clear the table, never scrape or stack dishes; instead, remove them two at a time. Salt and pepper containers, salad and bread plates, condiment dishes, and unused flatware can be taken away on a serving tray. Whenever something is whisked away to the kitchen, you can save time by bringing dessert plates (with or without dessert) on the return trip.

For a larger party, you may want to arrange ahead of time for a guest who is a good friend to help you with the clearing. If other guests offer to help, implore them to stay put: "No, thank you—really." Your other guests should be just that—guests—and remain at the table.

AFTER-DINNER COFFEE

Simply have three choices ready—a pot of brewed coffee, a pot of decaffeinated coffee, and a pot of hot water with a choice of tea bags, including both herbal and regular.

AFTER-DINNER DRINKS

Offering after-dinner drinks can bring an especially cordial touch to the evening's end. If you're serving coffee, a tray holding bottles of liqueurs, brandy, and Cognac—along with the appropriate glasses—may be brought in at the same time. Then ask each guest which he or she would prefer.

PLANNING AND HOSTING A BUFFET

There are several advantages to a buffet: For one thing, it lets hosts accommodate more guests than they can during a traditional sit-down meal. In addition, guests and hosts usually have more time to visit, since the meal can be prepared in advance and guests can serve themselves.

The menu for a buffet will depend partly on whether your guests will be seated at tables or dining from their laps. If the latter, choose foods that are easy to manage with a fork alone; also, avoid dishes that are soupy.

No matter what the seating arrangements are, steer clear of foods that have to be eaten just after being taken from the oven, such as soufflés. Beyond that, use simple common sense when planning the menu. When it comes to potatoes, for example, remember that French fries get soggy over time, while stuffed potatoes do fine at room temperature. Another bit of common sense: When serving cheese, meat, or anything else that needs be sliced, do all slicing in advance so that the buffet line doesn't come to a standstill as guests take on this task themselves.

SETTING UP

When ready to set out the food, stack the plates at one end of the buffet table. Next comes the food: the main course, vegetables, salads, bread, and sauces and condiments. The napkins and utensils come at the end, so that guests don't have to juggle them while they're serving themselves their meals.

If your party is fairly large, set up two lines for people to serve their food. If the room is spacious enough, place the buffet table in the center of the room with a line on either side. Or you can set up two lines on each end of a long table. Either way, guests will be able to get their food more quickly with two buffet lines.

THE FOOD IS SERVED

When all the guests have arrived and the allotted time for drinks is over, announce that dinnertime has arrived. Your guests, who are always served before the host and hostess, should then form a line around the table, helping themselves to the buffet. When finished, everyone removes their empty plates to a designated table or sideboard, unless there is a server to pick them up.

BUFFET BEVERAGES

If possible, place beverages and glasses on a separate sideboard or nearby table. If guests are seated at tables, place water glasses on the tables and fill them before guests sit down. Wineglasses should also be at each guest's place, but should never be filled in advance. One or two opened bottles of wine can be placed on each table and poured by anyone who chooses to.

As host, you'll be more relaxed at a large informal buffet—and your guests will be appreciative—if you set up an area for drinks and suggest that everyone help themselves. When you spot someone who's engaged in a conversation and holding an empty glass, do ask if you can refill it. Try not to interrupt, however: Instead, signal the guest with a questioning look—which will most likely be responded to with a smile and a glass held out in your direction.

If iced beverages are served, stacks of coasters should be set out around the room so that sweating glasses won't leave rings on tabletops.

If coffee has been placed on the sideboard, guests may serve themselves at any time. Otherwise, the host or hostess takes a tray set with cups and saucers, a coffeepot, brewed tea, and cream and sugar into the living room to serve after dinner.

THE BOSS IS COMING?

Inviting the person to whom you answer at the office into your home doesn't have to result in the nervous hand-wringing it classically calls to mind. Today's executives and managers run the gamut from the free spirit who arrives at work in jeans to the adamant defender of tradition. You may want to invite your boss and his spouse simply to introduce them to your family, or to repay an invitation previously extended to you. If your boss—or any other guest of high rank from your company—is of the old school, keep the following four things in mind:

- If you and your boss don't socialize regularly at work, you'll probably feel more relaxed if you include a few other guests. Select people with interests similar to his.

- Don't put on airs. Act as you normally act, and entertain as you normally entertain. Don't hire special help unless you would ordinarily do so, and don't serve a hard-to-carve roast unless you know you can handle it. In other words, be yourself. Being gracious and interested will impress the boss far more than trying to outdo yourself in a way that he, more than anyone, knows you can't afford.

- If you have small children, by all means introduce them to your guests, who will surely be delighted to meet them. After a few minutes have passed, however, retire the little ones to another room. Even though your boss may be fond of children, having them underfoot for most of the party can be wearying. If possible, hire a baby-sitter to keep them entertained in another room until they're called out to bid your guests good-bye.

- If you work in the kind of highly traditional office where workers address a person of higher rank as "Mr." or "Ms.," don't suddenly switch to "Ralph" or "Rhonda"—either in the invitation or while chatting during the evening. You and your spouse should shift to using first names only once you've been asked to.

LATECOMERS

The before-dinner drinks have been quaffed and the olive pits dispatched to the wastebasket, and the first course is ready and waiting. But a guest (or guests) has yet to show up. What to do? Etiquette says that the host waits for fifteen minutes before serving dinner. That's it. Take note: Tacking on even a brief grace period shows inconsideration to the many for the sake of the few. When the latecomer finally enters the dining room, he (or she or they) should immediately apologize to the group at large for delaying the meal. If the grace period has expired and the meal has begun, the tardy one is served whatever course is being eaten at the time. If this happens to be dessert, the host sees to it that he also gets a plateful of the main course from the kitchen—past its prime though it will be. The gracious host also refrains from making sarcastic or negative comments to the latecomer.

OFFICE PARTIES

Today's office parties serve to build morale and showcase the company. Office parties, especially the informal variety, also provide employees with the chance to become better acquainted and even to forge the bonds of real friendships—an important side benefit in a time when the workplace has become the principal venue for social contacts.

INVITATIONS

Whoever in the department is in charge of the party (or, if it's a company-wide affair, the company event planner) will send a memo on paper or by e-mail to each staff member. An example: "The production department will celebrate a good year and the holidays on Friday, December 23rd, in Meeting Room C. All work stops at 3:30 P.M. sharp for cocktails and a buffet. Will you join us?" When the party is to be held in a restaurant, hotel, or club, more formal invitations may be sent—handwritten for small groups, printed for large ones.

Spouses and dates may or may not be invited. If spouses and dates are included, the party invitation should be clearly addressed to "Mr. and Mrs. Brown" or "Miss Green and Guest."

OFFICE PARTY PITFALLS

People who drink too much at office parties risk serious harm to their professional careers. Sloppiness and lack of self-control become obvious to superiors, who will think twice—or, worse, never—about giving a big drinker future responsibilities. Belligerent and unruly behavior or sexual aggressiveness can lead directly to dismissal. Even relatively benign behavior while under the influence—laughing too loudly, talking too much, acting giddy, or becoming quietly morose—will be remembered and can soil a reputation. A good host keeps a careful eye on employees during an office party; fellow employees can help, too, by watching out for the coworker who is overindulging and steering her toward the coffee or even taking her home before the situation becomes obvious.

OFFICE PARTY DRESS

At a party held after work in the workplace, both men and women can simply show up in the clothes they have worn all day. Or they may opt to change into fancier dress in anticipation of the event.

At an office party held outside the office, both men and women may choose to change from work clothes into dress clothes. Because this is a business affair, overly dressy or revealing clothing is in poor taste. It's advisable to err on the side of conservatism. If you're unsure about the proper dress, check with a colleague who has attended these off-site social events in the past or with the person who's planning the event.

OTHER OFFICE OCCASIONS

Employers and employees often throw parties when someone leaves or retires, when a coworker is going to be married or about to have a baby, or when individual achievements are to be honored. Office sports teams traditionally celebrate with postgame get-togethers. Many businesses also have regular birthday parties for workers.

Special-occasion parties may be given by the boss or by the staff; they should include the entire department and possibly any special friends of the guest of honor who work in other areas of the company. While spouses aren't necessarily included in such events, especially if the party is given within regular office hours, the spouse of the guest of honor should be invited.

These informal parties may be given in the office, a conference room, or the cafeteria. Alternatively, a lunch or dinner can be held at a nearby restaurant. A staff committee or the boss's executive assistant is usually designated to handle the details, including time, place, menu, entertainment, and gifts. Bills should be given directly to the boss if he or she is throwing the party; if the staff is hosting, the bill is split among them. (If you are the party organizer, it's a good idea to collect party funds before you begin incurring out-of-pocket expenses.)

There are several important rules to remember when planning a special-occasion party:

- Clear the event with your superior. Be certain that the scheduled date and time don't conflict with important business.

- Reserve the party space well in advance.

- Don't impose your party planning on people who are trying to work. Be considerate of your coworkers' time and job responsibilities.

- Don't overdo your party privileges; a weekly—or even a monthly—party is simply too much. So is throwing a workplace bridal shower for your coworker's sister's granddaughter.

RESTAURANTS, BARS, AND AT-HOME PARTIES

Since your coworkers may be personal friends as well, it's normal to socialize with them at lunch, after work, or at home. Letting your hair down in a social setting should be done with care. In a relaxed atmosphere—especially if alcohol is present—tongues are loosened and defenses are dropped. Don't make the mistake of believing that off-the-premises conversations are also off the record. If you pass along a rumor, take potshots at an absent coworker or boss, or reveal a workplace confidence, you can be sure that what you said will get back to the office, sometimes faster than you do.

DINING OUT WITH COWORKERS

When you have lunch or dinner out with coworkers (see also "Business Meals," page 153), the big question is generally who will pay and how much. The absolute best way to ensure fair payments is for the group to reach an agreement *before* placing any orders. Ideally, everyone in the group agrees to split the bill evenly. On the other hand, if Lucy eats like a bird and everyone else is up for the Surf 'n' Turf, ask your server to bill Lucy separately, and split everyone else's bill even-steven. If orders promise to vary significantly, request separate bills for everybody. (Or, if you are blessed with a willing mathematical genius at the table, let that person handle the bill division, and don't quarrel when he or she rounds off numbers.) Tips should be evenly divided, because everyone received the same service, but bar bills should be divided among the drinkers only.

It is inappropriate to ask a server for separate checks at the end of the meal or to invite a newcomer to dine without making it clear at the outset that the meal is Dutch treat. Be conscious of what you order compared to your companions; if you owe substantially more than they do, take the initiative by speaking up and paying the piper. If someone offers to put the whole bill on her credit card in order to save time, be sure to pay her back immediately. People tend to forget small debts, but it is rude and thoughtless to expect a generous coworker to come around with hat in hand when her credit card bill arrives. Finally, if it's the Thursday before payday and you really can't afford a meal out, politely ask your coworkers for a rain check rather than borrowing from someone who's probably as short on funds as you are.

AT THE BAR

In groups of three or more, the smart course is to agree in advance to split the total bill at the end – even though this means controlling the impulse to buy a round for everyone. When a coworker agrees to be the designated driver for your group, be eternally grateful and pay collectively for his or her iced teas, colas, and bar snacks.

AT COUNTRY CLUBS

The country club is a mainstay of business entertaining – a place where company executives invite clients or customers to enjoy an afternoon in the sun, and their guests return the favor. Country club golf courses, tennis courts, and swimming pools have been the scene of countless friendly competitions between business associates of one kind or another. Indeed, it's long been said, only partly tongue-in-cheek, that more major business decisions are made on the green than in the executive office.

The country club is also an ideal place to entertain even when no sports are involved: The setting is superb, and there is usually only one sitting at lunch and dinner, which means you can linger at your table for as long as you like. When sports are the central activity, lunch or after-game cocktails are usually on the agenda to ensure that there is ample time to talk, whether about business or life in general. Lunch may be the climax of a morning spent on the golf links or tennis court, or the prelude to an afternoon game – assuming that no more than a half day is to be devoted to the outing.

WHO PAYS FOR WHAT?

Many businesspeople simply take turns paying for everything at their respective clubs. At other times, certain customs are common when a match is taking place:

- A one-day golf or tennis tournament typically has an all-inclusive price that includes greens fees and a meal; there is an understanding that the host usually takes care of the cost.

- Clubs have varying policies for charging greens fees and cart or caddie fees to a member's account. In some cases, it is mandatory that all fees are charged to the member's account. In this instance, the polite guest will offer to take care of the tips for the caddies. (Ask the member or the caddie master what an appropriate amount is at that club.) At the time of signing in, the guest should at least offer to cover his or her greens fees. The host will probably decline the offer. The best way to reciprocate is for the guest to extend a return invitation to an event at the guest's home course or club.

- Most clubs don't allow tipping of waiters and other staff. You should, however, tip any locker-room attendants who shine shoes or bring you a drink. Parking attendants also deserve a dollar or two.

THE SPORTING GUEST

Whenever you're invited to a business associate's country club for a round of golf or a game of tennis, don't automatically accept unless you (1) know the rules of the game and (2) can play well enough not to slow others down. Being honest about your knowledge and abilities will allow the host to decide whether to suggest another sport or to limit the occasion to lunch.

If you feel perfectly secure with the sport of choice, accept with enthusiasm. On the day of the game, make a point of arriving early: Road conditions and traffic are unpredictable, and you don't want to be the person responsible for getting things off to a late start. As a token of your appreciation, you might bring a sleeve of golf balls or a can of tennis balls. You should also offer to pay your own greens and caddie fees.

AT SPECTATOR SPORTS

A host who invites a business associate to a spectator sport of any kind—tennis or hockey, baseball or basketball—should always order tickets in advance. In addition, if the budget allows, reserving a car for transport to the stadium or arena will prevent any parking problems. During the event, the host should offer to purchase all food or drinks. The guest, on the other hand, will be wise to do the following:

- Take your cues from your host. Ask him what he's wearing before you don your jeans.

- Have a beer or other alcoholic beverage only if he does.

- Whether you support the same team or not, show your support by cheering, not jeering.

- If you are rooting for different teams, don't gloat if your team prevails.

- Volunteer to buy a snack and a drink for your host and any other guests.

- Stand and cheer when appropriate, but try to avoid shouting, "Down in front!" at other spectators.

- Try your best not to leave your seat while play is going on. If you must, get up and return only when there is a break in the action.

AT MEMBERS-ONLY SOCIAL CLUBS

Members-only social clubs are places where tradition is important: They typically feature dining rooms with a first-class menu and expert staff, a lounge, a library, and various fitness facilities. Unless a private room is rented for the purpose, business is not conducted in the public areas of most of these clubs. Many even have by-laws specifying that business-entertainment reimbursements from a member's company are not allowed; all expenses, including dues, must be paid personally. While business may be discussed, using an item of business paraphernalia, be it a cellular phone or a notepad, is usually off-limits.

When a guest is invited to a members-only club, he or she should ask the host what to wear; many have strict dress codes. For the host's part, it's never out of line for him or her to mention the type of dress expected at the club at the time the invitation is extended. Guests who are unaware of the club's customs will be grateful for the information; showing up badly over- or underdressed could end up embarrassing both parties.

Hints for guests:

- Don't strike out on a solo tour of the club. You should enter the library or lounge only if escorted by your host.

- If you have drinks at the bar before dinner, limit yourself to one. Also, remember that confining your drinking to soda or spring water is perfectly fine.

- Don't be stiff, but do behave impeccably. Here, your actions reflect not only on your company, but on your host as well.

AT THE THEATER

For culturally minded businesspeople, an invitation to a play, a concert, an opera, or a ballet is an excellent choice, particularly when spouses are included. Starting or ending the evening with dinner makes for an even more memorable occasion. Unless you, as the host, are already familiar with your guests' tastes in such things, ask which kind of entertainment they favor; people who love musical comedies might find it hard to stay awake at the ballet. Once you determine what best fits the bill, purchase tickets in advance and ask for the best seats possible; if that means settling for the peanut gallery, try another show of the same type.

ARRIVING AND BEING SEATED

It is mandatory to arrive on time—even more so if you are picking up the tickets at the box office. Most theaters hold reserved tickets until twenty minutes before curtain time and then sell them on a first-come, first-serve basis. Also remember that along with talkers, late arrivals are a major source of resentment for theatergoers. At most performances, latecomers aren't allowed to be seated until a scene change occurs.

Traditionally, there is protocol for seating, starting with the host taking the aisle seat after his guests have entered the row. If there are two couples, the spouse of the guest sits next to the host, and vice versa. When there are several couples, the host's spouse leads the way into the row and the others follow, with women and men alternating. If any of the party are carrying their coats (on the assumption that they'd otherwise face an interminable wait at the coat check), they should hold them close to their chests as they edge to their seats, so as not to brush the heads of the people in the forward row. They should also excuse themselves to every person they move past.

Any able-bodied person who is seated should stand up to let new arrivals into the row.

NOISE

Talking or whispering during the show is frustrating for those around you. Watch the show; talk later. Any theatergoer carrying a cell phone or pager should keep it turned off during the performance. Doctors and other audience members who must be on call are wise to bring a cell phone or pager that signals with a light or a silent vibration. If your watch makes a regular, audible beep, turn it off or leave it at home.

APPLAUSE

If you're not sure when to clap, wait to see what everyone else does; little is more embarrassing than breaking out in applause while the rest of the audience stays quiet.

DEALING WITH RUDE THEATERGOERS

What is the proper thing to do when someone nearby is talking and spoiling the performance for everyone in the vicinity? In the 1955 edition of *Etiquette*, Emily Post took up this question under the heading "Theatre Pests." The intervening years have offered no better solution than the one she presented then: "If those behind you insist on talking," she wrote, "it is always bad manners to turn around and glare. If you are young, they pay no attention, and if you are older, most young people think an angry older person the funniest sight on earth! The only thing you can do is to say amiably, 'I'm sorry, but I can't hear anything while you talk.' If they still persist, you can ask an usher to call the manager."

14 | *Table Manners: Navigating the Meal*

All the rules of table manners are made to avoid ugliness. To let anyone see what you have in your mouth is repulsive, to make a noise is to suggest an animal, to make a mess is disgusting.

—Emily Post on table manners

Emily Post got it right. In one sentence, she covered the principal reasons why table manners exist. Virtually all of the issues covered in this chapter have to do with avoiding one of these three sins. If you bring nothing else away from this discussion, remember her words: When you think about any action you take at a meal, ask yourself: "Does it have the potential to be repulsive, sound like an animal, or make a mess?" If it does, then don't do it.

Like it or not, table manners stand out as perhaps the single most important benchmark of etiquette. This is largely because of the nature of eating itself. Think about a typical meal: We sit at a table with other people, attempting to carry on a conversation, while we're busily cutting up food, manipulating this food into our mouths, and then mashing it into a pulp before swallowing it.

Table manners give us confidence by providing guidelines on what to do during this very public and rather gross activity. Of course, confidence is the name of the game when it comes to building strong relationships with people — and having confidence in your table manners as you eat is one of the surest ways to make a positive impact on your dining companions.

Good table manners are critical for another, related reason as well: The reality is, people judge other people by their table manners. We can forget to hold a door, but chew with your mouth open and it rises to the level of an unpardonable sin. In a business situation, table manners may well be the key factor that differentiates you from your competition.

THE MOST IMPORTANT THING TO DO

The ultimate reason for getting your table manners down cold is that it leaves you free to concentrate on the most important task of any social or business meal, which is to participate. This means being focused on the conversation. As a junior member of the party, you don't want to try to dominate the discussion, but you do want to make comments and ask questions. When the table isn't involved in a general discussion, be a good conversationalist with the people seated on either side of you.

As the host, it's your job to steer the conversation, to suggest topics for discussion, and to make sure that everyone at the table is given the opportunity to be part of the general conversation.

WHEN TO TALK BUSINESS

At lunch or breakfast, a business discussion can occur at any time during the meal. Most likely it will happen after orders have been placed for food. The host is responsible for starting the discussion at the meal—but a thoughtful host also realizes that one of the benefits of a business meal is the chance it offers participants to get to know each other better, personally as well as professionally, and so leaves plenty of time for non-business talk as well. Remember, the bonds forged at a meal can last long after the check has been paid.

At a business dinner, the goal is tilted much more toward building relationships than the nitty-gritty of business discussion. Typically, at a business dinner the host will hold off on any specific or focused business discussion until after the main course is finished. That way,

THE NO-SHOW

If it's fifteen to twenty minutes after the appointed time and your lunch or dinner date hasn't shown up, phone her office. If he's not there and an assistant can't tell you his whereabouts, wait another half hour at most. Then write a note and leave it with the maître d': "Jim, I waited almost an hour, and hope everything's all right. Would you please give me a call at the office? Rita." Before you leave, tip the maître d'; doing so acknowledges you've held a table that would otherwise have been occupied by paying customers. Later, when the no-show phones to explain, don't sound annoyed or out of sorts. Simply accept his apologies and reschedule the meal.

If you are running late, call your dining companion's cell phone or, if necessary, the restaurant to let your companion know you are on the way. When you finally arrive, don't waste even more time by offering an elaborate excuse, which might add insult to injury; a quick but sincere apology will do.

the participants can focus on getting to know each other and on enjoying the good food.

RESTAURANT PRE-MEAL PREP FOR THE HOST

If you're hosting a business meal, remember that a little careful preparation will go a long way toward keeping the occasion trouble-free.

- *Consider your guest's taste.* If possible, find out whether your guest(s) especially likes or dislikes certain foods or ethnic cuisines. You can simply ask when extending the invitation; or a call to an assistant might give you the answer. You could also give your guest a choice of two or three restaurants. If you're hosting a group, choose a restaurant with a wide-ranging menu so that everyone present can find something to his or her taste.

- *Choose a restaurant you know.* Even a popular new place with the hottest chef in town may have snail-like service or be so noisy or cramped that it's hard to carry on a conversation. Also keep in mind that if anyone is going to travel fairly far to reach the restaurant, it should be you and not your guest.

- *Invite well in advance.* You or your assistant should arrange any business meal at least a week in advance, so that the guest can fit it into his or her schedule and have time to prepare for the meeting.

- *Make it clear that you are—or aren't—the host.* So there is no question about who's footing the bill, ask, "Will you be my guest for lunch?" On the other hand, if you and the other person see each other frequently and have developed a close working relationship, you may want to go Dutch. If so, a simple "Do you want to have lunch next Tuesday?" or "How about if we split lunch next week?" is a graceful way to suggest this.

- *Tell your guest what to expect.* So that your meal partner can prepare and bring along any pertinent materials, be specific about business topics you want to discuss and how deeply you'll be delving into them.

- *Reserve a table ahead of time.* Failing to reserve a table risks getting the meal off to a late start—a real problem at lunch or breakfast, where time is at a premium. If you have a preference for seating—a spot that's especially quiet, for example—let it be known at the time the reservation is made.

- *Reconfirm with your guest.* This is a must, saving real embarrassment later on. Call on the morning of a lunch or dinner; if you've scheduled breakfast, call the day before. At the same time, you might want to tell the guest to go ahead and be seated if he or she arrives early.

THE SOLUTION TO ANY PROBLEM

One of the biggest problems people encounter at the table is the fear that they won't know what to do in a given situation. After all, no one wants to look foolish or ignorant. Fortunately, there's a simple solution to the problem: Whenever you aren't sure what to do, simply sit back and wait and watch. Notice how other people are handling the situation, or which utensil they are using, or which glass they are drinking from—and then follow their lead.

With that general guideline in mind, the following is a step-by-step guide to table manners, from first arrival to final thank-you. While the advice is geared to a restaurant setting (which is where most business meals take place), it is equally applicable to meals held in a private dining room, a club, or other locale.

ARRIVING FOR THE MEAL

The impression you make on your business meal companions starts when you first arrive at the restaurant, well before you lift your first utensil. In fact, the very first things you do are critical to the success of the rest of the meal. When you start off on the right foot, you can quickly focus on building a great relationship. Start off on the wrong foot, on the other hand—by being late, for example—and you'll have to spend valuable time trying to recover, rather than building rapport.

PRE-PLANNING

- **DON'T BE LATE.** It's appropriate that this is the first rule of table etiquette. It may also be the most important. *Don't* start off your encounter on the wrong foot by showing up after the agreed-upon time. Arriving even five or ten minutes late leaves a bad impression; any later than that sends a clear message of carelessness and thoughtlessness.

- **DRESS APPROPRIATELY.** Show respect for your host or guests by looking sharp. This is a time to dress up a little, rather than dress down.

WHEN YOU ARRIVE AT THE RESTAURANT

- **WAIT.** If your host hasn't arrived, wait in the lobby or waiting area for her. Don't go to the table and wait there. If you are the host, wait for your guest in the lobby. If some of your guests have already arrived, you should wait in the lobby only until the time you made your reservation for. Then proceed to the table and have the maître d' or waiter escort the late guests in when they arrive. (Note: When the establishment is filling up and you're advised by the restaurant staff that it is best to sit at the table, it's okay to do so.)

- **TABLE LOCATION**. The host deals with table selection. As a guest, do not check out the table location and then suggest that the waiter or maître d' change it. Your host may have asked for that table for a reason; it's not up to you to second-guess her.

AS YOU APPROACH THE TABLE

- **LOOK TO THE HOST FOR SEATING ASSIGNMENTS**. Your host may have a specific seating arrangement in mind, so you should let him point you in the right direction. As the host, be prepared to indicate where people should sit. The guest of honor should sit in the best seat at the table. Usually that is one with the back of the chair to the wall. This means that the guest of honor won't be sitting in a traffic area with waiters and busboys passing behind her. Once the guest of honor's seat is determined, the host should sit to her left. Other people are then offered seats around the table. If spouses are with you at a business dinner, the male host has the female guest of honor sit to his right while the female host has the male guest of honor sit to her right.

CHIVALRY NOW—
APPROACHING THE DINING TABLE

One of the hardest problems for men and women in today's world is drawing a distinction between a purely social setting and a business setting when it comes to amenities such as holding chairs. In our social lives, a man is expected to hold a chair for a woman when they are sitting down to a meal. When sitting down for a business breakfast, lunch, or dinner, however, the same gesture may be perceived as sexist. The man is caught in a trap: He can easily make the error of trying to hold a chair when the woman doesn't want him to—or just as easily make the mistake of *not* holding a chair for a woman who believes such a gesture is an integral part of the man's role, whatever the setting. What to do?

Communication is the answer. As the man and woman approach the table, the man simply says, "Can I get the chair for you?" Now she can make the choice: "Why, yes. How thoughtful. Thank you." Or "No, thank you, but it was nice of you to offer." Instead of a confusing, awkward moment occurring, the situation passes without a hitch, and they can focus on building a better relationship—which, after all, is the primary purpose of any business-related encounter.

AT THE TABLE

- **WHAT TO DO WITH THE NAPKIN.** When you sit, the first thing you should do is put your napkin on your lap. In some restaurants, the wait staff will hold your napkin and place it on your lap for you; the simplest thing is to let them do this rather than trying to do it yourself.

- **WHAT'S ALL THIS SILVERWARE?** Table settings are decoded in full in Chapter 15. The most important thing to keep in mind when deciding which fork or knife or spoon to use is this: *You always use the utensils on the outside of the place setting.* If you don't use a utensil for a particular course, then when the course is removed from the table, the waiter will remove the utensil for that course as well.

PLACING ORDERS

Once you are settled in your seats, you can expect a waiter to come to the table to take drink orders. The waiter may also bring menus if the food hasn't already been ordered for you.

WHEN THE WAIT STAFF ASKS FOR DRINK ORDERS

- **IF YOU ARE ASKED FIRST.** As a junior executive at the table, you don't know if you should order alcohol or not. In this situation, err on the side of safety and order something non-alcoholic. As the first person to order, you don't want to be in the situation where you are the only person at the table to order alcohol. If others, including your boss, order an alcoholic drink, you can either quietly change your order before the server leaves the table or opt not to have alcohol before the meal. Either choice is appropriate.

- **WHEN YOU ARE THE HOST.** When the server asks for drink orders, let your guests know your expectations for drinking at the table. By saying, "While John is deciding, I'll order. I'd like an iced tea, please," the host is signaling that this is a working meal where drinking isn't appropriate. Conversely, by saying, "While John's deciding, I think I'd like to order a Pinot Grigio," you've given your guests the signal that they may feel comfortable ordering something alcoholic if they wish. If you don't drink but would like your guests to be comfortable ordering cocktails, you can say, "Joe, please feel free to enjoy a glass of wine or a drink."

WHEN THE WAITER ASKS FOR YOUR FOOD ORDER

- **WHAT SHOULD YOU ORDER?** As you look over the menu, keep in mind three important guidelines to ordering:

  1 Order medium-priced dishes, not the most expensive items on the menu.

  2 Know the food you are ordering. This isn't the time to be adventuresome and order something you've never had before. Not only might you not like it, but also it might be difficult to eat. You want your focus to be on the people at the table and not on your food.

  3 Order food that is relatively easy to eat. Linguine with clam sauce is very tasty, but eating linguine is a challenge that's nearly certain to leave your tie or blouse spattered with sauce.

- **WHAT IS THE HOST'S OBLIGATION WHEN ORDERING?** First, the host should already have eaten at the restaurant previously. A smart host never takes guests to a place he hasn't already visited. That hot new restaurant may be the "in" place, but if the music is so loud you can't carry on a conversation, there really isn't much point in going there for a business meal. By checking out the restaurant ahead of time, you can also assure yourself that the food is good and familiarize yourself with some of the items on the menu. That way, when you return there as the host of a business meal, you'll be able to offer menu suggestions to your guests.

- **WHAT IF THE MENU IS PRE-ARRANGED AND YOU HAVE A SPECIAL DIETARY NEED?** If, for instance, you are a vegetarian, it is perfectly acceptable to quietly ask the waiter whether there is a vegetarian selection available. If there isn't, you can ask him or her to bring you a plate without the meat on it. The key is to make your request known without making a big deal out of it.

- **IS THERE ANYTHING YOU HAVE TO ORDER?** As you listen to other people ordering, you realize they are all having an appetizer, a salad, and a main course—while all you want is a main course. There is no requirement for you to order any course you don't want. Simply order the main course and politely say, "No, thank you" if you are asked whether you want anything else.

BEFORE THE FIRST COURSE ARRIVES

Drinks and bread will soon arrive at the table. These mark your first opportunity to deal with food at the same time you are trying to carry on a conversation.

- **WHAT DO YOU DO WITH THE BREAD BASKET?** Bread is most often placed on the table in a basket that everyone shares. If the bread is placed in front of you, feel free to pick up the basket and offer it to the person on your left. Then take a piece yourself and pass it to the right.

- **WHY PASS TO THE RIGHT?** It simplifies life at the table if food is passed in just one direction. For instance, if the bread starts out to the right and the butter to the left, at some point halfway around the table a person is going to be faced with the problem of trying to handle both the bread and butter at the same time. It's easier if everyone simply passes in one direction. Thus, for the sake of practicality, the guideline is to pass right rather than left, since most people are right-handed. They receive the plate or basket with their left hand, which leaves their right hand free to easily serve the food to themselves. (Note: When someone near you on your left asks for something to be passed, it's okay to take the more direct route and pass left.)

- **NOW THAT YOU HAVE BREAD AND BUTTER, WHAT DO YOU DO?** You place the bread and butter on your butter plate—yours is on your left—then break off a bite-sized piece of bread, put a little butter on it, and eat it. Don't butter the whole piece of bread and then take bites from it.

APPETIZERS AND SOUP

The first course to arrive will be your appetizer or soup, if you ordered one. Appetizers are typically eaten with a fork and knife, though in some cases they will be eaten with your fingers. If you do eat food with your fingers, try to take bite-sized pieces rather than bringing a big piece of food to your mouth and then tearing a bite off with your teeth.

- **WHAT ABOUT SHRIMP COCKTAIL?** Shrimp cocktail typically arrives in a glass with a long stem, set on a small plate. It takes a little practice to learn to eat the shrimp with a small fork (known as a shellfish, or oyster, fork—see "The Formal Place Setting," pages 197–200), but it's a skill that's easily mastered. If the shrimp is small enough to be eaten in one bite, pick it up with the fork and enjoy. If the shrimp is bigger than one bite's worth, then spear it with your fork and cut it on the plate on which it's served. When faced with shrimp cocktail and no fork, simply hold the shrimp by the tail, dip it into the sauce, and take a bite. Fork or no fork, when the shrimp is big and the sauce is yours alone, you are free to double dip. If the sauce is communal, no double dipping, please.

■ **CLAMS AND OYSTERS.** It's great fun to pick up a clam shell or oyster shell and slurp the shellfish directly off it into your mouth. Just not at a business meal. Instead, use the little oyster fork to get the clam or oyster to your mouth.

■ **WHAT'S THE PROPER WAY TO EAT SOUP?** Dip the spoon into the soup to get a spoonful with a motion that takes the spoon away from you rather than toward you. You can gently rub the bottom of the spoon on the edge of the cup or bowl to catch any drip. The reason for the motion away from you is to avoid inadvertently directing a drip into your lap.

■ **CAN YOU TIP YOUR SOUP BOWL OR CUP?** Yes, it is acceptable to tip the bowl – but only for the last drop or two. Again, tip the bowl away from you rather than toward you.

■ **WHAT DO YOU DO WITH OYSTER CRACKERS?** If oyster crackers come with the soup, place them on the underplate (the plate the bowl is sitting on) and add a few at a time to your soup; using your fingers for this is fine. Larger crackers, however, should stay out of the soup; eat them with your fingers instead of crumbling them into the bowl.

■ **WHERE DO YOU PUT THE SPOON WHEN YOU'RE FINISHED?** If the soup is served in a cup, it will come on a saucer. When you're done, place the spoon on the saucer. If the soup is served in a shallow bowl, place the spoon in the bowl with the handle positioned at four o'clock (pointing to the lower right). This position lets the waiter know you're finished with the soup.

SOME GENERAL TABLE MANNERS

Throughout the meal, you will encounter a number of situations that can occur during any course, such as passing the salt and pepper, putting your utensils down while eating or when you're finished, and the issue of whether a man should stand when a woman excuses herself to the restroom.

■ **WHAT ABOUT SALTING AND PEPPERING FOOD?** Be sure to taste the food before putting salt or pepper on it. That way you can be sure it needs the seasoning. It would be a shame to ruin good food because you salted before you tasted. In addition, some people regard those who season their food before tasting in a negative light. Fair or not, those who are fast with seasoning may be thought of as making decisions too hastily about other, non-food matters as well.

- **HOW DO YOU PASS THE SALT AND PEPPER?** Always pass them together. If a person asks for just one, pass both anyway.

- **WHEN CAN YOU START EATING?** In business situations, it's best to wait until everyone is served and the host has started eating. This is true for all the courses served at the meal. The host, in turn, should respect the fact that good food should be eaten while it's hot. Once three people are served, the host should consider giving those guests who have been served permission to start. She might say something like this: "This restaurant serves great food and it should be enjoyed hot. So, please, if you've been served your food, start eating and enjoy."

- **CAN YOU PUT YOUR ELBOWS ON THE TABLE?** Between courses, it's perfectly acceptable to put your elbows on the table. In fact, from the perspective of body language, by leaning forward with your elbows on the edge of the table and your hands clasped in front of you, you are projecting an image of being attentive and listening closely to the speaker.

- **WHERE DO YOU PLACE YOUR UTENSILS IF YOU'RE NOT FINISHED EATING?** While you are still eating you may want to put your utensils down. Simply place the utensil(s) on the edge of the plate. Do not place used utensils on the table or tablecloth.

- **WHERE DO YOU PLACE YOUR UTENSILS WHEN YOU'RE FINISHED EATING?** At the end of a course, the utensils are placed side by side diagonally across the plate, roughly in the four o'clock to ten o'clock position. Imagine your plate is a clock face: Now, place the tip of the knife or the tips of the fork tines across the center so they point toward ten o'clock, and position the handle so it points to the four o'clock position (toward the lower right). When servers see utensils set in this position, they recognize it as a sign that they can remove the plate.

- **IS THERE ANY SENSE TO HOW SERVERS BRING FOOD AND TAKE AWAY EMPTY PLATES?** Actually, there is a protocol for serving and removing: Serve from the left and take away from the right. The server will approach you from the left side to bring your food to you, and he or she will approach from the right side to remove a plate or bowl.

AMERICAN VERSUS CONTINENTAL STYLES OF HOLDING UTENSILS

There are two styles for handling the knife and fork while dining: the American style and the Continental (also called European) style, which is used not only by Europeans but also by some Americans who prefer it. Is one more proper than the other? Certainly not. In fact, there's no reason not to use both during a meal: You might want to cut the meat in the Continental way, for example, and eat the other dishes American-style.

- *American Style.* This entails cutting food with the fork in the left hand and the knife in the right (or reversed, if you're left-handed). Then you place (not prop) the knife on the edge of the plate and switch the fork to your right hand before raising it, tines up, to your mouth. The fork should rest on the middle finger of your hand, with your index finger and thumb gripping the handle slightly above.

- *Continental Style.* In the European style, the food is cut in the same way. The knife, however, is kept in the cutting hand while the other hand lifts the fork to the mouth. The fork is held tines down with the index finger touching the neck of the handle. (Note: The "tines down" rule is by no means written in stone. But whichever style you choose—American, Continental, up, down—never grip the fork in your fist and use it as a spear or shovel.)

Usually, you see a person eating Continental-style with the fork in the left hand and the knife in the right hand. Once in a while, someone will have the fork in the right hand and the knife in the left. Again, either way is acceptable.

The method for cutting food is the same in both styles: Hold the knife in the right hand with your index finger pressed just below where the handle meets the blade. Hold the fork, tines down, in your left hand and spear the food to steady it, pressing the base of the handle with your index finger. As you cut the food, keep your elbows just slightly above table level—not raised high.

- **SHOULD YOU PICK UP YOUR FORK IF IT FALLS ON THE FLOOR?** No. Leave it there; tell the server and ask for another fork.

- **WHAT DO YOU DO IF YOU SPILL FOOD OR DRINK ONTO THE TABLE?** Quickly pick up the fallen glass and if the spill is going to run off the table, place your napkin over it. Get the server's attention and ask him or her to bring you a fresh napkin, then finish covering the mess. If your spill gets onto another person's clothing, it is very important that you offer to get the affected garment cleaned.

- **HOW SHOULD YOU SIGNAL A SERVER?** Look at the server quietly and say "Waiter" (or "Waitress"). If he is across the room and you can catch his eye, gently raise your hand to shoulder level and motion to him. At no time is it appropriate to call out to a server or to wave frantically (unless it's an actual emergency).

- **SHOULD A MAN STAND AS A WOMAN EXCUSES HERSELF TO THE RESTROOM?** In business, the basic rule of thumb is to keep things gender neutral. If you wouldn't do it for another man, don't do it for a woman. That said, if a man is at a meal with an elderly woman or a client who would clearly appreciate his standing as a gesture of respect, then he should be all means do it. As with so much of etiquette, a little common sense goes a long way in making the right choice.

- **IS IT ACCEPTABLE TO BLOW YOUR NOSE AT THE TABLE?** Really, it's not. (The one exception is a quick, slight dabbing—not blowing—of the nose). Any blowing of your nose into a tissue should take place *away* from the table, preferably in a restroom. Don't even think about sitting at the table and blowing into your napkin—or a tissue, for that matter. Both sneezing and nose-blowing should be followed by a quick visit to the restroom to wash your hands and clean up.

- **WHAT ABOUT PASSING GAS?** This is a potentially embarrassing natural bodily function. So treat it as such by excusing yourself from the table to take care of the matter in the restroom.

- **WHERE DO YOU PLACE YOUR NAPKIN WHEN YOU EXCUSE YOURSELF FROM THE TABLE?** The best thing to do is to loosely fold it so that no soiled areas are showing and then place it to the left of your place setting. Do this whenever you leave the table, either during the meal or at the end of the meal. By having just one resting spot for your napkin, you don't have to worry about inadvertently sending a signal to your waiter according to where you place it.

  Once in a while, you may find your napkin placed on your seat or seat back when you return. Some restaurants have their servers take this liberty. If so, check the seat or seat back for any food that may have spilled from the napkin, then simply pick up the napkin and sit down.

- **WHAT DO YOU DO WITH A FINGER BOWL?** When you encounter a finger bowl, use it either after eating a hands-on meal such as lobster (in this case there is often a lemon slice in the water) or, at a more formal meal, when dessert is served. Dip your fingers, one hand at a time (not one finger at a time), into the water and then dry them on your napkin. If the finger bowl is brought out just before dessert is put on the table, it is sometimes set on the dessert plate, sitting atop a doily. If this is the case, lift the doily and bowl as a unit and set them at the upper left of your place setting.

■ **WHAT SHOULD YOU DO IF YOU HAVE SOMETHING IN YOUR MOUTH YOU WANT TO REMOVE?** Believe it or not, the easiest—and also the most appropriate—thing to do is to raise the utensil you are using to your lips and gently push the offending article onto the utensil. Then deposit it on the edge of your plate. The exception is when you have a large mouthful of gristle and fat. In this case, excuse yourself to the restroom and remove it. No one will want to look at that on the side of your plate, and it does not belong in your napkin.

ALL THINGS WINE

Literally for millennia, the enjoyment of good wine with a meal has been a real social pleasure. Today is no different. However, it is equally important to note that at no time should a person feel compelled to drink wine if he or she doesn't want it. The following are wine guidelines for the business meal:

■ **WHAT DO YOU DO IF YOU DON'T WANT WINE?** Don't turn your glass upside down or put your hand over the glass as the server is about to pour. The easiest thing to do is simply to say to the server, "No, thank you," as she approaches to pour wine for you. If you don't notice the server and she pours you wine, just leave it in the glass and continue with your conversation. That's much more important than whether you have wine in your glass.

■ **HOW DO YOU POUR WINE?** You may be asked to refill your partner's glass. Fill a white wine glass to about two-thirds full. Fill a red wine glass to about one-half full. As you finish pouring, tip the bottle to cease the flow and twist the bottle at the end of the movement. This small twisting motion as the flow stops will prevent drips from falling from the bottle and landing on the tablecloth or, worse, the person you are pouring for.

■ **CAN YOU DRINK BOTH RED AND WHITE?** Yes, although you should finish one before switching to the other. For instance, you may start with white during the appetizer or, at a formal dinner, during the fish course and then switch to red for the main course.

"WHY DON'T YOU CHOOSE THE WINE?"

The menus have been perused and the chitchat is gathering steam, when your host abruptly thrusts a wine list the size of a small book in your direction: "Harry, why don't you choose the wine?" Bewildered, you haven't a clue where to start.

One response is to be honest: "I'd love to, but I know so little about wine I think I should leave it up to you." (Note: Never be embarrassed by your lack of wine savvy; truth be told, it's the person who sees you as somehow lacking who has the problem, and even alleged "wine experts" are often clueless about pairing wines with food.) An alternative is to ask the other guests for suggestions as you glance over the list: "Which red do you think will go best with the dishes we're having?" What you should *never* do is fake it; otherwise, you could end up with a wine that overpowers the food and pleases no one—with you as the guilty party.

With this default option in mind, learning a few wine basics will put you on relatively safe ground for the future. (If, after reading this, you want to bone up further, it's easier than you might think: A number of excellent small books on wine appreciation are available that take the mystery out of choosing—and are entertaining to boot.)

Listed below are wines that generally go well with certain kinds of dishes. Although the wines are grouped as whites and reds, the recommendation of each is based less on color (the old advice being to stick with white wine for fish or chicken and red wine for meat) than on the balance of sweetness and acidity that makes for a food-friendly wine. Some wines, especially American ones, are named for the grape variety, such as Chardonnay and Pinot Noir; others, usually European varieties, are named for the region where the wine originated, such as Burgundy and Bordeaux.

FISH, MILD

Whites: Chablis, German Riesling, Loire Sauvignon Blanc (Sancerre, Pouilly-Fumé)
Light Reds: Dry rosé, Beaujolais, lightest Pinot Noir

FISH, OILY

Whites: New Zealand or Loire Sauvignon Blanc (Sancerre, Pouilly-Fumé),
Chenin Blanc, Gewürztraminer, white Burgundy
Light Reds: Pinot Noir, Beaujolais, Barbera, Loire Cabernet Franc

SHELLFISH

Whites: Loire Sauvignon Blanc (Sancerre, Pouilly-Fumé), Muscadet, dry Chenin Blanc

OYSTERS

Whites: Chablis, Austrian Grüner Veltliner, dry sparkling wines, dry German Riesling

POULTRY

Whites: German or Alsace Riesling, Chardonnay, Pinot Blanc
Reds: Australian Shiraz, California Syrah, Zinfandel, Pinot Noir

PORK

Whites: French Chardonnay, Chenin Blanc, German or Alsace Riesling
Reds: Pinot Noir, Cabernet Franc, Chianti, Spanish reds (Rioja)

BEEF AND LAMB

Reds: Cabernet Sauvignon, Merlot, Rhone reds, Zinfandel

VEAL

Whites: German Auslese Riesling, Alsace whites, Rhone whites
Reds: Loire Cabernet Franc, Pinot Noir, Chianti, Spanish reds (Rioja)

GAME

Reds: Burgundy, Rhone reds, Australian Shiraz, Zinfandel

GAME BIRDS

Reds: Cabernet Sauvignon, Amarone, Burgundy, Rhone reds

PASTA WITH RED SAUCE

Whites: New Zealand Sauvignon Blanc
Reds: Barbera, Chianti, Zinfandel, Loire Cabernet Franc

PASTA WITH CREAM SAUCE

Whites: Soave, Pinot Grigio, Sauvignon Blanc, Champagne

SALAD AND VEGETABLES

Whites: Sauvignon Blanc, dry Chenin Blanc, dry Riesling, Austrian Grüner Veltliner

INDIAN, CAJUN, AND OTHER SPICY FOODS

Whites: German Gewürztraminer, German Riesling, Chenin Blanc, Sauvignon Blanc
Reds: Beaujolais, Barbera, Pinot Noir, rosé

THE SALAD COURSE

In most restaurants and homes, the salad course will be served after the appetizer and before the main course. Occasionally, in a more formal setting, the salad will be served after the main course. In a home setting, salad may also be passed around the table during the main course.

- **WHICH SALAD IS YOURS?** Food for your place setting will be put on your left and drinks will be placed on your right. This means that if salads are already on the table as you sit and one isn't immediately in front of you, your salad is the one just to the left of your fork(s). If salad is served as a course, it will be placed in front of you. If you don't want to eat it before your main course, simply move the salad to the left of your fork. If the waiter makes a motion to take it away, simply tell him to leave it and that you'll finish it later.

- **CAN YOU USE A KNIFE TO CUT YOUR SALAD?** Sometimes it can be hard to cut the lettuce with the edge of your fork. In this case, yes, you can use a knife, particularly if there are large lettuce leaves. Leave your knife on the salad plate when you are finished. If the server starts to place it back on the table, ask him to bring you a clean knife instead.

- **HOW DO YOU EAT...?**

  □ *Cherry tomatoes:* Very carefully. Try to spear the tomato with your fork and cut it in half. (This isn't always easy.) If you put a whole cherry tomato in your mouth, close your lips tightly before biting into it. If you don't, you will likely spray seeds and tomato juice across the table, much to your embarrassment.

  □ *Olives with pits:* You should use your fork to move the olive to your mouth. If it has a pit, you can discreetly remove the pit from your mouth with your fingers and put it on the side of the plate.

  □ *Asparagus spears:* Asparagus is often described as a finger food. At a business meal, however, you should err on the side of caution and use a fork—especially if the asparagus is limp or is served with any kind of sauce.

THE MAIN COURSE

If you order for yourself, you can avoid some of the potential difficulties of a main course by ordering food that is easy to eat and that you know you enjoy. In some business situations, however, the meal is pre-ordered for you—which means you may be faced with food you either don't like or don't know how to eat.

- **WHAT DO YOU DO WITH BONES?** At a business meal, don't pick up a bone and eat it in your fingers unless you see your host doing it. One exception would be eating foods that are clearly finger foods, such as chicken wings served as an appetizer, or spare ribs, or possibly fried chicken. (Even with fried chicken, check out how your host is handling it before you pick it up with your fingers.) The considerate host, meanwhile, noticing that someone has ordered lamb chops, will say, "You know, Tom, I hate leaving those last great flavorful bites on the bone. It really is okay if you want to pick up those bones." With that permission, gently go ahead and enjoy.

- **SHOULD YOU CUT OFF ONE BITE OF MEAT AT A TIME, OR SEVERAL BITES?** You should cut one bite of any food and then eat it before cutting the next.

- **HOW ABOUT LINGUINE OR SPAGHETTI?** When you are at home, practice twirling linguine or spaghetti onto a fork. Use the side of your plate or a spoon to twirl against. If you select one or two strands at a time to twirl, you shouldn't get an overly large mouthful. Don't use your knife and fork to cut the plate of spaghetti up into small bits.

- **DO YOU EAT VEGETABLES SERVED ON A SIDE PLATE DIRECTLY FROM THE PLATE?** If the plate of vegetables is just for you, you can eat directly from the side plate. If you are sharing the vegetables with other people, transfer your serving from the side plate to your plate.

- **CAN YOU SHARE A TASTE?** Accepting another person's offer to taste a morsel of her dish—or offering a bite of yours—is fine as long as it's handled unobtrusively. Either hand your fork to the person, who can spear a bite-sized piece from her plate and hand the fork back to you, or (if the person is sitting close by) hold your plate toward her so that she can put a morsel on the edge. Don't be tempted to hold a forkful of food to somebody's mouth or reach over and spear something off someone else's plate.

It's the rare restaurant meal during which at least one perplexing question doesn't arise ("Should I ask for a doggy bag?") or a glitch doesn't occur ("Is that a foreign body in my water?"). These pointers will help you cope:

- *The food arrives at different times?* At a business meal with a colleague or client, if your dining partner's food arrives before yours does, encourage her to eat it before it gets cold. Likewise, if your own food has to be sent back for any reason, urge her to continue eating. If you are at a meal with your boss or other people who rank higher than you, wait for a signal from them that you may begin eating. At a meal with people of similar rank, if three or so people at a large table receive their food and there is a wait for the rest, they may start eating so their meals won't get cold. At a buffet it is acceptable to start eating once you have returned to the table.

- *Your fork or glass is unclean?* If your yet-to-be-filled water goblet seems soiled, or any utensil shows a bit of dried crust, don't announce it to everyone at the table—especially the host. The next time a server stops by, discreetly ask for a replacement.

- *You spot a hair or bug?* If there is a speck floating in your water or a hair or a pest of some kind in your food, simply refrain from drinking or put down your fork until you catch the attention of the waiter. While it's probably impossible to keep the rest of the table from knowing something is amiss, try your best not to cause a fuss.

- *Your dining partner has food on his face?* If you notice a speck of food on someone's face (or, in the case of a man, on his beard), you're doing them a favor by subtly calling attention to it. Do so with a light "Oops, there's something on your cheek." You might signal silently by cocking an eyebrow while using your index finger to lightly tap your chin or whatever part of the face is affected. As prevention for yourself, the occasional dab with your napkin will help ensure no wayward bits of food stay put for long.

- *You have spinach in your teeth but don't know it?* Occasionally running your tongue over your teeth may let you know whether you have food (the usual culprit: spinach) caught between your teeth. If you can execute a quick wipe of your teeth with your napkin without attracting attention, do so. If the food stays lodged there, it may be better to excuse yourself from the table and go to the restroom to remove it rather than worrying about it for the rest of the meal.

- *You're finished but your plate is still half full?* At a business meal, forget the doggy bag unless you're going Dutch and are with a good friend. Even then, don't load up the bag with butter, sugar packets, or any other ancillary items.

- **IS IT ACCEPTABLE TO SOP UP SAUCE WITH BREAD?** Don't do this at a business dinner unless the host says this is acceptable or does it himself—in which case it's okay. Remember, don't hold the bread in your fingers and push it around in the sauce. Instead, break a piece of the bread off and then use your fork to spread some sauce on it and eat it.

- **WHAT IF YOU DON'T LIKE THE FLAVOR?** It happens: You're served a beautiful, carefully prepared dish, and you take one bite and don't like it at all. Maybe it has blue cheese in it, and you can't stand blue cheese. Don't make a fuss or comment. Simply eat the other food on the plate. If the host says something to you, reply that you appreciate the effort that went into making it, but it's not for you. At a restaurant, don't ask the server to bring you something different—you ordered the dish, so now it is yours.

- **WHAT IF THE FOOD HAS SOMETHING WRONG WITH IT?** In that case, ask the server to take it back. It's perfectly acceptable to expect to get what you ordered. Perhaps you wanted medium-well-done meat and it came out rare. They will either fix the problem and then return that food to you or bring you another serving.

DESSERT

- **SHOULD YOU USE A SPOON OR FORK TO EAT PIE WITH ICE CREAM?** It's your choice. You can use either a fork or a spoon or both—the fork for the pie, and the spoon for the ice cream.

- **WHAT ABOUT FRESH FRUIT?** While fruits like grapes, cherries, and berries can be eaten directly with your fingers, don't simply pick up larger fruits like apples or peaches and take a bite out of them. Quarter large fruit with your knife, remove the seeds or pit, then pick up a section and eat it.

- **WHAT IF YOU DON'T WANT COFFEE?** Simply tell the server promptly. Don't turn your cup upside down on your saucer. At banquets and large events, there are times when different servers will repeatedly ask if you want coffee. The easiest thing may be to let one of them pour a cup and then leave it. That will stop the interruptions.

- **WHAT DO YOU DO WITH A TEA BAG?** If you are served tea in a cup with a saucer, simply place the tea bag on the saucer. If you are served it in a mug, place the tea bag on your dessert plate (or other nearby plate at your place setting). If you don't have a plate available, place the tea bag in the bowl of your spoon. Or you can ask the server for a saucer when she serves you the tea in a mug. Do not, under any circumstances, place the tea bag directly on the tablecloth. Also, forgo winding the string around the tea bag to squeeze the tea bag dry.

PAY AHEAD OF TIME

Nothing is more impressive than to be able to say at the end of a meal, "Sally and Jim, I've enjoyed our conversation. I think it's been a productive meal as well as an enjoyable one. We can go; the check is all taken care of." Instead of having to fumble with your cash or a credit card and calculate a tip, you can stay focused on your guests. To do this, simply ask at the time you make your reservation how you can best arrange for payment ahead of time—and then ask the restaurant to add a 20 percent gratuity to the bill.

THE MEAL IS OVER

When the meal is through, you still have several things to think about as you prepare to leave the restaurant.

- **WHO PAYS?** The person who does the inviting does the paying. If someone invites you to lunch and the server places the check on the table, don't make a grab for it. Let the person who invited you have the opportunity to pick up the check and deal with it.

- **WHAT IF THE SERVER GIVES THE CHECK TO YOUR GUEST?** This is an especially common situation when the host is female and the guest is male. In this case, be firm and say, "Jim, I invited you to lunch. Please, let me have the check. I'll take care of it." A simple way to prevent this from happening, whether you are male or female, is to let the server or maître d' know in advance that the check should be brought to you.

- **DO YOU WRITE A THANK-YOU NOTE?** A note sent by the guest serves as a thank-you for the meal and an enjoyable time, as well as a confirmation of any decisions that were made. The host should also write, telling the guest how nice it was to dine with him or her and briefly recapping any business details. A follow-up phone call by either party could be made instead, but a note has two advantages: It doesn't interrupt the other person's day, and it comes across as warmer and more gracious.

- **DO YOU HAVE TO RECIPROCATE WITH AN INVITATION?** Does inviting someone to a business lunch, dinner, or breakfast mean they are obligated to reciprocate, tit for tat? Not necessarily. The rules governing the reciprocation of invitations vary from situation to situation.

  ▫ You are not expected to repay an invitation to a strictly-business meal (especially one charged to an expense account), no matter who invited you—a customer, a client, or your boss. But you may certainly do so if you have continuing business together.

  ▫ A client who is entertained by a salesperson or supplier is not expected to return the invitation, even if his or her spouse or family was invited.

  ▫ Do return social invitations from coworkers and other business associates, whether they've extended the hand of friendship to cement a business relationship or you simply enjoy one another's company away from the office. You needn't reciprocate in kind. For example, you could have your associate join you for a cookout as your thank-you for a restaurant dinner.

TIPPING

Whoever is paying the bill should make sure a gratuity hasn't already been included in the total—something that is standard procedure at some restaurants. Other restaurants may include an automatic gratuity only for large groups. On most occasions, you'll be tipping not only the waiter but other restaurant staff as well. (See also "How Much to Tip?" pages 276–278.) Tip according to these general guidelines:

- **The Waiter or Waitress.** 15 to 20 percent of the total bill before tax is added
- **The Sommelier, or Wine Steward.** Either 15 to 20 percent of the cost of the bottle or $3 to $5 per bottle. If you tip a sommelier, remember to deduct the cost of the wine from the bill before figuring the tip for the wait staff.
- **The Bartender.** 15 to 20 percent of the tab, with a minimum of 50 cents
- **The Coatroom Attendant.** $2 for the first coat and $1 per additional coat
- **The Parking Valet or Garage Attendant.** $2

THE THANK-YOU NOTE

A handwritten thank-you note sent the next day to express your appreciation for being hosted at a business meal accomplishes two things: It sets you apart from your competition, in cases where they don't send notes, and it gives you a reason to make another contact with your host—which keeps you at the top of her mind in a very positive way.

> *Dear Larry,*
>
> *Thanks so much for the lunch today—and for introducing me to the Café Rouge. I can understand why it's your favorite restaurant. The conversation was almost as delicious as the Beef Bourguignon, and I really appreciated your wise counsel about the transfer offer.*
>
> *Yours,*
> *Sarah*

Or, in a somewhat more formal tone:

> *Dear Ms. Jones,*
>
> *Thank you so much for lunch today. The restaurant was elegant, and the meal was delicious. Most of all, I appreciate your ideas and guidance about my decision to transfer to the Seattle office. Your suggestions really helped me to get my priorities in order. I look forward to entertaining you on your next visit to the Northwest.*
>
> *Sincerely,*
> *Mark Dawson*

15 | *Decoding the Table Setting*

While your knowledge of table manners (see Chapter 14) is critical to your success at a business meal, knowing how to decode the intricacies of the table setting will also help make you a more confident and comfortable participant. This confidence allows other people to focus on what you have to say, rather than what you are doing—increasing the likelihood that they'll feel comfortable doing business with you.

Place settings vary greatly depending on the formality of the event or the locale. Settings can also be traditional or inspired by a local custom. For instance, utensils are traditionally positioned with forks on the left side of the plate and knives and spoons on the right. A country club may bring your utensils wrapped in a napkin, however, leaving you to position them yourself. It is imperative, therefore, to understand not only how a place setting is conceived but also what each utensil is and what it's used for.

Regardless of the formality of the event or the place where it's being held, unless your business meal takes place at a diner or deli, the table will hold more than one plate, as well as any number of utensils, glasses of different shapes, and an assortment of other items. The easiest way to become comfortable approaching a table setting is to learn the function of all the different items—and then to learn how those items have actually been arranged quite thoughtfully for your use.

THE FORMAL PLACE SETTING

Large business events are the most likely places to encounter formal table settings, complete with a full array of drinking glasses and flatware. Even for the table-savvy, a refresher briefing on table settings can be extremely helpful.

PLATES, ET CETERA

At formal occasions, you'll often have these at your place setting at the very beginning: a service plate, the large plate at the center of the place setting (also known as a charger or a place plate); and a bread plate (just above the forks and slightly to the left). Small first-course and salad plates will be brought out by the server as needed and then set on the service plate. (Note: In certain circumstances, the salad plate may already be on the table, in which case it is placed to the left of the napkin.) The service plate will be replaced by your plate of food when the main course is served.

If you encounter a salt cellar (a small open dish) rather than a traditional shaker, use the accompanying small spoon to salt your food. If no spoon comes with the cellar and you are sharing the cellar with others, dip the tip of your unused knife into the salt and deposit a little mound of it on the edge of your dinner plate. If you have your own cellar at your place setting, taking a pinch of salt with your fingers shouldn't raise any eyebrows. (Note: Do taste your food before salting it.)

GLASSWARE AND NAPKINS

The most common glasses you're likely to encounter are the water goblet (placed just above the knife) and two wineglasses (just above the right-hand utensils)—the larger one for red wine, the smaller for white. At more formal table settings, there may be additional glasses: the cylindrical champagne flute, which is better at keeping the wine bubbly than the saucer-shaped champagne glass of old; and a sherry glass, also cylindrical but smaller. The napkin, either folded into a rectangle or rolled and inserted into a napkin ring, will be to the left of the forks or in the center of the service plate. Napkins that have been decoratively folded (such as in a fan shape) are sometimes set inside the water goblets.

UTENSILS

The number of courses in a formal dinner runs from four to six, with all the necessary utensils made available for the diner. In Victorian England, the determination of the newly rich to maintain class distinctions led to the design and manufacture of so many new utensils for dining—as specific as a sauce-tasting spoon (used at the table)—that even the most avid social climber was at a loss for what to do with which. Thankfully, since then most of these contrivances have fallen out of fashion, and working one's way through a formal place setting is no longer as daunting as it once was.

Today, at most formal establishments, tables are rarely set with every utensil under the sun—the daunting ten-piece place settings that run the gamut from oyster fork to fruit knife. Utensils are usually limited to what is needed for a typical meal, with additional ones brought out whenever ordered dishes require them. However lavish or sparse the table setting, having a rudimentary knowledge of utensil placement will make any diner feel more comfortable.

The classic traditional place setting is managed from the "outside in," meaning you start with the outermost utensils and work your way toward the plate. Some other setting styles are more or less free-form, or even unique to a particular place. For this reason, it helps to be able to recognize utensils by shape as well as by order of use.

Let's take a closer look at a full formal place setting, starting at the outside and working in:

On the Left Side of Your Formal Place Setting

- **FISH FORK.** This fork appears in a place setting when a first course of fish is served. It is at the outside left of the place setting, since it is the first fork used.

- **DINNER (ENTRÉE, OR PLACE) FORK.** This largest of the forks at a place setting is used to eat the entrée and side dishes. At times, the dinner fork (rather than a fish fork) is used to eat the fish course as well.

- **SALAD FORK.** This smaller fork is likely to be set to the right of the dinner fork, meaning that the salad will be served after the entrée in the formal (and European) tradition.

And on the Right Side

- **OYSTER (SHELLFISH) FORK.** This small utensil is used for oysters, shrimp, clams, and similar first-course shellfish. It is the only fork placed on the right side of the place setting, beyond the spoon and sometimes resting in the bowl of the soupspoon.

- **SOUPSPOON/FRUIT SPOON.** If soup or fruit is being served as a first course, this spoon is the outside utensil on the right side of the plate.

- **FISH KNIFE.** This is positioned to the left of the soupspoon/fruit spoon, and to the right of the dinner knife.

- **DINNER KNIFE.** This large knife is used for the entrée, and is placed just to the right of the plate.

- **STEAK KNIFE.** If you have ordered beef or game, this knife might be brought out by the waiter as a replacement for the dinner knife.

Other Utensils at Your Formal Place Setting

- **BUTTER KNIFE.** This small knife is placed across the edge of the bread plate. It is replaced there after each buttering.

A Formal Place Setting

- **DESSERTSPOON AND DESSERT FORK**. At most formal meals, the dessertspoon and dessert fork are brought in just before dessert is served. Sometimes they are paired and placed above the dinner plate from the beginning of the meal.

- **TEA OR COFFEE SPOON**. This small spoon is presented to the diner at the end of the meal, when coffee and tea are served.

THE INFORMAL PLACE SETTING

There's no mystery to setting a proper table—especially an informal one, which calls for fewer utensils. The basic rule: Utensils are placed in the order of use, from the outside toward the plate. A second rule, although with a few exceptions: Forks go to the left of the plate, knives and spoons to the right.

The typical place setting for an informal three-course dinner includes these utensils and dishes:

- **TWO FORKS**. A large one (the dinner fork) for the main course and a small one for a salad or appetizer. If the salad is to be served as the first course, the small fork goes to the left of the dinner fork; if the salad is served after the main course, then the smaller (salad) fork is placed to the right of the dinner fork.

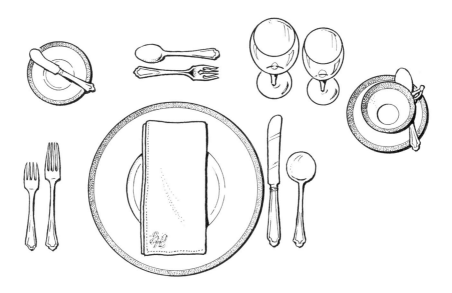

- **DINNER PLATE**. Sometimes there are no dinner plates on the informal table when diners sit down. The plates are brought out by the server just as the food is ready, making sure food stays warm while everyone at the table is being served.

- **ONE KNIFE**. The dinner knife is set immediately to the right of the plate, its cutting edge facing inward; it may be a steak knife if the main course is meat or chicken. It can also be used, if necessary, with any first course.

- **SPOONS**. Spoons go to the right of the knife, with a soupspoon (used first) farthest to the right and a dessertspoon (used last) to its left.

- **GLASSES**. A water goblet and one wineglass (or two, if two wines are being served) are placed at the top right of the dinner plate. If wine is not a part of the meal, the goblet can be used for either water or iced tea.

- **NAPKIN**. A folded napkin is placed in the center of the place setting or to the left of the forks.

  Other dishes and utensils are optional, depending on the menu or the style of service.

- **SALAD PLATE**. This is placed to the left of the forks. If the salad is to be served with the meal, rather than before or after, it may be served directly on the dinner plate—but this is done only at meals where the main course won't come with a pool of sauce or gravy.

- **BREAD PLATE WITH BUTTER KNIFE.** The bread plate is placed above the forks, with the butter knife resting across the edge.

- **DESSERTSPOON AND DESSERT FORK.** These can be placed either horizontally above the dinner plate (the spoon at the top and its handle to the right; the fork below and its handle to the left) or beside the plate. If beside the plate, the fork goes on the left-hand side, closest to the plate; the spoon goes on the right-hand side of the plate, to the left of the soupspoon.

- **COFFEE CUP AND SAUCER.** If coffee is to be drunk during the meal, the cup and saucer go just above and slightly to the right of the knife and spoons. If it is served after dinner, the cups and saucers are brought to the table.

GLASSWARE

Aside from the water goblets and wineglasses on the table, cocktail, liqueur, or punch glasses may be used at various times during the party, with a server bringing them out as necessary. Knowing their finer differences may be of some value on future occasions. Following is a guide:

- **WATER GOBLET.** This bowl-shaped glass with a stem is correct for both formal lunches and dinners. The usual capacity is 10 ounces or slightly more.

- **ALL-PURPOSE WINEGLASS.** A straight-sided glass with a capacity of 6 to 9 ounces may be used for both white and red wine. It is filled three-quarters or less full.

- **RED WINE GLASS.** The classic bowl has a slight tulip shape. Although the total capacity is 8 to 10 ounces, the glass should be one-half or less full.

- **WHITE WINE GLASS.** This differs from the red wine glass by having straight sides and a smaller capacity—5 to 8 ounces. It is filled three-quarters full or less.

- **SHERRY GLASS.** The traditional shape is a narrow V, and the total capacity is from 2 to 3 ounces. Fill to about half an inch from the top.

- **CHAMPAGNE GLASS.** Called a flute, this cylindrical glass has replaced the traditional saucer-shaped glass because it keeps the champagne bubblier. Its capacity is 5 to 7 ounces.

- **MARTINI GLASS.** This wide V-shaped glass holds from 4 to 6 ounces and should be filled to about ¾ inch from the top.

- **HIGHBALL GLASS.** Used for the gin-and-tonic and similar cocktails served on the rocks, this straight-sided glass holds 10 to 12 ounces.

- **OLD-FASHIONED GLASS.** This glass can be used for any drink on the rocks. The standard size has a capacity of 8 ounces, but taller versions are also seen.

- **SHOT GLASS.** This is for drinking whiskey neat. The most popular size is 1½ ounces, but some shot glasses hold 3 ounces.

- **LIQUEUR GLASS.** Also called a cordial glass (cordial being another name for liqueur), this small glass has a capacity of 1 to 2 ounces.

- **BRANDY SNIFTER.** The design of this glass—a small neck and a balloon-shaped bowl—is meant to hold in the brandy's aroma. Snifters range in capacity up to 20 ounces or so, but only about 2 ounces of liquor are poured into the snifter at one time. Brandy may also be served in a liqueur glass.

- **PUNCH CUP.** The total capacity is usually 4 to 5 ounces. Fill two-thirds full.

Red Wine Glass, White Wine Glass, Champagne Glass

PLACE CARDS AND SEATING

Place cards are expected at formal affairs. If you see place cards on a table, do not change the location of your seat so you can have a "better" seat or sit with a friend. In fact, there is a standard protocol regarding who sits where. As with introductions, "importance" comes into play, regardless of gender. Tradition says that a guest of honor (not necessarily someone for whom the party is given, but sometimes a person of rank instead) is always seated to the host's right, with those lower in the business hierarchy seated progressively farther down the table.

If this arrangement seems shockingly undemocratic, keep in mind that top executives and foreign visitors often adhere to protocol and expect the same of everyone else. In any event, that some seats at the table are better than others is rarely apparent to observers.

If there are no place cards, be wary as a junior member of the team of taking the best seat in the house (the one with the seat back to the wall). Also, try seating yourself with people you don't know and make an effort to get to know them rather than safely sitting with a friend. The business meal is an opportunity to broaden your horizons and make new contacts.

ENTERTAINING AT HOME: THE DINNER PARTY

Inviting people into your home for a meal is a wonderfully personal way to entertain your business associates. But hosting even a casual business dinner requires putting thought into how to set the table and how you want it to look. While the most important consideration is the happiness of your guests, the nuts and bolts of entertaining have to be sorted out beforehand. When will you serve the salad? Should you serve liqueurs after dinner? What do you do when you have twelve guests but only eight place settings of your good china? All of these factors come into play in arranging your table settings. When planning your table, simply follow the guidelines outlined in this chapter—while also keeping in mind the following:

TABLECLOTHS AND PLACE MATS

Although a formal dinner calls for either a tablecloth or place mats, at informal dinners a tablecloth is largely a matter of choice. A bare table with place mats is the alternative.

You may think a tablecloth essential to the overall look you want to achieve, or it may serve to hide the scratches on a less-than-perfect table. On the other hand, the wood surface of a table can become a design element in itself. The gleaming mahogany of a fine dining table is set off nicely by crisp white broadcloth place mats and napkins paired with copper or pewter serving dishes. The weathered wood of a rustic table makes a good foil for terra-cotta or hand-painted Italian serving bowls and platters, which can be combined with napkins and mats in natural earth tones.

CHINA AND FLATWARE

If your good china and flatware won't stretch to meet the number of guests, you have two alternatives. The first is to set a second, smaller table with your pottery or everyday dinnerware, or even with dishes and place settings borrowed from a relative or friend.

The second choice, appropriate for truly casual affairs, is to mix and match. After all, making sure that every piece of china and flatware matches is less important than the conversation and the quality and presentation of the food. Worn or chipped plates, cups, and saucers won't make the grade, but using different patterns or colors is acceptable as long as they're somewhat in keeping with the occasion—no plastic wineglasses with bone china, please. The idea is to create a harmonious whole.

CENTERPIECES, CANDLES, ET CETERA

The centerpiece is just that: flowers or something else ornamental placed in the exact center of the table. Fresh flowers are the obvious choice, but an arrangement of imitation flowers crafted from silk or glass can also be used. Alternatives to flowers are bowls of fruit (think of a still life by an old master) or ornamental vegetables or a striking antique or contemporary glass ornament. Whatever you choose, make sure the centerpiece doesn't stand so tall that your guests can't see over it.

Candles, if meant to be merely ornamental, are placed on either side of the centerpiece. If you want to create a more dramatic mood by using candles as the only source of light, you might want to place one above each place setting so that guests can clearly see their food. While white is the traditional candle color for a formal dinner, color isn't an issue at informal affairs: Simply choose whatever you think looks best with the china and linens you're using.

If your table seats eight or more, place a set of salt and pepper shakers or grinders at each end. At even the most informal meal, these two basics should be a cut above those you use every day. Wooden, pewter, and smartly designed clear glass shakers or grinders are just some of the countless choices that are available.

PART FOUR

COMMUNICATION

16 | *The Good Conversationalist*

No matter what field of business you're in, the way you speak is fundamental to how you are perceived. People who use incorrect grammar, are indifferent listeners, or talk mostly about themselves are seen in a less-than-positive light. Whether you're making a sales presentation or chatting with your supervisor, the ability to reach and influence a listener with your speaking voice is one of the most valuable assets you have.

Speaking poorly, on the other hand, can have serious consequences: Eighty percent of executives questioned in a recent study by a Midwestern university cited a lack of communication skills—not technical expertise or overall performance—as the main reason employees were held back in their careers.

THE IMPRESSION YOU MAKE

Every time you speak, the listener is subconsciously registering the quality of your voice, your enunciation, your grammar, and your choice of words. Most often, it is only when one of these elements deviates from the norm that it's noticed—for better or worse.

- **VOLUME.** It goes without saying that a mid-range between loudness and softness is most desirable. A too-loud voice almost always annoys or unnerves other people, while a too-soft delivery can make you seem uncertain, vulnerable, or shy or make you difficult to understand.

- **TONE.** Don't speak in a monotone, which flattens not only your message but the listener's interest as well.

- **RATE.** The rate at which you speak is important. Fast talkers are harder to understand than slow talkers, and they frequently have to repeat themselves. Slow talkers merely make the listener impatient.

- **ENUNCIATION**. Don't swallow syllables, slur words together, or drop final letters. Dropping letters—the *g* in words ending with *-ing* being the prime example—should be reserved for informal talks among friends; when speaking over the phone or engaged in a business conversation, enunciate the entire word.

- **ACCENT**. So long as your grammar and word usage are correct, you should never be embarrassed by a regional, ethnic, or foreign accent. Your accent is a drawback only when it's strong enough to hamper communication.

GRAMMAR AND WORD USAGE

Some grammatical rules have relaxed in recent years, more so in conversation than in writing. But don't be fooled into thinking that correct grammar no longer matters—it does, a lot. Although putting a preposition at the end of a sentence is no longer frowned on (with "That's the store I went to" now preferred over the awkward "That's the store to which I went"), the basic rules still hold fast.

Brushing up on grammar doesn't have to be a chore. A number of easy-to-understand and entertainingly written wordbooks are sold today, and they bear little resemblance to the dry textbooks you probably remember. Buying one is a particularly smart investment for anyone in business. These three books make an excellent start:

- *English Grammar for Dummies,* by Geraldine Woods (John Wiley and Sons, 2001)

- *The Grammar Book for You and I (Oops, Me),* by C. Edward Good (Capital Books, 2002)

- *New Fowler's Modern English Usage,* 3rd ed., by H. W. Fowler and R. W. Burchfield, ed. (Oxford University Press, 2000)

VOCABULARY

Having a good vocabulary doesn't mean using big words in place of small ones; it's the precise meaning of a word, not its length, that matters. In most conversation, using *endeavor* for *try, conclude* for *end,* and *prognosticate* for *predict* sounds unnatural and forced. Strive instead for a vocabulary that's wide-ranging yet direct. Carefully chosen, descriptive words improve communication and leave the listener with a positive impression in the process.

Interjections to banish: *you know, uh, er, like,* and other fillers. Even the broadest vocabulary is sabotaged by continually dropping these meaningless utterances between your words.

PRONUNCIATION AND MEANING

If you are unsure how to pronounce a certain word, or you hear someone else using a pronunciation for a word different from the one you've been using, your best course is to look the word up in a dictionary as soon as possible. A good dictionary will always include a guide to pronouncing each word listed. This same advice holds if you aren't sure of the meaning of a word you've just heard or read. (Many people make a point of keeping a dictionary on their office bookshelf for just these purposes.)

JARGON

The world of business has done more than its share to inject jargon into American speech. "Corporate speak" is responsible for enshrining words such as *leveraging, downsize, value-driven,* and *proactive* in the jargon pantheon — while turning the nouns *impact* (as a replacement for *affect*), *transition* (for *change*), and *reference* (for *refer*) into verbs.

While many people think that using jargon makes them appear more professional, the fact is that jargon tends to muddy language, robbing it of sharpness and power. Stating your thoughts in clear, descriptive terms is usually preferable to couching them in jargon — though not always. If, for example, everyone in your company uses a certain term — *media opportunity* for *press conference* — it's better to grit your teeth and adopt its use.

SLANG

There is nothing inherently wrong with slang. Slang words lend vigor to speech, so long as they don't descend to the vulgar. Still, most obvious slang words, terms, and phrases should be used sparingly during a serious business discussion or formal meeting. When talking business in a more casual setting, how much slang you use will depend on both the demeanor and the vocabulary of your conversation partner.

THE ART OF CONVERSING

Being a good conversationalist is less a matter of eloquence than of adequately hearing others out and getting one's message across — a simple interaction that is vital to conducting business. In the 1937 edition of *Etiquette,* Emily Post wrote, "Ideal conversation must be an exchange of thought, and not, as many . . . believe, an eloquent exhibition of wit or oratory." She held that the secret to an effective dialogue with another person was not cleverness, but rather learning to "stop, look, and listen." "Stop," wrote Mrs. Post, means "not to rush recklessly forward" — that is, don't start talking merely for the sake of filling dead air. "Look" means to look the person to whom you are speaking in the eye. And "listen" means exactly that; it is, she said, "the best advice possible . . . since the person whom most people love . . . is a sympathetic listener."

Besides observing these timeless fundamentals, the businessperson who strives to become a good conversationalist remembers to do some things and avoid doing others. The pointers that follow apply equally whether you work in a software company where unconventionality reigns or in a workplace where staidness is more the style:

TALKING BUSINESS

Whenever you are discussing a contract, forging a deal, or doing business of any kind, think of your conversation in terms of three stages: the warm-up, the core, and the wrap-up.

The Warm-Up

Once you and your business companion have said your hellos and taken your seats, engage in a little small talk—chat that can range from the day's top news story to your golf handicap to, yes, the weather. A minimum of five to ten minutes is usually devoted to this opening stage. Throughout, camaraderie is punctuated by smiles and laughter, but only when genuinely called for. (See also "Small-Talk Tips," pages 56–57.)

The Core

After an appropriate amount of time, the talk turns to the business at hand. Make clear your personal investment in this longer portion of the conversation by sitting erect and making eye contact. As the conversation gets rolling, keep in mind that you are engaged in a dialogue, not a monologue. Even if you're launching into a lengthy explanation of a complicated new technology, draw the other person into the conversation by pausing occasionally to ask questions such as, "Am I making sense to you?" or, "What do you think so far?" Also be careful to use the word "you" as often as "I"; this conveys a message to your partner that you consider him or her integral, not tangential, to the business being discussed.

Although you should put smiles aside during this stage for the most part, don't abandon altogether the occasional snippet of small talk; leavening the conversation with the occasional funny aside or pertinent anecdote keeps the atmosphere more relaxed and helps you get your message across. Hammering your point too aggressively or relentlessly, on the other hand, can have the opposite effect.

The Wrap-Up

Ending with a brief recapitulation of any decisions made during the conversation ensures there are no misunderstandings. But once you've wrapped up your business and resumed your small talk, stick with it. Letting go of the business topic and ending the conversation on a purely social note is an implicit acknowledgment of the friendly nature of the business relationship.

THE ART OF LISTENING

The ability to listen is one of the most important talents you can bring to business conversations. What it takes to listen well is illustrated by this scenario:

A young woman named Leigh, then recently hired by a large bank based in Denver, had been looking forward to taking a vacation day on Friday. But she changed her plans on learning that she and a small group of other employees were invited to a Q&A session with a financier of some note. She was also nervous. "I'm really thrilled to be invited," she confided to a friend, "and you can bet I'll listen as hard as I can. But I just hope I *hear.*"

In her own way, Leigh perfectly described the three essential pieces of what psychologists call active (as opposed to passive) listening. They apply to telephone conversations as well as face-to-face meetings.

- **BE THERE**. If a session where valuable information will be exchanged is scheduled, attend it; even if it's at an inconvenient time, don't enlist a surrogate. You don't want to count on someone else to tell you about what was discussed. And when you do show up, be present mentally and emotionally as well; if your attention wanders, you're not really there.

- **LISTEN CAREFULLY**. Listen to every word, every tone, every pause. Take notes if the situation permits it. (Taking notes isn't usually a problem during telephone conversations—so keep pencil and paper near the phone.) If you're not sure about the propriety of notes (at lunch, for instance), the simplest thing to do is ask: "Mind if I jot down a couple of your points?"

- **HEAR**. Once you've grapsed the first two pieces, this one is the easiest. It is really an elevated form of hearing—fully mulling over and absorbing what the speaker is saying, why he is saying it, and what it means for your future association. With this step you become an active participant in an exchange of information, even though you may not have uttered a word for half an hour.

As for the young banker, she was there, she listened, and she heard—very successfully, it turned out. Her questions so impressed the financier that a year later, when she applied for a higher position at another bank, the financier wrote her a glowing letter of recommendation that eased her climb up the ladder.

THE ART OF QUESTIONING

Asking the right questions can set you on the road to success, whether you're participating in a meeting, dealing with a customer, or evaluating a new client, vendor, or other prospective business partner. Some people mistakenly believe that by asking questions, you're ceding control of the discussion to whoever is responding. Producing answers, they reason, is more impressive than questioning. But in reality, the reverse is true: Using questions creatively is actually a way of artfully guiding the discussion in the direction you want.

Asking questions has another benefit, as well: In business, as much as in social situations, most people really enjoy being afforded the chance to talk about themselves—their likes and dislikes, their views and opinions. You may have noticed that anybody with a reputation as a good conversationalist is less likely to be a raconteur than a person who asks thoughtful questions and listens well. When you encourage someone to talk, you will almost always learn things about them that you wouldn't learn if you chose to dominate the conversation—and you'll also leave a much more favorable impression.

THE GOOD LISTENER

In the corporate world, it's not only discourteous but also unprofessional to be an indifferent listener. Supervisors claim they can easily tell whether a subordinate has been listening by the quality of the questions asked at the end of a discussion, along with the accuracy of his or her summation. Score high as a listener by remembering to do the following:

- *Concentrate.* Pay close attention to what the other person is saying, no matter how tempted you are to let your mind wander. Also try your best to be patient with someone who's speaking too slowly or faltering in getting their message across.
- *Reconfirm.* To show you understand, occasionally paraphrase what the speaker is saying. Once you've picked up the rhythm of the other person's speech, you should be able to do this without seeming to interrupt.
- *Wait.* In conversation, patience is a virtue and interrupting is a sin. Remember that there's a fine line between the occasional interruption made to confirm or question a particular point and one that's made because the speaker is bursting to throw in his two cents' worth.
- *Question.* If you don't understand something, ask for an explanation. A likely time: when talk turns to computers or other technical subjects.
- *Respond.* Use positive body language to show you're paying attention. Lean slightly toward the speaker, and react to what he says with the occasional nod, smile, or cocked eyebrow.
- *Keep still.* If you're at your desk, don't shuffle papers or make a halfhearted effort to continue whatever you're working on. When standing, refrain from any distracting gestures, such as rattling the change in your pocket.

GENTLE GUIDANCE

The simple technique of seeming interested in what a person has to say can dissolve barriers of suspicion and build feelings of friendship and trust, allowing people to open up. It is a skill long used by successful diplomats, winning politicians, and the best salespeople. If you move the conversation along with gentle, intelligent questions, you'll more than likely gain valuable information, given freely, without seeming nosy or intrusive—information that makes all the difference in the outcome of a business transaction of any kind. Here are some conversational gambits that will help you get into areas that might be sensitive, and make your partner more likely to be forthcoming:

"I hope you don't mind my asking, but . . ."

"I was talking to an old friend the other day and he said the marketing plan looked a little weak, and I don't know if I agree. What do you think?"

"I read an industry report the other day about Behemoth Booksellers that claimed a merger was in the offing. . . . Have you heard anything like that?"

"If you don't think it's a good idea to tell me, please know I completely understand, but I was wondering . . ."

"My boss was delighted to hear that I was having lunch with you today. She's really sorry she couldn't join us, and she asked me to ask you if your company still plans to bid on the Epsom & Saltz project."

Note the frequent mention of third parties—"an old friend," "my boss," "an industry report." This helps remove your questions from the realm of personal curiosity to a more general, shared level of interest.

ABOUT BODY LANGUAGE

At times, the words and tone of the speaker may be enough to gauge the meaning of what is being said. But a person's posture, facial expressions, and gestures also send messages—some of which are open to interpretation, others of which come through loud and clear.

- **STANCE.** Someone who stands with back straight, shoulders back, and chin up flashes a message of self-confidence and ambition. Also note that standing with your hands clasped behind you is a more graceful and authoritative pose than sticking your hands in your pockets. Do not stand with your ankles locked or your arms crossed in front of you, nor should you hold on to one of your arms at the elbow; these poses signal shyness and insecurity.

- **SITTING.** Slouching in a chair conveys laziness, tiredness, even disrespect. Some body-language experts see crossing one's legs while seated as a defensive gesture, yet many people (men and women alike) simply find this position more comfortable. A less ambiguous signal is jiggling the knee, which communicates insecurity or apprehension, especially during an interview.

- **FACIAL EXPRESSIONS.** A smile denotes warmth, openness, and friendliness. But don't overdo it. False smiles make you look phony, whereas never-ending smiles invite suspicion. On the other side of the coin, a frown or a furrowed brow suggests anger or worry, even if your words are positive.

  Then there is the poker face. The desire to achieve this blank, noncommittal expression—believed by many to be an advantage when negotiating a deal—has led some businesspeople to get injections of Botox (short for botulinum toxin), a bacterial substance that works by paralyzing certain facial muscles and that eliminates wrinkles for a period of three to five months. Enthusiasts of the procedure—an extreme measure, but one that speaks to the temper of the times—have claimed that it keeps tension frowning to a minimum and makes them look more relaxed.

- **EYE CONTACT.** Looking into the other person's eyes shows your interest in the conversation. Do not, however, go to the other extreme: Staring can look threatening, not to mention strange. The desirable middle ground is reached by shifting your focus to other parts of the face from time to time.

- **GESTURING AND FIDGETING.** Go easy on the gestures: Using your hands to emphasize a point is fine, but overdoing it makes you look too excitable. Movements to be avoided include playing with your hair, tie, or jewelry; biting your lip; drumming your fingers; unconsciously snapping the clip on a ball-point pen; and jiggling the change or keys in your pocket.

- **NODDING.** Nodding doesn't necessarily mean you agree, but that you understand. Be careful, though: Too much positive head-nodding can make you seem like a kiss-up, especially when directed to your boss.

INTRODUCTIONS

Although the ways of going about an introduction are less rigid than they once were—a reflection of the casualness that has entered all segments of American life—the act itself remains as important as ever. Effective introductions put people at ease and serve to draw new acquaintances into a smoothly flowing, cohesive conversation. Learning how to do introductions effectively and then performing them with polish will also make you look confident and professional to coworkers, bosses, prospects, and clients. On the other hand, failing to introduce a newcomer or a stranger, whether a business associate at a meeting, a visitor to the office, or a guest at a party, is a serious social error.

THE ALL-IMPORTANT HANDSHAKE

Most people are sizing you up as they shake your hand. As straightforward as this everyday gesture may seem, take into account the following:

- *When to do it.* A handshake is in order not only when you're being introduced but also when you welcome people into your office, when you run into someone you know outside of work, when you say good-bye, and whenever another person offers his or her hand.

- *The gender question.* Until recently, it was considered polite for a man to wait for a woman to extend her hand before extending his own, but this is no longer customary—especially in business. Furthermore, women should shake hands with other women, even if hesitant to do so. Today a handshake is usually expected, regardless of one's gender.

- *The proper grip.* Your grip speaks volumes: A limp one suggests hesitance or timidity, and a bone-cruncher can come across as overly enthusiastic or domineering—not to mention painful. A medium-firm grip conveys confidence and authority. Also make sure your shake is palm-to-palm (not fingers-to-fingers), and keep your hand perpendicular to the ground. An upturned palm may subconsciously signal submissiveness; a downward palm, dominance.

- *The two-hand shake.* This involves clasping the outside of the greeter's hand with your free hand. While this kind of handshake signals warmth, it can seem presumptuous or insincere when used in a first meeting. Take care: Some people consider the two-hand shake too intimate for business, while others see it as a "power" move, intended to subtly intimidate the recipient.

- *Gloved handshakes.* When winter gloves are worn outdoors, common sense prevails: You needn't take them off to shake someone's hand. A woman attending an event that calls for formal attire leaves her gloves on when shaking hands, but she takes them off when it comes time to eat.

THE NON-SHAKER

From time to time, you may meet someone who doesn't offer their hand to be shaken. This may be due to a fear of germs, or the person may be from another country with different customs. If you are faced with a non-shaker, withdraw your hand as unobtrusively as possible and move on.

   If you are concerned yourself about coming into contact with another person's germs, take this far less rude approach: After introductions are made, keep your fingers and hands away from your mouth and eyes. Then, as soon as you can politely excuse yourself, make a trip to the restroom to wash your hands. Not shaking is a quick way to sour a potentially valuable relationship. Once you start off on the wrong foot, it is very hard to recover.

THE FOUR ESSENTIALS

Whether introducing yourself or being introduced by others, smile and stay relaxed. Always do the following:

- **STAND UP.** Today this rule applies to men and women alike. If there's no room to stand—you're wedged behind a table at a restaurant, for instance—briefly lift yourself out of your chair, extend your hand, and then say, "Please excuse me for not standing. I'm pleased to meet you."

- **SMILE AND MAKE EYE CONTACT.** Your smile conveys warmth, openness, and interest in the person you're meeting. Making eye contact shows that you're focused on her and her alone.

- **STATE YOUR GREETING.** The direct "How do you do?" or "Hello" or "It's so nice [great] to meet you" are excellent openers. Repeating the person's name—"How do you do, Ms. Dowd?"—not only is flattering but also helps you remember the person's name.

- **SHAKE HANDS.** A proper handshake lasts about three seconds; the clasped hands are pumped two or three times, after which you let go and step back

WHEN YOU'RE THE INTRODUCER

When it falls to you to make an introduction, remember two things: (1) Offer snippets of information about the people you're introducing (their professions, perhaps, or where they're from), and (2) state their names in full. "Ms. Dawson, this is Scott Bernstein, our marketing assistant. Scott, meet Carol Dawson, from Wilde and Wooley." Information about the person (in this case, the client) puts him or her into a context and provides an opening for conversation: "Wilde and Wooley? They've been going great guns lately, I hear." Or, "Do you know Karen Nelson? I used to work with her before she joined your firm."

Your choice of words when making an introduction is flexible. "I'd like you to meet . . ." or "May I introduce . . . ?" or any other reasonably gracious phrase you feel comfortable with is fine. When you are introducing people of unequal rank or age, use professional titles if they are called for. For example, a young salesman meeting a physician would be introduced to Dr. Michael Yamaguchi. An official title such as governor, congressman, or one of the various military ranks is retained even if the position is no longer held.

WHO'S INTRODUCED TO WHOM?

The question of who to introduce to whom is solved by following one simple rule: Talk to the more important person first.

- If you're talking to a client and your boss approaches you, say to the client, "Mr. Client, I would like to introduce you to my boss, Mr. Manager." Then, turning to your boss, you say, "Mr. Manager, I would like you to meet Mr. Client. Mr. Client is CEO of . . ."

- If you are talking to your boss and a client approaches you, say to your boss, "Excuse me." Then turn to the approaching client and say, "Mr. Client, how nice to see you. I would like to introduce you to my supervisor, Mr. Manager." Then turn back to your boss and say, "Mr. Manager, I would like you to meet Mr. Client. Mr. Client is CEO of . . ."

Importance can be defined in many ways: by job level, age, experience, and degree of public recognition. A client or prospect is always considered more important than a supervisor or boss. If you're not sure who takes precedence, make an arbitrary choice and forge ahead with the introduction. A slight error in protocol is much less of a misstep than failing to make the introduction at all. When introducing peers of equal status, it doesn't matter whom you talk to first—again, what matters is that you make the introduction.

INTRODUCING SOMEONE TO A GROUP

If you find yourself introducing someone to a group—a circle of friends at a cocktail party, for example—wait for a conversational opening to present itself, then grab your chance: "Hi, everybody. I'd like to introduce you to Sandy Vail, who's in from Tennessee." Next, introduce the people standing near Sandy by name. Others can introduce themselves later. If, however, the person you are introducing is one of your clients and the group is made up of colleagues, then the client is the "important" one to whom the others are presented: "Linda Ambrose, I'd like you to meet our sales staff."

HUGS AND KISSES

Hugs and kisses in greetings usually take these five forms:

- *The kiss.* Kisses on the cheek are better left to social situations. In business, men and women executives should refrain from kissing in public, since even a peck on the cheek might be misconstrued. The occasional peck on the cheek is the exception when the parties know each other well, especially when they greet each other at a quasi-social event like a convention.

- *The air-kiss.* What began as a way of avoiding lipstick traces and smudged makeup is now a fad. The lips are puckered and the cheek is put alongside the other person's cheek; a full-fledged air-kiss repeats the gesture on the other cheek. The habit of air-kissing often looks artificial in a business setting: To the person watching, it looks insincere; to the recipient, it may seem all the more artificial.

- *The bear hug.* Save this two-armed hug for old friends or for business associates with whom you're especially close and haven't seen for a long time.

- *The semi-hug.* Engaging in a momentary clutch (each person placing his or her arms briefly around the other person's shoulders) is sometimes appropriate among businesspeople of the same sex, but only if they have a close personal friendship as well.

- *The shoulder clutch.* This involves grabbing each other's right upper arm or shoulder with the free hand while shaking hands. It is best used by business associates who haven't seen each other for a long time but maintain a warm relationship.

No matter what profession you're in, avoid close contact with another person when you are ill. It's more welcoming to tell someone you have a cold and keep your distance than to risk infecting him or her.

WHEN YOU ARE INTRODUCED

When you are the one being introduced, be sure to follow the four essentials for an introduction—beginning with standing up. If the person making the introduction is having trouble remembering your name, rescue the situation by offering your name to the introducer or extending your hand and saying your name directly to the other person.

If an introducer gets your name wrong, mispronounces it, or relays inaccurate information about your job or background, politely make the correction without embarrassing him or her. "Actually, it's June, not Joan." Getting your name straight matters most when

(1) you expect to see the person you're being introduced to again or (2) the person will be introducing you to others. If you're permanently parting ways, it's best to let the error slide.

INTRODUCING YOURSELF

If you're attending a business meeting or social gathering and no one introduces you, jump right in. Just step up and say, "I don't believe we've met. I'm Mary Buchwald from Hill and Dale." Be sure to state your first and last names and, if necessary, ask others to state both of theirs.

Refrain from putting a courtesy title or honorific before your name when introducing yourself: "Hello, I'm Mary Buchwald"—not Mrs. Mary Buchwald. Doctors and Ph.D.'s show themselves in a better light if they drop the "Dr." and use only their names. Leaving a title unstated suggests self-confidence and humility; if need be, one's credentials will be revealed in due course.

CONCERNING NAMES

Etiquette says you shouldn't use a person's first name until he asks you to do so; at the same time, rigid adherence to this custom can make you look obsequious or pretentious.

Take your cue from the person you're greeting. If he immediately calls you Jack, there may be an unspoken understanding that you're on a first-name basis. When in doubt—if the person is elderly, for example, a top-level executive, or even a public figure—test the waters before taking the plunge. One use of "Mr. Quinby" will usually give you the answer. Unless he says "Please call me Roy," keep using "Mr." or the appropriate honorific, or simply refrain from using his name for the rest of the chat.

REMEMBERING NAMES

For many people, names go in one ear and out the other during introductions. Their minds suddenly go blank and nervousness sets in the moment they have to shake hands. If they concentrate on anything, it's themselves—the impression they're making and whether they're saying the right thing—rather than on mentally registering the other person's name.

Overcome this problem by putting the focus on the other person as you're being introduced. When someone offers her hand, make a point of listening to her name, repeating it in your greeting, and then imprinting it in your mind by visualizing how it would look written down—or even emblazoned across a billboard.

Associating a person's name with a visual image is another method advised by some experts. If you're lucky, the person's name will easily lend itself to associations: for Mr. Green, a golf course or green piece of clothing; for Miss O'Hare, a rabbit or a head of bushy hair; for Mr. Baker, a loaf of bread or a chef's toque.

FORGOTTEN NAMES

If you suffer a memory lapse when greeting or introducing someone you've met before, don't be ashamed to admit it. Be honest and calm: "I remember meeting you, but I simply can't recall your name." Instead of concentrating on your own embarrassment, try to put the other person at ease. It's much better to admit your memory lapse than not to do the introduction.

Try to avoid bluntly saying, "What did you say your name is?" Better excuses are "I've just drawn a blank" or "My memory gets worse by the day," which puts the blame on you. If you recall anything at all about the person, bring it up: "I clearly remember the conversation we had about Fiji, but your name seems to have slipped my mind. What is it again?" Or you could look incredulous and utter something such as "I can't believe I've forgotten your name. I'm so sorry!"

DIFFICULT NAMES

If the name of someone to whom you're being introduced is misunderstood or highly unusual, ask for it again: "I'm sorry, I didn't quite catch your name." Making sure that you have a name correct shows respect and consideration. If the name is especially complicated and you expect to see the person again, ask him or her to give you a business card.

If someone mispronounces your name and does it more than once, gently correct them (in private, if possible) with a word association: "It's SHILL-er, as in thrill." You could also make a joke of it: "I've heard people pronounce my name thirty different ways, but it's actually . . ." A smile on your face as you say this shows that you don't take the mistake personally.

WHEN INTRODUCTIONS ARE UNNECESSARY

If you're walking with a group and meet someone you know coming in the opposite direction, etiquette says you're not required to pause and make introductions. If you stop to chat briefly, the group should continue on while you finish your conversation and catch up. Likewise, if you're dining with a group and someone you know walks by your table, you're not obliged to introduce them to your assembled friends. If you want to exchange a few words with the person, step away from the table. On the other hand, if there is any question in your mind as to whether you should make introductions, then by all means make them.

17 | *On the Telephone*

Thirty years ago, who could have dreamed that placing a call to a business or government department would be as frustrating as it is today? Being put on hold indefinitely or hearing a recorded voice telling us to "press 1 for . . ." slams an electronic door on us and our simple wish to connect with a human being. We press and press again, our blood pressure rising, until we finally reach the desired person—on tape, as often as not, asking us to please leave a message. But here's the bottom line: Whether or not you're ultimately successful in completing a call, any frustration must be brushed aside. Smart businesspeople treat even a recording device with courtesy. A message left in an upbeat tone of voice gives the recipient of your call confidence in both you and your company; an irritated tone does quite the opposite.

PLACING BUSINESS CALLS

Before placing your call, prepare by writing down any questions you want to raise, along with the specific topics you want to cover. Even if an item seems minor, jot it down; it's easy to forget something once the conversation starts rolling. Then place these notes by the phone so you can refer to them throughout the call. If your phone call involves facts and figures, gather together all data sheets or other reference materials you might need. Also, have a blank pad and pen handy, so you can take notes during the conversation, and a desk calendar, in case you need to set dates.

No matter who answers your call—the person you're trying to reach, a receptionist, an assistant, or your contact's voice mail—identify yourself at once. Unless you're calling someone with whom you regularly do business, identify your company, too: "This is Katherine Bowlin of Sellmore Marketing." Give your full name even if you talk with the person fairly often, since he may not be as familiar with your voice as you think. Using your first and last names each time you call will also reinforce your name recognition.

Next, quickly explain why you've called and ask if this is a convenient time to talk. (Failing to ask this question is one of the most common of all telephone errors.) If he says talking now is fine, state the purpose and estimated length of the call: "Mr. Peterson, I have a question about the marketing proposal. It should take about five minutes." Try to be honest: If you suspect five minutes is a conservative estimate, say so.

If the person you call says he's busy, ask when you might call back. Try to avoid having him return the call—this may put you in the awkward spot of not having your thoughts collected or your notes at hand when the call comes out of the blue.

WRONG NUMBERS

If you've dialed a wrong number, admit it and apologize. Don't just hang up. Instead, simply deliver the line that has done service in the cause of good manners for generations: "I'm sorry. I must have dialed the wrong number." Then give the person the number you were trying to reach, to make sure you don't make the same mistake twice.

YOU'RE PUT ON HOLD?

If you reach a receptionist who transfers incoming calls or an assistant who takes calls for her boss, chances are, you'll be asked if you mind being put on hold. If pressed for time, tell the person answering that you'd prefer simply to leave a message—then leave your name, your company name, a brief reason for the call, and either when you can be reached or when you'll call back.

If you are placed on hold and more than three minutes pass, it's perfectly proper to hang up and call back later. Even though you've been treated badly, try not to betray your annoyance. Politely say that you were unable to hold, and leave it at that: No explanation is required.

USING A SPEAKERPHONE

A cardinal rule for using a speakerphone: Immediately tell the person on the other end of the line that you are using one. If he or she expresses any hesitation, explain why you feel it necessary to be on speaker—because you'd like other people in the room to be included in the conversation, for instance, or because it makes it easier for you to take notes. Most people won't mind as long as they're asked beforehand and they understand the reason for using the device.

If others are present, identify them at the very start of the conversation: "There are three people from marketing who'll be joining in—Leslie Marshall, Andy Armistead, and Kathy Kincannon." The participants should then introduce themselves so that the person on the other end can begin to link voices to names—sometimes a difficult task, since voices emanating from these devices often sound as if they were coming from a well. Confusion will be kept to a minimum if each participant identifies himself when he speaks to the listener: "Tom, Andy here." You can also make it clear who's talking by saying "I agree with what Kathy just said" or "I see Leslie has a question for you."

ANOTHER IMPORTANT TIP. Close your office door before making any call using a speakerphone. Even though voices are amplified by a speakerphone, people generally tend to talk louder than usual when using one. The result? Workmates within earshot are disturbed by the noise.

PHONE-CALL FAUX PAS

Following are telephone errors made by even the best-behaved businesspeople. Most apply to phone calls in general, not just those from the office.

- Don't do other things at your desk while talking on the phone. Typing or shuffling papers suggests that your attention is elsewhere.

- Eating while on the phone is not only distracting but also subjects the other person to unnerving smacks and crunches. Because sounds are magnified over the telephone, even a cough drop in the mouth can make its presence known.

- Don't leave a radio playing or office equipment running in the background. These sounds, too, are magnified over the phone.

- Never chew gum while talking on the phone. While gum chewing may not be offensive to some people, you have no way of knowing whether your phone mate considers it unprofessional and crass.

- Don't sneeze, blow your nose, or cough directly into the receiver. Either excuse yourself for a moment or turn your head away.

- If you have to put the receiver down during the conversation, set it gently on the desk to avoid startling your phone mate with a sudden bang.

- Don't address a business associate by his or her first name in sentence after sentence: It sounds insincere and patronizing.

- You wouldn't abruptly end a face-to-face encounter just because another colleague walked into your office—so why do so many people feel it's okay to break off a conversation to take a phone call? If you're holding a meeting in your office and the phone rings, don't answer unless you're expecting an important call—in which case you should apologize to those present for the interruption. If possible, make arrangements before the meeting to have all calls channeled to voice mail or to an assistant's or coworker's phone; or if you have a "Do Not Disturb" button on your phone, use it.

- For practical reasons, some executives have assistants stay on the line for the entire call. Even if the conversation is about business and business only, letting your phone mate know that someone else is listening in is without doubt the best thing to do.

ANSWERING BUSINESS CALLS

Never underestimate the importance of how you answer the phone. You never know when it may be the first call from a potential client or customer. Your attitude and demeanor, in turn, will form her initial impression of your company, and you want it to be positive, not poor. Two other considerations:

- An incoming call answered by an actual person instead of a machine will not only make a good impression; it will also earn the caller's eternal gratitude by not putting her in electronic limbo.

- Forget your personal problems. Your voice should sound pleasant and calm whenever you answer the phone, no matter how overworked or rattled you feel. Remember, you're speaking for the company, not yourself.

Whenever possible, answer the phone promptly—that is, by the third ring. Answering with your full name is an absolute necessity whenever a call is coming from outside. Then what to say? Although "Helen Bonner speaking" is not impolite, "This is Helen Bonner" may sound somewhat less abrupt to some ears. Then follow with something on the order of "Can I help you?"

If you work in a company with several departments, state your department after your name: "This is Angela Dixon, Rights and Permissions." This saves time for both you and the caller, eliminating the need to ask "Is this Mr. Worsham's office?" or "Have I reached the accounting department?"

You're terribly busy? If you don't have an assistant to field incoming calls and a client or customer calls at an inconvenient time, give her precedence over any work you're doing if at all possible. If this is impossible, explain your predicament and tell her you'll phone back whenever it suits her. Agree on a time, and then keep your word. If you do have an assistant, ask her to take messages or route calls to your voice mail when you're busy; or if your phone system allows, press the "Do Not Disturb" button.

IF YOU SHARE AN EXTENSION

When answering a phone shared by others, state the department name before giving your own: "Quality Control, Bill Fryer speaking." If the call is for someone else, say "Just a moment, please" before handing over the receiver. If the person isn't in, tell the caller when he's expected back, if you know, and offer to take a message. Don't volunteer gratuitous information about why someone's not available. If the person is in a meeting or on vacation, say so. Otherwise, don't feel you have to explain his whereabouts. "He's not back from lunch" and similar comments risk raising questions about his work habits.

If you go in search of the person being called, tell the caller how long it will take: "If you can wait two minutes, I'll try to find him." If you haven't located the person within the allotted time, return to the phone with your update. "I'm sorry, but I couldn't find him. If you give me your name and number, I'll leave them on his desk." An alternative is to ask if the caller wants to be routed to the person's voice mail to leave the message himself.

RETURNING CALLS

The number of businesspeople who prefer to hide behind their voice mail is growing by leaps and bounds. Don't be one of them. If someone leaves a message asking you to call back, do so as soon as possible—or at least on the same day the call was received. Twenty-four hours is as long as a call can go unreturned without violating the precepts of good manners. This golden rule is also good business practice—yet it is broken more than almost any other.

If it's an especially busy day and you suspect the call will take more time than you can spare, call the person back, explain the situation, and ask if you can set a time to talk later. Or if you have an assistant, ask him or her to call back and explain the delay, and then arrange a callback time that will be convenient for both parties.

TRANSFERRING CALLS

If whoever you're talking with needs to be transferred to someone else in your company, first give the caller the correct extension in case she is disconnected. Then tell the person to whom the call's being transferred who is on the line and why she is phoning; this spares callers from having to repeat themselves.

THE ART OF THE HOLD

If not handled properly, the words "Hold please" can be two of the cruelest in the English language. Receptionists, assistants, secretaries, and all others who field incoming calls need to be sympathetic to the holder's dilemma. Doing the following will help keep frustration and annoyance to a minimum:

- Never tell someone to hold; ask them instead. More important still, wait for the answer. The question "Could I please put you on hold?" is doubly irritating when immediately followed by silence or recorded music.

- Give the reason for the hold. "Ms. Tomkins is on another line," for example. Or "She's somewhere nearby; I'll have to page her" or "I'll have to check to see who can handle that."

- When someone is holding, deliver a progress update every 60 seconds: "I thought she was almost done with her call, but she's still on the line." At the second or third check, ask whether the person would like to keep waiting or would rather leave a message.

- When you finally transfer the call, give the caller your colleague's name and extension in case he or she becomes disconnected.

SCREENING CALLS

Assistants also bear the burden of screening calls for their bosses and others. This is an area where touchiness abounds. A caller who's asked his name, put on hold, and then told the desired person is unavailable, for example, may feel he has been deemed unimportant. Similarly, a caller who's asked "What does this call concern?" might resent having an assistant determine whether his call is worth putting through. (By the way, if you are asked that question, it's your obligation to answer, even if the matter is a complicated one; the briefest summary — "It has to do with the new banana importing law" — should be satisfactory.)

It is up to those whose calls are being screened to furnish their assistants with the language to be used. It's then the assistant's job to use that language with a courteous tone.

POINTS OF POLITENESS

As you mind the more obvious p's and q's of telephone manners, adopting the following three practices will help you make an even better impression:

- *Hold back on first names.* If you haven't met someone and have some reason to suspect she doesn't share your informal nature, don't call her by her first name straight off. Unless she has started the talk with "Call me Rhonda. What can I do for you?" address her as Ms. Jones. An assumption from the outset that the two of you are on a first-name basis can be a mistake; to many people, especially those who are older, it is overly familiar and impolite.

- *Go easy on "you."* During the course of the call, be careful not to overuse the word "you" — especially when your phone mate hasn't met a deadline or taken care of a problem. "You forgot" or "You neglected to" can sound accusatory on the phone, even when said in a pleasant tone. Putting your comments in the form of a question is preferable: "Could you get that to me by Friday?" or "Did you complete the report on that project?"

- *Listen carefully.* The impersonal nature of a phone call makes it easy for you to tune out, even when a business call requires your utmost attention. Listening closely not only is courteous but also ensures you won't miss any details. Also be sure to let the caller know you're listening. Since you can't show this with a nod, a smile, or other visual responses, use verbal responses instead: "Yes, I understand," "Of course," and "I see." (See "The Art of Listening," page 213.)

CALLER ID

Caller ID devices, which attach to your phone and display the number and sometimes the name of the person placing the call, can be both beneficial and bewildering. A positive: They allow you to prepare for a call before answering it. A negative: Answering your phone and using the caller's name at the outset may throw him or her off guard; you may come off as being sneaky — plus, the caller may not be the person identified on the screen.

BUSINESS CALLS IN PROGRESS

Once you do get through to the person you're calling, keep in mind that the impression you make depends entirely on your voice and choice of words, not your appearance; this makes it all the more important to sound professional and personable. Even when rushed, make an effort to speak slowly and distinctly. One much-advised technique for sounding upbeat is to smile as you speak—the theory being that a smile makes the voice brighter and more pleasant. Even the way you hold the receiver matters: Tucking it under your chin or holding it below your mouth makes you harder to understand.

Follow cues from the person you're speaking with to establish the call's tone. If someone is all-business and no-nonsense, you should be, too. Others may be informal and chatty. In the latter case, indulging someone who strays off the business subject may have the benefit of leading to the discovery of common interests or backgrounds, provided the tangent doesn't distract you from the purpose of your call. People who've never met face-to-face sometimes click and establish a kind of telephonic bond. The goodwill that results makes it all the easier for you to keep the business relationship running smoothly.

CALL WAITING AND OTHER INTERRUPTIONS

Being interrupted by a second call is less common than it once was, now that most office phone systems have voice mail, which automatically records a message from a second caller if you're on the phone. If your office phone still has call waiting without voice mail and it clicks on, apologize to the first caller and say you'll return immediately; put him or her on hold and quickly explain to the other caller that you'll have to call back.

When you switch to the incoming caller, try your best to keep a conversation from starting: Your responsibility is to the first caller, who should never be left on hold for more than thirty seconds; even this brief period can seem like an eternity when a conversation that's going full steam is interrupted. If the incoming call is extremely urgent or from overseas, however, explain to your first caller why you must hang up and set the time you'll call back.

When you have to put someone on hold for other reasons—retrieving data sheets from another office, for example—apologize and tell them how long you'll be off the line. Then return when promised, even if you haven't found what you're looking for. If necessary, explain that you'll need a few more minutes and will call back as soon as your search is successful.

When a coworker arrives at your office door and sees you are on the phone, he should have the courtesy to leave. If he hovers and becomes a distraction, stop the conversation at an opportune moment and say, "Will you excuse me for a moment? There's someone at the door." Then quickly determine why the other person is there, or mouth, "I'll see you later."

MECHANICAL GLITCHES

When a disconnection occurs, it is the caller's responsibility to call back. If you initiated the call, immediately redial the person and apologize, even if you're not at fault: "I'm sorry; we somehow got disconnected. I think we left off with the annual report." Redial even if the conversation was nearing an end; not calling back is like walking off in the middle of a face-to-face talk.

If you're the one who was called, stay off the line. If the person who made the call doesn't ring back within five or six minutes, you may then call him or her, saying, "I'm not sure we were through talking when the line went dead."

If a bad connection or static on the line makes it difficult to hear, don't be embarrassed to ask the other person to hang up so that you can try again. A second call often solves the problem, even when placed right away.

USING VIDEOPHONES AND TEXT TELEPHONES

Workplaces staffed largely with young, technology-minded employees are more likely to be equipped with videophones, which use a built-in camera to project your image to the caller. These devices can also be used as regular phones by simply switching off the camera. No special rules apply: A call on a videophone involves no more preparation than getting ready to answer the front door—you just have to look presentable enough for a face-to-face encounter.

Also coming into wider use for people who are deaf or hard-of-hearing are text telephones, also called teletypes (TTYs) or telecommunication devices for the deaf (TDDs). These devices, which look like small typewriters, permit two people to communicate by typing back and forth in a conversational manner over a phone line.

If your office isn't equipped with a TDD, you can still communicate with the deaf or hard-of-hearing by using a relay service. In this case, the hearing caller speaks to a mediator, who relays words to the recipient by teletyping them into a console; the words then appear in the display window of the recipient's device.

If conversing with a deaf or hard-of-hearing person over a TDD, keep the following two things in mind:

- Address him directly, as if the mediator weren't present. Do not say, "Tell him that . . ." or "Ask him to . . ."

- As with any other call, adhere to the precepts of telephone etiquette.

CLOSING A CALL

When you end a business call, don't leave matters hanging. Wind things down with a conclusive statement: "I'll get the final figures to you by noon Friday" or "I think we agree we need more research. Shall we talk again, maybe tomorrow?" Then sign off on a positive note with a polite acknowledgment: "Thank you for calling" or "It's been nice talking with you."

A few minutes spent discussing things that have nothing to do with the business at hand are perfectly in order after callers have established a friendly relationship. But don't overdo it: Without any visual clues from your phone mate, it's hard to tell when you're wearing out your welcome.

THE CELL PHONE

Cell phones are great when used properly; they allow the user to be more immediately reachable. Their very utility, however, is also their downfall. Inappropriate use of cell phones does more to damage business relationships than almost anything else. When a businessperson becomes a slave to the phone rather than the master of it, she has crossed the line and will end up using it inappropriately.

Here are five critical tips every cell phone user should know and use:

1   Don't let your phone ring if the ringing will disturb others around you. Meetings, presentations, plays, and movies—these are all times when turning the cell phone off (or at least setting it to vibrate) is mandatory.

2   Don't take your phone out and start using it if there is any possibility the people around you will be bothered by your use of it. Also, don't assume they won't listen to your conversation. Remember: It's much harder to ignore a conversation when you hear only one side of it than when you hear both people talking.

3   Absolutely never say anything confidential, personal, or private if others can overhear you. Instead, stop the conversation by telling the other person you'll call back when you can talk privately.

4   Speak quietly. Most people's phone voices are consistently louder than their regular voices. When speaking on a cell phone, you need to be especially careful not to shout—otherwise you'll end up sharing your conversation with everyone in the waiting room.

5   Don't overdo it. One brief conversation isn't likely to disturb anyone, but an hour and a half of continuous use may drive those around you crazy.

ON THE STREET

Cell phones come into their own on the sidewalk or in a cab, when there is often good reason to use one: You've left the office and are delayed for an appointment, or you've forgotten to relay an urgent piece of information to someone, or you suddenly remember you need another set of figures for a meeting. Just remember not to shout into your phone while walking down the street: It's you, not your phone mate, who is contending with traffic noise. What's more, talking loudly may leave the impression to passersby that you're eager to call attention to yourself. Another consideration: Remember safety and pay attention to your surroundings, especially when crossing intersections or maneuvering on crowded sidewalks.

IN RESTAURANTS

While cell phones have a place in business, using them in a restaurant is another matter entirely. That old rule of "a time and a place for everything" applies here especially: After all, restaurants are places where people come to relax and dine, as a respite from the workday grind. Some restaurants, in fact, require cell phones to be checked at the door or to be used only outside the dining areas. The rule is simple: Excuse yourself from the table and make or take the call in an anteroom, a restroom, or a lobby or step outside. There are exceptions to this rule, of course—for example, a doctor who is on call. At business and social meals alike, making or receiving a phone call at the table is both inconsiderate and intrusive.

So what if the person at the next table is gabbing away on a phone while you're trying to talk business? If his voice is rising above the ambient noise, a dirty look will probably be little more than water off a duck's back. Instead, ask the waiter or manager to talk with the offender. Never approach a stranger and try to correct his behavior. You have no idea how he will react, and the result could be an unpleasant—and unhelpful—confrontation.

IN THE CAR

Phoning from moving vehicles brings up the question not only of etiquette but also of safety. Carrying on a phone conversation diverts the driver's attention from the road, and driving with only one hand heightens the danger even more. Many states are jumping on the bandwagon and making it illegal to use handheld cell phones in an automobile—so be aware of the laws in your area. The use of a portable speakerphone, a built-in phone, or a hands-free device (a headband with a mouthpiece that plugs into a cell phone) will lessen the risk, but the smartest choice is to pull over to the side of the road before making a call.

ANOTHER NECESSARY COURTESY. Let your phone mate know if there are other people in the car who will be privy to the conversation.

PAGERS

The annoyance potential for pagers, or beepers, is as high as that for cell phones. Those who use them should remember that however urgent the page, the pager should be turned off at once, especially at a public gathering.

Happily, the days of the audible pager are numbered. Just as the boom box has been largely replaced by portable CD, tape, and MP3 players and earphones, noisemaking pagers are being supplanted by ones that signal a page with a light, a low-volume tone, or a silent vibration; newer models also feature voice mail and numeric and alphanumeric messages.

ANSWERING MACHINES AND VOICE MAIL

Whether you use an answering machine in a home office or are connected to a voice mail service at your company, there are certain practicalities and civilities you need to keep in mind:

MESSAGE CHECKLIST

When you take a telephone message, both the caller and the person you're taking the message for will appreciate it if you do the following:

- *Get the name and number right.* Ask the caller's complete name. Also ask for the spelling, since many names can be spelled more than one way—for example, Jean or Jeanne, Allen or Alan, Deborah or Debra, Anderson or Andersen. Then read the phone number back to the caller.

- *Ask the name of the caller's company.* This may help the person for whom you're taking the message identify the caller more easily. It also provides an idea of what the call may be about.

- *Note the date and hour.* Jot down the time the call came in, so the person knows how long the message has been sitting there.

- *Add your initials or name.* Do this in case the person receiving the message wants to know more about the call.

- *Deliver your message.* All your good effort to write the information down will be wasted if you don't make sure the message gets to the intended recipient.

RECORDING A GREETING

On your office phone, a no-nonsense, straightforward greeting is the better choice by far. Short and sweet is the goal—your full name, your company name, and a request that the caller leave a message: "This is Miguel Hernandez at Johnson-Cowles. Please leave your name and number and I'll call you back."

You may also want to change your greeting daily to give callers an idea of your schedule: "On Tuesday, July 12, I'll be in a meeting in the early afternoon, but I should be in my office for the rest of the day. If you leave a message, I'll call you back as soon as possible." You might also refer callers to an assistant or someone else in your department: "If you need to speak with someone immediately, you can call Cassandra Reagor at extension 7131."

When you're going away on a business trip or vacation, change your greeting before you depart. After identifying yourself, say "I'll be out of the office until Monday, August 17. Please call back then." (For safety and security, if you work at home, do not leave this message. Instead, simply ask callers to leave their name and number.) You should also give the name and number of someone else in your department to contact if an issue needs to be discussed before you return.

LEAVING A MESSAGE

A cardinal rule when leaving a message is to state your name and number slowly and clearly at the start of the message. Many people ramble on until they realize they're about to be cut off, then recite their number so quickly that it's often indecipherable. Also, keep your message short: Since most people have little tolerance for long messages, you risk getting passed over or deleted if you don't get straight to the point. Worse still, long messages can overwhelm a voice mail system. Finally, repeat your name and number at the end of the message.

RETURNING CALLS

Return all calls left on your answering machine or voice mail within twenty-four hours. If you are the one leaving a message, reduce the potential for telephone tag by stating where you can be reached and when—then make it a point to be available at that time. If something comes up and you can't keep your promise, leave a second message explaining the circumstances and saying when you plan to call again. Then do it: Not calling back when you said you would is the equivalent of standing someone up.

18 | *The Good Writer*

In our so-called Information Age, no skill is more important than the ability to organize and convey information with clarity and coherence. Ultimately, this means being able to write effectively. Virtually every form of business requires writing of some kind—letters to clients, memos to coworkers, reports, requests, recommendations, manuals, newsletters, PowerPoint presentations, even notes for the office suggestion box. Some types of business writing are highly formalized, such as the financial section of a company's annual report. Others are extremely informal: interoffice e-mail, for example. Most of the material today's businessperson is expected to write falls into the category of "general writing"—more organized and attentive to correct grammar and construction than spoken conversation, but not nearly so rigid and rule-bound as legal or scientific writing. Whatever the format, however, all good writing must meet four basic tests:

- Is it accurate? (Does it correctly describe the situation?)

- Is it clear? (Have you said what you intended to say?)

- Is it coherent? (Will it make sense to the reader?)

- Is it correct? (Are there any misspellings, typos, grammatical mistakes, or structural errors?)

THE IMPORTANCE OF GRAMMAR

It is interesting how often we use the language of building when discussing writing. We "construct" sentences. We "structure" paragraphs. Words are the basic building blocks of writing . . . and grammar is the blueprint.

If your grammar is poor, you won't be able to say what you mean; you may even convey messages that you don't intend. Your audience—the reader—may form a negative opinion of your competence or your seriousness. It is not exaggerating to say that the writer of an ungrammatical letter (a job-application cover letter, for example) may live to regret it.

There are numerous excellent books that detail correct grammar use and elegant writing. Buy at least one and keep it handy as a reference source. These include but certainly are not limited to

- *The Elements of Style*, 4th ed., by William Strunk Jr. and E. B. White (Pearson Education, 1999)

- *On Writing*, by Stephen King (Simon & Schuster, 2001)

- *Chicago Manual of Style*, 15th ed., by the University of Chicago Press, ed. (University of Chicago Press, 2003)

- *Eats, Shoots & Leaves: The Zero Tolerance Approach to Punctuation*, by Lynne Truss (Gotham Books, 2004)

SELF-CHECK: READ IT ALOUD

When you receive an important communication, try reading it out loud. Voicing the words of others literally forces you to slow down and hear the way the words are put together.

Similarly, if you're stuck on a writing project, take a few minutes to explain what you're trying to say to a colleague—then write that explanation. If no one is available, visualize such a conversation instead.

Finally, once you've finished a piece of writing, make a point of reading your writing out loud. You'll quickly hear the spots where your argument sounds forced, your phraseology is clichéd, or your grammar falls short. If you're repeating yourself or taking too long to make your point, that will quickly become apparent as well.

ORGANIZE AND OUTLINE

Many people can write a grammatical sentence but are unable to put together a coherent paragraph. Their ideas tumble around like clothes in a dryer, making it impossible to sort the shirts from the socks. Even the most indulgent reader won't put up for long with confused, chaotic writing.

To avoid this fate, always take time to outline your thoughts before you actually start writing. Begin by jotting down the main points you want to make, then look over your notes and decide how best to organize them. Here are two ways:

- *The step-by-step outline.* This works best when you want to explain a process. If a step is out of order, you'll be able to spot the error in your outline and make the correction.

- *The cause-and-effect outline.* Use this when you want to describe how something happened. Make an outline that clearly relates the cause and the ensuing consequences.

Outlining may seem time-consuming, but down the line it will save you much rethinking and rewriting. (Happily, word-processing software is available that aids the outlining process.) An outline will also help you stay on track as you write. It's often tempting to follow an interesting tangent, add unnecessary details, or drop in an amusing comment or personal story. But your readers have time constraints, too. They want you to get to the point quickly and make your case clearly; every extraneous bit of information becomes a distraction and a delay.

BE CONSISTENT

When Ralph Waldo Emerson opined that "a foolish consistency is the hobgoblin of little minds," he wasn't writing a business letter. Consistency in business writing is a virtue: It's essential to clarity, and brings an important unity to your writing in terms of point of view, tense, and mood. As you compose your rough draft and then edit it, keep the following factors in mind:

POINT OF VIEW
When you begin a piece of writing, you first have to decide what point of view to use in telling your story—either the first person (*I, me, my, mine, we, us, our, ours*), the second person (*you, your, yours*), or the third person (*he, she, it, him, her, his, hers, its, they, them, their, theirs*). Your job is to select a point of view and then stick with it. Readers will find it hard to follow writing that shifts from one perspective to another.

FIRST PERSON
Business writers frequently use this point of view, especially in letters, memos, and internal reports. It offers an individualized, personalized perspective. The first person can also be found in formal writing, but it is most often used when the writer wishes to set a friendly, more casual tone.

SECOND PERSON
This point of view is less common because it adopts the viewpoint of the reader rather than the writer. It is most appropriate in writing that instructs (this book, for example). The second per-

son can also be used in letters. Be careful, though: Second-person writing can easily become accusatory, judgmental, and hostile: "You should know that . . ." or "Your duty is to . . ."

THIRD PERSON

This is an objective viewpoint. It allows the writer to maintain a detached perspective—an observer of the action, rather than a direct participant. The third person generally sets a more formal tone than the first person. In the language of journalism, it is the reportorial, not editorial, point of view.

TENSE

Tense indicates when an action or event takes place. All verbs have tenses to indicate whether something is happening in the present, happened in the past, or will happen in the future: "I'm eating at the Greasy Spoon"; "I ate at the Greasy Spoon last Tuesday"; "I will eat at the Greasy Spoon next week." Unless there is a clear difference in time ("We received your broken fax machine yesterday, and we will repair it next week"), select the tense that expresses the time frame of your writing and use it consistently.

MOOD

A final unifying element in writing is mood. This is the attitude of the writer, reflected in the tone of the writing. You may wish to take a serious tone that reflects your knowledge and professionalism when writing a report or proposal. Conversely, you might choose a light, joking tone when writing a memo about the annual Christmas party to members of your work team. You will probably want to adopt a conciliatory and polite tone when writing to a customer with a complaint, whereas a tougher, no-nonsense tone could be the best choice in a performance review for an employee who constantly procrastinates on assignments.

Whatever mood you adopt, be sure that it is the one that's most appropriate for your purpose: "Boy, did we have a wild year!" hardly sets the right tone for the annual report of a company that has suffered major financial losses. Once you've decided on the right tone, maintain it throughout. Sudden changes in mood—what might be called manic-depressive writing—disorient the reader and leave the impression that the writer is uncertain or conflicted about the subject.

PROOFREAD

Once you've gone through a series of drafts and arrived at a piece of writing you're happy with, your job still isn't done. No matter how organized you are or how cogent your presentation may be, all your best efforts will go down the drain if you make grammatical errors, misspell words, or don't know the difference between a comma and a semicolon.

When people read your writing, they'll focus on the argument so long as they don't stumble across any errors. The minute a mistake is spotted, however, the reader's attention turns to the mistake, distracting attention from the points you're trying to make.

The bottom line: An ounce of prevention is worth a pound of cure. Proofread *everything* before sending it out into the world — especially those e-mails you rip off in a flash. For a formal letter or a report, have a colleague go over the piece with a fine-tooth comb (and be ready to reciprocate when she asks you to do her the same favor).

EFFECTIVE BUSINESS LETTERS

The old-fashioned personal business letter — written on pristine, high-quality paper, sealed in an envelope, and delivered by post or by hand — remains the single most impressive written ambassador for your company. A letter has a dignity that cannot be equaled by electronic mail or faxed correspondence. E-mail and faxes have a spontaneous, off-the-cuff quality akin to a telephone call. A letter, by contrast, says that someone has planned, written, edited and revised, typed, and perhaps retyped a message. In other words, the sender has expended time — that most precious commodity — to communicate with the recipient.

It's a shame, then, that so many businesspeople regard the writing of business letters as a chore. But it doesn't have to be that way: If you keep in mind the tests of accuracy, clarity, coherence, and correctness and follow the basic rules of form and grammar, you can master the craft of writing business letters — and even come to enjoy the process.

THE PARTS OF A BUSINESS LETTER

The format of the standard business letter includes these parts:

DATELINE
This consists of the month, day, and year. The month should be spelled out in full, and all numbers should be written as numerals (January 1, 2005, not Jan. 1 or January 1st). The date is typed two to six lines below the letterhead, usually on the right side of the page, although flush-left and centered datelines are also perfectly acceptable.

REFERENCE LINE
Some letters require specific reference to file, account, invoice, order, or policy numbers. These references are usually typed below the dateline, but they may also be centered on the page. When the letter runs longer than one page, the reference line should be repeated on each subsequent sheet.

WAYS TO A SUCCESSFUL LETTER

Most of the fundamentals for creating successful business letters have to do with simplicity and directness—the hallmarks of good writing. Here are some tips to help you get there:

- *Let it simmer.* Organize your thoughts before you start, and always write a rough draft of your letter. If you have the time, put your draft aside for at least a half hour. You will be amazed how you can improve your writing if you allow it to "simmer" for a while.

- *Keep it short.* Write only as much as you need to get your message across. But don't be so terse that you leave out important information that supports your case.

- *Write in the first person.* Avoid the "royal *we*" unless you are writing as a representative of your company as a whole.

- *Be natural.* Make your writing as much like your manner of speaking as you can. But always write in complete sentences, and leave out interjections and excessive use of pronouns and contractions.

- *Avoid clichés and buzzwords.* If you use a word such as *paradigm* or *leveraged,* be sure you know what it means.

- *Avoid jargon.* Avoid technical jargon and specialized language unless you are certain your reader is familiar with the field.

- *Proofread.* Read and reread your letter for spelling, grammar, and punctuation errors. Never rely totally on your computer's spelling- and grammar-checking programs: "Pleas sea hour lay test add" will pass the spelling checker as easily as "Please see our latest ad."

SPECIAL NOTATIONS

When necessary, letters may include notation of the means of delivery—"certified mail" or "registered mail"—or on-arrival instructions, such as "personal" (to be opened and read by the addressee only) or "confidential" (for the addressee or other authorized personnel). These lines are typed in all capital letters and placed flush left, four or five spaces below the dateline, and two lines above the inside address. On-arrival notations are also printed in capital letters on the face side of the envelope.

INSIDE ADDRESS OF THE RECIPIENT

The inside address is usually typed three to eight lines below the dateline. When a letter is addressed to an individual, the inside address includes the following:

- **ADDRESSEE'S COURTESY TITLE AND FULL NAME.** When writing to a woman you don't know, you can address her as "Ms." For unisex names like Pat, Jan, Leslie, Alex, Hillary, and Lynn, however, a phone inquiry to the recipient's firm to confirm his or her gender will save potential embarrassment. Names from other cultures can also be problematic. If you cannot discover the sex of the person, you should drop the courtesy title in the address and the salutation ("Jan White"; "Dear Jan White"). It's awkward, but better than risking an unintended insult. In addition, if your recipient holds a doctoral degree, you'll need to do some research to determine whether he or she uses the courtesy title "Dr." (Some Ph.D. holders revere their hard-earned title, while others dispense with it entirely.) For physicians, either "Dr. Smith" or "Jane Smith, M.D." is acceptable.

- **ADDRESSEE'S BUSINESS TITLE, WHEN REQUIRED.** When an individual holds more than one position in a company, your decision to use all titles or just one will depend on the purpose of the letter and the recipient's preference. Do not substitute a business title for a courtesy title, however: Address your letter to "Mr. Richard Lambert, President, Alpha Company," not "President Richard Lambert."

- **NAME OF THE BUSINESS.** It is equally important to write the name of the company or organization exactly. Look for details: Is "Company," "Corporation," or "Incorporated" spelled out or abbreviated? Does the company name include commas, hyphens, periods, or ampersands? Are words run together? Which letters are capitalized? Find out by checking letterhead, corporate publications, the firm's Web site, or the phone book.

- **FULL ADDRESS.** In the address, numbers are generally written in numeral form unless they are part of the name of a building (One Town Plaza). As a rule, street numbers are written in numerals (123 East 17th Street), though First through Twelfth are often written in full. Also, spell out any number that may cause confusion. City names are written in full unless an abbreviation is the accepted spelling (St. Louis). State names can be written out or the two-letter Postal Service abbreviation can be used—followed by the ZIP code. Foreign addresses should conform to the standards in the country of receipt. For a letter to a business or organization, the address line includes the following:

  - Full name of the company, firm, or organization

  - Department name, if necessary

  - Full address

- **TO THE ATTENTION OF.** If you are writing a company or company department, you may also want to include an attention line that directs your letter to a specific individual ("Attention: Mr. Benjamin Hayes" or "Attention: Director of Health Benefits"). The attention line is placed two spaces below the address and two lines above the salutation; the salutation itself is directed to the company or department.

SALUTATION

Your salutation is your greeting. In most cases, it is a simple "Dear Mr. ____" or "Dear Dr. ____," followed by a colon. It is a rule of thumb that you salute a person in a business letter with the same name form you use in person; so a business salutation uses a first name only when you know the addressee well or have agreed to correspond on a first-name basis. (For a complete chart showing forms of address, see pages 252–257.)

What to write when you are addressing a company rather than an identifiable person? The old-fashioned "Gentlemen" is obviously unacceptable unless the organization includes no females. "Sir or Madam" and "Ladies and Gentlemen" sound stilted. "To whom it may concern" is acceptable but rather formal and clichéd. The best solution is probably to address the company ("Dear Blue Sky Investments") or department ("Dear Investor Relations") or to direct your salutation to a specific position ("Dear Human Resources Director"). A salutation such as "Dear Sales Representative" is also acceptable.

BODY

Whether your letter consists of a single paragraph or several, the chief rule here is brevity. Business letters should never go beyond one page unless absolutely necessary. The trick is to be concise and to the point, but never discourteous.

ENDING

When ending your message, stay friendly and brief. If you know the recipient, it's fine to end on a personal note: "Please give my best to your wife" or "I enjoyed seeing you at the trade show and hope your trip home was as pleasant as you expected." Even if you don't know the person, your closing can be friendly and helpful. ("I look forward to talking with you soon." Or "Please call me directly at 555-1212 if you need additional copies of the brochure.") It is always polite to say thank you for a service or attention. Do not, however, thank someone for something they have not yet done: "Thank you in advance" is presumptuous.

Complimentary close and signature. A complimentary close is used on most letters, typed two lines below the last line of your message and usually positioned flush left on the page. In most business letters, you want to end on a friendly but not too familiar note. Use variations of "truly" ("Yours truly," "Yours very truly," "Very truly yours") or "sincerely" ("Most sin-

BUSINESS-LETTER CHECKLIST

This checklist will help you decide whether your letter meets the basic requirements of effective business writing:

- Does your letter follow the standard business format described on pages 241–246 ?
- Did you begin with an outline of your major points as described on pages 238–239 and then write a rough draft?
- Is your message stated clearly and concisely?
- Did you include all necessary information, and are you sure the facts are accurate?
- Have you set a friendly, natural tone? Even when a letter conveys negative criticism or bad news, it should be courteous and considerate of the reader.
- Finally, did you check and double-check every detail—including grammar, spelling, and punctuation—before adding your signature?

cerely," "Very sincerely," "Sincerely yours," "Sincerely"). "Cordially" and its variations are proper closings for general business letters, especially when the writer and the recipient know each other. If you are on a first-name basis with your addressee, informal closings are appropriate ("As ever," "Best wishes," "Regards," "Kindest regards," "Kindest personal regards"). Closings such as "Respectfully" and "Respectfully yours" indicate not only respect but also subservience; although seen in diplomatic and ecclesiastical writing, they are too obsequious for most business letters.

Your handwritten signature will appear below the complimentary close, followed by the typed signature. Your business title and company name may be needed, but don't repeat information that already appears in the corporate letterhead. Your name is typed just as in the handwritten signature. The courtesy title "Mrs.," "Miss," or "Ms." may be added to indicate the writer's preference. Academic degrees (Ph.D., LL.D.) and professional ratings (CPA) may also be included in the typed signature. If more than one writer is signing a letter, the written and typed signature blocks can be placed either side by side or vertically.

FINAL NOTATIONS.

If your letter is typed by someone else, the typist's initials may be included two lines below the signature block. Once standard in business letters, the use of initials is now a matter of corporate style.

When you are enclosing materials with your letter, the notation "Enclosure," "enc.," or "encl.," sometimes with an indication of the number of enclosed pieces—"Enclosures (2)"—

is typed below the signature block. The notation "Separate mailing" or "Under separate cover" followed by the name of the piece or pieces ("Separate mailing: 2004 Annual Report") appears when materials are being sent separately.

Courtesy copies—notated as "cc:" or "Copies to"—indicate that your letter is to be distributed to other people. The names of these recipients are listed alphabetically, and you may also include their addresses if this will be helpful to your recipient.

A postscript, or P.S., can be added below the last notation and should be initialed by the letter writer. Postscripts are a common tactic in contemporary direct-mail advertising, as if the writer had one last brilliant reason for you to buy the product. With word processing, however, P.S.'s are rarely necessary and may signal to the reader that you did a poor job of organizing your thoughts if you left important information out of the body of your letter.

WRITING MEMORANDA

By definition, a memorandum—memo—is an informal written communication, usually sent within an office or company for quick and concise communication of news, requests and responses, procedures, and some employment-related information.

The format for memos differs from business letters in address, salutation, content, and close. Memos can be typed on letterhead, but companies often have a standard memo form, printed or part of a word-processing program. The basic address style is

TO: Name(s) of primary recipient(s) or group
FROM: Name of sender
DATE: Day of sending
SUBJECT or RE: A brief but precise title, such as "Thursday's New Business Presentation" or "Changes in Employee Health Insurance"
COPIES: Name(s) of other recipient(s)

List names by order of established management hierarchy—highest to lowest position—or alphabetically. Use an alphabetized listing when the recipients are roughly on the same job level or share responsibility for a project. For memos with wide distribution, you may want to address them to a group ("The Staff," "Purchasing Department," "Birthday Party Planners").

A memo does not have a "Dear ____" salutation; a memo gets to the point in a more direct manner than a typical business letter. The tone is usually casual and friendly, though the rules of good grammar and clear construction are always in effect. The informality of memos means that the writing is closer to conversational style. Still, a business memo is not a personal letter, and memos should never include private information or waste the reader's time by straying from the topic into marginal or unrelated issues.

Memos do not include the complimentary closing of business letters and are not signed by the sender, although some writers initial their memos. But it never hurts to conclude with thanks or compliments or words of encouragement. ("We all know that this project is our first real shot at national recognition, and I really appreciate your willingness to burn the midnight oil.")

INVITATIONS

When planning a company-sponsored event, it's important to set the right tone from the get-go, beginning with your invitations. The company person in charge of drawing up the guest list should start by consulting every department head to make sure no key clients or customers are overlooked. Once the list is compiled, the invitation is written so that recipients are told everything they need to know before accepting and attending. For a large event, invitations should be mailed four to six weeks in advance; for cocktail parties or less formal events, two to three weeks in advance.

Whether your invitation is formal or fanciful, the envelope addresses can be typed or printed, though handwritten is preferred. Use a fountain pen, not a ballpoint. Don't go overboard with showy calligraphy, and never use address labels. The invitation should include the following:

- Who is hosting, including the senior officer or CEO

- The purpose of the event

- The style of dress

- Whether there will be food and/or dancing

- How to reply

- Other enclosures, such as a map or instructions about transportation routes and the availability of parking; or an admission card, which will note whether the invitation admits one or two.

A formal invitation is traditionally engraved in black on white or ecru quality paper and is usually a double-fold card. But unless the company's image calls for such formality, lighter designs that set the mood are perfectly acceptable.

Formal invitations are set in a traditional cursive typeface; the numbers are spelled out. For a more personal touch, the example shown here includes the recipients' names, which are handwritten.

> [corporate logo]
> In honor of
> The Zerfoss Group, Limited
> Judith Alexander
> of Alexander & Anderson Industries
> requests the honor of
>
> Mr. & Mrs. Richard Bailey's
>
> presence at a cocktail buffet
> on Wednesday, January twelfth
> Two thousand and five at
> six o'clock
> The St. Regis Hotel
> New York City
> RSVP Card Enclosed ▪ Black Tie
> Dancing

An invitation for a more informal event uses numerals for the date and time as well as a less traditional typeface. Information for RSVPs — name, address, and telephone number — is also supplied

> [CORPORATE LOGO]
> GORDON & MUSE ADVERTISING
> JAMES EVANS
> PRESIDENT
> REQUESTS THE PLEASURE OF YOUR COMPANY
> IN HONORING
> MOLLY COLLINS OF BLACKLOCK PRODUCTS, INC.
> AT A COCKTAIL BUFFET
> ON TUESDAY, SEPTEMBER 29
> 6 TO 9 P.M.
> ATLANTA BOTANICAL GARDENS
> RSVP ▪ BUSINESS DRESS
> LILY YARBOROUGH
> 71 PINE DRIVE
> ATLANTA, GA 30305
> (404) 555-1212

FORMAL ANNOUNCEMENTS

From time to time, companies send out formal printed announcements—notices of change of address and new office openings, additions to staff, promotions, deaths. Whether these announcements are conservative or creative depends on the company's general graphic standards, its corporate image, and the occasion. Announcements should focus on a single item and, as with all good business writing, should quickly get to the point. Grammatically, a company or business name is always treated as a singular noun and requires a singular verb: "Smythe, Smythe & Jones is pleased to announce . . ." but "The Directors and Officers of Jones Company are pleased to announce . . ." Announcement cards and matching envelopes are ordered when needed. A formal announcement would read

THE BOARD OF TRUSTEES OF HIGH Q UNIVERSITY
IS HONORED TO ANNOUNCE THAT
MICHAEL KEMERLING, PH.D.
HAS BEEN ELECTED TO
THE FORTESCUE CHAIR OF MEDIEVAL LITERATURE
AND WILL ASSUME THE POST
ON THE FIRST OF FEBRUARY
TWO THOUSAND AND FIVE.

THE STATIONERY DRAWER

Think of business stationery as a form of public relations. Whenever a piece of paper goes out, it should look good and suit the occasion, because its appearance will reflect on the image and character of the business. If you place large or frequent orders for stationery, establish a relationship with a printer and paper supplier who will watch out for your interests and see that your stationery standards are maintained. The effective businessperson's stationery drawer should contain the following:

- **CORPORATE LETTERHEAD.** This is an 8½" × 11" sheet of good-quality (high-cotton-fiber) paper that is imprinted with the company name and other pertinent information, including full address and telephone number, fax number, and e-mail address. Law firms, medical partnerships, and other professional groups may include a complete list of partners on the letterhead. (Note: This can be costly, considering that the letterhead must be reprinted whenever a partner joins or leaves.)

    If the name and title of a company officer or a partner are printed on the letterhead, that paper is to be used only by that person. Otherwise, letterhead can be used by anyone in the company for official correspondence. The name and address of the company should be printed on the face side of the matching envelope.

If a letter runs to more than a single page (generally, it should not), then second sheets are of the same paper but do not carry the letterhead. If you are responsible for ordering letterhead, remember to order matching plain sheets.

- **MONARCH SHEETS**. Also called executive sheets, these measure $7\frac{1}{4}" \times 10\frac{1}{2}"$ and are used by individuals for personal business letters. Monarch sheets and their matching envelopes are imprinted with the name of the individual and the address of the business, but not the business name.

  Monarch sheets are sometimes used as business letterhead by physicians, lawyers, consultants, and other professionals. In this instance, it is correct to print the name of the company or firm, address, and telephone and telecommunications numbers on the sheet. Monarch sheets used as corporate letterhead also may require second sheets in the same paper.

- **CORRESPONDENCE CARDS**. These are used for short, personal messages, including thank-you notes. The cards are printed with the individual's name only; the name and business address are printed on the matching envelope. Usually $4\frac{1}{2}" \times 6\frac{1}{2}"$, these cards are made of a heavier weight paper and do not fold.

- **ENVELOPES**. Envelopes should match your corporate letterhead and other papers in size, quality, color, and printing style. Generally, return names and addresses are printed on the face side of envelopes to meet postal regulations. In fact, before placing any stationery orders, it's a smart idea to check with your local postal authority for the most up-to-date rules. This applies to all mailings you send out, including windowed billing envelopes and response envelopes, as well as prepaid stamped envelopes of any kind.

- **BUSINESS CARDS**. The last basic item in the stationery drawer is the business card, which is customarily presented during business occasions. Although there seems to be no end to the gimmicks offered for these small essentials, the standard is a $3\frac{1}{2}" \times 2"$ card of heavy paper stock in white or ecru, printed in black or gray ink. The card should include only pertinent information: name and business title, business name, address, telephone and fax numbers, and e-mail address. If your name is ambiguous (Marion, for example, or Pat), include your courtesy title (Mr. Marion Brown, Ms. Pat Di Beradino); otherwise, use your full name only. (See also the box "Your Trusty Business Card," page 141.)

A card printed on a special form to fit roll-style address holders can be a real convenience for clients, suppliers, and others who frequently contact you by phone, fax, or e-mail. Naturally, these cards should include the same information as your business card.

Companies may also provide their employees with social business cards—printed with only the name and business telephone number of the individual—for use on strictly social occasions. Business and social business cards should always be handed out discreetly (never give out your card in the first minutes of meeting someone or during a meal) and accepted graciously. The information on your cards should also be kept up-to-date, and the cards themselves should be clean and never folded.

LOGOS AND GRAPHICS

The look of business stationery was once limited to white, ecru, or pale gray papers and black or gray ink. Today, businesses are free to be as creative as they like. Major businesses spend small fortunes on the development of complete graphics programs, and your company may have a standards manual that specifies the exact look, placement, and use of everything from invoice forms to parking lot signage.

A word to the wise: Before spending a great deal of money on graphic design development, think carefully about what your real needs are. Don't overlook the traditional forms just because they are traditional, and beware of relying on gimmicks. In the long run, your smartest investment may well be the quality of the paper and the visual clarity of the design you select—not the flash or glitter.

Finally, keep your readers' needs in mind when printing any written material. If you print your letters and reports in gray ink on blue paper, your written communications may be too hard to read. Your word-processing program offers a wealth of typefaces, but many of them—old-world and script styles—are also difficult to read on the printed page, and may look frivolous to boot. For printed text, select readable typefaces—serif styles—in sizes of at least 10- or 12-point type.

WHAT'S IN A NAME?

In business correspondence, getting a person's name and title correct is essential. Not only do name and title identify a person, but they also signify position and rank, achievement, and even self-concept. The person who receives your letter has an ego, and it may be a large one. If you have a history of correspondence, check your file letters from him or her; the courtesy or business title from the typed signature line will indicate how the person prefers to be addressed. This information may also be found on an executive letterhead or in a company directory or annual report. If necessary, there's nothing wrong with calling your addressee's business and making inquiries; asking for the right name—including spelling—and title shows concern on your part.

FORMS OF ADDRESS

	INSIDE & ENVELOPE	SALUTATION
CLERICAL AND RELIGIOUS		
Pope	His Holiness the Pope *or* His Holiness Pope Paul	*Your Holiness; Most Holy Father*
Patriarch	His Beatitude the Patriarch of ___	*Most Reverend Lord*
Cardinal	His Eminence Ian Cardinal Green *or* His Eminence Cardinal Green	*Your Eminence; Dear Cardinal Green*
Archbishop	The Most Reverend Archbishop of ___ *or* The Most Reverend Ian M. Green Archbishop of ___	*Your Excellency; Dear Archbishop Green*
Catholic Priest	The Reverend Father Green *or* The Reverend Ian M. Green	*Dear Father Green*
Episcopal Bishop	The Right Reverend Ian M. Green Bishop of ___	*Right Reverend Sir (Madam); Dear Bishop Green*
Methodist Bishop	The Reverend Ian M. Green Bishop of ___	*Dear Bishop Green*
Mormon Bishop	Bishop Ian M. Green Church of Jesus Christ of Latter-Day Saints	*Dear Bishop Green; Sir*
Protestant Clergy	The Reverend Jane F. Jones *or* The Reverend Dr. Jane F. Jones	*Dear Ms. Jones; Dear Dr. Jones*
Rabbi	Rabbi David A. Schiff *or* Rabbi David A. Schiff, D.D.	*Dear Rabbi Schiff; Dear Dr. Schiff*

GOVERNMENT OFFICIALS—UNITED STATES

	INSIDE & ENVELOPE	SALUTATION
President	The President *or* The Honorable Ian A. Green President of the United States	*Mr. (Madam) President;* *Dear Mr. (Madam)* *President*
First Lady	Mrs. Green (*no first names*)	*Dear Mrs. Green*
President-Elect	The Honorable Jane F. Jones President-Elect of the United States	*Dear Madam (Sir);* *Dear Ms. Jones*
Former President	The Honorable Ian A. Green	*Sir (Madam);* *Dear Mr. Green*
Vice President	The Vice President *or* Vice President Jane F. Jones	*Madam (Sir);* *Dear Madam (Mr.)* *Vice President*
U.S. Attorney General	The Honorable Jane F. Jones Attorney General	*Dear Madam (Mr.);* *Dear Madam (Mr.)* *Attorney General*
U.S. Cabinet Officer	The Honorable Ian M. Green Secretary of ___ (*or* The Secretary of ___)	*Sir (Madam);* *Dear Mr. (Madam)* *Secretary*
U.S. Postmaster	The Honorable Jane F. Jones Postmaster General	*Madam (Sir);* *Dear Madam (Sir)* *Postmaster General*
Supreme Court (Chief Justice)	The Chief Justice of the United States The Supreme Court of the United States *or* The Chief Justice The Supreme Court	*Sir (Madam);* *Dear Mr. (Madam)* *Chief Justice*
Supreme Court (Associate Justice)	Madam Justice Jones The Supreme Court of the United States	*Madam (Sir);* *Madam (Mr.) Justice;* *Dear Madam Justice* *Jones*
Federal Judge	The Honorable Ian M. Green Judge of the United States District Court for the ___ District of ___	*Sir (Madam);* *Dear Judge Green*
U.S. Senator	The Honorable Jane F. Jones United States Senate (*Use same forms for state senators,* *with the indication* The Senate of ___.)	*Madam (Sir);* *Dear Senator Jones*

	INSIDE & ENVELOPE	SALUTATION
U.S. Representative	The Honorable Ian M. Green United States House of Representatives (*Use same forms for state representatives, with indication* House of Representatives, State Assembly, *or* House of Delegates.)	*Sir (Madam);* *Dear Representative* *Green;* *Dear Mr. Green*
State Governor	The Honorable Ian M. Green Governor of ___	*Sir (Madam);* *Dear Governor Green*
State Supreme Court	The Honorable Jane F. Jones Chief Justice of the Supreme Court of ___ The Honorable Ian M. Green Associate Justice of the Supreme Court of ___	*Madam (Sir);* *Dear Madam* *(Mr.) Chief Justice;* *Sir (Madam);* *Dear Justice Green*
Mayor	The Honorable Jane F. Jones Mayor of ___	*Dear Madam (Mr.) Mayor;* *Dear Mayor Jones*
Alderman or Councilman	The Honorable Ian M. Green *or* Alderman Ian M. Green	*Dear Mr. Green;* *Dear Alderman Green*
(Alderwoman or Councilwoman)	The Honorable Jane F. Jones *or* Councilwoman Jane F. Jones	*Dear Ms. Jones;* *Dear Councilwoman* *Jones*

FOREIGN AND DIPLOMATIC

Foreign Head of State	His Excellency Ian M. Green Premier (President) of ___	*Excellency;* *Dear Mr. (Madam)* *Premier*
Prime Minister	Her Excellency Jane F. Jones	*Excellency;* *Dear Madam (Mr.) Prime* *Minister*
Canadian Prime Minister	The Right Honorable ___, P.C., M.P. Prime Minister of Canada	*Sir (Madam);* *Dear Mr.* *(Madam) Prime Minister*
Royalty (Correct form is to address a representative of the royal person.)	The Private Secretary to Her Majesty, the Queen (His *or* Her Royal Highness *for members of royal families*)	*Sir (Madam)*

	INSIDE & ENVELOPE	SALUTATION
U.S. Ambassador	The Honorable Ian M. Green American Ambassador (*In Canada and Latin America:* The Honorable Jane F. Jones Ambassador of the United States of America)	*Sir (Madam);* *Dear Mr. (Madam)* *Ambassador*
Foreign Ambassador	His Excellency Ian M. Green Ambassador of ___	*Excellency;* *Dear Mr. (Madam)* *Ambassador*

U.S. MILITARY

	INSIDE & ENVELOPE	SALUTATION
	Military titles are numerous. The basic address form is Rank, Full Name, Service Initials. *In the address, rank may be written in full or abbreviated* (Major, Maj., *or* MAJ).	*Salutation style is* Dear Rank *or* Mr./Ms./Miss Surname
Services	United States Army (USA); United States Navy (USN); United States Air Force (USAF); United States Marine Corps (USMC); United States Coast Guard (USCG)	
Examples	General Jane F. Jones, USA (*or* GEN Jane F. Jones)	*Dear General Jones*
	Commander (*or* CDR) Ian M. Green, USN	*Dear Commander Green*
	Colonel (*or* Col.) Jane F. Jones, USAF	*Dear Colonel Jones*
	First Sergeant (*or* 1SG) Ian M. Green, USA	*Dear Sergeant Green*
	Lieutenant (j.g.) Jane F. Jones, USCG *or* LTJG Jane F. Jones, USCG	Dear Ms. Jones (*Use Mr., Ms., or Miss for Navy and Coast Guard officers below the rank of lieutenant commander.*)
Military Academy	Private (Pvt) Ian M. Green, USMC	*Dear Private Green*
	Cadet Jane F. Jones United States Military Academy *or* United States Air Force Academy	*Dear Cadet Jones*
	Midshipman Ian M. Green United States Naval Academy *or* United States Coast Guard Academy	*Dear Midshipman Green*
Retired Officers	Major Jane F. Jones, USA, Retired	*Dear Major Jones*

INSIDE & ENVELOPE		SALUTATION
PROFESSIONAL TITLES		
Attorney	Ms. Jane F. Jones, Attorney-at-Law *or* Jane F. Jones, Esq.	*Dear Ms. Jones*
Certified Public Accountant	Ian M. Green, C.P.A. *or* Mr. Ian M. Green *(Follow this address form for all professionals whose names may be followed by credentials, as* Ian M. Green, R.N. *or* Mr. Ian M. Green.*)*	*Dear Mr. Green*
Dentist	Jane F. Jones, D.D.S. *or* Dr. Jane F. Jones	*Dear Dr. Jones*
Physician	Ian M. Green, M.D. *or* Dr. Ian M. Green	*Dear Dr. Green*
Veterinarian	Jane F. Jones, D.V.M. *or* Dr. Jane F. Jones	*Dear Dr. Jones*
College/University Officers	Dr. Ian M. Green President (Chancellor, Dean) *or* President Ian M. Green	*Dear Dr. Green*
Professor	Dr. Jane F. Jones *or* Jane F. Jones, Ph.D., Professor of ____ *or* Professor Jane F. Jones	*Dear Dr. Jones; Dear Professor Jones; Dear Ms. Jones*
MULTIPLE NAMES		
Men with Different Surnames	Mr. Ian M. Green Mr. James L. Black *or* Messrs. I. M. Green and J. L. Black *or* Messrs. Green and Black	*Dear Mr. Green and Mr. Black; Dear Messrs. Green and Black; Gentlemen*
Women with Different Surnames	Mrs. Jane F. Jones Mrs. Ann B. Smith *or* Mesdames J. F. Jones and A. B. Smith *or* Mesdames Jones and Smith	*Dear Mrs. Jones and Mrs. Smith; Dear Mesdames Jones and Smith; Mesdames* (*Use* Mrs./Mesdames *for married women;* Miss/Misses *for single women;* Ms. *for women whose status is unknown or who prefer the generic title:* Ms. Jane F. Jones and Ms. Ann B. Smith/ Dear Ms. Jones and Ms. Smith.)

	INSIDE & ENVELOPE	SALUTATION
Men or Women with the Same Surname (Because these forms imply familial relationships, you may want to use them for related persons only.)	Mr. Ian M. Green Mr. Richard Z. Green *or* Messrs. I. M. and R. Z. Green *or* The Messrs. Green	*Dear Messrs. Green;* *Gentlemen*
	Miss Jane F. Jones Miss Betty B. Jones *or* Misses Jane and Betty Jones (Mesdames) *or* The Misses Jones (The Mesdames)	*Dear Misses Jones;* *Dear Mesdames Jones;* *Dear Ms. Jane and Betty* *Jones*
Physicians in Joint Practice	Dr. Ian M. Green, Dr. Jane F. Jones, and Dr. Ann B. Smith	*Dear Drs. Green, Jones,* *and Smith*
Married Couples	Mr. and Mrs. Ian M. Green *or* Mr. Ian M. Green and Ms. Jane F. Jones	*Dear Mr. and Mrs. Green;* *Dear Mr. Green and* *Ms. Jones*
	President and Mrs. Ian M. Green *or* The President and Mrs. Green	*Dear President and* *Mrs. Green*
	Dr. Ian M. Green and Dr. Jane F. Jones	*Dear Drs. Green and* *Jones*
	Dr. Ian M. Green and Dr. Jane F. Green	*Dear Drs. Green*
	The Reverend Jane F. Green and Mr. Green	*Dear Rev. and Mr. Green*
	MAJ Jane F. Green and CPT Ian M. Green *(Address married couples in the military* *in order of higher rank.)*	*Dear Major and* *Captain Green, USA*

19 | *Communicating Electronically*

The business etiquette of electronic communication is constantly evolving, and what passes for manners in this brave new world often reflects the enthusiasms of the media's youthful masters. (The coinage of the term *netiquette* for on-line etiquette is just one example of the playful approach to good behavior on the Internet.) That being said, the basic rules of consideration and respect still hold, even in the relatively informal realm of cyberspace.

THE BASICS

For businesses, e-mail can be an efficient saver of time and paper. Consider its advantages:

- E-mail eliminates the need for many types of printed memos.

- It facilitates the exchange of computer files.

- It allows off-site employees and contract workers to cooperate on projects as easily as if they were in neighboring cubicles.

- It enables quick transmission of data between businesses and greatly speeds approvals and authorizations.

But because it is so easy and ubiquitous, e-mail is also ripe for abuse—as anyone who faces the daily deletion of a flood of pointless, useless, and irrelevant messages from their in-box can testify.

HANDLE WITH CARE

Making mistakes or misusing e-mail can have consequences a letter writer never dreamed of. Keep the following points in mind at all times:

- **PUBLIC OR CONFIDENTIAL?** *Never* send confidential or sensitive-information materials—contracts, business plans, salary and sales information—electronically. E-mail is *not private,* and messages can easily be intercepted (accidentally or intentionally) or forwarded to unintended recipients without your knowledge or consent. Encryption programs are available, which code your message so that it cannot be read until it's decoded by the recipient. But it is generally more prudent to use the post office, express mail, or other traditional forms of transmission for private materials.

- **PRIVACY**. E-mail privacy is an oxymoron, a contradiction in terms. Every e-mail you compose, send, or receive on your office PC or laptop, whether it travels over an interoffice network or the Internet, belongs to your employer, and your employer has the right to read it. After all, he owns the computer, your time, and the work you produce while in his employ. In short, think of your e-mails as postcards that anyone in your company can read.

- **KNOW WHEN IT'S INAPPROPRIATE**. The more serious the message, the less appropriate e-mail becomes as the medium. E-mail isn't appropriate for formal communications, such as invitations or birth announcements. Plus, it is potentially dangerous to rely on e-mail for any kind of truly important message because it can easily be duplicated, altered, and forged. Remember: Once your e-mail is sent, it is no longer within your control.

Nor is e-mail the appropriate medium for delivering bad news of any kind. Never, for example, send an e-mail letter of resignation. Similarly, don't issue serious complaints or criticisms by e-mail; try to arrange a personal meeting to discuss problems, or write a business complaint letter or confidential memo if a one-on-one conversation isn't possible.

- **RECOVERING FROM A MISTAKE**. So what do you do in case of accidents? If you've mistakenly sent something private to the wrong individual (not group), immediately phone her and apologize. (Asking her not to read it is an invitation to have her open it immediately.) If your errant message has gone out to virtually everyone, all you can do is transmit a blanket apology and say you hope no one has been offended or angered.

  If that e-mail was about a manager and it mistakenly ended up on her desk, you need to make a beeline for her office and offer your apology ASAP. Much better for you if you take responsibility for your actions than if you wait for her to come find you to discuss your transgression.

SALUTATIONS, SIGN-OFFS,
AND MASS MAILINGS

There's no denying that an e-mail is inherently more informal than a typed letter sent via snail mail—but that doesn't mean you can forget all about appropriate salutations. Begin all e-mails addressed to your boss, a client, or anyone in senior management with a formal greeting—"Dear Bob" or sometimes even just "Bob"—but never "Hey there!" Even with close colleagues whom you e-mail back and forth with frequently, it is thoughtful to employ some sort of salutation, at least on your first e-mail of the day. In subsequent e-mails, use your common sense: If you're firing ideas back and forth every few minutes—the equivalent of instant messaging—then it's acceptable to drop all salutations.

The same goes for signing off on an e-mail. For supervisors, clients, and upper management, a formal sign-off is required: "Warm regards," "Best wishes," or "Sincerely yours" concludes your note with a tone of respect and warmth. For closer colleagues, you may evolve to a more abbreviated sign-off—but again, except for the case where the e-mails are flying fast and furious, it's always appropriate to sign at least your name or initials at the end of your message.

What about when you're sending out a mass e-mail to 100 of your closest associates? The greeting can be generic—"Dear All" or "Greetings, everyone"—while the sign-off should be the same as for an individual e-mail. One caution: When you send group e-mails, be careful that the program you're using isn't the kind that reveals all of the recipients' e-mail addresses in the address field. Some people equate this kind of mass exposure with giving out their home phone number to a telemarketer. Instead, use a program that displays only the address of that specific recipient on each e-mail.

- **NO ALL CAPS.** Another on-line convention is to avoid typing in all capital letters, because caps indicate that you are shouting your message. Readability studies also show that all-caps messages are much harder to read. Use capitalized words sparingly, for emphasis: They are the e-mail equivalent of italics in regular writing.

- **PERSONAL USE.** Virtually everybody uses office e-mail for communicating with their friends, and few companies place such back-and-forthing off-limits. But if your correspondence with friends becomes voluminous, it can become an issue—especially if the company happens to do a random check and decides that your "Sent" file might be interesting reading.

E-MAIL HELL

Pity the poor person who intends something for one coworker's eyes only and accidentally hits "Memo All." E-mail's ability to blanket the masses has proved the undoing of more than a few hapless employees. The horror stories are legion: The intern who criticized the way the company was run in less than polite language; the woman who trashed her new boss; the man who made mincemeat of a rival coworker. In short, pay attention to addresses when transmitting a message. Once you've clicked on the "Send" button, e-mail can rarely be retrieved. Even better, never e-mail any comments about someone that you wouldn't say to their face.

QUESTIONS OF SECURITY

Unfortunately, along with all the benefits of computer technology comes the Web's dark side: Computer security is more important today than ever before. The cleverness of virus writers is remarkable: Every time a new security safeguard is put in place, hackers and virus writers view it as yet another challenge to be overcome.

Ultimately, our fate is in the hands of the cybersecurity experts. But here are some basic tips to help safeguard your computer and your company's network:

- Use virus detection software.

- Avoid opening e-mails from people you don't know.

- Never open an attachment from a person, even someone you know, unless you're expecting an attachment from them.

- If you have doubts about an unexpected attachment from a colleague, check with him or her before opening it.

SURF WARNINGS

The Internet should be a boon to workers, allowing them to get information quickly that once took hours of digging and multiple trips to the library. But the Internet is much more than a research tool. Games, sports scores, market updates, the latest news and gossip, recipes, catalog shopping, music, movie reviews, chat rooms, even day trading on the stock market—it's all just a click or a keystroke away. Problem is, much of what workers do on the Internet isn't work—and as a result employers, in self-defense, are increasingly monitoring workplace Internet use.

As with e-mail, there is no privacy protection for on-the-job Internet surfers. Employers can monitor and audit their employees' computers for Internet use, checking on sites visited, time spent at each site, and software downloads. Downloading software is a particular concern because of the danger of violating copyrights or a company's purchasing policies, as well as the possibility of importing viruses into the company's system.

An employee who accesses pornographic material or engages in sexist, racist, or other prejudiced on-line conversation can put the company in jeopardy of sexual harassment and discrimination charges or defamation actions.

The absence of a stated company policy on Internet use does *not* mean employees are free to surf at will. Internet usage should be strictly confined to job-related tasks. Some companies limit Internet access to specific computers or personnel, and these restrictions should be respected. Before spending any questionable time on the Internet or downloading any software, check with a supervisor or the company's information systems specialist.

Internet access is available in your office for a reason. If you're caught idly surfing, 'fess up and hope it doesn't cost you your job, your bonus, or your promotion.

A Special Warning. Never do job-hunting research or apply for a job on the Internet at your workplace. Having your boss or anyone else in your company come across it means the cat's out of the bag and you will have to suffer the consequences.

WATCH THE BASICS, EVEN WITH E-MAIL

E-mail is not an excuse for misspellings, grammatical errors, or punctuation mistakes. Your familiarity with such rules should shine through at all times, no matter what medium you use. The spelling checker found in many modern e-mail programs can help, but it's far from perfect (see the box "Ways to a Successful Letter," page 242).

Tone matters, too. *Flaming* is the on-line term for sending messages that are highly emotional, angry, or insulting. Although flaming is most likely to occur in chat rooms, when members of a group are engaged in back-and-forth conversation, it can occur in any message—especially if the writer is feeling strong emotions. It's also important to carefully monitor your tone when expressing criticism, no matter how mild—otherwise, even a simple request can come across as an attack.

E-mail software often contains a variety of emoticon characters, which you can use to indicate your mood: ☺ ☹ ☹ . Similarly on-line users have developed a vocabulary of keystroke symbols to indicate emotional state, including the following:

:-)	"happy, laugh"	:-O	"yelling, shocked"
:-(	"sad, unhappy"		

These are perfectly fine so long as they are part of the electronic parlance of the people you do business with; if they aren't, then use of these symbols may mean nothing to the recipient and annoy at the same time. The same goes for on-line abbreviations—IMHO for "in my humble opinion," IOW for "in other words," BTW for "by the way." If you use these as a matter of course in every e-mail you send, there's a very good chance that at least some recipients will have no idea what you mean.

A RIGHT TO PRIVACY? FORGET IT

Face this fact: Unless laws are enacted, your employer has the right to monitor and intercept your e-mail, to access e-mail you have received, even to retrieve from your computer's hard drive e-mail that you long ago dumped or deleted—and your employer is also free to act on what he or she finds.

Remember that sending racist or sexist jokes to a workmate is the same as telling them in the office corridor. Posting pornographic writing or pictures by e-mail is the same as tacking nudie pictures to your office wall. Sending proprietary company data to a friend is the same as stealing confidential documents from a file. And insulting bosses or the company in an e-mail note is the same as slapping them in the face.

More companies are setting e-mail policies and communicating them to workers and are requiring new employees to sign statements that they have read and understand these policies. Some employers post warnings on their office computers. But it's a mistake to assume that in the absence of a policy statement, you are free to use office e-mail as you like.

PART FIVE

ON THE ROAD— HERE AND ABROAD

20 | *The Thoughtful Traveler*

For men and women caught in the throes of making travel plans, packing, and preparing for whatever business awaits them, etiquette is probably the last thing on their minds. After all, isn't behaving well a given? The answer should be a resounding yes, but business travelers will do well by themselves and other people when they take a few extra things into account. One is the value of self-reliance, which places fewer burdens on their hosts. Another is the importance of choosing carefully what to take along—a habit that helps make trips glitch-free.

Just as important is remembering to respect the rights of fellow travelers, a dictum that today includes coping cheerfully with the growing frustrations of airplane travel and keeping your cell phone calls in check. The less bumpily things run on a business jaunt (and the less annoyance you cause), the easier it is to focus on the trip's objectives. (See also Chapter 22, "Doing Business in Another Country," page 285.)

BE SELF-RELIANT

Unless a corporate travel office is handling your travel arrangements, build self-reliance into all your plans. Your hosts shouldn't have to tend to things you can easily handle for yourself.

- Once the date and time of the visit are set, tell your host that you'll make your own hotel reservations. Or if your company has a travel department or an affiliation with a travel agency, leave the reservations to them. If your host insists on making them herself, let her do so; the hotel chosen will no doubt be in a place convenient to you both, which is what you want.

- Don't overlook the fact that many large hotel chains offer special rooms for business travelers. Amenities range from data ports for laptops to two-line phones to highlighters and Post-it pads. Another hotel amenity is the on-site business center, equipped with copiers, fax machines, computers, and Internet acess—all for the benefit of businesspeople. Ask the reservationist about special services of this kind and any other perks. You might find that the hotel caters to solo business travelers by setting aside group tables in the restaurants; a few even organize wine tastings.

- Businesswomen will be wise to ask about other amenities. Babysitting services and creative programs to keep children occupied may be offered for women who take their kids along, an increasingly common choice among those who travel frequently.

- If you're going to meet a client at your hotel, arrange in advance for the use of a meeting room. A note of caution: Having a business meeting in your hotel room is usually considered too personal these days, especially when it is with a member of the opposite sex.

- If the journey is a long one, plan to arrive in town the day before the meeting, so that you'll be refreshed and at your best. If you have an appointment scheduled for the day you arrive, book a flight that leaves plenty of room for unexpected delays. The same holds true if you're driving: Get an early start.

- Make your own arrangements for traveling from the airport to the hotel. If you must go straight from the airport to your meeting, think twice about taking a taxi; the line at the taxi rank may be long on a busy day. A safer alternative, if cost permits, is to arrange for a car service; the driver knows your destination in advance and will be waiting when you arrive.

- If you're scheduled to give a presentation, plan on arriving the day before. Take any visual aids with you, including equipment for presenting them, or send them ahead or arrange for them to be available to you. Don't assume that the office you're visiting has, say, an overhead projector for your slides.

- When all of your arrangements are final, prepare an itinerary for your host, your office, and your family. Include the following:

  □ Your flight schedule, with flight numbers and times of departure and arrival

  □ The name, address, and telephone number of your hotel

  □ The times and locations of your meetings, with telephone numbers where you can be reached

  □ The name and telephone number of the contact person in the office you're visiting

THE CELL PHONE—
PUBLIC NUISANCE NUMBER ONE?

Today, respecting the rights of fellow travelers threatens to boil down to one overriding rule: Keep your cell phone calls to a minimum, especially when you're on a train or in any other enclosed area trapping those around you as unwilling listeners. Don't enter into heated discussions while on your phone, and absolutely do not discuss confidential information while anyone is near you who can overhear your conversation. Declaring a moratorium on cell phone use while traveling may be unrealistic, but remember that in an airport lounge or equally crowded place, idle phone chats with friends contribute to the din. Do your part to keep the peace by making your call in an out-of-the-way place.

If you must use your wireless phone on a train, speak softly and briefly and save any calls that aren't urgent for later. Use airphones only when absolutely necessary, and try to keep your voice to a reasonably low level when you do.

TROUBLE-FREE CLOTHING

Pick out the clothes in your wardrobe that are best suited to business travel. They should be lightweight (unless the climate dictates otherwise), wrinkle-resistant, and stylish but not flashy.

- Choose washable shirts or blouses.

- Wear comfortable shoes, but take along a better pair for business meetings and evenings. Leave the sneakers at home.

- Pack enough underwear and socks or panty hose for each day; don't rely on having the time to rinse out small items at night.

- Make sure you have everything you need in your cosmetic or shaving kit; unlike leisure travelers, business travelers often can't afford the time to buy items they forgot.

- If exercise is part of your daily routine, pack your swimsuit or workout gear; a hotel that offers exercise and sport facilities will provide towels at the gym or pool.

- Pack a collapsible umbrella.

What to wear on a plane? Both men and women may be tempted to don jeans and sneakers for the flight, especially since they know they'll be squeezed into a tight seat and could run into delays. Just remember, airlines cater to business travelers. Look the part by dressing appropriately, and you may find you get an added measure of service. Also, by dressing in business casual for travel, if a checked bag is lost, you won't have to arrive at a meeting looking as if you've just come from mowing the lawn or shopping for groceries.

DIFFERENT CLIMATES, DIFFERENT STYLES, DIFFERENT TIMES OF DAY?

Choosing a travel wardrobe becomes trickier when you travel to a part of the country where the climate is different from your home region. You might assume, for instance, that if you're going to the Deep South, you'll find businessmen in shirtsleeves in summer. But you probably won't, since business dress codes are fairly standard throughout the country, with long-sleeved shirts the rule. Guard against sartorial missteps by asking the advice of workmates or friends who are familiar with the region's customs.

If you are making a presentation or attending a meeting at another company, wear your usual business clothes; then wait until you are invited to remove your jacket before taking the liberty of doffing it.

Dressing for evenings calls for more attention. Men might learn, for example, that a blazer is expected with the usual khakis-and-sport-shirt uniform worn for casual events. Likewise, in some places women dress more formally in the evening than during the day, with a beaded top instead of a twin set; accordingly, a woman should pack a dressier garment than she might be wearing for her business dealings. As a practicality, those who travel frequently can invest in one of the stylish daytime-to-evening outfits that are designed with the traveling businesswoman in mind.

EN ROUTE

Trains, planes, and automobiles: Each of these modes of transportation presents its own set of concerns for the business traveler.

UP, UP, AND AWAY
Airline travel is complicated by (1) the penchant airlines have for changing their rules and (2) the fact that in the post-9/11 world, airports have stricter rules regarding security. Take note: If there's one place on earth where an ordinary citizen must *always* follow directions, it's an airport.

Luggage and ID. So there won't be any surprises, before you pack your bags check with the airline regarding size limits for carry-on luggage and the number of pieces allowed. You will be asked for a photo identification when you check in and will be barred from boarding if you can't produce a driver's license or some other form of photo ID. If a glitch does occur, you can exhibit your first courteous act of the trip by not arguing with airline employees or making a scene. To avoid problems, get in the habit of jotting down a checklist of essential articles and then running through it before you leave for the airport—wardrobe items, toiletries, business papers, and personal documents, with your photo ID and/or passport at the top of the list. Tip: Check the expiration date on your driver's license and/or passport. It would be frustrating (to say the least) to have a security officer refuse to let you through the security checkpoint because your documentation had expired.

In the air. As amazing as it seems, the bad behavior of some airborne passengers qualifies as a threat to safety, with alcohol often to blame. Notorious cases abound: The man who wrestled with an attendant for a liquor bottle, shouting obscenities; the enraged woman who knocked an airline attendant to the floor because there were no more sandwiches; and incidents even more appalling. As for minor incivilities, you might as well just grin and bear them. If you don't respond to boorish behavior with similar reactions, your journey will at least *feel* a lot smoother. Any truly unacceptable behavior, however, should always be reported to the flight attendant.

Some airplane do's and don'ts:

- DO tell the flight attendant if you need to deplane quickly. He or she may be able to move you to a seat closer to the front.

- DO carry on at least a brief conversation with the stranger next to you, but only if you are sure he or she invites it. Conversely, politely cut off unwelcome chitchat by excusing yourself to read a magazine or to do your work.

- DO ask anyone seated next to you whether they will be bothered by the clicking of your laptop computer.

- DO treat airline attendants politely. Be patient when you make a request, say "Please" and "Thank you," and thank them when you deplane.

- DON'T try to board before your seat number is called. Never try to push ahead of fellow passengers while walking down the boarding ramp, and be careful not to block the aisle for more than a few seconds when putting luggage in an overhead compartment.

THE AIRPLANE SEAT

Nothing is more frustrating than sitting down in your cramped-space seat and just after liftoff having the person in front of you drop his or her seat back practically into your lap. One of the most selfless courtesies you can extend to your fellow travelers is to refrain from reclining your seat or to do so only a little.

- DON'T crush other people's belongings in an overhead compartment to make room for your own. If there's no room for your luggage, ask the flight attendant for help. If he or she has no solution, accept that you must check the bag; personnel are usually standing by to make sure it gets into the cargo hold.

- DON'T embarrass the helpless parents of a crying child. If a noisy infant or restless youngster disturbs you, leave your seat and scout the plane to see if a vacant seat is available. If, as a rule, you find crying babies intolerable, add earplugs to the items in your carry-on bag.

- DON'T overdo the alcohol. Watch your drinking or avoid it altogether, especially if you're going to attend a meeting after arriving. No matter how liberal your corporate culture, you don't want to be met by a colleague—or even more important, a client—with liquor on your breath.

ON A TRAIN

Businesspeople who travel between major cities in the same general part of the country have the luxury of choosing rail over air. Naturally, the tenets of courteous airplane travel apply equally to travel on a train, whether for a business trip or the daily commute. One becomes even more key: the use of electronic devices. Unlike airline passengers, railroad travelers are able to use their personal cellular phones to conduct business, ring up friends, or check the football scores if they so wish. A simple rule of thumb for cell phone use: If using the phone will disturb the people around you in any way, don't use it. And if you do use it, don't talk about anything confidential or personal. (Note: Many trains today have cars designated as "quiet cars," on which use of cell phones or other electronic equipment is prohibited.)

Above all, don't emulate those most thoughtless of business travelers who have a way of turning their seats and nearby vacant ones into an office of sorts, spreading out papers and tapping away on a laptop when not shouting into a phone. They are the reason an extended trip on a train has even more potential than an airline flight to make life miserable for travelers. (See also "The Cell Phone," pages 232–233; "Pagers," page 234.)

ON THE ROAD

It's stating the obvious to say that someone driving to another town for a meeting should allow plenty of time to reach their destination. If you realize you're going to be late, pull to the side of the road and use your cell phone to give your estimated time of arrival. Notification enables your clients or colleagues to continue with their own routine until you arrive; not only will they appreciate your thoughtfulness, but your own anxiety will also be relieved.

Another reason to build extra time into your schedule is concern for your own safety: You won't have to floor the gas pedal to make your appointment. The most common cause of accidents is speeding. Drive at the speed limit, turn on your blinker before changing lanes, and don't tailgate cars in front of you. Keep in mind that speeders and tailgaters also run the risk of eliciting so-called "road rage" on the part of other drivers, an eventuality to be avoided at all costs. Wouldn't it be the icing on the cake to gesture rudely toward the driver of another car, then arrive at your afternoon appointment only to see the same driver walking over to greet you?

IN A TAXI OR LIMOUSINE

Time was, out-of-town arrivals at an airport or train station had to be wary of literally being taken for a ride by unscrupulous taxi drivers. Today, however, the fares between most airports and major train stations and nearby destinations are strictly regulated, with the stan-

POINTERS FOR CAR PASSENGERS

A car passenger traveling with fellow businesspersons should watch his or her p's and q's. Jabbering on about something can distract the driver, who may be reluctant to tell you so. You'll have to use your experience or intuition to gauge the appropriate level of conversation. Other hints:

- Don't lose yourself in your laptop unless there's urgency to make a deadline that the driver shares. Withdrawing completely is as discourteous as talking someone's ear off.

- Before turning on the radio, ask your companions' permission and what kind of station they prefer.

- Use your cell phone only when really necessary or when a business call is being made on behalf of you and any others in the car. If you are the driver, remember that safety comes first.

- By all means don't smoke, especially in someone else's car. If you must have a cigarette, wait for a rest stop.

dard charges posted both at taxi stands and in the cabs themselves. Reconfirm this fare before stepping into the taxi, however. For extra certainty, call ahead to your host or hotel to check on taxi availability and rates as well as the best route to your destination.

Paying. Make sure you have small bills in your wallet in case the driver isn't able to make change; although it is the driver's responsibility to be able to change at least a $20 bill, this doesn't guarantee he or she can. Tip the driver 15 percent of the fare.

Livery service. The change problem can be avoided altogether by arranging to have a car or limousine service pick you up at the airport or train station. These services allow you to pay by credit card, with the cost determined up front—which means no surprises. Better still, the car will be ready and waiting when you arrive, relieving you of having to scramble to find a taxi.

All-day service. Travelers with hectic schedules should consider a third alternative: hiring a limousine and driver for a full day or even the whole trip. The driver will be at your service for as long as necessary, patiently waiting at the curb whenever you have to be picked up. This kind of arrangement doesn't come cheaply, but the peace of mind you gain may be worth the extra cost.

TRAVELING WITH YOUR BOSS

If you find yourself setting off on a business trip with the boss, keep two words in mind: *respect* and *deference.* No bowing and scraping is in order (nor should your boss expect it), but holding doors, seeing to it that she has the more comfortable seat, and letting her initiate a conversation shows an unspoken understanding of your respective ranks. Unless your executive traveling companion insists on doing them herself, you should take charge of various tasks—hailing cabs, checking in at the hotel, making restaurant reservations, and tipping service people. Stay on your toes in all regards: Traveling with the boss gives you the opportunity not only to let her get to know you better but also for you to shine.

AT YOUR DESTINATION

No matter how weary you feel, be gracious as you check in at your hotel. If you have to make any special requests, a polite demeanor will get you further than a brusque one. If, say, you failed to reserve a meeting room in advance and one isn't available, you may need to ask whether you can use a table in the dining room or cocktail lounge during off-hours.

Remember these tips as you check in and get settled:

- For safety's sake, don't confirm your room number aloud when you are given your key, electronic or otherwise. On the off chance a disreputable character in the lobby has spotted you as a likely target, the whereabouts of you and your belongings will remain a secret.

- If you find something about your room you don't like, call the front desk and ask for a change, giving the reason: The room is too noisy, too near the elevator, or has a poor view. Most hotels will try to accommodate your requests, depending on availability.

- Call your host to let him or her know you've arrived. Confirm the time of your meeting: "I'll be there at eight o'clock sharp tomorrow morning. Look forward to seeing you then!"

DEALING WITH HOTEL STAFF

Large hotels have full-service staffs to assist their customers. Although the staff may be extremely deferential and willing to handle most requests, don't treat them as servants. Instead, make a point of being courteous and don't skimp on tipping. Not only is this the right thing to do, but word spreads about rude or difficult guests, who can expect no more than the minimum of attention. (See also "How Much to Tip?" pages 276–278.)

In some hotels you'll find a fridge full of snacks and beverages there for the taking. The guest selects an item and checks it off an attached bill; the mini-bar and food costs are then added to your room charge at checkout. There should also be an attached price list. Look it over carefully: The markup for this convenience is considerable, and if you aren't careful, it will add a surprising amount to your bill. The same holds for in-room phone calls, which can carry substantial premiums; check all phone tariffs before using, and bring a prepaid phone card if you plan on making extensive use of the phone.

DINING OUT

On a business trip, dining out is an inevitable part of the package, whether the occasion is a business meal or a social one. If you find yourself dining solo in your hotel, don't feel awkward. (Remind yourself that in Europe and much of the rest of the world, dining alone is nothing to be embarrassed about.) A book will keep you occupied while you're waiting for your food. If, however, you prefer to have company, check with the maître d' or host to see if group tables are set aside for business travelers. (For a full discussion of dining out, see "Business Meals" and "Breakfast, Lunch, or Dinner?" pages 153–154.)

WHEN YOU'RE THE HOST

When you're the visitor but are playing the host for a meal, ask your hotel's concierge or front-desk personnel for restaurant recommendations. You'll want a place that's reputable enough to do your company credit, but reasonable enough so that you won't have to watch what your guests order. Even if your expense account has no limits, avoid very expensive restaurants; your client may take it as a sign of fiscal irresponsibility. When calling for a reservation, it's fine to ask the average cost of a meal or what the price ranges are for main courses, appetizers, and wine. Having made reservations, you'll also find it easier to resist a guest's suggestion of a pricey restaurant.

If your dining partners are customers or clients, it's understood that you will pay the tab. Use a credit card, having made sure beforehand that the restaurant accepts the one you plan to hand over. (Although it's the rare restaurant that doesn't take credit cards, never take a chance; the embarrassment of being caught without enough cash is one of the business traveler's worst nightmares.) Also, consider arranging for payment beforehand. It's a great feeling to be able to leave the table without spending time reviewing the check or figuring the tip. Instead, your focus is on your guests.

If you and your guests have overcoats, check them and pay the tip ($2 for the first coat and $1 per additional coat) when you leave. To keep a guest from insisting on paying for the retrieval of his coat, go quietly ahead to the coatroom and tip the hostess in advance.

WHEN YOU'RE THE GUEST

It is likely that you'll be invited to dinner by the business associate you've traveled to meet, which means that he or she expects to pay. Accept graciously, even if your expense account is the bigger one.

Even if you're taken to a five-star restaurant, be modest in what you order. Never go straight to the highest end of the menu, which might put your host in an uncomfortable position down the road. In addition to being wined and dined, business travelers are entertained in other ways. For tips on attending private clubs, the theater, and sporting events, see Chapter 13, "Business Events," page 153.

HOW MUCH TO TIP?

Whether to tip—and how much, of course—is always a matter of concern when you're traveling on business. For starters, remember three key things: First, always tip discreetly. Second, the longer the task takes, the larger the tip should be. Third, don't tip too much; anyone who flashes tip money or lavishes inappropriate tips on waiters, doormen, or anyone else will come across as foolish in the extreme. Some other rules of thumb for tipping:

- **SKYCAP AT AIRPORT**. The standard tip for the skycap who checks your bags at curbside is $2 for the first bag and $1 per additional bag. A skycap who carts your bags to the check-in counter or elsewhere deserves double that.

- **TAXI AND LIMOUSINE DRIVERS**. The standards for tipping cab and limousine drivers vary from place to place, with some local drivers expecting no tip at all. Unless you're in a cab with someone who can tell you what's customary, assume a tip of 15 percent will be appropriate. Be sure you have enough change and small bills on hand at all times so that you and your companions can get out of the cab without delay.

- **DOORMAN**. It's not necessary to tip a hotel or restaurant doorman on arrival unless he takes your bags out of the car and readies them for the bellman. Follow the rule of $2 for the first bag and $1 per additional bag. If he hails a cab for you, tip him $1 for every person in your party. If the doorman has been particularly helpful during your stay, you may decide an extra $5 is in order.

- **BELLMAN**. When the bellman arrives at your room with your luggage, give him $1 or $2 for every bag he has carried.

- **PARKING VALET/ATTENDANT**. At your hotel or elsewhere, the attendant who parks and retrieves your car gets $2.

- **HOUSEKEEPER**. If you happen to see the person who cleans your room, you may hand her an envelope with your tip and a thank-you. If you are staying for a few nights, you can leave a tip on the desk in the room with a note: "Thank you, Housekeeping." If you are staying for a longer time, leave a tip every couple of days, as the personnel may change. The standard is $2 for each night.

- **CONCIERGE**. In large hotels, this is the staff member to ask for help with theater tickets or dinner reservations; a $5 (or $10 for hard-to-get tickets) tip will do for these services or any other special help. Whenever the concierge gives you directions around the hotel or the city, no tip is expected.

- **WAITER**. The waiter receives 15 to 20 percent of the tab (excluding tax), regardless of your opinion of service provided. This applies across the board, from the corner coffee shop to a posh restaurant. If the service was unacceptable, you may reduce your tip, but not less than 10 percent. A small tip doesn't correct the problem; it simply hurts all the employees sharing in the tip pool—and the others may have given you very good service. Instead, leave a regular tip but be sure to talk to the manager about the problems so she can correct them for the future.

- **HEADWAITER/CAPTAIN**. This employee usually receives a tip that is 25 percent of the tip to your waiter, but only if he has been actively involved in serving you. In this case, tip him separately.

THE SAFETY-MINDED BUSINESSWOMAN

If you're a woman on a business trip, don't be lulled into thinking that your briefcase, laptop, and no-nonsense attire protect you against unwanted attention. Balance a desire to be friendly and to learn about your surroundings with a healthy dose of common sense—especially if you're traveling alone. Doing the following will increase your sense of security:

AT YOUR HOTEL

Electronic keys have reduced the incidence of hotel room break-ins dramatically since their introduction, but you can also take extra precautions. Some hotels have floors with keyed elevator access, which are great for added safety. At hotels lacking such facilities, it's a good idea to ask for a room near the elevator, so you won't have to travel down a long corridor. Have your key or door card in hand before you arrive at your room, in order to avoid fumbling through your handbag at the door. If you stay in a motel, make sure it's one with only interior entrances to the rooms.

Once you're settled, don't allow anyone into your room unless he or she is expected and you're absolutely positive you know who it is. Even though the chambermaid who comes in the evening to turn down your bed will have a key, she should always knock first and announce who she is when you answer the door. Other hotel personnel should be announced by the front desk before showing up at your room. Never open your door without first checking through the peephole to confirm that it is either a service you ordered or someone you know.

Use discretion when getting into an elevator with a sole male occupant. If you become uneasy once inside, push the button for the next floor and get out. Many hotels will also see to it that you are escorted to your room at off-hours.

OUT AND ABOUT

If you've driven to your destination and find yourself driving at night, park in a visible, lighted place. Look around before getting out of the car. Get your car keys ready when returning to the car, and then glance under the car and in the backseat before getting in. If someone appears to be following you as you're walking to your car, walk past it to find help. Likewise, if you're walking on the street and sense you're being followed, do an about-face, cross the street, or duck into a store.

21 | *Conventions, Trade Shows, and Other Off-Site Events*

While most of your time is spent at your office or with a client, from time to time you find yourself traveling off-site to a convention, a trade show, a seminar, or possibly a course for management training. Whatever the reason, just because you are "off-site," it doesn't mean you can suddenly ignore the basic tenets of behavior. In fact, because you are off-site and because you are representing your company, you should focus that much more closely on making sure your actions reflect positively on you and your company.

HOW MUCH FUN?

Because attending an off-site event usually means traveling to another city or a resort, a social aspect is always present. A holiday spirit takes hold after hours, with merriment the rule in convention hospitality suites—rooms rented by participating companies to provide their delegates with a space where they can relax and entertain. Golfing and group excursions to city restaurants and tourist sites are other standard activities.

While the chance to have fun is an integral part of any off-site event, don't let your hair down too enthusiastically. The last thing you want to be is a stick-in-the-mud, but bear in mind that your conduct reflects on your company—after hours as well as during the formal proceedings. Remember, too, that poor opinions of someone who drinks irresponsibly or dresses in a way that attracts the wrong kind of attention have the habit of finding their way back to the home office.

TRAVELING WITH YOUR SPOUSE

If your spouse or partner is coming along to an out-of-town event, make sure he or she understands that this isn't just another vacation, especially if the company is footing the bill. Although wives, husbands, and significant others are free to entertain themselves by shopping or sightseeing during the day, the company may be hosting evening receptions or other events that everyone is expected to attend. To fit in, well-meaning spouses make an effort to learn something about whatever topics are the focus of the convention, allowing them to join in conversations in a reasonably knowledgeable way. Making this effort demonstrates an appreciation of the event's actual purpose.

After-hours activities not sponsored by the company—a foray into the entertainment district, for example, or a group visit to a dance club—are another matter, and neither the delegate nor spouse should feel an obligation to take part. Dancing away the wee hours at the hottest new nightclub in town may be an experience to remember, but it may also have consequences the next morning, when there are meetings and conferences to attend.

GETTING DOWN TO BUSINESS

It goes without saying that the meetings are the real business of an event, which means you should practice more than your golf swing in advance. In a word, go prepared. (See also "Pre-Meeting Preparation," pages 112–113, and "If You're Attending," page 116.)

- Review the agenda beforehand. You might discover that a subject you feel passionate about is the focus of one of the seminars and decide to get involved. List the points you want to make (if only in the question-and-answer period), and arm yourself with any facts and figures needed to back up the contentions you plan to put forward.

- If you have questions you want answered or issues you think worth bringing up, write them down. Then rehearse asking them until each is the very model of conciseness. Rambling on at the mike won't win you points with anyone present, and may garble your questions to boot.

- Learn as much as you can about the principal speakers, not just by reading their biographies in the program but also by asking workmates if they can flesh out the speakers' backgrounds in any way; doing this will allow for a more meaningful conversation if you happen to be introduced to one of them.

NAME TAG ETIQUETTE

Your name tag will contribute to the overall impression you make. These unassuming little plastic badges are subject to certain rules.

- Wear a pin-on name tag on the right side of your chest, about four inches below the shoulder. This positioning will ensure that it is in clear view when you are shaking hands during introductions.

- Don't wear your name tag outside the convention hall. Ideally, the tags should be small enough to be easily slipped into a pocket or handbag while you go to and from meetings.

- Don't write "Mr.," "Mrs.," or "Ms." in front of your name on the card. Technically, a professional title such as "Dr." may be added, but this is determined by how much the wearer wants to advertise his or her credentials.

- At business (not social) events, it's appropriate to add your title under your name: "Bryce Walker, Production Manager." Unless the convention is confined to fellow employees, add your company name as well.

Once the event is in progress, observe two important rules: The first and most obvious is to show up for the meetings, sessions, or classes you're scheduled to attend. Even if the topic isn't all that pertinent to your daily work back home, you have the obligation to participate after money has been spent to get you there. The second rule is to be punctual. Coming in late is disruptive and casts a poor light on you and your company—the name of which, remember, is emblazoned across your name tag.

Make a point of taking your own notes, since relying on the minutes to be distributed later can be a big mistake. Also, many of the points and insights you find important may be overlooked by the minutes taker.

MAKING A PRESENTATION

You may be asked to make a presentation at an event. As a presenter, not only are you giving information on which you are an expert but you are also representing your company. Therefore, the quality of your presentation will reflect directly on you and your firm. As you approach your task, consider the following tips:

- PRACTICE. Have your presentation ready with enough time to spare that you can fit in several dress rehearsals. If you're using a computer-generated presentation, practice with all the equipment and become familiar with the talking points at which you will click to the next image.

- **PROOFREAD**. Review all your hand-outs and presentation images for accuracy. If you make a typo, someone is bound to point it out to you. Remember, you're the expert now—so let your material reflect this.

- **ARRIVE EARLY**. If you have to travel, especially by airplane, plan on arriving the night before. Not only will you be fresh and ready to make your presentation, but you won't have to worry about getting to the venue on time.

- **SET UP EARLY**. Go to your presentation space at least a half hour early, and plug everything in to make sure it is working properly. You can choose to distribute hand-outs ahead of time or have them on a table ready for distribution at the end of the presentation. Also, check the functionality of your microphone and test the volume levels.

- **TAKE FIVE**. Five minutes before your presentation, head to the restroom for one final pit stop. Do a quick check in the mirror. Take several deep breaths, give yourself a big smile, and head back to the presentation room.

- **THANK THE HOST**. At the start of the presentation, thank the host or sponsor for inviting you. Remember to give credit to any other people who helped you prepare it, stating their names in full.

- **SPEED KILLS, SO DOES MONOTONE**. Public speakers tend to accelerate their speech, so consciously work to slow down your pace of delivery. Speak clearly, and engage the participants by looking them in the eye. Use your voice volume and inflection to drive home your points and to make your presentation lively. Step away from the podium from time to time, and use your hands to make your points. And don't forget to smile.

- **LISTEN**. When someone asks a question or makes a point, really listen to what they are saying, then respond directly to their question or point. If you don't know the answer, or need to get additional information to respond, say so—and then be sure to follow up.

- **THANK THE AUDIENCE**. At the end of the session, be sure to thank the audience for attending. Provide contact information and then be prepared to meet and greet participants afterward.

NETWORKING

Off-site events, especially conventions and trade shows, offer the perfect opportunity to network. During breaks, make it a point to meet people from other companies or from out-of-town branches of your own firm. It may be tempting to spend all your time with your chums from the home office, but if you do, you're missing a key opportunity. Remember: The very fact that you and the strangers around you work for the same company—or in the same field—means that you have something in common. You never know when a perfunctory first meeting might one day blossom into a valuable business relationship. (See also "Introductions," pages 217–222.)

TRADE SHOWS

Crowds, banners, color, music, noise: An atmosphere this overwhelming can grow wearying after a while, making it all the more important for exhibitors who tend booths to keep their cool and treat even casual browsers as their best customers. As an exhibitor, remember that you are seen not as an individual, but as the embodiment of your company.

WITH PROSPECTIVE CUSTOMERS

At a trade show, it's the nature of the beast for people to make snap judgments when they pause at a booth. This means that it's doubly important for you to use good business etiquette as you demonstrate your product. When meeting potential buyers

- Dress as if you were meeting an important client back at the office

- Always stand when talking

- Shake hands

- Express interest in the person

- Give him or her your undivided attention

The trickiest part of your job is when you're faced with the task of balancing several customers at once without offending any one of them. Have business cards at the ready, and use them to momentarily placate any visitors awaiting their turn. Much in the manner of putting someone on hold on the telephone, utter a quick "Please excuse me" to the person you're talking with, turn to the bystander, and hand him or her a card and say, "Would you mind waiting a bit? I'll be right with you." If you see that a booth mate is free, direct the prospect to him or her. Or, if possible, quickly set up an appointment to meet later in the day.

Even if you're making small talk with a potential customer, it's not a good idea to invite another prospect to join in unless your intuition tells you otherwise: The best tack is always to give undivided attention to one person at a time. The same rule applies to product demonstrations. If someone is standing by observing, that's fine—but you should direct your demonstration to the person you're dealing with at the moment. At the same time, make it clear to the other person that you'll attend to him or her as soon as you have finished.

WITH OTHER EXHIBITORS

If you attend trade shows regularly, more than likely you'll be acquainted with many of the booth-tenders from other companies. While you'll no doubt want to catch up with them, and perhaps make plans for the evening, remember that you're not at a high school reunion. The less time you spend schmoozing with old friends, the more time you'll have to meet with potential customers.

For the sake of your fellow booth mates, be punctual when it is your turn to take over the post. Getting sidetracked at a huge show is easy, and keeping people waiting can cause a ripple effect for some time afterward.

FOLLOWING UP

A handwritten note to each prospective customer you talked with will have more impact than a typewritten one, which could look suspiciously like a form letter. Tell the recipient how nice it was to meet him, and that you hope the interest he expressed in your product will someday result in an order. A reference to a non-business topic you discussed—a new grandchild, for example—personalizes the letter further and lets it stand out from the norm.

"WHICH WAY TO THE SNACK BAR?"

Considering the number of people streaming by your booth, it is inevitable that you'll be asked for directions to restrooms, snack bars, the lost and found, and, yes, the often-elusive information booth. The very fact that you've staked out a space in a gargantuan hall marks you as a fixture of sorts, if only temporarily. As a consequence, in the minds of the ebbing and flowing army of booth-browsers, you know the lay of the land.

The wise booth-tender will make sure he or she can politely provide the needed answer, even if the directions are to a competitor's booth. On the first day, make yourself familiar with the layout of the floor by taking a walking tour, with the show directory as your guide. Then keep the directory close at hand for the rest of the show. When people who find themselves without a directory ask the way to a specific company's booth, look up its number and respond cheerfully. Your kindness to a stranger might open up a conversation that could lead to interest in your product.

22 | *Doing Business in Another Country*

While the United States has the world's largest economy and its business practices are for the most part respected, the way business is done in the rest of the world remains strictly local. Take this statement very seriously: Unless you accept the validity of other cultures' ways of conducting business and try to abide by them, your dealings will be less effective than they could be—or, worse, you'll fail completely. The major differences you encounter will often have less to do with negotiating tactics and decision-making than with how effectively you are able to communicate with your foreign counterparts and how well you understand the social aspects of doing business with them.

Social aspects? Yes. In the United States, efficiency comes first and foremost when doing business, but the American production-line mentality doesn't always carry over in other countries. Though your training and inclination may tell you to get right down to brass tacks, on other continents such haste may be considered inappropriate. In the Middle East, for example, your host may serve rounds and rounds of tea before touching on business matters.

How the finer points of negotiating and decision-making are handled will depend on the specific organization with which you're dealing, and the country and field with which you're involved. For these particulars, an excellent teacher can be a fellow American who has had experience doing business at the same company in the same setting and can tell you what to expect.

BEFORE YOU GO

The slogan "Be prepared" takes on new meaning whenever you travel to another country with the aim of doing business. As an American, when you land on foreign soil, pass through customs, and step out into an unfamiliar world, always remember this: You are representing your country as much as your company. How you behave will either reinforce or counteract your hosts' conception of Americans—and this, in turn, will affect the outcome of your business negotiations.

Two recent developments in particular have changed both how Americans view the rest of the world and how the rest of the world views Americans: the rise of the global economy and the events of September 11, 2001. Business is now routinely conducted on a global basis. Therefore, American businesspeople have to be more prepared than ever to interact with people from different cultures. At the same time, because of September 11, the business traveler must be more aware of the security concerns that affect not only her travels but the travels of anyone working for her. The result of these changes is an ever-wider array of customs and courtesies to be mastered. Embarking on this respectful undertaking shows your cultural sensitivity and your willingness to learn and adapt.

TRAVEL WARNINGS

Naturally, one of the first steps you or your company should take before venturing abroad is to find out whether there are any U.S. State Department warnings you should know about before traveling to your destination. The State Department's Web site at http://travel.state.gov/travel_warnings.html gives you not only warnings of political unrest but also updates on currency, entry regulations, driving conditions, and more.

That done, you should prepare an itinerary for your hosts, your office, and your family. (See Chapter 20, "The Thoughtful Traveler," page 267.)

CUSTOMS AND CULTURE

At minimum you should know the basic facts about the country you're visiting. But when you exhibit more than a nodding acquaintance, you impress your hosts and all others you meet with your appreciation of the nation, the culture, and the individuals themselves.

Begin your mini-course on a country by skimming the surface and then digging deeper. Start your search on the Internet, which offers a wide array of sites where you can find key facts and explore specific areas of a country's culture. While the Internet is great for basic facts and information, travel guidebooks can provide an in-depth background on the history and culture of the country you are visiting. Once you arrive at your destination, keep abreast of local events by reading regional English-language newspapers.

Be warned, however, that culture is not determined solely by national boundaries. For example, the Basque Country and Andalusia, regions of Spain, have distinctly different cultures, as do Sicily and Tuscany in Italy. Nor does language determine culture—witness the Americans and the British.

SEX, POLITICS, AND RELIGION

The old saying that you should never discuss sex, politics, or religion in polite company applies twice over in foreign countries. Sex as a topic (in the sense of gender as well as in the sense of sexuality) is definitely off-limits.

A HOT TOPIC

Politics is a hot topic in much of the world—usually too hot to touch. Never criticize the leaders or government of your host country, and never criticize your own. If, as is likely, you're quizzed about American politics or policy (either national or international), graciously admit that you're no expert in such matters. Remember, too, that a businessperson is more of an ambassador for his or her country than is a garden-variety tourist.

CONCERNING RELIGION

Wherever you're headed, make yourself aware of the country's dominant religions. Also take note of its religious and secular holidays. You don't want to ask for a business appointment on July 14 in France—that's Bastille Day—and neither do you want to attempt to conduct business in Jerusalem on a Friday afternoon, when everything is closed in preparation for the Jewish Sabbath.

Religious customs are a still more important concern. If traveling to Thailand, have you learned that it's sacrilegious to photograph any statue or other image of Buddha? Or that if you're accompanying your Muslim host in Saudi Arabia, he must stop to pray several times during the day? Such are the vagaries of religions of which you may know little, but whose orthodoxies and conventions you must nonetheless respect. This, in turn, shows respect for your host and translates into more successful business dealings.

PRACTICAL CONCERNS

What do passports, visas, credit cards, currency, and other paraphernalia of overseas travel have to do with behavior? Nothing in themselves—but your lack of attention to such items can disrupt your visit (and wreak havoc in some cases), creating embarrassment for you and inconvenience for your hosts. The following information may save you considerable hassles once you embark on a business trip:

- If you lose your passport in the United States, notify the nearest passport agency or Passport Services in Washington, D.C. If the loss occurs in a foreign country, report it to the nearest U.S. Embassy or Consulate or the local police department.

- It's easier to replace a lost passport if you photocopy the data page ahead of time and keep the copy in a separate place when you travel.

- Certain countries will not allow you to enter without a visa. To find out whether a visa is required and how to obtain one, call the consulate or embassy of the country you plan to visit, not an agency of the United States; the responsibility to grant and issue visas is the country's alone.

- Check to see if your destination has ATM service readily available. Many airports have ATM machines easily located where you can get funds in the local currency even before you get your baggage. If ATMs won't be available, traveler's checks and some U.S. currency is advisable along with a couple of credit cards.

- Let your credit card companies know that you're traveling, and where. Given the eagerness of credit card companies to prevent fraud, the computer may reject your card in a new, faraway place, thinking it might have been stolen.

- If you use a corporate credit card, make sure your company authorizes your use of it abroad; otherwise, it, too, could be rejected.

- Photocopy your credit cards before you leave, and carry these copies separately from your cards. If a card is lost or stolen, you'll have the number on hand to report it.

- Take along copies of the toll-free numbers of your credit card companies.

IN CASE OF EMERGENCY

The U.S. Consulate is the first place to call in emergencies, so note its location and telephone number in the country you're visiting. Should you need the name of an English-speaking doctor or a hospital, the consulate can give you one. Their personnel can also help if you should get into trouble with the police or want to know whether a political crisis warrants your leaving the country. If you're going to be in the country for any length of time or are concerned about potential danger, be sure to register with the consulate once you've arrived. Registering will give them permission to give your family and friends information about your welfare if need be.

BUSINESS CARDS

One writer on international trade declares that your business card, carefully created for use in the country you visit, is the one card you should never leave home without. But what should you put on it for the convenience of your international cohorts?

- After your name, your title—as well as your function—should be shown. For example, if you function as the associate director of training for the human resources department, give an additional title if you have one, such as assistant vice president. In case your title or position is one that a foreigner might not understand, consider putting a "plain English" version in parentheses—for example, "Human Resources (Personnel)."

- Don't omit your title, even if it's a junior one. In many countries, particularly Latin American ones, hosts who don't know your title won't know how to treat you or whom they should designate to do business with you. But avoid any temptation to exaggerate your position—being found out could have serious consequences, even to the point of wrecking the planned negotiations.

- If English isn't commonly spoken in your destination, print one side of your card in English and the other in the native language. Even in countries where English is the second language, you're less likely to find English speakers in small towns than in the larger centers of trade.

EXCHANGING CARDS

In many countries, the exchange of cards follows a certain protocol. There may be a designated time for presenting cards—for example, at the beginning of a meeting or after you've been introduced. In some countries, good manners dictate that you present the card with both hands, or with the foreign-language side up. When you receive a card, don't just stick it in your pocket. Read it right away and then place it in your own card case or briefcase.

You may be surprised at how many cards identify the person as "Doctor," particularly in Europe. Unlike in the United States, men and women with advanced degrees, or even university graduates, legitimately go by their academic titles. Even if, to you, the title doesn't seem meaningful, it's a faux pas not to use it.

FORGING PERSONAL RELATIONSHIPS

In many countries, forming personal relationships is an all-important part of your business dealings. While socializing, your hosts get to know you. If you're patient, you'll establish trust—an important element in your foreign counterparts' decisions to do business with you. Conversely, if you appear too eager to talk business, they may think you begrudge the time you spend with them.

Learn to be the gracious guest, starting with your self-taught mini-course on the culture of the country. Answer questions about American life in a way that can't be perceived as boasting. Don't be surprised if the conversation turns to music, gardening, good places to vacation in winter, or preferences in wine or beer. Such sociability does not, however, give you permission to ask personal questions; the American's readiness to "open up" is not typical of the rest of the world.

THE IMPORTANCE OF NAMES AND TITLES

As for names, don't confuse developing social relationships with familiarity; remember that for an American, foreign names and forms of address are rife with the opportunity for mistakes and embarrassment. Doing research ahead of time helps, but you still need to pay especially close attention to names during introductions—a truth well illustrated by the fact that in Spanish-speaking countries a person bears both of his parents' surnames (see page 300).

Always address people by their proper titles. "Señor" and "Madame" are straightforward, but others can be confusing—for example, when in England, don't automatically call a dentist "Doctor"; surprisingly, "Mr." or "Ms." is the proper title. An engineer in the United States is known simply as "Mr." or "Ms.," but in South America, Europe, and Asia, address him or her as "Engineer."

About the use of first names: In most countries outside the United States, it will be a long time before you're on a first-name basis with your host and others you meet formally—perhaps never. Let your overseas business colleague suggest using first names, but do not do it yourself.

DEFERRING TO AGE

Show respect for businesspeople who are older than you are—even those in a lower position. Be deferential, holding the door for them and allowing them to be seated first. Show similar respect for anyone who has a more senior position than you do. If you happen to be younger than anyone around, dress and act in the most mature manner you can muster, a way of demonstrating your business experience and acumen.

RESPECTING WORK ETHICS

Don't be surprised when you don't meet a lot of workaholics abroad. In many places, family and private life, not work, is the most important part of the businessperson's world. Even if you feel you could close the deal if you and your host were to work for an extra couple of hours, resist the temptation to suggest it; it's likely you'll be either rejected or resented. Never interpret this difference in attitude to mean that your foreign counterparts are lazy or indifferent. They may be every bit as serious and meticulous about their work but may simply have a different attitude toward timing than many Americans have; in general, closing shop for the day is not seen as a reason for feeling guilty.

A QUESTION OF TIMING

Workweeks and business hours vary around the globe. In Italy, Greece, and some Latin American countries, it's commonplace practice to close for two or more hours in the afternoon and then to stay open until 7:00 P.M. or later. Shops as well as offices may also close on Saturday afternoons. In China, the business week is Monday through Saturday, as it is in Japan and other non-Muslim countries in Asia. In Israel, the workweek is Sunday through Friday, with stores and offices closing on Friday at about noon. Muslim countries observe Friday as their Sabbath, and no business is done that day, with Thursdays sometimes only a half day as well. (This doesn't necessarily mean, however, that some people don't work beyond their official business hours.)

Punctuality will not be faulted in any country, but don't consider it an affront if you're kept waiting for half an hour or so, especially in Latin America. Also, don't forget that traffic jams are hardly confined to the industrialized West.

SPEAKING ENGLISH ABROAD

American English is loaded with idioms and eccentric circumlocutions, and people who speak English as a second language may be familiar with all or none of them. While you may think they understand what you're saying, they may be hearing something else. Conversational bloopers may make funny stories over the dinner table, but when you're in a business situation they can have serious consequences. Do everything you can to help other people understand you, and to make your conversation in English clear for them.

- Speak clearly and not too fast, enunciating carefully.

- Don't use slang, regionalisms, colloquialisms, or euphemisms. If you say that something is "a slam dunk" or "a no-brainer," anticipate a puzzled look.

- Make sure that your overseas counterpart has the same understanding of all business and legal terms as you. It may be that in your field the same terminology is used worldwide—but you shouldn't assume so.

- When using numbers in a business discussion, it may be necessary to write them down and show them, since numbers can be expressed verbally in different ways.

- If your host seems at all puzzled or hesitant as you're speaking, pause immediately and ask whether he or she is having problems understanding you.

UNDERSTANDING BODY LANGUAGE

Two thoughts about body language: (1) Know what your body language is saying to others and (2) learn how to read other people's body language. Although your facial expressions, stance, and gestures are basic to communication, they are also easily misunderstood. For example: In the United States, looking directly at the speaker's face in a meeting shows that he or she has your full attention, but in Asian countries, making eye contact is considered impolite. Even in the United States, extended eye contact or staring is rude, and in some countries it could get you into real trouble.

Gestures are similarly perilous. In some countries, showing the bottoms of your feet is an insult. You'll also be well advised to check on local customs before pointing with your finger or snapping your fingers in public. Beckoning with a curled index finger is widely considered offensive, as well. Waving your hand, arm raised, in greeting or to get someone's attention may be misunderstood as a "no" signal.

In addition, the following gestures should be avoided unless you're absolutely sure that they have the same meaning in your host country as in the United States:

- Thumbs up

- The "okay" sign—making a circle with your thumb and forefinger (obscene in Japan and elsewhere)

- "V" for victory

PERSONAL SPACE AND OTHER BASICS

Once you've been in a country for a while, you'll probably get the feel of the local body language. Meanwhile, here are a few guidelines:

- **SPACING YOURSELF.** The distance maintained between yourself and others is important; getting too close or moving too far away can be misconstrued as unwanted familiarity or standoffishness. North Americans and Europeans are comfortable standing some two to three feet apart. The Japanese and other Asians require more space, but the rest of the world likes to get closer than we're accustomed to.

- **HANDSHAKES.** In North America and Europe, a firm handshake is an appropriate form of greeting. In Asia and the Middle East, where handshaking is still relatively new, the customary grip is gentler; a too-hearty grip could be interpreted as aggressive. In Islamic countries, offering your hand to a woman is highly offensive. At the other extreme, it's said that you can never shake hands too much in France, where women shake hands as freely and as often as men.

- **BOWING AND SIMILAR GREETINGS.** In Japan and some other Asian countries, the bow is the equivalent of the handshake. In rank-conscious Japan, the person of inferior rank bows first and lowest. The Indians and Thai may place their hands together at the chest in a prayerlike gesture as a form of greeting.

- **TOUCHING.** North Americans don't engage in casual touching, but Latin Americans and southern Europeans do. If a native jabs you with his or her finger to make a point or touches your arm in conversation, don't be offended. In Middle Eastern, Southeast Asian, and Pacific Island nations, a man may even find his male host taking his hand. Do not misconstrue these gestures, but don't try to copy them either.

SPEAKING IN A FOREIGN LANGUAGE

It is a courtesy to your foreign hosts to have some small familiarity with their language—knowing at least the words for "please," "thank you," "good morning," "good afternoon," "good night," "hello," and "good-bye." Carry a pocket foreign-language dictionary so that you can look up words and communicate with people who may not understand English—hotel and restaurant employees, for example.

USING TRANSLATORS AND INTERPRETERS

While English is often used for international business dealings, there may be times when negotiations will be conducted in the host language of the country you're visiting. Unless you are fluent in this language (and oftentimes even if you are), you'll want an interpreter present.

The word *interpreter* usually brings to mind those phenomenal men and women who translate as the speaker speaks, their words following at a fast clip. Known as simultaneous translators, they are not the kind of interpreter the average businessperson uses. More widely used are consecutive interpreters, who speak after the speaker has completed a few sentences. To make sure you get what you bargained for, use only professional translators. To avoid a conflict of interest, make sure that they are in your employ, not hired by your counterpart. Ask for recommendations from friends who have done business in your destination, or see whether your company can handle the hiring.

BEFORE THE MEETING

To let your interpreter get acquainted with your way of speaking, spend some time with her beforehand. This will also help you to gauge whether your interpreter's English is idiomatic. Go over the agenda for the meeting, and make sure she can handle technical as well as business terms.

Prepare visual aids, if possible, to clarify and reinforce your and your translator's spoken words. Use both languages on charts and graphs, which can also serve later as confirmation of what you said. Acquaint your interpreter with the visual aids before the meeting.

Also, make sure to let your interpreter know the appropriate dress for the occasion. If you think she should wear business clothes, say so. In general, your interpreter's clothing should be subdued and unobtrusive; it is you, not she, who's the center of attention. If the occasion is formal, ask her to wear a formal dress; for a male interpreter, ask him to wear black-tie attire, or at least a dark suit.

AT THE MEETING

The translator is usually seated at the table between the two major players who need her— for example, you and your host. On more formal occasions, such as a dinner, she will sit slightly behind them. Although she does not expect to join you in eating dinner, see to it that she has a meal either before or after the occasion.

When you speak through an interpreter, many of the same rules apply as when you speak English with a non-native speaker. Speak slowly and distinctly, avoid slang and regionalisms, and watch the host for signs that he's tuning out. Always address the listener, not the interpreter.

Keep your sentences short, and speak only a few before stopping for translation.

Intermittently ask your host whether he is clear about what you're saying or has any questions. Be expressive as you speak, and show concentration as you listen. Smile, but don't tell jokes; despite your interpreter's best efforts, humor rarely translates well.

Don't interrupt your interpreter, but also don't hesitate to stop the meeting to ask her about anything that isn't clear to you. When the meeting is over, have the interpreter go over what was said and her impressions of your counterpart's reactions. Also ask her about anything you did not understand. Finally, draft and circulate to all participants a report in English of the conclusions or agreements reached during the meeting.

TO TRANSLATE CORRESPONDENCE?

In most cases, you won't need a translation for your English-language correspondence with an overseas organization. Many businessmen who wouldn't trust themselves to negotiate with you in English verbally are perfectly able to read and understand your letters and to answer them in English. When you do need a translator for your business letters, make sure you hire a true professional—one who can convey your meaning, not one who will merely translate words literally from one language to another.

DIFFERENCES IN DRESS

Whether the adage "Clothes make the man" holds true today is debatable, but clothes do reveal the businessman and businesswoman. Until you've visited a country a few times and know the dress code, dress conservatively. For men, a dark suit and dark tie are safe bets, and white shirts are the prevailing choice in most countries. Although the buttoned-up look may not appeal to you, you discard it at your own risk—and the risk of your business. For women, sticking to the traditional dress code is key, and on the modest side at that.

MEN'S CLOTHING

First check with your host to see whether it is appropriate for you to wear the traditional garment. If you get the go-ahead, don't scour your hometown in search of such shirts; wear your own white shirt until you have the chance to buy some local garb. In warmer climates, men can wear light-colored suits. For cool comfort, do as the natives do: In Singapore, men wear long-sleeved shirts and carry their jackets (in case of over-air-conditioned rooms). In Latin American countries, men wear loose shirts called guayaberas, which are not tucked in, and some Asian countries have similar comfortable regulation dress for men.

Ties, too, can be problematic. In England, if you wear a striped tie, there's the chance you could be sporting some Englishman's "old school tie." In other countries, certain colors are inappropriate; white, for example, is a color symbolic of mourning. To be safe, stick to dark, solid colors.

WOMEN'S CLOTHING

Businesswomen should generally choose conservative suits and dresses and "sensible shoes" with medium-height heels. Skirts and dresses should not go far above the knee in Western countries; in other countries, keep the hemline below the knee and avoid sleeveless blouses and tops, as well as scoop-neck or other low necklines. Avoid excessive, flashy, or (in destinations where it may be an issue) overtly religious jewelry, and keep your cosmetics understated as well.

NOTE OF CAUTION. Acceptability of slacks for women varies from country to country.

DINING AND DRINKING

Whether you are the guest or the host, be prompt. As the host, make arrangements in advance. If you need help finding a suitable restaurant, ask for the hotel concierge's assistance. When ordering dinner or wine, you may ask your guests if they can suggest local specialties. When invited to someone's home, send flowers or take along a box of fine chocolates.

During the meal, do as your mother told you when she said to pick up the same fork your hostess does. In other words, always watch your native host or guest and follow his example. If you're traveling to China or Japan, you should learn to handle chopsticks. In Middle Eastern countries, never eat with your left hand, which is considered unclean. If you find yourself being served a strange dish anywhere, eat it whether or not you like it—or even know what it is. One travel expert suggests that you never ask what animal the dish came from—it's easier to down a sheep's eyeball when it remains unidentified.

TOASTING

Except in Muslim countries, drinking usually accompanies dining—and drinking calls for toasting. (Remember that if you're a non-drinker, this is one time that your host should show his understanding; it's perfectly fine to toast with a drink that is non-alcoholic.) For occasions that are somewhat formal, you should have a toast prepared in advance unless you're an accomplished extemporaneous speaker. Make it short and gracious, acknowledging the hospitality of your host. Wherever you are, etiquette calls for the host to make the first toast, so you can take your cue from him. Don't attempt a humorous toast—it could be misunderstood or considered in bad taste.

When drinking informally, you may be expected to utter a short one-word or one-phrase toast—"A votre santé" in France, or just "Santé" (health); in Germany, "Prosit" means the same. Americans unaccustomed to toasting may find themselves drinking more than they intended, so beware.

FOREIGN-LANGUAGE TOASTS

If you have to give a toast to an overseas host, or you want to make a toast to someone visiting the United States who speaks a different language, make a point to learn his or her country's traditional toast—which is usually the equivalent of "To your health!" or "Cheers!" Following is a sampling of international toasts, with their pronunciations shown in informal phonetics; capital letters indicate the syllable(s) to stress.

LANGUAGE	TOAST	PRONUNCIATION
Cantonese	Yung sing	YOUNG-SING
Czech	Nazdraví	nahz-DRAHV-ee
Dutch	Proost	PROWST
Finnish	Kippis	KIP-pis
French	A votre santé	ah-votruh-san-TAY
German	Prosit	PROHST, with guttural R
Greek	Stin egia sas	steen-ee-YAH-sahs
Hebrew	L'Chayim	luh-CHI-um, with guttural CH
Hungarian	Egészségedre	eh-geh-sheh-GEHD-ruh
Italian	Salute	sah-LOO-tay
Japanese	Kampai	KAHM-PYE
Korean	Gan bei	kahn-BAY
Malaysian	Slimat minim	seh-lah-maht MEE-noom
Polish	Na zdrowie	nahz-DROH-vee-ah
Portuguese	Brindare	brin-DAH-ray, first R slightly trilled
Russian	Na zdorovie	nahz-doh-ROH-vee-ah
Scandinavian*	Skål	SKOAL
Spanish	Salud	sah-LOOD
Thai	Choc-tee	chock-DEE
Turkish	Serefe	sheh-REH-feh

*Danish, Swedish, Norwegian

GIFTS

Any gifts to your hosts should be tasteful but not too expensive. Moreover, they should be fitting. What you give or send to the host who has entertained you one evening in his home is not what you should give a department head who has spent one or two days attending your presentations, introducing you to her colleagues, and arranging meetings for you. To the former, you might bring fresh flowers or a box of fine chocolates. To the latter, you should give a more lasting present—one from the United States or, better yet, from your state; it is acceptable to send it after you return home. The more you research the customs of your host's country and his or her individual taste, the more likely you are to select a gift that successfully conveys your appreciation.

23 | *Adjusting Your Cultural Lens*

Good business etiquette really means showing consideration and understanding to your colleagues and associates at all times, with the goal of establishing mutually respectful relationships—personal links that will enable you to work together as smoothly as possible in pursuit of your business goals. When traveling to a new culture, the importance of personal consideration takes on a whole new dimension. As a guest, it's incumbent on you to respect and follow the customs of your host—many of which may be quite different from what you're used to. Understanding the local business etiquette is the essential starting point for everything else you hope to accomplish.

Since customs can sometimes vary even within a country, the most important thing you can do in this regard is follow the lead of those around you and ask others for guidance when necessary. As a thoughtful traveler, however, you can make things easier for your host by doing some preliminary research on the basic customs of the place you're planning to visit. Many excellent books offer in-depth discussions of business traditions and taboos around the world; at the end of this chapter, we list a number of them for your further reading. In the meantime, here are thumbnail sketches of the main regions of the globe and the business cultures that prevail there.

LATIN AMERICA

Latin America encompasses a wide variety of national and local styles, from the teeming sprawl of Mexico City to freewheeling Rio de Janeiro to the ultra-cosmopolitan Buenos Aires. Still, certain customs of doing business hold throughout the region. Above all, Latin Americans like to conduct business at a leisurely pace, preferring to establish a friendly relationship before moving on to work matters. Personal connections mean everything in this part of the world; before doing business with any new contact, you'll first need to get a third-party introduction—either through an institution such as a bank, law firm, or consulting firm or through a mutual professional acquaintance or friend.

DOING BUSINESS

All business meetings should be arranged at least two to three weeks in advance (showing up at a business or government office without an appointment is unacceptable in Latin America) and confirmed both before you leave and once you arrive in the country you're visiting. Personal assistants typically act as gatekeepers for executives, and treating these employees with the utmost politeness is essential when scheduling appointments.

Optimal meeting times are in the morning between 10:00 and 12:30, and in the afternoon between 3:00 and 5:00. Set aside two to three hours for each session, and don't be surprised if a morning meeting stretches into a business lunch, since meals play an important part in Latin American business dealings.

All meetings will generally begin with social conversation, designed to get to know you as a person (one exception is Venezuela, where businesspeople tend to get straight to the point). When business discussions do start, they tend to proceed relatively slowly. It may take a number of meetings, and even several visits to the country, to conclude your negotiations. It's vitally important that you never express any impatience or anger at the tempo of the proceedings.

While you're expected to be punctual for all meetings, your host is likely to be up to thirty minutes late (bringing along some reading material is always a good idea). Be prepared to be greeted with a friendly, somewhat prolonged handshake. Male friends may also embrace in an *abrazo* (a warm hug), while close women friends will lightly kiss each other on both cheeks accompanied by a light touch on the arm. Business cards can be presented at this time, but discreetly. Your cards should have information in Spanish (or Portuguese, in the case of Brazil) on one side, and that side should be presented face up so that your host can read it.

In addressing your host, remember that most Latin Americans have two surnames; the first is from their father, the second from their mother. Use the first when addressing someone. For example, Señor Eduardo Perez Montaldo would be greeted as Señor Eduardo Perez. Titles such as "Doctor" and "Professor" are important, so be careful not to leave them out when introducing or greeting someone. Latin Americans also like to stand closer to the person with whom they are talking than you may be used to, and may casually touch your arm during conversation. Don't pull away—it's considered rude—and be sure to maintain solid eye contact with your host at all times.

ENTERTAINMENT

Establishing a friendly relationship also means plenty of socializing—and Latin Americans love to entertain, both in restaurants and in their homes. While business lunches are the mainstay here (typically lasting one and a half to two hours), business dinners are also popular. Be warned, though: In most Latin American countries dinner is a late affair, sometimes not starting until 10:00 P.M. or later.

If you've been invited to a party or dinner at someone's home, it's considered polite to arrive at least fifteen to thirty minutes late. In general, you should never discuss business topics at a meal or a party—be it in a restaurant or a private home—unless your host raises the topic.

LOOKING THE PART

The Latin American business culture places a high priority on being well-dressed and well-groomed. For the most part, the business casual look is frowned upon here. All business attire should be conservative, elegant, and up to date. For men, dark suits of gray or blue, with a well-pressed white shirt, a conservative tie, and polished dress shoes, are standard, while a tuxedo may be required for more formal affairs.

Women should opt for conservative clothing—generally dresses, suits, or pantsuits, neither flashy nor revealing, worn with heels and makeup. Jewelry should be kept to a minimum. For dinner, an elegant conservative dress or an elegant skirt and blouse ensemble are appropriate, while a cocktail dress or evening gown is the choice for more formal occasions.

EUROPE AND RUSSIA

With the fall of the Iron Curtain, the adoption of the euro, and other steps toward economic integration, business practices across Europe and Russia are becoming increasingly standardized. Still, significant differences remain in how business is conducted in various regions: Delays and legal red tape tend to predominate in newly capitalist eastern Europe, while a more formal style reigns in northern Europe and a more relaxed approach that emphasizes personal ties marks Mediterranean business dealings. One common thread is that vacations and holidays are held dear across the continent—meaning business slows to a crawl in August and at year's end.

DOING BUSINESS

As you move from the north of Europe to the south, the most obvious differences in manners concern time and space. Scandinavians, Germans, Britons, and other northern people place a very high value on punctuality, while standards are looser in the southern regions. In Spain or Portugal a visitor might be kept waiting thirty minutes before being greeted with the utmost courtesy. Southern Europeans also have a more intimate personal comfort zone, preferring to stand about two feet apart when they converse. For northerners, the acceptable distance is about four feet, and anything closer is seen as an invasion of privacy.

The standard greeting throughout Europe is the handshake, for both men and women. It is usually polite for a woman to extend her hand first. Most continentals shake hands before and after each meeting, while in Great Britain a single introductory shake is sufficient. Throughout Europe, formality in address is the rule: Never call another person by his or her first name until clearly invited to do so, and be careful to use any professional titles such as "Doctor," "Professor," or "Advocate." Since many European businesspeople speak English, an English-language card is usually acceptable, although a card printed on one side in your host's language is considered a sign of courtesy in southern European countries (and is a must in Spain).

In general, all business and social appointments should be scheduled at least two weeks in advance. In northern countries, being exactly on time is essential; meetings start promptly, move quickly to the matter at hand, and tend to follow a tightly scripted agenda. In southern countries such as Spain and Greece, while you should plan to be on time, your host may not be. Meetings are more likely to start late, interruptions are not unexpected, and there is no attempt to hurry the outcome. In these regions, patience and courtesy are the keys to successful business negotiations.

In eastern Europe, with its relatively undeveloped infrastructure, the etiquette tends to revolve around logistical challenges. Be sure to set up meetings far in advance; it may take months to finalize visas and other travel arrangements. Once you arrive, multiple meetings will likely be required to wrap up business dealings. This is especially true in Russia, where extreme caution in making decisions is the norm and being too ready to compromise is regarded as a sign of weakness.

ENTERTAINMENT

In northern Europe, business entertainment tends to center on lunch or dinner at a restaurant, where an earlier business discussion may or may not be continued. In Germany, for instance, it's acceptable to talk about business before or after the meal, but never while eating. Dutch and Scandinavian businesspeople, on the other hand, have no problem mixing food and business, and all the French ask is that you give the food equal attention. In Great Britain, it's considered bad form to talk shop after hours, while in Portugal discussing anything business-related over a festive dinner is out of the question.

The evening meal plays an even larger role in the business dealings of southern and eastern Europe. In Italy, restaurant dinners are an important part of doing business and should never be turned down (and since generosity is prized, don't be surprised if your host insists on picking up the tab). Accept any invitation offered in Greece, as well: Hospitality is a tradition here, and it's not uncommon to be welcomed into a host's home (a rare honor in most European countries). Be ready for a late night, however: In Spain, despite the fact that the traditional afternoon siesta has given way to a shorter mid-afternoon break, it's still fashionable to start dinner at ten o'clock and continue well past midnight.

In eastern Europe, long, lavish dinners are the rule—typically accompanied with copious amounts of vodka or other alcoholic beverages, consumed in endless rounds of toasts. (Note: It's perfectly fine, in most countries, to take a sip of your drink after each toast rather than downing the entire glass.)

LOOKING THE PART

Conservative business attire prevails throughout Europe, although this varies by profession: As in the United States, an investment banker is expected to wear a suit, while an editor is more likely to wear a sport jacket or blazer and tie. In general, jackets stay on in offices and restaurants, and women wear skirts, not slacks.

From London to Moscow, dark suits, white shirts, and subdued ties, worn with laced dress shoes (not loafers), are standard formal business attire for men, although men in the south of France often substitute a blue blazer and slacks in summer, while many Scandinavian men may switch to sport jackets with or without ties.

Women traveling on business in Europe should dress stylishly but conservatively. Always wear skirt-and-jacket suit ensembles in business settings (exceptions are the dress-friendly countries of Greece and Spain, and Italy, where fashionable slacks or dresses are acceptable), and keep jewelry to a tasteful minimum. Women and men alike should save their most elegantly cut suits for Italy and France, where fashion standards are particularly high.

THE MIDDLE EAST

There are two things to keep in mind when doing business in the Middle East. The first is that nothing is more important in this part of the world than the give and take of personal relationships. Whenever possible, business is conducted according to whom you know rather than through official channels. Courtesy and hospitality are considered extremely important, and all business dealings proceed on a basis of friendship and personal respect.

The second is that religion is a dominant fact of life in the Middle East. In most countries the predominant religion is Islam, whose influence pervades even secular states like Turkey, where people drink wine, women dress European-style, and the government is nonclerical. In traditional societies, such as Saudi Arabia, Islam touches every corner of life. Here, the workweek runs from Sunday through Thursday (the Sabbath being Friday) and prayers are said five times daily: at dawn, midday, afternoon, evening, and night; all business stops at these times. Dogs are unclean, drinking alcohol or eating pork is forbidden, and Saudi women (who by law wear veils in public) are deemed invisible. So strict is the separation between the sexes in some Arab states, in fact, that it is a breach of manners to ask the health of your counterpart's wife or daughters.

The degree of strictness you'll have to observe will vary from country to country. In some Middle Eastern nations, such as the Gulf States of Kuwait, Qatar, Bahrain, Oman, and the United Arab Emirates, the business sector has been thoroughly Westernized and women generally enjoy greater freedom. Still, it's important always to be sensitive to protocol: Alcohol should be consumed in private; use of your left hand should be avoided (it's symbolically unclean); and women should dress modestly at all times—meaning long sleeves, hemlines that go below the knee, and a scarf or other head covering when appropriate. This same advice holds when visiting Israel, where kosher diet restrictions and other Jewish customs should be respected.

DOING BUSINESS

Make appointments well in advance, preferably with a letter of introduction from a mutual friend. All appointments are generally scheduled for the three intervals between the first four prayer sessions of the day. Since the traditional emphasis on hospitality can cause delays, meetings may be scheduled for a time of day, rather than a specific hour. In either case, arrive on time—but don't expect your counterpart to follow suit. Throughout the Middle East, it is customary to make visitors wait. The exception to this is Turkey, which tends to follow Western time schedules.

A Western-style handshake is the standard greeting in Turkey and Israel, but in other Middle Eastern countries you can expect a warmer, more effusive greeting, with the hand often grasped and held rather than shaken. Arabs may also hug or kiss each other. Despite this warmth, formality is the rule in address: Always call people by their professional titles, followed by their last names. First names connote much more familiarity in the Middle East than they do in the West. (The big exception here is Israel, where an informal business culture tends to prevail, and people move to a first-name basis almost immediately.) In Turkey, people may address each other by occupational title alone—saying simply "Doctor."

Although English is spoken widely throughout the region, all business cards should be bilingual.

Meetings generally start with extensive small talk, designed to establish friendship and trust, and tend to follow an "open door" pattern that traces back to when tribal leaders held court in their tents. When you do get down to business in Arab countries, expect lengthy conversations, multiple participants, frequent interruptions, and numerous cups of coffee or tea. In Turkey, the interruptions may be fewer, but expect plenty of haggling; age is particularly respected here, and the eldest participants are the ones likely to make any final decisions.

ENTERTAINMENT

The role of host is taken extremely seriously in the Middle East. Businesspeople in the Arab nations like to entertain visiting guests at home, and their hospitality is proverbially lavish. Go with an empty stomach, refuse nothing, and eat with relish—but not with your left hand. Turkish business meals are generally held in restaurants; courses are typically ordered one at a time, and invited guests aren't allowed to pay for a thing. Israelis, too, will generally take the lead in arranging business meals, which may be held in a restaurant or a private home and often feature a selection of Western and Middle Eastern foods. In all cases, if your stay is long enough, you may eventually be honored with the chance to reciprocate by hosting a meal in a restaurant.

LOOKING THE PART

In the Arab nations, modesty is all. In Saudi Arabia, women are required to be completely covered and veiled in public. In less strict societies like the Gulf States, dresses or skirts may be worn, but dresses should be long-sleeved and hemlines should be below the knee. While your Arab host may wear traditional desert robes, visiting men should dress in suit and tie, unless invited by their host to wear traditional garb. In Turkey, conservative business attire is standard, including dark suits and subdued ties for men, and long dresses or skirts with heels for women. As for making concessions to the heat, follow your host's lead: In Turkey, for example, jacket and tie may both be doffed on a hot day, while a jacketless wardrobe of long-sleeved shirt and trousers is starting to catch on in Jordan.

The big exception to all of the above is the informal business culture of Israel, where many men wear slacks and open-necked shirts to work. Show up to your first meeting in a suit and tie, however: It shows respect to your host and gives him or her the opportunity to suggest something more casual for your next meeting. For women visiting Israel, conservative suits or dresses are appropriate; if visiting a traditional area, be sure your outfit covers your elbows and knees.

ASIA

Asia is the most culturally diverse region on earth. Each time you get off an airplane in Asia, you can expect to encounter a whole new set of customs—including language, manners, religion, and social outlook. For all their differences, however, the people of Asia share a common trait: A rigorous, deeply ingrained sense of courtesy, which includes respect for the elderly, personal humility and a readiness to subordinate one's self to the group, and meticulous avoidance of any controversy or confrontation. Nothing must disturb the harmonious flow of proper social intercourse, since such a disruption could well cause individuals to lose face (suffer public embarrassment)—a disgrace that Asians will go to extremes to avoid.

Respecting these boundaries and taking the time to build solid personal relationships is the key to success in Asia. In order to save face and maintain harmony, Asians will avoid bringing up inconvenient facts or ideas, and the thoughtful visitor will avoid putting his or her host on the spot. Requests are rarely answered with the word "No." Instead, you'll receive a polite evasion such as "Perhaps, but not yet" or "Very interesting—we'll consider it." For the same reason, decisions tend to be reached by consensus, which takes time. In general, no agreement is final until each issue is resolved to everyone's satisfaction. Not surprisingly, one of the supreme Asian virtues is patience.

DOING BUSINESS

Try to make all appointments in Asia as far ahead of time as possible—two months is the advised lead time in some countries. When dealing with China, it often helps to work through an established public relations firm when setting up appointments (the U.S. Department of Commerce may be helpful in this regard as well). It's also customary in China to send a list of your delegation before every meeting, along with a detailed agenda. The Japanese, too, like to set the agenda beforehand and then stick to it.

When you show up for a meeting, be on time: In most Asian countries, arriving even just a few minutes late to a business engagement is considered an insult. There are exceptions, but they apply only to your host; in Indonesia, for example, people of higher rank may be intentionally late to a meeting as a sign of status. Indians respect punctuality but don't always observe it themselves; keep flexible to allow for sudden rescheduling.

Greeting styles vary. In China, a gentle bow of the head and a handshake are appropriate. In Indonesia, the handshake precedes a slight nod or bow, while Japanese businesspeople often shake hands with Westerners while bowing to one another. The traditional Thai salutation is the *wei*—palms together at chest level with head inclined in a slight bow. Again, however, Westerners are likely to be greeted with a handshake—and the same holds for South Korea and the Philippines. In India, a handshake is standard for everyone. In general, avoid touching your host after the initial greeting.

Bilingual business cards are essential throughout Asia. After greeting someone, present your card foreign-language side up. In China, South Korea, and Japan, hold it with both hands and take your host's the same way. When a card is presented to you, read it carefully before putting it into your pocket (not your wallet).

Professional titles are very important throughout Asia. Unless invited to do otherwise, address people by their titles (use the equivalent of "Mr." if they don't have any) and their family names. In China, Japan, and other Far Eastern countries, the family name comes first rather than last (as it does in the West). Li Wu Chin belongs to the Li family, and his given name is Wu Chin—so he should be addressed as Systems Director Li. Similarly, Yamamoto Lobo is Associate Manager Yamamoto. (Japanese businessmen who deal frequently with foreigners sometimes reverse this traditional order and put their family names last.)

ENTERTAINMENT

Meals form the core of business entertainment in Asia. Eating together is considered essential for building good relationships, and all invitations should be accepted. In China, expect lavish restaurant banquets lasting two hours or more, with numerous courses and many toasts. In India, entertaining usually takes the form of lunch, while in the Philippines you may dine in your host's private home, with many guests and abundant food (return the favor by hosting a restaurant dinner after the deal closes). Spouses are expected to attend business dinners in Thailand but are rarely invited along in Hong Kong. Japanese dinners often segue into a trip to a karaoke bar—in which case, be prepared to stay out until the wee hours.

In Asia, punctuality is less important in social affairs than it is in business. While the Chinese tend to show up on time or even a few minutes early, guests in most other countries are expected to arrive a bit late (fifteen to thirty minutes is standard in India). Check beforehand to see if you should bring a gift to your host and what form your thanks should take. In China, a thank-you the next day is proper etiquette. In India, thanking your host after a meal is considered insulting—far better to offer a meal in return.

Whatever the country, always wait to be seated, since many Asian societies have elaborate seating hierarchies; let your host bring up any business topics; and be careful to leave a bit of food on your plate. (A clean plate suggests there wasn't enough to eat.) Remember, too, that attempts to use chopsticks are always appreciated.

LOOKING THE PART

The biggest factor in Asian business attire is the climate. In temperate countries like China, Japan, and Korea, standard Western business dress is the norm: Dark suits, dress shirts and ties for men, and skirt-jacket ensembles for women (pant suits and slacks are also popular among women in Japan). Bright colors are frowned on for either sex in China, while in Japan, tastes in men's dress shirts have lately been trending toward pastel and beyond. In Japan and Korea, where guests may be asked to remove their shoes in a home or restaurant, slip-on dress shoes are appropriate for men. Women should avoid excessively high heels in China.

In hotter countries, the emphasis shifts to comfort. Follow your host's lead: In Hong Kong and Indonesia, suit jackets are often doffed as the day heats up, while businessmen in Singapore may forgo jackets completely, wearing only a long-sleeved (or sometimes short-sleeved) shirt and a tie with trousers. For women visiting these countries, a blouse and a skirt is appropriate (with long sleeves and a below-the-knee hemline, in the case of predominately Muslim Indonesia). In India, the casual look of slacks and a short-sleeved shirt is standard for men, but a jacket is advised for initial meetings. Women can wear slacks and a jacket over a long-sleeved blouse, or a dress, provided the hem is below the knees.

AFRICA

Africa is a vast and complex region, home to more than 50 nations and many distinctive and disparate cultures. Arabic and Islamic culture prevails in northern countries such as Egypt and Morocco, while the countries of Central Africa are made up of a varied and volatile mix of ethnic groups (Nigeria alone is home to 250 different tribes). The southern part of the continent is dominated by South Africa, the continent's economic powerhouse, whose customs reflect the checkered legacy of 300 years of Dutch and English influence. Throughout Africa, great importance is placed on establishing warm, friendly relations between business associates. It makes sense to enjoy the process, since business dealings on the continent tend to proceed at a significantly slower pace than in Europe and the United States, and transactions can often become ensnared in governmental red tape.

DOING BUSINESS

Because of the ongoing civil conflicts in many parts of Africa, check U.S. State Department advisories before making travel plans. English is spoken by businesspeople in much of Africa, although business in West African countries is typically conducted in French, the language of their one-time colonial ruler. Make all appointments a month or two in advance (a letter of introduction from a mutual acquaintance will help pave the way), leave a local contact number, and call a day or two before to reconfirm. A good time for doing business is first thing in the morning, before the midday heat. Arrive on time to every meeting, but don't expect the same from your host. Keeping visitors waiting is standard practice in many countries.

A gentle, warm handshake is the accepted form of greeting across Africa—different ethnic groups may have their own subtle variations—and you should shake the hand of everyone in the room when you arrive and when you leave. People should be addressed by either their professional titles or the equivalent of "Mr.," followed by their surnames, and prolonged eye contact should be avoided. Present your business card with your right hand to each person upon meeting him or her.

Greetings are generally long, effusive, and endlessly upbeat—implying that everything in life is fine. Be prepared to do a good deal of casual chatting, designed to build rapport, before getting to your agenda; pushy business dealings are considered rude in Africa. You can also expect to have a large number of people present at meetings, and interruptions are common—in Egypt, for example, mid-meeting visits from friends and phone calls from family members are expected and take priority. Since pre-business socializing can keep business matters at bay for some time, meetings frequently extend beyond their scheduled length—so leave plenty of space between appointments.

ENTERTAINMENT

African people tend to be very courteous, friendly, and giving, and they love to entertain business guests—typically over a meal in a restaurant or a private home. Dinners may go late into the evening, particularly in West Africa and the northern Arabic countries. When dining in a private home, be ready to eat with your hands, since some traditional households don't use utensils (your host will be glad to show you how). In South Africa, business matters are put aside at social occasions. Barbecues, called *braais*, are a favorite form of entertaining. If invited to one, contribute by bringing a bottle of wine or a dessert.

LOOKING THE PART

For visiting men, lightweight business suits are the conservative dress standard throughout sub-Saharan Africa. Many equatorial countries, however, favor business attire even more conducive to the climate; in West Africa, cotton safari suits are common, while open-necked shirts are often worn by businessmen in Central Africa. In South Africa, dress codes can swing from medium-weight suits in the relatively cool winter months to open-necked shirts and slacks (or even Bermuda shorts) in the summer.

Women in sub-Saharan Africa should wear light dresses or skirt-and-blouse ensembles. In the winter in southern Africa, wool suits or dresses with a light topcoat may be needed.

In Egypt and the other Islamic countries of northern Africa, dress standards are much closer to those of the Middle East. In general, men should choose conservative dark suits and ties, while women should wear clothing that covers their arms, legs, and neckline—no matter how warm the weather.

SUGGESTED READING FOR BUSINESS TRAVELERS

- *Kiss, Bow, or Shake Hands: How to Do Business in Sixty Countries,* by Terri Morrison, Wayne A. Conaway, and George A. Borden (Adams Media, 1994)

- *Doing Business Internationally: The Guide to Cross-Cultural Success,* 2nd ed., by Danielle Medina Walker and Thomas Walker (McGraw-Hill, 2002)

- *Do's and Taboos Around the World for Women in Business,* by Roger E. Axtell, Margaret Corcoran, Tami Briggs, and Mary Beth Lamb (John Wiley & Sons, 1997)

- *International Business Etiquette: Latin America: What You Need to Know to Conduct Business Abroad with Charm and Savvy,* by Ann Marie Sabath (Career

Press, 1999). (This is one of a series by Sabath. See also *International Business Etiquette: Europe; International Business Etiquette: Asia and the Pacific Rim.*)

- *The Global Etiquette Guide to Europe: Everything You Need to Know for Business and Travel Success,* by Dean Foster (John Wiley & Sons, 2000). (This is one of a series by Foster. See also *The Global Etiquette Guide to Mexico and Latin America; The Global Etiquette Guide to Africa and the Middle East; The Global Etiquette Guide to Asia.*)

PART SIX

THE JOB APPLICANT

24 | *The Job Search*

So what does etiquette have to do with a job search? A great deal indeed. Your stops along the path to employment include meeting new people, communicating your abilities, and proving that you not only have what it takes but would also be nice to have around. Etiquette gives you confidence as you move through this process, letting you focus on the tasks at hand instead of worrying about how to comport yourself.

This chapter takes you on a quick tour through job-hunting territory, with pointers on how to travel it with self-assurance and civility. Forming the framework are the ins and outs of networking, setting up informational interviews, making cold calls, and consulting an employment agency. Advice is slanted toward how you should act in the process and applies to job-hunters of any kind: the new college graduate seeking her first job; the worker looking for a change; the unlucky soul who suddenly finds himself out of a job. (For more on the last two cases, see "Leaving Your Job," page 90.) Even though, on the surface, job-hunters may appear to be very different in attitude and style—compare the buzz-cut computer genius sporting a Hawaiian-print shirt to the budding stockbroker in the expensive Italian suit – their concerns and course of action are more or less the same.

NOTE. Bookstores offer a wealth of job-search guides that leave no stone unturned in the pursuit of the perfect job. The classics of this genre are often updated and will take you through the finer points of job-hunting in a way that, because of space limitations, this book cannot. Browse the shelves until you find a guide that appeals to you and then strike out on your search, knowing that you already have the all-important tenets of good behavior firmly in place—the finer points that give you the competitive edge.

THE SAVVY NETWORKER

How you behave when networking is as important as the effort itself. The smart networker respects the opinions (and time) of others, helps other people as much as she is helped, and establishes rapport long before asking a favor or even offering a business card. A bad networker is a name-dropper who brags about her connections and comes across as being more concerned about what can be done for her than what she can do for someone else. It's not hard to guess which of the two has a greater chance of success!

STAYING IN TOUCH

The first rule of networking is to do it all the time, not just while job-hunting. Keeping in touch, as well as helping out people on your networking list whenever possible, ensures that when you actually do need help finding a job, you can easily call in your chits. When that moment comes, tell everyone you know that you're job-seeking and then leave it at that. As eager as you'll be to whip out your résumé, it's up to someone else to ask for it. Also be careful not to come off as a shameless self-promoter, grabbing every chance to spout off your accomplishments. A low-key mention of your job search is all that's needed; anyone who's interested will probably ask questions or offer to help.

Following are some ways to stay in touch with people in your network, even when you're not actively looking for work. (Note: Passing along the lame joke that was forwarded to you on e-mail by your ex-college roommate isn't one of them.)

- Meet for a bite to eat

- Invite to a party

- Invite to a baseball game or a play when you have an extra ticket

- Mail an article that would be helpful or interesting

- Send holiday, birthday, congratulatory, and get-well cards when appropriate

- Share information about job openings

When anyone, either inside or outside your network, says he'll be happy to help, graciously accept the offer. Note the type of job you're looking for in a handwritten or e-mail note to your helper or referral, pointing out whatever qualifications and experiences make you think you can handle it. If the helper says he wants to tell a friend about you, follow through immediately by sending him a résumé along with a brief letter detailing your career goals. If the helper gives you the name of someone to call, tell that person you're calling at the suggestion of (helper's name). If you're lucky, you might have found the first link in a chain that leads to an informational interview (see pages 320–321) or even a job interview.

Word process or e-mail a thank-you note to everyone who has offered help in any way. If, for example, you chat with someone at a cocktail party who says she thinks she'll mention you to her boss, your note will serve as a reminder. Just remember never to assume the favor has already been performed.

Notes like this one can set the stage for things to come:

Dear Jane:

I enjoyed meeting you at Sharon Stewart's party last weekend—especially since I never dreamed of crossing paths with a Braves fan in Pittsburgh. Of course, I also really appreciate your offer to mention me to your boss. Your company sounds like the kind of place I'd be interested in knowing more about. Thanks!

Sincerely,
[Signature]
Chris Cavanaugh

If you're using stationery or a correspondence card and it isn't printed with your address and phone number, write them under your signature. Even if you exchanged cards with the recipient, she may have lost or misplaced yours.

Keep a list of the people who have helped you (or even expressed interest in your job search) so that as soon as you're hired you can deliver the good news to all. A note of thanks also lets you say, "Please call on me if I can ever help you in any way"—an obligation for the nice-guy networker.

THE RIGHT TOOLS

Finding a job is, first and foremost, an exercise in communication, both oral and written. Assembling the communication tools you'll need is the first step in a successful job search. Today, most companies expect job applicants to have access to rapid messaging (many firms require employment applications to be faxed or e-mailed, for instance), but that doesn't mean that a letter is a thing of the past. Correspondence on high-quality paper, when done right, can make an especially good impression—particularly when the inclusion of your e-mail address shows that you could have taken the easier way out.

- **VOICE MAIL/ANSWERING MACHINE.** Make it easy for people to reach you over the telephone by having an answering machine or a voice mail service at home. Leave a professional-sounding message by clearly announcing your first and last names and phone number. Speak as you normally do; you don't want to over-enunciate and sound as if you're trying too hard. Don't get creative: You have no way of knowing what a prospective employer will think of background music or jokey spiels explaining why you're not at home. (See also "Recording a Greeting," page 235.)

- **FAX/E-MAIL.** Having a fax machine or e-mail at home isn't essential (the cost may be prohibitive), but you should know how to gain quick access to either. Regular mail will usually do when sending a résumé and cover letter, but if an employer asks you to fax or e-mail your material ASAP, get moving to the nearest all-service copy shop.

- **PERSONAL BUSINESS STATIONERY.** When sending something by regular mail, never use company letterhead to conduct personal business—especially when looking for a job. For all job-search letters, buy the best-quality personal business stationery you can afford; the favorable impression made by a heavy-bond 100 percent cotton paper is worth the cost. Business stationery can be either 8½"× 11" or 7½"× 10" and makes the best impression when printed (black ink is the fail-safe choice) with your name, address, telephone number, and e-mail address and fax number. (See also "The Stationery Drawer," pages 249–251.)

- **CORRESPONDENCE CARDS.** A handwritten note makes an indelible impression in the electronic era, especially in more traditional fields. While cover letters and other formal correspondence should be word-processed on your business stationery letter sheets, thank-you notes and personal notes to business associates can be written on a correspondence card. (See also "The Stationery Drawer," pages 249–251.)

- **PERSONAL "BUSINESS" CARDS.** Job or not, a job-seeker should have a printed card of some kind—it's the most efficient way to give someone you meet enough information to reach you in the future. Make sure the card is of high-quality stock and printed with a readable font. Include your full name, home address, home phone number, and, if applicable, a home e-mail address and fax number. Once you've had cards printed, put a few in each coat or suit pocket, handbag, or briefcase, so that you'll have one handy when needed.

If you are employed but simultaneously looking for another job, consider having a personal card printed with only your name, home and e-mail addresses, and telephone and fax numbers. Having both this card and your company card at the ready lets you choose between handing out one or the other as called for. (See also "Your Trusty Business Card," page 141.)

LETTERS AND PHONE CALLS

Your first contact with a potential employer may result from successful networking, in which case you'll probably have a referral. In this case, a letter or phone call to your contact—mentioning who referred you, of course—is appropriate. Alternatively, you may be starting out cold. If that's the case, you'll be writing an unsolicited letter or phoning a potential employer who has never heard of you. A well-composed letter on paper may give you a leg up, if only because it allows you to show off your writing skills in a time when good business writing is at a premium. (Job application letters are given full treatment in Chapter 25, "Résumés and Application Letters," page 323.) When it comes to picking up the telephone, the chance of a cold call paying off may be only a little better than being struck by lightning—but, as they say, "You never know. . . ."

TELEPHONE TIPS FOR JOB-SEEKERS

Whether you're trying to get through to someone to schedule a job interview or an informational interview or to ask about job openings, keep in mind the following tips. (See also Chapter 17, "On the Telephone," page 223.)

- *Best times of day to call.* Typically, the best time to reach someone is between 11:15 A.M. and noon, when morning meetings have adjourned and the lunch hour hasn't started. Another time when people are more likely to be free is after 4:00 P.M.

- *Voice mail as a tool.* Placing your call very early or very late in the day, when the call-screener (typically a nine-to-five employee) isn't likely to answer, often gives you the opportunity to leave a voice mail message on the person's direct line. Play on the person's ego by mentioning positive things you've heard or read about him that have sparked your desire to meet him.

- *The right attitude.* Be friendly and upbeat every time you call. Never act annoyed that someone from whom you need a favor hasn't returned your call, much less acknowledged your existence. Always be considerate of other people's time by being direct, courteous, and to the point.

- *The call-screener.* Don't try to become friends with a call-screener, but do sound friendly and positive. A secretary or assistant who finds you to be aggressive or curt will undoubtedly find reasons not to put your call through. State that you know the person you're trying to reach must be very busy, and then ask the most convenient time of day for her to be reached. If your mission is accomplished, a second thank-you to an especially cooperative and cordial call-screener is deserved.

COLD CALLS

After preparing for your call, take the plunge. Don't worry too much about having to make repeated efforts to reach someone: Polite, positive persistence is an admirable quality in the business world. At the same time, listen for signs of exasperation from the assistant when he realizes that it's you yet again. If you sense any irritation, make your next contact a letter.

Once you've been put through to the person in charge of hiring, don't jump into a discourse: Someone who tags you as long-winded is unlikely to be eager to meet you. Simply introduce yourself, give the name of whoever suggested you contact the firm (if applicable) and a brief description of your relevant professional experience and your current job (if any), and say that you're interested in learning about potential openings in her department. If the person seems receptive, ask if you can go ahead and send a cover letter and résumé (check to see whether she prefers e-mail or paper). Don't bring up meeting in person unless you perceive some genuine interest on her end. Before hanging up, thank the person by saying something like, "I know how busy you must be, and I really appreciate your taking the time to talk with me."

CHECKING OUT WANT ADS

In this age of the Internet, you're just as likely to find an ad for a job opening on a job-postings Web site as you are in the newspaper want ads—so keep an eye on both. Be aware, though, that some companies post ads only as a backup, preferring to hire either from within the organization, through referrals, or through employment agencies.

Some companies give post office box addresses to respond to; others, fax numbers and e-mail addresses. A company that lists only an e-mail address expects you to be fully wired, while one that gives only a post office box would probably be impressed by a perfectly executed letter on good-quality stationery.

Be sure to read a job advertisement carefully and try to figure out what kind of employee the company wants, and then use your cover letter to sell yourself accordingly—noting, when possible, experience and accomplishments that meet their needs. Such careful attention to detail will make your letter stand out among the potentially hundreds of responses. So will express-mailing a letter to a post office box, which is money well spent. (Note: Packages from FedEx and other private express-mail companies cannot be sent to U.S. Postal Service boxes.)

If the ad lists a phone number and nothing more, call and ask for the name and title of the person to whom your résumé and cover letter should be sent. And make sure everything about the name is correct: Getting the right spelling of an unusual name just may give your letter the edge it needs.

SIGNING UP WITH EMPLOYMENT AGENCIES

Just what do employment agencies do? First, you should understand that most private agencies represent not the job-seeker, but rather companies that are looking for employees. In these cases, you do not pay a private employment agency to help find you a job; the tab is paid by the companies enlisting the agency's help. Companies looking for employees generally list job opportunities and look for prospects in the open market, so you'll be missing out if you rely too heavily on openings provided by an agency. Consider agencies as only a part of, not the be-all, of a job search.

ANOTHER BIT OF ADVICE. Never sign up with a private employment agency without doing a little detective work. Ask for recommendations for agencies from any friends who have experience with them, or even from a friendly interviewer who isn't able to offer you a job. On your own, find out something about the agency's history: how long they've been in business and the professions they specialize in. Also make a call to the Better Business Bureau, who will tell you if any complaints have been filed against the firm.

MEETING THE RECRUITER

Try to meet in person with an employment agency recruiter before he or she presents you as a candidate to an employer. This meeting is as important as a job interview, so dress the part, arrive on time, bring a résumé and list of references, and be prepared to speak succinctly about your goals, accomplishments, and skills. Also do everything you can to show respect for the recruiter's expertise and time. Courteous behavior will reap benefits; like a potential employer, a recruiter is looking for strong social skills as part of the package.

One explicit difference between an *employment agency* interview and a *job* interview is how forthcoming you are about unfavorable information in your personal or job history. While you would never actually lie during a job interview, you wouldn't necessarily bring up being fired, for example, unless you were asked the question. Not so with a recruiter. Present yourself in a positive light, but avoid unwelcome surprises by telling the person anything about your employment or personal history that could be construed as negative. Because recruiters are answering to the employer, they don't want to be caught unawares after giving a glowing recommendation. Similarly, if your radar tells you that a former supervisor might give you a less than flattering recommendation, prepare the recruiter for this possibility.

Remember that the recruiter's job is finding the perfect employee for the employer, not the perfect job for you. With this in mind, be as specific as possible when describing your needs so that you aren't seen as fitting a job that doesn't appeal to you. Also face the fact that the recruiter is not a job counselor. Expect an agency to represent you positively to companies, to keep your job search confidential, and to tell you why a particular employer isn't offering a job—but not to provide career advice.

TEMPORARY EMPLOYMENT AGENCIES

Approach an interview at a temp agency just as you would any job interview; the more impressed they are, the better the assignments you'll be offered. An agency will need copies of your résumé, so have it ready before calling. Then be specific about what kind of job you're looking for and in what field. If, for example, your goal is to work as a paralegal at a law firm, you could shoot for *any* job (secretary, for example, or receptionist) at *any* law firm. Working as a temp is a way to get your foot in the door and meet the people who can hire you permanently, assuming they're going to recognize your skills and talents. Once inside, you'll be privy to job openings in other departments and able to apply for positions as they become available.

ABOUT SALARY. When working through a temp agency, you'll be paid an hourly wage consistent with the industry standard for your geographic location and level of experience. (It is the agency that determines your salary, not the company.) Salaries aren't set in stone, and it's acceptable to negotiate an hourly rate with the temp agency that meets your needs and expectations.

THE INFORMATIONAL INTERVIEW

The purpose of the so-called informational interview is to learn about a person's career, company, or industry, with the ultimate aim of advancing your job search. (This kind of meeting is not—repeat, not—an opportunity to flash a résumé or ask for a job.) Through your networking contacts or your own research, identify several successful people within your field of choice or an influential person within a company that you'd like to learn more about. Then begin the process of requesting a brief meeting:

- Send a short letter of introduction (or, in fields that don't stand on tradition, do it via e-mail) stating your background, your career goals, and your reason for wanting to meet.

- End the letter with a promise to call.

- Follow through later in the week, phoning to ask about scheduling a meeting.

GETTING IN

The easiest way to get an appointment is to already know someone or be referred by a mutual friend. If you're making a cold call (ringing up a person who doesn't know you or doesn't expect your call), you'll have to work much harder, since getting a response may require writing more than one letter and making several phone calls to an assistant. With each call, strike a balance of politeness, deference, charm, and self-confidence, but be careful not to become a pest: Use your intuition to gauge whether the person you're calling is rolling his or her eyes at yet another entreaty. While persistence with charm often pays off, with the wrong person it can backfire.

PREPARING

Once a meeting is scheduled, make the most of it by preparing thoroughly, scouring the Internet and appropriate publications. Learn as much as you can about both the company and the field and be ready (1) to state what you hope the meeting will accomplish and (2) to talk about your career goals. Put your questions in writing, keeping in mind that your aim is to learn as much as possible while making a good impression.

Call the morning of the meeting to confirm the start time, then arrive five minutes early. Dress professionally, giving as much attention to looking spiffy and well-groomed as you would for an actual job interview. Bring a résumé in a folder or briefcase, but don't offer it unless it is asked for. Also bring paper and a pen to take notes. (Forget your tape recorder, which would not only set the wrong tone but also probably make the person you're speaking with less inclined to open up.) Wear a watch, since you'll want to be the one to end the meeting when the allotted time is up.

MEETING

During the course of the meeting, play up the pupil-teacher relationship—particularly if you're a recent graduate. Without seeming to pry, ask the person what she learned along the way before succeeding in her career. Take note of any career moves she says were beneficial, plus any that were not. If you can convince the person that you want her advice because you admire her accomplishments, you may well gain a mentor and an ally—a contact who knows just the people who can open doors for you.

THANKING

Follow up an information interview with a thank-you note. (Send it on the same day of the meeting or, at the latest, the morning after.) Thanking the person for her time—and for sharing insights into her career or company—not only makes her feel good about helping you but also reinforces the positive impression you hope you made.

25 | *Résumés and Application Letters*

As you prepare to fax, e-mail, or post your résumé to points near and far, face up to a blunt reality: In today's time-conscious world, people are looking for reasons to dispose of it. The person who receives your résumé is under no obligation to actually read it or respond—and is all the less likely to if it's not well presented or contains a misspelled word. To lessen the chance of your résumé being directed toward the wastebasket or deleted with the click of a mouse, make it easy to read, to-the-point, and error-free. Remember: The care with which it's done announces your professional abilities loud and clear.

For all the attention that goes into creating a résumé (ideally, it should be tailored to the desired job), the end product should be short and sweet—one page or, if you have extensive work experience, two. A "quick take" shows consideration of the reader's time, a fundamental of business etiquette. This is true whether you're applying cold for *any* job opening within a particular company or for a *specific* job opening you found in an ad, or you're sending your résumé and cover letter to someone to whom you've been referred.

The cover letter you send along with your résumé should also be limited to a single page. This cover letter is actually a letter of application—and it needs to be a well-crafted piece of salesmanship that separates you from the pack. While your résumé effectively telegraphs the bare bones of who you are and what you are seeking, the letter allows you to expand on how your background makes you a good fit for a specific company or job.

THE BASICS

Paring down your résumé and letter means taking the trouble to organize and present information so that it's readily accessible; likewise, making sure that it's free of any grammatical and spelling errors shows you as not only meticulous but also respectful—the compositional equivalent of not slouching in your chair. Your dictionary, a brush-up on grammar, and perhaps one of the myriad résumé- and cover-letter-writing guides on the market (each with a somewhat different theory of what's best) will be your tools. No matter which style or format you choose, be mindful of these four basics:

- Make certain your résumé and cover letter are completely accurate and a true reflection of your experiences.

- Illustrate your skills and abilities by relating your specific accomplishments instead of merely listing the jobs you held.

- If you're mailing your résumé and cover letter, use 8½" × 11" sheets of good-quality (high-cotton-fiber) paper in white, off-white, or a muted neutral color.

- Use a readable typeface. Steer clear of trendy or unusual fonts, and keep the size at 12 points—no larger, and never below 10 points.

TO TELL THE TRUTH

A cardinal rule for the job applicant: Don't even *think* of lying or exaggerating anything in a résumé or cover letter. Assume that the truth will come out and have severe, even lifelong, consequences. But then, given that reality, how do you write about something in your background that is less than favorable—or at least sounds that way?

Just how negative that "something" is determines what you write. For example, when an applicant has family obligations that make relocation impossible, it's best to make this point up front. If, however, you were fired or laid off from your last job, it's probably better not to include this. Chances are good that anything written about this kind of experience will sound defensive and even hostile. But do be prepared to confront the question in an interview.

Women who left the workforce to raise a family, even for several years, have nothing to be ashamed of. When bringing up such gaps in employment in your application letter, put them in the most positive light by noting any continuing education, volunteer work, or life experiences that would be viewed as beneficial by a potential employer.

CHRONOLOGICAL OR FUNCTIONAL?

The two classic résumé styles are the reverse chronological résumé, which lists the jobs you've had going backward in time, from the current one to your first, and the functional résumé, which describes your skills, abilities, and accomplishments as they relate to the job you seek. Employers are most accustomed to the chronological style, but if you have little work experience or some gaps in employment, a functional résumé shows your skills and talents in the best light.

SAMPLE FUNCTIONAL RÉSUMÉ

THERESA MONTALVO

211 Elmwood Drive

Houston, TX 77110

(713) 555-1212

OBJECTIVE

Entry level position in accounting, where exceptional math skills, mastery of applicable software, attention to detail, a willingness to work hard, and a positive attitude are required.

EDUCATION

Currently enrolled in night classes at University of Houston, working toward degree in accounting that will enable me to reach my goal of becoming a CPA.

Graduated in 2002 from Hillsboro Junior College, in top 15 percent of class.

EXPERIENCE

2003 to present   Assistant Bookkeeper, Moonbeam Computers, Katy, TX

- Created linked spreadsheets to track travel and entertainment using Excel
- Maintained an Access database to record additions to fixed assets
- Downloaded mainframe queries to Excel for account analysis
- Designed an information systems improvement that made cost reports available 20 percent sooner

SUMMARY

Creative problem solver who works well with people. Fluent in Spanish. In junior college, awarded Moore Math Medal two years in a row.

Using the functional résumé style, this aspiring accountant shows she's serious by including her eventual goal in her résumé – to become a CPA. Because her experience is thin, she first details her education, then specifies her duties in bulleted entries, with the last showing her as the kind of person who does more than is required. The inclusion of her math award backs up her claim to superior math skills.

SAMPLE CHRONOLOGICAL RÉSUMÉ

MICHAEL COLLINS
4620 Carroll Street
Laramie, WY 82002
(307) 555-1212

OBJECTIVE

Join a leading company in the HVAC industry in a key sales-management position, with responsibility for sales and service administration in both domestic and international markets.

SUMMARY

Over 8 years of customer service and inside sales experience in the HVAC industry, with emphasis on hydronic systems and mechanical components. Advance training in the application of chillers, boilers, pumps, and related equipment.

EXPERIENCE

2003–present   Manager of Customer Service, Cool Breeze, Inc., Laramie, WY

Key responsibilities include processing of all orders, dealing with representatives on technical issues, coordinating deliveries with production, and reviewing all purchase orders and other legal documents. Initiated regular weekly meetings with purchasing and production departments to reduce lead time on orders. Recognized as employee of the year, 2004.

1999–2002   Manager of Warranty, Cool Breeze, Inc.

Reviewed all incoming claims under the standard warranty policy. Approved payments or arranged for appropriate action. Reported to senior management on a weekly basis a summary of all claims and reported any critical areas of concern or developing trends to the Engineering and Corporate Safety Coordinator. Reduced the cost of warranty claims by 35% compared to budget for 3 years running.

1995–99   Field Service Technician (repairing HVAC equipment), Cool Breeze, Inc.

Managed field service and start-up crew working in the Southwest. Responsible for work-order scheduling and crew training. Devised a job-planning program that reduced average service time by 30%. Received company award as top service team 4 out of 5 years.

KEY SKILLS

Experience in telephone sales
Good working knowledge of order entry
Proficient in use of Internet and Excel, Word, and PowerPoint

Bachelor of Business Administration, University of Wyoming (1999)

Associate Degree in HVAC systems design and operations, Holbein Institute (1996)

Certificate in advanced air-conditioning repair, Vo-Tech of Laramie (1995)

Summer intern, Hot Stuff Pump Company (1994). Worked with Chief Engineer on the development of a new heat exchanger. Prepared drawings using AutoCAD 13. Earned 60% of funds needed for college expenses.

Using the chronological résumé style, this manager in the heating, ventilation, and air conditioning (HVAC) business is looking for a higher position in another company. Because he is experienced, he focuses his résumé on his work and then lists his educational background at the end. His track record shows him to be a self-reliant person who continues to advance.

USING A RÉSUMÉ SERVICE

If your design skills on the computer end with word processing, consider hiring a service to prepare and print your résumé. But be aware that there are two schools of thought on the wisdom of pursuing this route: Proponents say that besides adding technical finesse, a résumé service can take your list of previous jobs and wordsmith it into a maximum-impact marketing tool. Skeptics counter that your résumé will end up looking like it came off the assembly line.

If you are considering hiring a service, ask to see several samples—not just one—of their work. Then politely suggest that your participation in the creative process would be a condition of signing up.

Two additional sources of help. (1) Web sites on the Internet that walk you through the process of writing your résumé and (2) special software programs that will format your résumé for you.

CONCERNING REFERENCES

While it's a good idea to have four or five references who can speak to your capabilities and accomplishments, remember not to incorporate them into your résumé or cover letter. Instead, list them on a separate page, after double-checking the addresses and phone numbers. Take the list to an interview in case you are asked for it; if you're caught without it, have it delivered by the next business day.

ASKING SOMEONE TO SERVE AS A REFERENCE

Choose your references carefully: Go with people who know your professional skills and capabilities but aren't threatened by your success. Though it's tempting to include relatives and friends, they are never suitable as references unless you've actually worked for them. If you are a recent graduate, you might include professors who can confirm your academic accomplishments and contributions in the classroom.

Once you've made up a list, call potential references and ask if they are willing to be named. If they are, show concern for their time constraints by asking if they'd rather have their home or office phone numbers listed. If you receive anything less than an enthusiastic response, reevaluate your decision to include that person, and consider finding someone else.

After the initial call, offer to get together for a cup of coffee or lunch (your treat, of course) so that you can personally hand over your résumé. If the invitation is accepted (and don't be surprised if it isn't, in these harried times), be as aware of your clothing and personal image as you would for a job interview (see "Dress One Notch Up," pages 337–340). Think of meeting with a reference as an exercise in networking; he or she may be able to give you a referral as well.

If a face-to-face meeting isn't feasible, mail your résumé to a reference. In a separate note, include examples of your work so that the person will be prepared to speak about your capabilities in specifics: "She doubled her sales quota every month" will have more impact than "She's a real go-getter."

THANKING REFERENCES

Thank each reference twice: when he or she accepts the role of reference and when you accept a job. A typed letter is appropriate, but a handwritten note on your best stationery is more personal. By all means, keep your references abreast of your job search, especially when you've had success.

Once hired, it's acceptable to ask your new employer which references he or she contacted, so you can write a second note of thanks. Even if references weren't called, thank them for offering their assistance; your diligence will pay off in the future if you need to call on them again. Mention in your correspondence (and in person, when possible) your eagerness to return the favor in some way whenever you can.

THE APPLICATION LETTER

The goal of your cover letter—technically an employment application letter—is to successfully apply for an interview. A good application letter, supported by a concise résumé, should make the reader *want* to meet the writer in person. (See also "Effective Business Letters," page 241.) It is not, however, going to get the job for you.

Whether you are writing unsolicited, responding to an advertisement, or writing with a personal referral, be sure you have the correct spelling of the recipient's full name as well as her correct courtesy and business titles. If "M. J. Jones, Human Relations Director" is Mary Jane and your salutation is "Dear Mr. Jones," your carefully written letter may hit the recycling bin. If you do not know the correct person to address (as often happens when you respond to a blind ad), call the company and ask. If you can't pin down a contact name, then it's appropriate to address the company or a specific department or position.

KEY COMPONENTS OF A GREAT APPLICATION LETTER

As you compose your application letter, keep firmly in mind what you're selling—your abilities, your skills, your experience, and your education *as they relate to the employment needs of the company.* There will be many things about you that a potential employer does not want to know. Your family, hobbies, politics, religion, and personal traits are of interest only if they bear directly on the job. You have to convince the reader that you are the best person for the position; do this by stating what you can do for the company, not what the company can do for you. (An employer, for example, doesn't want to hear that an applicant regards a job as "an opportunity to improve my financial management skills.") Here are some tips to make your letter shine:

Quality materials. First of all, use personal stationery and your personal address. Quality writing paper and envelopes reflect directly on you, so make the effort to purchase the best stationery possible. Writing on the letterhead of a current employer is deceptive—and will make a potential employer question your common sense.

Make every letter an original. You may be sending out dozens of résumés, but each cover letter should be individualized. You can use your computer to develop a basic format for application letters, but use this format only as a starting point—not as a tool for churning out duplicate letters.

A good start. Make your opening sentence and paragraph dynamic. What can you say in your first sentence that will compel the recipient to read on? An example: "For the past year, I have been honing my sales skills in my position as right-hand person to GHI's top salesperson. I relish the opportunity to put those skills to work for you." Aim for a grabber lead, and avoid openings that are predictable, dry, or hackneyed. If you are writing as the result of a personal referral or recommendation, say so in the first sentence. Include any titles or information that will immediately identify your referral: "Our friend Dr. Robert 'Bob' Johnston, who is still the best physician ever to care for us Western College football players, recommended that I contact you about the sports reporting position with your newspaper." This opening not only identifies the referral by name and title, but also establishes a connection between the writer and the reader, provides a key piece of information about the writer, and clearly states the purpose of the letter.

Keep it short. Never write more than one page. Use your cover letter to point out and expand on information that is directly applicable to the job you're seeking. You'll also want to briefly explain specific experiences or capabilities you bring to the table, such as overseas service and fluency in a foreign language, so long as they are relevant.

No apologies necessary. Remember that you're seeking a job, not begging for clemency. Even if you're a first-time job applicant, your cover letters should reflect self-confidence and competence. You don't have to humble yourself or plead—and never apologize. "My experience as a radio producer has taught me how to deal with last-minute problems and still meet every deadline" shows confidence and professionalism without being boastful.

Bringing up salary. In general, address the issue of salary in an initial letter only when the employer asks for your salary requirements or when the amount of your compensation is your first consideration. If you have to make $50,000 a year, you might as well say so in the beginning and let the chips fall. Many potential employers use salary figures as a means to cull applications, and it's frankly pointless to pursue a job that can't meet your financial needs. If an employer asks for salary requirements, you may give either the actual amount of your present salary or a range. It is also perfectly acceptable, however, to say that your current salary is "consistent with standards in the market," or that your needs are negotiable.

AN EXEMPLARY COVER LETTER

The letter on the opposite page is an example of a professional and attention-getting application. It is written on the recommendation of a supervisor. It is also an unsolicited letter and must consider the fact that no position may be available. Note that the writer cites a number of concrete, proven skills that she brings to the table—focusing on her account work, rather than her lengthy experience as a traffic director, since account service is the area in which she desires employment. She also cites specific, though not confidential, numbers to demonstrate the success of the project she has managed. The writer's one personal remark—about returning to her hometown—is relevant to the job because it establishes her roots in (and knowledge of) the recipient's territory.

WINSTON R. SMITH
Vice President, Account Services
Big Bang Advertising Agency
4321 Creative Boulevard
Chicago, IL 60000

Dear Mr. Smith:

Meredith Gregory, my supervisor at Flotsam, Jetsam & Associates, has recommended that I contact you about an account service position with Big Bang. During six years as Flotsam's traffic director, I have had behind-the-scenes involvement in virtually every aspect of the business. But direct client contact is what I do best.

Two years ago, in addition to my normal duties, I became the account manager for Fido Dog Food, then a small division of the Big Cheese Food Products account. The work has been long, hard, and always satisfying, and now I plan to move into account service full time. It is the area where I can make the most productive use of my organizational skills, my persistence in bringing every project to successful completion, my commitment to measurable results for the client and the agency, and the "grace under fire" that is the chief asset of every traffic manager worth her salt.

I am very proud of what I've accomplished on the Fido account, especially my direction of the repositioning campaign that has raised the brand from near-generic status to a major regional name. In two years, Fido has expanded distribution, enlarged its product line, and seen a remarkable 73 percent growth in sales. Flotsam has benefited as well, with a fourfold increase in billings, from $500,000 to $2 million.

Why do I want to leave such a booming account? I am known at Flotsam as "the traffic director who does account work," and a full-scale transfer to the account side would be difficult to achieve here. I can bring Big Bang a broad-based knowledge of product and service accounts—as you know, Flotsam has a diverse client list. I am also a great admirer of Big Bang's strategic planning and implementation, as well as the creative work that you consistently provide. And on a personal note, I would like to return to Chicago, the city of my birth.

Ms. Gregory tells me that she is looking forward to appearing with you on the research panel at the marketing convention next week. As I know how exhausting these events can be, I will call you in two weeks to see if we can arrange a meeting. (My daytime number, should you want to reach me, is 212-555-1212.) I realize that you may have no immediate openings, but I would like to discuss future opportunities with Big Bang.

Thank you very much for your consideration.

Sincerely,
[SIGNATURE]
Dorothy B. Gale

Closing the letter. Notice that the sample application letter on page 331 closes with a commitment to act. It also includes a telephone number where the writer can be reached during business hours. If you're available only at certain times, give that information as well. If you can't take calls during business hours, say so and provide a number for an answering service or a machine or an e-mail address. (If you use a machine or voice mail, be sure that your answering message is clearly audible and professional, and that you include your name.) Do not, however, expect an employer to track you down. Make your follow-up calls on schedule.

End with gracious, but not effusive, thanks. Concluding sentences such as "Thank you for your time and consideration" and "Thank you for considering my application for the position" are always correct.

Never send photocopies, and always sign each letter. (If you're of the old school and want to send an actual letter, you should never handwrite it, although you may address an envelope by hand.)

Finally, don't automatically blame your letter if you fail to get an interview. There are many reasons why you may not get to the next step in the process: The position may have been filled; the employer may have received applications from more qualified people; there may have been no job in the first place. (For corporate visibility, some companies continuously run classified ads even when they have no openings.)

PROOFREADING YOUR WORK

Any mistake in your letter can cost you the job. There is no excuse for misspelling, poor grammar, or bad punctuation. Unless you're very secure with your writing skills, have someone else proofread your résumé and all cover letters. A new, objective pair of eyes can find mistakes and give suggestions for rewording or deleting information. Another trick is for you to read the letter from right to left, one line at a time; this forces you to look at each word separately. Move a piece of paper down the page to track each line. Always wait at least one day between creating a document and proofreading it, so that you bring a fresh, objective eye to the task. This waiting period between creating and proofing allows you to be less biased about your own work.

WHAT TO LEAVE OUT

As important as knowing what to put in your résumé is knowing what to leave out. Just as you want your writing to be concise, the style and content of your résumé should also follow the classic dictum "less is more."

- *The word* "résumé." Putting this at the top of the page is not only unnecessary but takes up precious space. The same applies to the line "References available upon request," which is generally understood.

- *References.* Don't add these to the résumé (or cover letter) itself. List them on a separate page and hold on to it until references are requested.

- *A photo.* Even if you're drop-dead gorgeous, you want to be hired for your mind, experience, and accomplishments—not your looks.

- *Age, etc.* Don't list strictly personal information that is not related to the job, such as age, height, weight, marital status, or health.

- *Your GPA?* At some point, usually five years after your graduation, leave off your college accomplishments and your GPA, even if it was a 4.0. Use your own discretion: A forty-year-old would seem foolish noting that he served as president of his social fraternity, but a twenty-one-year-old with limited job experience should include such an accomplishment because it demonstrates leadership skills.

- *Salary needs.* Avoid including salary needs unless the advertisement you're responding to specifically asks for them. In that case, include them in the cover letter. Your résumé is never the place to broach the subject of salary.

26 | *The Job Interview*

Congratulations! Your job skills—all those abilities and all that experience that you wrote about in your résumé and application letter—have gotten you in the door. Now it's time to sell yourself and to stand out from the other interviewees. This is when your people skills bear fruit. Your expertise and experience are vital, but your attitude, your appearance, and how you handle yourself can either clinch or ruin your chances. Remember: The interview is your opportunity to start building the best relationship possible with the interviewer. And that is what etiquette really is all about—building great relationships.

INTERVIEW TOP FIVE

Sometimes the amount of information thrown at you to prepare for an interview can literally be overwhelming. These top five job-interview manners are the cream of the crop. Pay attention to these five potential deal-breakers, and you will significantly increase your chances that you will get the job.

1 Don't be late

2 Be prepared

3 Dress one notch up

4 Smile, speak clearly, and look your interviewer in the eye

5 Thank them twice

1 DON'T BE LATE

No choice here. Late means late, even if you're just one minute late. Your best bet is to travel to the site of the interview the day before, to be sure you know how long it takes to get there. Then add an extra ten to twenty minutes to your schedule as margin for error. Once there, visit a coffee shop or wait outside so you can enter five minutes early. Perfect.

While waiting, be cordial but professional (in other words, not overly familiar) with everyone you meet. You never know how much influence the receptionist or assistant might have. When you come face-to-face with the interviewer, extend your hand in greeting: "Hello, Ms. Philpot. Thank you for calling me in." Don't forget to smile. (See also "The All-Important Handshake," page 217.)

Don't be surprised if you're interviewed by two people at once, or by two or more people separately. If you're faced with a panel of interviewers, make eye contact with all of them at different points, and don't concentrate your attention on one at the expense of others. Instead of letting a multiperson interview cow you, consider it an opportunity to find out even more about the company. The more answers to your questions, the better.

Once you're seated (stand until you're offered a chair), the interview will no doubt begin with small talk. Then come the pertinent questions:

2   BE PREPARED

Some interview questions you can anticipate, others you can't. The best way to stay calm is to recognize what you can control and prepare for that. Improve your odds with some research and self-examination:

- **READ UP ON THE COMPANY.** Resources such as Dun & Bradstreet, leading business magazines, the company's annual report, and its Web site will fill you in on the company's profile and its general attitude. Collecting information not only helps you anticipate the qualities your interviewer is looking for, but also gives you ideas for questions to ask the interviewer (see page 343). Ideally, you'll be able to talk about the company's chief products, prime markets, and even plans for future growth. If you're applying for a specific job, ask the firm's human resources department for the job description beforehand so you'll be able to answer questions in that context, highlighting any skills that directly apply.

- **KNOW THYSELF.** Because you'll be asked about your strengths, aptitudes, and experience, it's essential to have a concrete idea of your strengths before articulating them to your interviewer. Spend some time reviewing your résumé, refreshing your memory of dates of employment and exact job titles and, if necessary, revising it to highlight the most relevant areas of your experience. Know your résumé by heart. During the interview, having it firmly in your head enables you to point out or discuss certain parts of it without consulting a hard copy.

- **PRACTICE.** Ask yourself the questions you're likely to be asked (see pages 340–341), and practice answering them aloud.

READY? SET? BEFORE YOU GO...

Here's a checklist of things to remember before you set out for your interview. Tick them off one by one, and you're all set. (See also box, "Interview Faux Pas," page 345.)

- Your shoes are clean.
- Your clothes are pressed and stain-free.
- Your nails are clean.
- Your hair is neat.
- You've removed all extra jewelry.
- You have clean copies of your résumé.
- You have the address and phone number of the meeting place.
- You know how to get there and how long it will take.
- You know the names of everyone you are meeting and how to pronounce them.
- You have your notebook and pen.
- There is nothing extraneous or bulky in your bag.
- You are prepared for rain, sleet, or snow, and your coat is in good condition.
- For women, you have a powder compact, lipstick, and an extra pair of panty hose.

3 DRESS ONE NOTCH UP

Like it or not, the clothes you wear to your interview invite snap judgments that are hard to overcome, no matter how well you conduct yourself as a conversationalist and thinker. Here's how to get your wardrobe right, every time: Remember when you visited the company to see how long it took to get there? Consider extending that trip so that you also stop into the firm's reception area briefly and check out how people dress. If you can't make a pre-interview visit, call and ask a human resources representative what the office dress code is. If all else fails, ask whoever answers the phone.

Next, when selecting clothes for your interview, be careful to dress one notch better than the standard office wear of the company that you're applying to. For example, if the men in the office normally wear slacks and a sport shirt, you should wear slacks, a button-down shirt and tie, and a sport coat. If management has a different dress style than the office rank and file, then your clothes should be a conservative version of what you would wear to work there if your job level were one notch above the position you're applying for.

Avoid items that draw attention. Gold chains or pinkie rings alone may screen out a male before a word is spoken, and a female wearing pink patterned hose is also jeopardizing her chances. Yes, dressing is personal and a way of expressing yourself, but clothing yourself for a job interview often requires a measure of compromise, especially in traditional fields. Your clothes are one expression of how you see yourself fitting into the company.

Remember to plan for *all* of your wardrobe; any coat, umbrella, handbag, or briefcase should be as presentable as the rest of your outfit. Try to carry as little as possible, so you don't find yourself loaded down as you walk into your appointment. Do bring a small leather notebook or planner: You shouldn't take notes during the interview, but it's smart to have a presentable notebook on hand in case you need to take down phone numbers and such at the end. Also carry with you at least one copy of your résumé—clean, unsmudged, and ready to make a powerful impression on whoever receives it.

The advice that follows is slanted toward businesses on the conservative side and will usually put you on safe ground. At the same time, dressing *too* traditionally could hurt your chances in fields such as information technology, music, and fashion. Again, tailor your wardrobe to the expectations of the company.

Interview Clothes for Men

Following are the best interview clothing choices at most companies. (See also "Business Clothes for Men," pages 27–31.)

- SUITS. Unless you're interviewing in a field where a suit would look out of place, wear one. Natural fabrics in solid dark blue or gray suggest authority and quality, while all but the most subtle of patterns are risky. It must be perfectly clean and pressed; spots and wrinkles leave a poor impression.

- SHIRTS. As a rule, the simpler the better in conservative environments—no bright colors, no patterns, no French cuffs, no monograms.

- TIES. In general, now is not the time to use your tie as an expression of your individuality. To play it safe, choose the traditional silk tie in relatively muted colors and patterns (foulard, stripes, paisley, or solid). It may also be wise to avoid ties with large images and designer logos.

- SOCKS. These are easy: Choose a color that coordinates with your suit (usually black, dark gray, dark brown, or dark blue), and make sure they're long enough not to expose bare skin when you're sitting or crossing your legs.

- SHOES. Wing tips or slip-on dress shoes in black or brown leather are the classics. Avoid any "dress" shoes with thick rubber soles. As important as the style is the condition: Shoes should be newly polished, and heels shouldn't be visibly worn down.

- JEWELRY. Limiting jewelry to a wedding band and class ring is the safest choice. In some creative fields, a small earring is more acceptable than a pinkie ring, neck chains, or bracelets, which are a bad idea most anywhere.

- **COLOGNE**. Here, less is more. Splashing on too much can be the kiss of death. Confine any scent to a subtle aftershave, used sparingly.

- **BRIEFCASE**. A slim leather attaché or portfolio is the best choice. Make sure the contents are orderly in case you have to open it.

Interview Clothes for Women

Women have more to think about, and often have to spend more, than men when putting together an interview outfit. On the other hand, they have a wider range of clothing choices than men, especially when it comes to colors, patterns, and fabrics. (See also "Business Clothes for Women," pages 35–40.)

- **SKIRT SUIT**. This is the risk-free choice for an interview. While natural fabrics were once the only way to go, today knits and natural-synthetic blends are perfectly acceptable.

- **BLOUSES**. Choose a long-sleeved blouse that shows a little cuff beyond the jacket sleeve. Short-sleeved blouses may be fine for work in summer, but not for your interview. A sleeveless blouse? Never—at least in conservative fields. For an interview, a cotton or silk blouse in a neutral color and with a simple collar is still the safest choice.

- **SCARVES**. A classic 34-inch square silk scarf that complements your suit in color and pattern brings an elegant touch to your outfit.

- **SHOES**. Pumps with a 1½-inch heel (and in perfect condition) are standard. Choose a color that complements your suit and handbag—black, brown, burgundy, or navy. Avoid open-toed shoes.

- **STOCKINGS**. Choose a shade that approximates your skin color or is a bit darker.

- **BRIEFCASE**. A status briefcase is preferable to a purse for an interview, conveying more authority. A small purse kept inside the case will hold your lipstick and other grooming essentials.

- **JEWELRY**. Earrings or bracelets that dangle, sway, jangle, or gong should be left at home, as should any rings other than a wedding band, an engagement ring, and perhaps one more of simple design. Non-ear piercings will be greeted with alarm at the more traditional workplaces, and necklaces should be confined to small-scale silver or gold chains or classic pearls.

- **PERFUME.** Minimalism is the rule for perfume as well: Choose a light, not romantic, scent—and wear it very sparingly.

- **MAKEUP.** Subtle makeup that doesn't call attention to itself is without doubt the best choice in any but the most nonconventional workplaces. Save the brown lipstick and heavy eyeliner for weekends.

Grooming and Hygiene

While you want to be *seen* to your best advantage during an interview, you never want to be *smelled,* except for perhaps the slightest hint of perfume or cologne. Shower or bathe, wash your hair, and use deodorant. And don't forget your breath: Try not to eat before the interview—nothing should come between it and your last tooth-brushing (especially alcohol, which will "loosen you up" right out of a job). Avoid eating garlic or onions even the night before; in some people, the odor of both can emanate from the pores for eighteen hours or more. The same applies to liquor, beer, and cigarettes: If you've overindulged the night before, your interviewer's nose may tell him so—and he'll mark you as undisciplined or worse. Don't rely on breath mints to mask such a serious lapse in judgment.

Finally, try to visit a washroom just before going to the interview for a final check of your clothing, face, and hair.

4 SMILE, SPEAK CLEARLY, AND LOOK YOUR INTERVIEWER IN THE EYE

Engage the interviewer, and let your personality shine through. You are showing her that you will represent her company well, and that you are a confident, can-do person.

Answering Questions

Answer questions in a clear and confident manner, but be careful not to come off as a know-it-all. Start your statements with "I think . . ." or "I imagine . . ." or "As far as I can tell . . ." instead of "There's no doubt that . . ." or "Everyone knows that . . ." or "It's clear that . . ."

Here are three questions that are usually asked, either directly or in a roundabout way:

- **WHAT ARE YOUR STRENGTHS?** This question can be answered in two ways: (1) with a list of your virtues or (2) with concrete examples of your good points at work. The latter is far more effective in making a lasting impression; the interviewer is more likely to take note of your anecdote about how you took charge of the office when your supervisor was ill than something on the order of "I'm good at assuming responsibility when I see a job that needs doing."

- **WHY DO YOU WANT A NEW JOB, AND WHY WITH US?** Put a positive spin on this one. For example, if you're currently employed, avoid saying you feel your talents aren't sufficiently appreciated, you dislike your boss, or anything else negative;

instead, say you've gained enough experience in your current job to make you ready to tackle new challenges, and you believe this new position could give you the chance. Back this up with your knowledge of how the company operates (something you've learned in your earlier research). Woe to the interviewee who is asked "What do you know about us?" and finds himself at a loss for words.

- **WHAT WAS THE HARDEST THING YOU EVER FACED IN A JOB?** This question *demands* prior preparation. The idea is not to recount the story of a disastrous situation, but to talk about a problem that you were instrumental in solving. This shows that you are ready and able to cope with difficulties that may come your way.

Fielding Inappropriate Questions

The Equal Employment Opportunity Act outlaws job-interview questions about age, national origins, marital status, sexuality, or religion. Most interviewers know the law and won't ask. Still, be prepared for the possibility. First, decide whether you'll confront or deflect the issue. If you choose confrontation, simply reply, "I'm sorry, but I'm not required by law to answer that question." Realize, however, that acting offended or invoking the law will jeopardize your chances of getting the job, even though you're within your rights.

If a question truly offends you, you could thank the interviewer for her time and indicate that, based on the question, this is not the kind of company you're interested in. A less rash course is to give her the opportunity to reexamine the appropriateness of the question. But do it by questioning the *question*, not the questioner: "I'm surprised by that question. I thought it was off-limits."

YOU'RE OVERQUALIFIED?

If you are interested in a job that you're overqualified for, your interviewer will doubtless want to know why you're willing to take a step down and, in most cases, accept a lower salary. You can explain that you'll simply be happier with a less demanding position, or that you want to spend more time with your family or do more volunteer work—whatever the case may be. But realize that employers are wary of hiring overqualified candidates, seeing them as less likely to be satisfied and therefore more likely to leave. For this reason, convey a message of real dedication to the job, along with a valid reason for wanting it.

You may also want to change the format of your résumé from the traditional chronological form, which stresses the upward direction your career has taken in the past and highlights the fact that the new position would be a step down. Instead, organize your employment history by areas of experience, which shows your qualifications without pointing out the downward move. (See also "Chronological or Functional?" page 324.)

Or try humor. "How old are you?" answered by "Old enough to have seasoned like a good wine" won't sound confrontational. However you respond, ask yourself whether you want to work for a company that not only asks questions that are personally invasive but also flouts the law in the process.

- **HOW OLD ARE YOU?** Age discrimination is prohibited by law, so this question is unlikely; anyway, the interviewer will be able to judge your approximate age from the dates on your résumé. If you're over forty and the interviewer alludes to your age in any way, turn it to your advantage: "I really feel I'm at the top of my game now that I'm in my forties and have so much experience under my belt."

- **WHERE WERE YOU BORN?** If you're a member of an ethnic minority and are asked "Where were you born?" just give the name of the city and state if you were born in the United States. If you were born elsewhere but are an American citizen, say "I was born in Paraguay but am proud to say I became a U.S. citizen in 1991." If you're not a citizen, say you're in the process of becoming one, if this is the case. Understand that by law the potential employer has to check documentation of your citizenship or valid alien status.

- **MARRIED WITH CHILDREN?** At the heart of the questions "Are you married?" and "Are you thinking of having children?" is another: "Are family obligations going to affect your job?" Answering the first one is easy: Just say something on the order of "Yes, I'm married, but my husband and I have known from the start how important it is to keep our family and work lives separate." The second one, almost always directed to women, is thornier. Instead of questioning the relevance of a question about having children, answer honestly but with qualification: "No—not at present, at least." Or "Yes, someday down the line. But it really depends on how my career goes."

- **WHAT'S YOUR SEXUAL ORIENTATION?** If you are openly homosexual, being asked this question is your answer to whether you want to work there—and the answer is almost always no. Accordingly, politely pose a question of your own: "I'm gay, but what does that have to do with my fitness for this job?" The very fact that the question was asked shows that the company, if it's not actually anti-gay, considers sexuality an issue. If you're closeted but refuse to lie, look surprised and lightly brush the question off with "Gee, is that question really appropriate?" Then let the chips fall where they may.

- **WHAT'S YOUR RELIGION?** If you choose to answer, be general: "My own spirituality is important to me, but I make a practice not to discuss it, especially at work."

Asking Questions

At the end of the interview, you'll more than likely be asked whether you have any questions of your own. This is not merely a courtesy, but a continuation of the interviewer's investigation. Make your questions specific to the company or the job; they should also reflect your respect for the interviewer and your seriousness about your job search. Rely on the interviewer to have insights about the company and its employees, but don't ask for the kind of information that could easily be gleaned from the company's annual report; otherwise, you'll reveal that you haven't done your homework. Here's a sampling of pertinent things you might ask about:

- **COULD WE TAKE A FEW MINUTES TO REVIEW MY RÉSUMÉ?** This question allows you to make sure the inerviewer(s) have read your résumé without embarrassing them. It also gives you an opportunity to verbally recap your qualifications, highlighting your assets that best fit the job.

- **WHICH OF THE JOB'S RESPONSIBILITIES ARE MOST IMPORTANT?** You may have read a job description for the position you're applying for, but a boilerplate outline often fails to reflect which of the duties take priority. The interviewer's elaboration on the written description will help you tailor your discussion of your skills to fit the job's most significant aspects.

- **WHAT ARE THE COMPANY'S STRENGTHS?** Ask the interviewer his or her opinion of the company's strong points. This allows you the chance to demonstrate your knowledge of the business, which you gained in your preparation stage.

Discussing Salary and Benefits

Let the interviewer bring up salary. If he does, it won't necessarily mean you have the job, but it's a good sign. The rationale for waiting: If you broach the subject, the interviewer may not have had time to decide that you're a prime possibility for the job, and he therefore may quote the lower end of the range.

It's fine to respond to the interviewer's salary question with a question: "Could you give me an idea of the range?" Once you have an idea of your market value and the company's resources, offer a range of about $5,000 to $10,000 within which you're willing to negotiate. Wait until you've discussed other benefits and compensation before you make your decision on what you would accept. And remember that you don't have to answer on the spot: It's perfectly fine to ask for more time to consider the amount.

THE HOLE IN THE RÉSUMÉ

If you have a gap in employment of more than a year, you may be asked why. The reasons for dropping out of the workforce range from matters of choice (taking time off to raise kids or earn an advanced degree) to the unavoidable (being injured, downsized, or fired).

If you chose to stop working, dwell less on justifying why you thought it a good idea than on how your time off improved you—juggling a houseful of kids honed your organizational skills, for example. Taking time off to pursue an MBA or other degree speaks for itself, showing that you're serious about making the most of your career. Likewise, absences from work because of serious injury or downsizing are self-explanatory. It's only when you've been fired for misbehavior or poor performance (not job elimination) that you have your work cut out for you when you're asked "You weren't employed in '98 and '99? Why?" Rather than replying evasively, answer that you and your boss were having differences and couldn't resolve them (which is true)—so you were let go. The worst thing you can do is say anything negative about your former employer or claim that you were wronged. Approach it from the positive side, saying you've grown from the experience and have corrected any shortcomings, and that you're eager to put your newfound knowledge to work.

Whatever the reason for a gap in your employment, it is important to present yourself as someone who hasn't been living in a cave for several years, emphasizing that you remain interested and involved in your career. You should also use the functional-style résumé (page 325), which won't emphasize the obvious hole in employment the way a chronological résumé would.

5 THANK THEM TWICE

The first thank-you comes at the end of the job interview, along with a firm handshake and a clear statement of your appreciation for the time to meet. Then, that night at home, word-process your second thank-you on executive or standard 8½" × 11" paper.

This second thank-you doesn't have to be lengthy: Three or four brief paragraphs should do the trick. There's no reason to restate your qualifications, although you may want to address any specific requirement that came up in the interview. (If, for example, you learned that the position involves some contact with trade press, you would want to mention that you were editor of your college newspaper and are familiar with the fundamentals of press releases and interviews.)

Use your thank-you letter to recall strong points from the interview, to answer any questions that may have arisen, and to provide information you have promised: "I was very impressed during my tour of your facilities, and my conversation with Dr. Mitchell was particularly helpful. I am enclosing a copy of my paper on car phone safety issues that we discussed." End on an upbeat note by thanking the interviewer and expressing your hope for a positive outcome: "Thank you for your time and interest. I look forward to the possibility of joining your staff." Or "Thank you again for meeting with me. I look forward to hearing your decision about the position."

Put it aside and reread the note the next morning to be sure it is error-free. Then put it in an envelope and mail it or, if you're applying for an internal job, send it via interoffice mail.

INTERVIEW FAUX PAS

As important as the do's that apply to an interview are the don'ts, both in dress and behavior. You may be partial to chewing gum and wearing loud-colored clothes, but doing either is a major faux pas in all but the most unconventional companies. Here are some things to avoid:

- Arriving late
- Bringing shopping bags or boxes
- Loud colors in your outfit
- Plopping into a chair before the interviewer offers you one
- Using first names unless asked to
- Chattering on and on
- Chewing gum
- Smoking
- Jiggling your knee
- Playing with your hair
- Fidgeting in general

WAITING TO HEAR

Waiting to hear whether you've been accepted for the job is one of the most stressful parts of the job search. But face up to the fact that you must do just that: Wait, and be patient. Sending in still more samples of your work or yet another reference can make you look pushy. No matter how important the job is to you, remember that you're only one of the hiring manager's many concerns. Nevertheless, it's best to have some contact with the company (in addition to your always-essential thank-you note) within three weeks of your interview, lest you appear to have drifted off to some greener pasture. If you haven't heard from anyone within the time frame the interviewer specified, make a brief call saying that you're just checking in to see if there's anything else you should send. If you know when the company intends to make a decision and you haven't been notified, call a day or two after that date has passed to ask whether a decision has been reached and to reiterate your interest in the job.

RESPONDING TO AN OFFER

All your preparation has paid off; you've landed a job offer. No matter how thrilled you may be about it, however, *don't* succumb to pressure to give an answer right away. Instead, say something to the effect of, "Thank you for the offer. This is very exciting! I'd like some time to consider it. Can I have a couple of days to respond?"

If you have contacts at the company, now is the time to talk to them to learn more about the culture of the company, your immediate supervisor, and the team of people who will be your workmates. Also use this time to consider carefully your salary range and benefits needs.

When you meet again with your prospective employer or call to give your response, be aware this is the time when you have maximum leverage. Be sure to hammer out the details of your benefits package and salary before formally accepting the job. Now is also the time to ask about the potential for upward mobility and growth. If you're currently employed elsewhere, seek agreement from your potential employer to start at least two weeks after your acceptance, so that you can give your present employer adequate notice. Then, if everything is satisfactory to you, accept the offer with enthusiasm.

RESPONDING TO A REJECTION

So it didn't work out this time? Sending a brief note acknowledging that you've been rejected is better than just slinking off and acting as if you'd never had personal contact with a company. Thanking the company for considering you will show that you are a person of substance and good manners. And who knows? There's always the chance that you missed being hired by a hair and could be considered for a job in the future.

INDEX

RSVP, for formal meeting, 110
rumors, handling harmful, 55
rush jobs, 140
Russia
    business culture, 301–3
    Russian-language toast, 297

safety, traveling, 275, 278
salad
    cutting with knife, 190
    placement of, 190
    wine accompanying, 189
salad fork, 199, 200
salad plate, 198, 201
salary
    application letter, 330, 333
    asking for raise, 89
    job interview, 343
    résumé, 333
    temporary worker, 320
salt and pepper
    passing, 184
    shakers or grinders, 205
    using, 183–84, 198
salt cellar, 160, 198
salutation
    business letter, 244
    clerical and religious, 252
    e-mail, 261
    foreign and diplomatic, 254
    multiple names, 256–57
    professional titles, 256–57
    U.S. government officials,
        253–54
    U.S. military, 255
Sarbanes-Oxley Act of 2002,
    18, 21
sauces
    dipping into, 182
    sopping up with bread, 193
Saudi Arabia, 303, 305
Scandinavian-language toast,
    297
scarves, women's, 34, 35, 39,
    339
scents. See cologne; perfume
schedule
    for home-based worker, 125,
        128
    keeping contractor to, 142
screening telephone calls,
    228

seating
    airline travel, 272
    formal dinner, 159, 204
    home dinner, 163
    job interview, 345
    meeting, 119
    office visitor, 73
    restaurant meal, 179
    theater, 174
second-person writing style,
    239–40
security
    air travel, 271
    computer, 262
    office building, 64
    post-September 11 foreign
        travel, 286
    See also safety
self-introduction, 157, 221
self-regulation, 11
self-reliance, 267–68
Senator (U.S.), forms of
    address, 253
server. See waiter
service plate, 159, 197, 198
serving food, 164, 184
sex
    as taboo conversational
        subject, 287
    See also romantic relation-
        ships
sexism, 71, 263, 264
sexual harassment, 13, 91–96
    complaint about, 85
    definitions of, 93–94
    hostile environment as, 94
    quid pro quo as, 93
    responding to, 94–95
sexual orientation, 97–98,
    342
shaking hands. See handshake
shaving, 31
shellfish
    eating etiquette, 182–83
    wine accompanying, 188–89
shellfish fork, 182, 199
sherry glass, 198, 202
shirts, men's, 28, 33, 338
shoes
    Asian customs, 307
    business travel, 269
    care of, 32, 338

men's, 30, 32, 33, 301, 303,
    338
women's, 34, 36, 40, 296,
    307, 339
shot glass, 203
shrimp cocktail, eating eti-
    quette, 182–83
shrimp fork, 182, 199
sick days, 16
signature
    application letter, 332
    business letter, 245
silk scarves, women's, 34, 35,
    39, 339
silverware. See utensils
sincerity, importance of, 7–8
single hosts and hostesses,
    163
sit-down dinner
    formal, 159–60
    home entertaining, 163–65,
        204–5
    serving and passing food,
        164
sitting, body language of, 216
skirt lengths, 296, 307
slacks
    men's, 28, 33
    women's, 34, 35, 307
slang, 211, 291
slow talkers, 209, 214
slurping, 70
small talk
    African business meetings,
        308
    Middle Eastern business
        meetings, 304
    tips, 56–57, 158
smells. See odors
smile
    during introduction, 216,
        218
    during job interview, 335,
        336, 340
    during presentation, 282
    during telephone call, 230
smoking, 57–58, 345
    in car, 273
    sidewalk, 64–65
sneezing, 186, 225
snooping, 68
social clubs, 173

EMILY POST

JAMES MONTGOMERY FLAGG

EMILY POST 1873 TO 1960

Emily Post began her career as a writer at the age of thirty-one. Her romantic stories of European and American society were serialized in *Vanity Fair*, *Collier's*, *McCall's*, and other popular magazines. Many were also successfully published in book form.

Upon its publication in 1922, her book *Etiquette* topped the nonfiction bestseller list, and the phrase "according to Emily Post" soon entered our language as the last word on the subject of social conduct. Mrs. Post, who as a girl had been told that well-bred women should not work, was suddenly a pioneering American career woman. Her numerous books, a syndicated column, and a regular network radio program made Emily Post a figure of national stature and importance throughout the rest of her life.

"Good manners reflects something from inside—an innate sense of consideration for others and respect for self."

—EMILY POST